DATE DUE

SOMETHING ABOUT THE AUTHOR

ISSN 0276-816X

sometHInG ABOUT tHe AUthOR

**Facts and Pictures about Authors
and Illustrators of Books for Young People**

EDITED BY
ANNE COMMIRE

VOLUME 40

GALE RESEARCH COMPANY
BOOK TOWER
DETROIT, MICHIGAN
48226

Editor: Anne Commire

Associate Editors: Agnes Garrett, Helga P. McCue

Senior Assistant Editor: Joyce Nakamura

Assistant Editors: Dianne H. Anderson, Linda Shedd, Cynthia J. Walker

Sketchwriters: Rachel Koenig, Eunice L. Petrini

Researcher: Kathleen Betsko

Editorial Assistants: Lisa Bryon, Carolyn Kline, Elisa Ann Sawchuk

Permissions Assistant: Susan Pfanner

Production Director: Carol Blanchard

External Senior Production Associate: Mary Beth Trimper

External Production Associate: Dorothy Kalleberg

Internal Production Associate: Louise Gagné

Internal Senior Production Assistant: Sandy Rock

Layout Artist: Elizabeth Lewis Patryjak

Art Director: Arthur Chartow

Special acknowledgment is due to the members of the *Contemporary Authors* staff
who assisted in the preparation of this volume.

Publisher: Frederick G. Ruffner

Executive Vice-President/Editorial: James M. Ethridge

Editorial Director: Dedria Bryfonski

Director, Literature Division: Christine Nasso

Senior Editor, Something about the Author: Adele Sarkissian

Contents

5

Z

Introduction

As the only ongoing reference series that deals with the lives and works of authors and illustrators of children's books, *Something about the Author (SATA)* is a unique source of information. The *SATA* series includes not only well-known authors and illustrators whose books are most widely read, but also those less prominent people whose works are just coming to be recognized. *SATA* is often the only readily available information source for less well-known writers or artists. You'll find *SATA* informative and entertaining whether you are:

> —a student in junior high school (or perhaps one to two grades higher or lower) who needs information for a book report or some other assignment for an English class;

> —a children's librarian who is searching for the answer to yet another question from a young reader or collecting background material to use for a story hour;

> —an English teacher who is drawing up an assignment for your students or gathering information for a book talk;

> —a student in a college of education or library science who is studying children's literature and reference sources in the field;

> —a parent who is looking for a new way to interest your child in reading something more than the school curriculum prescribes;

> —an adult who enjoys children's literature for its own sake, knowing that a good children's book has no age limits.

Scope

In *SATA* you will find detailed information about authors and illustrators who span the full time range of children's literature, from early figures like John Newbery and L. Frank Baum to contemporary figures like Judy Blume and Richard Peck. Authors in the series represent primarily English-speaking countries, particularly the United States, Canada, and the United Kingdom. Also included, however, are authors from around the world whose works are available in English translation, for example: from France, Jean and Laurent De Brunhoff; from Italy, Emanuele Luzzati; from the Netherlands, Jaap ter Haar; from Germany, James Krüss; from Norway, Babbis Friis-Baastad; from Japan, Toshiko Kanzawa; from the Soviet Union, Kornei Chukovsky; from Switzerland, Alois Carigiet, to name only a few. Also appearing in *SATA* are Newbery medalists from Hendrik Van Loon (1922) to Robin McKinley (1985). The writings represented in *SATA* include those created intentionally for children and young adults as well as those written for a general audience and known to interest younger readers. These writings cover the spectrum from picture books, humor, folk and fairy tales, animal stories, mystery and adventure, science fiction and fantasy, historical fiction, poetry and nonsense verse, to drama, biography, and nonfiction.

Information Features

In *SATA* you will find full-length entries that are being presented in the series for the first time. This volume, for example, marks the first full-length appearance of Chinua Achebe, Maurice Duggan, Vachel Lindsay, Elisabeth May Ogilvie, Baroness Emmuska Orczy, David Palladini, and Lotte Reiniger, among others. Since Volume 25, each *SATA* volume also includes newly revised and updated biographies for a selection of early *SATA* listees who remain of interest to today's readers and who have been active enough to require extensive revision of their earlier entries. The entry for a given biographee may be revised as often as there is substantial new information to provide. In Volume 40 you'll find revised entries for Russell C. Hoban, Eve Merriam, and Jane Yolen.

Brief Entries, first introduced in Volume 27, are another regular feature of *SATA*. Brief Entries present essentially the same types of information found in a full entry but do so in a capsule form and without illustration. These entries are intended to give you useful and timely information while the more time-consuming process of compiling a full-length biography is in progress. In this volume you'll find Brief Entries for Thomas M. Batiuk, John Burstein, Stephen E. Cosgrove, Linda Heller, Hugh Lewin, Stephen Manes, Chiyoko Nakatani, Michael Rosen, and Julian F. Thompson, among others.

Obituaries have been included in *SATA* since Volume 20. An Obituary is intended not only as a death notice but also as a concise view of a person's life and work. Obituaries may appear for persons who have entries in earlier *SATA* volumes, as well as for people who have not yet appeared in the series. In this volume Obituaries mark the recent deaths of Claude B. Aubry, Ben Lucien Burman, Dorothy M. Johnson, and others.

Each *SATA* volume provides a cumulative index in two parts: first, the Illustrations Index, arranged by the name of the illustrator, gives the number of the volume and page where the illustrator's work appears in the current volume as well as all preceding volumes in the series; second, the Author Index gives the number of the volume in which a person's biographical sketch, Brief Entry, or Obituary appears in the current volume as well as all preceding volumes in the series. These indexes also include references to authors and illustrators who appear in *Yesterday's Authors of Books for Children.* Beginning with Volume 36, the *SATA* Author Index provides cross-references to authors who are included in *Children's Literature Review.*

Illustrations

While the textual information in *SATA* is its primary reason for existing, photographs and illustrations not only enliven the text but are an integral part of the information that *SATA* provides. Illustrations and text are wedded in such a special way in children's literature that artists and their works naturally occupy a prominent place among *SATA*'s listees. The illustrators that you'll find in the series include such past masters of children's book illustration as Randolph Caldecott, Kate Greenaway, Walter Crane, Arthur Rackham, and Ernest L. Shepard, as well as such noted contemporary artists as Maurice Sendak, Edward Gorey, Tomie de Paola, and Margot Zemach. There are Caldecott medalists from Dorothy Lathrop (the first recipient in 1938) to Trina Schart Hyman (the latest winner in 1985); cartoonists like Charles Schulz, ("Peanuts"), Walt Kelly ("Pogo"), Hank Ketcham ("Dennis the Menace"), and Georges Rémi ("Tintin"); photographers like Jill Krementz, Tana Hoban, Bruce McMillan, and Bruce Curtis; and filmmakers like Walt Disney, Alfred Hitchcock, and Steven Spielberg.

In more than a dozen years of recording the metamorphosis of children's literature from the printed page to other media, *SATA* has become something of a repository of photographs that are unique in themselves and exist nowhere else as a group, particularly many of the classics of motion picture and stage history and photographs that have been specially loaned to us from private collections.

What a *SATA* Entry Provides

Whether you're already familiar with the *SATA* series or just getting acquainted, you will want to be aware of the kind of information that an entry provides. In every *SATA* entry the editors attempt to give as complete a picture of the person's life and work as possible. In some cases that full range of information may simply be unavailable, or a biographee may choose not to reveal complete personal details. The information that the editors attempt to provide in every entry is arranged in the following categories:

1. The "head" of the entry gives

  —the most complete form of the name,
  —any part of the name not commonly used, included in parentheses,
  —birth and death dates, if known; a (?) indicates a discrepancy in published sources,
  —pseudonyms or name variants under which the person has had books published or is publicly known, in parentheses in the second line.

2. "Personal" section gives

  —date and place of birth and death,
  —parents' names and occupations,

—name of spouse, date of marriage, and names of children,
—educational institutions attended, degrees received, and dates,
—religious and political affiliations,
—agent's name and address,
—home and/or office address.

3. "Career" section gives

—name of employer, position, and dates for each career post,
—military service,
—memberships,
—awards and honors.

4. "Writings" section gives

—title, first publisher and date of publication, and illustration information for each book written; revised editions and other significant editions for books with particularly long publishing histories; genre, when known.

5. "Adaptations" section gives

—title, major performers, producer, and date of all known reworkings of an author's material in another medium, like movies, filmstrips, television, recordings, plays, etc.

6. "Sidelights" section gives

—commentary on the life or work of the biographee either directly from the person (and often written specifically for the *SATA* entry), or gathered from biographies, diaries, letters, interviews, or other published sources.

7. "For More Information See" section gives

—books, feature articles, films, plays, and reviews in which the biographee's life or work has been treated.

How a *SATA* Entry Is Compiled

A *SATA* entry progresses through a series of steps. If the biographee is living, the *SATA* editors try to secure information directly from him or her through a questionnaire. From the information that the biographee supplies, the editors prepare an entry, filling in any essential missing details with research. The author or illustrator is then sent a copy of the entry to check for accuracy and completeness.

If the biographee is deceased or cannot be reached by questionnaire, the *SATA* editors examine a wide variety of published sources to gather information for an entry. Biographical sources are searched with the aid of Gale's *Biography and Genealogy Master Index*. Bibliographic sources like the *National Union Catalog*, the *Cumulative Book Index*, *American Book Publishing Record*, and the *British Museum Catalogue* are consulted, as are book reviews, feature articles, published interviews, and material sometimes obtained from the biographee's family, publishers, agent, or other associates.

For each entry presented in *SATA*, the editors also attempt to locate a photograph of the biographee as well as representative illustrations from his or her books. After surveying the available books which the biographee has written and/or illustrated, and then making a selection of appropriate photographs and illustrations, the editors request permission of the current copyright holders to reprint the material. In the case of older books for which the copyright may have passed through several hands, even locating the current copyright holder is often a long and involved process.

We invite you to examine the entire *SATA* series, starting with this volume. The following section describes some of the people in Volume 40 that you may find particularly interesting.

Highlights of This Volume

PIERRE CULLIFORD......Belgian author, illustrator, and animator—who may be better known by the pseudonym Peyo—is the creator of the "Smurfs." When the popular blue dwarfs made their debut over twenty-five years ago, they became such a success that Culliford was forced to abandon work on his other cartoon characters. Since that time, the Smurfs have been featured in more than fifty books like *The Hundredth Smurf, Smurphony in C*, and *The Smurfs and the Howlibird.* They also have their own television series. Culliford keeps a watchful eye on the television production, being somewhat wary of his little characters becoming too Americanized. "The only thing I insisted on from the start," he confesses, "was that the Smurfs not chew gum and not drink Coca-Cola."

PENELOPE FARMER......who emphasizes she usually doesn't "write for any particular age group. . . .I just write it as it comes and let the publishers decide." She is decidedly the author of more than a dozen books for children, including fantasies like *The Summer Birds, Emma in Winter, Charlotte Sometimes*, and *A Castle of Bone.* As far as Farmer is concerned, writing a book is a continuously developing process. She always allows for change in plot and characters. Plots, she observes, can come "spontaneously, all at once." Creating characters, on the other hand, "is something you feel. . . .a feeling of balance and contrast."

JOHN GARDNER......the late educator, editor, and author of adult novels and fairy tales for children. When he was a child, Gardner's favorite authors were "God, Dickens, and Disney." "God is an extremely uneven writer," Gardner noted, "but when He's good, nobody can touch Him." Although he later developed affinities for the New Criticism and medieval literature, Gardner was influenced by his three favorite authors throughout his writing career. "From artists like Dickens and Disney," he conceded, "I get my morbid habit of trying to make the reader fall into tender weeping." In addition to adult novels like *The Wreckage of Agathon* and *October Light*, Gardner produced the fairy tales *Dragon, Dragon, The King of the Hummingbirds*, and *Gudgekin, the Thistle Girl*, among others.

RUSSELL C. HOBAN......author of over fifty books for children. Despite his art background, which includes work as a magazine and advertising artist, Hoban has illustrated only a few of his books. More than twenty of them have been illustrated by his former wife, artist Lillian Hoban. In the beginning, Russell Hoban's career as a children's writer was very much a family affair. "There was always a child less than three-feet high around," he explains, "and that is the point of view I've generally written from." Since those early days, Hoban has branched into writing fiction for adults but continues to write for children of all heights. A sampling of his books includes *Bread and Jam for Frances, Charlie the Tramp, The Sorely Trying Day, The Mouse and His Child*, and *Emmet Otter's Jug-Band Christmas.*

DHAN GOPAL MUKERJI......Newbery Award-winning author who was born of Brahmin parents in a small village near Calcutta. One of Mukerji's earliest memories was of the jungle: "I was overawed by the fierce power of life, and I watched in silence the tremendous black masses of dark trees with the emptiness gleaming all around them...." As an adult, Mukerji emigrated to the United States but never forgot his cultural origins. "It has been the ambition of my life," he revealed, "to put into the hands of American boys and girls. . .a document that will portray the living soul of a Hindu boy." Mukerji instilled the mystique of India in his books for children like *Kari, the Elephant, Ghond, the Hunter, Hindu Fables*, and his Newbery Award-winner, *Gay Neck: The Story of a Pigeon.*

JANE H. YOLEN......best known for her original fairy tales written in the tradition of Howard Pyle and Oscar Wilde. Yolen believes that "literature should begin in the cradle. . . . The best readers. . .develop a love of reading early from the strong, beautiful, moving books of childhood." She was an avid reader as a child, beginning with the Andrew Lang fairy stories and going on to Tolkien and C.S. Lewis. Yolen's lifetime love of fantasy is reflected in award-winning books like *The Emperor and the Kite, The Girl Who Cried Flowers,* and *The Moon Ribbon.*

These are only a few of the authors and illustrators that you'll find in this volume. We hope you find all the entries in *SATA* both interesting and useful. Please write and tell us if we can make *SATA* even more helpful for you.

Forthcoming Authors

A Partial List of Authors and Illustrators Who Will Appear in Forthcoming Volumes of *Something about the Author*

Abels, Harriette S.
Allard, Harry
Allen, Agnes B.   1898-1959
Allen, Jeffrey   1948-
Anders, Rebecca
Anderson, Leone C.   1923-
Andrist, Ralph K.   1914-
Ardley, Neil (Richard)   1937-
Austin, R. G.
Axeman, Lois
Ayme, Marcel   1902-1967
Bains, Rae
Baker, Olaf
Balderson, Margaret   1935-
Barkin, Carol
Bartlett, Margaret F.   1896-
Barton, Harriett
Bassett, Jeni   1960(?)-
Batey, Tom   1946-
Bauer, Caroline Feller   1935-
Bauer, John Albert   1882-1918
Beckman, Delores
Beim, Jerrold   1910-1957
Beim, Lorraine   1909-1951
Bernheim, Evelyne   1935-
Bernheim, Marc   1924-
Betancourt, Jeanne   1941-
Birnbaum, Abe   1899-
Boegehold, Betty   1913-
Boning, Richard A.
Bonners, Susan
Bourke, Linda
Bowen, Gary
Bracken, Carolyn
Brewton, Sara W.
Bridgman, Elizabeth P.   1921-
Bromley, Dudley   1948-
Bronin, Andrew   1947-
Bronson, Wilfrid   1894-
Brooks, Ron(ald George)   1948-
Brown, Roy Frederick   1921-
Brownmiller, Susan   1935-
Buchanan, William   1930-
Buchenholz, Bruce
Budney, Blossom   1921-
Burchard, Marshall
Burke, David   1927-
Burstein, Chaya M.
Butler, Dorothy   1925-
Butler, Hal   1913-
Calvert, Patricia
Camps, Luis   1928-
Carley, Wayne
Carlson, Nancy L.

Carrie, Christopher
Carris, Joan D.   1938-
Carroll, Ruth R.   1899-
Cauley, Lorinda B.   1951-
Chang, Florence C.
Charles, Carole
Charles, Donald   1929-
Chartier, Normand
Chase, Catherine
Chessare, Michele
Cline, Linda   1941-
Cohen, Joel H.
Cole, Brock
Cooper, Elizabeth Keyser   1910-
Cooper, Paulette   1944-
Cosgrove, Margaret   1926-
Coutant, Helen
Dabcovich, Lydia
D'Aulnoy, Marie-Catherine
   1650(?)-1705
David, Jay   1929-
Davies, Peter   1937-
Davis, Maggie S.   1942-
Dawson, Diane
Dean, Leigh
Degens, T.
Deguine, Jean-Claude   1943-
Deweese, Gene   1934-
Ditmars, Raymond   1876-1942
Drescher, Henrik
Dumas, Philippe   1940-
East, Ben
Edelson, Edward   1932-
Edens, Cooper
Edwards, Linda S.
Eisenberg, Lisa
Elder, Lauren
Elwood, Roger   1943-
Endres, Helen
Eriksson, Eva
Erwin, Betty K.
Etter, Les   1904-
Everett-Green, Evelyn   1856-1932
Falkner, John Meade   1858-1932
Fender, Kay
Filson, Brent
Fischer, Hans Erich   1909-1958
Flanagan, Geraldine Lux
Flint, Russ
Folch-Ribas, Jacques   1928-
Foley, Louise M.   1933-
Fox, Thomas C.
Freschet, Berniece   1927-
Frevert, Patricia D(endtler)   1943-

Funai, Mamoru R.   1932-
Gans, Roma   1894-
Garcia Sanchez, J(ose) L(uis)
Garrison, Christian   1942-
Gathje, Curtis
Gelman, Rita G.   1937-
Gemme, Leila Boyle   1942-
Gerber, Dan   1940-
Goldstein, Nathan   1927-
Gordon, Shirley
Gould, Chester   1900-
Graeber, Charlotte Towner
Greenberg, Polly   1932-
Gregory, Diana   1933-
Grimm, Cherry Barbara   1930-
Gross, Alan   1947-
Gutman, Bill
Haas, Dorothy F.
Harris, Marilyn   1931-
Hayman, LeRoy   1916-
Healey, Larry   1927-
Heine, Helme   1941-
Henty, George Alfred   1832-1902
Herzig, Alison Cragin
Hicks, Clifford B.   1920-
Higashi, Sandra
Hockerman, Dennis
Hollander, Zander   1923-
Hood, Thomas   1779-1845
Howell, Troy
Hull, Jessie Redding
Hunt, Clara Whitehill   1871-1958
Hunt, Robert
Inderieden, Nancy
Irvine, Georgeanne
Iwamura, Kazuo   1939-
Jackson, Anita
Jackson, Kathryn   1907-
Jackson, Robert   1941-
Jacobs, Francine   1935-
Jameson, Cynthia
Janssen, Pierre
Jaspersohn, William
Jewell, Nancy   1940-
Johnson, Harper
Johnson, Maud
Johnson, Sylvia A.
Jukes, Mavis
Kahn, Joan   1914-
Kalan, Robert
Kantrowitz, Mildred
Kasuya, Masahiro   1937-
Keith, Eros   1942-
Kirn, Ann (Minette)   1910-

Koenig, Marion
Kohl, Herbert   1937-
Kohl, Judith
Kramer, Anthony
Kredenser, Gail   1936-
Krensky, Stephen   1953-
Kurland, Michael   1938-
Lawson, Annetta
Leach, Christopher   1925-
Lebrun, Claude
Leckie, Robert   1920-
Leder, Dora
Le-Tan, Pierre   1950-
Lewis, Naomi
Lindgren, Barbro
Lindman, Maj (Jan)
Lines, Kathleen
Livermore, Elaine
Lye, Keith
MacKinstry, Elizabeth   (?)-1956
Mali, Jane Lawrence
Marks, Burton   1930-
Marks, Rita   1938-
Marryat, Frederick   1792-1848
Marsh, Carole
Martin, Dorothy   1921-
Marxhausen, Joanne G.   1935-
May, Dorothy
Mayakovsky, Vladimir   1894-1930
McCannon, Dindga
McKim, Audrey Margaret   1909-
McLoughlin, John C.   1949-
McReynolds, Ginny
Melcher, Frederic G.   1879-1963
Miller, J(ohn) P.   1919-
Mills, Claudia   1954-
Molesworth, Mary L.   1839(?)-1921
Molly, Anne S.   1907-
Moore, Lilian
Moskowitz, Stewart
Muntean, Michaela
Murdocca, Sal
Nickl, Peter
Nicoll, Helen
Obligado, Lillian Isabel   1931-
Odor, Ruth S.   1926-
Oppenheim, Shulamith (Levey)   1930-
Orr, Frank   1936-

Orton, Helen Fuller   1872-1955
Overbeck, Cynthia
Owens, Gail   1939-
Packard, Edward   1931-
Parker, Robert Andrew   1927-
Paterson, A(ndrew) B(arton)   1864-1941
Patterson, Sarah   1959-
Pavey, Peter
Pelgrom, Els
Peretz, Isaac Loeb   1851-1915
Perkins, Lucy Fitch   1865-1937
Petersen, P(eter) J(ames)   1941-
Peterson, Jeanne Whitehouse   1939-
Phillips, Betty Lou
Plowden, David   1932-
Plume, Ilse
Poignant, Axel
Pollock, Bruce   1945-
Pollock, Penny   1935-
Polushkin, Maria
Porter, Eleanor Hodgman   1868-1920
Poulsson, Emilie   1853-1939
Powers, Richard M.   1921-
Prager, Arthur
Prather, Ray
Pursell, Margaret S.
Pursell, Thomas F.
Pyle, Katharine   1863-1938
Rabinowitz, Solomon   1859-1916
Rappoport, Ken   1935-
Reese, Bob
Reich, Hanns
Reid, Alistair   1926-
Reidel, Marlene
Reiff, Tana
Reiss, Elayne
Reynolds, Marjorie   1903-
Rohmer, Harriet
Rosier, Lydia
Ross, Pat
Roy, Cal
Rudstrom, Lennart
Sargent, Sarah   1937-
Saunders, Susan   1945-
Schneider, Leo   1916-
Sealy, Adrienne V.
Seidler, Rosalie
Shea, George   1940-

Shreve, Susan   1939-
Silbert, Linda P.
Slepian, Jan(ice B.)
Smith, Alison
Smith, Betsy Corington   1937-
Smith, Catriona (Mary)   1948-
Smith, Ray(mond Kenneth)   1949-
Smollin, Michael J.
Steiner, Charlotte
Stevens, Leonard A.   1920-
Stine, R. Conrad   1937-
Stubbs, Joanna   1940-
Sullivan, Mary Beth
Suteev, Vladimir Grigor'evich
Sutherland, Robert D.   1937-
Sutton, Jane   1950-
Sweet, Ozzie
Thaler, Mike
Thomas, Ianthe   1951-
Timmermans, Gommaar   1930-
Todd, Ruthven   1914-
Tourneur, Dina K.   1934-
Treadgold, Mary   1910-
Velthuijs, Max   1923-
Villiard, Paul   1910-1974
Wagner, Jenny
Walker, Charles W.
Walsh, Anne Batterberry
Watts, Franklin   1904-1978
Wayne, Bennett
Werner, Herma   1926-
Weston, Martha
Whelen, Gloria   1923-
White, Wallace   1930-
Wild, Jocelyn
Wild, Robin
Winter, Paula   1929-
Winterfeld, Henry   1901-
Wolde, Gunilla   1939-
Wong, Herbert H.
Woolfolk, Dorothy
Wormser, Richard   1908-
Wright, Betty R.
Yagawa, Sumiko
Youldon, Gillian
Zaslow, David
Zistel, Era
Zwerger, Lisbeth

In the interest of making *Something about the Author* as responsive as possible to the needs of its readers, the editor welcomes your suggestions for additional authors and illustrators to be included in the series.

Acknowledgments

Grateful acknowledgment is made to the following publishers, authors, and artists
for their kind permission to reproduce copyrighted material.

ABINGDON PRESS. Illustration by Gordon Laite from *Young Reader's Book of Christian Symbolism* by Michael Daves. Copyright © 1967 by Abingdon Press. Reprinted by permission of Abingdon Press.

ADDISON-WESLEY PUBLISHING CO., INC. Illustration by Alain from *One, Two, Three, Going to Sea: An Adding and Subtracting Book* by Alain. Copyright © 1964 by Alain./ Jacket illustration by Susan Paradis from *Revenge at the Spy-Catcher's Picnic* by Anna West. Text copyright © 1981 by Anna West. Both reprinted by permission of Addison-Wesley Publishing Co., Inc.

AMERICAN LIBRARY ASSOCIATION. Sidelight excerpts from *British Children's Authors: Interviews at Home* by Cornelia Jones and Olivia R. Way. Copyright © 1976 by American Library Association. Reprinted by permission of American Library Association.

ATHENEUM PUBLISHERS. Illustration by Jean Bartenbach from *Rockhound Trails* by Jean Bartenbach. Copyright © 1977 by Jean Bartenbach./ Illustration by Victoria Forrester from *The Magnificent Moo* by Victoria Forrester. Copyright © 1983 by Victoria Forrester./ Illustration by Al Lorenz from *Ab to Zogg* by Eve Merriam. Copyright © 1977 by Eve Merriam./ Illustration by Joseph Schindelman from *There Is No Rhyme for Silver* by Eve Merriam. Copyright © 1962 by Eve Merriam./ Illustration by Malcolm Spooner from *It Doesn't Always Have to Rhyme* by Eve Merriam. Copyright © 1964 by Eve Merriam./ Illustration by Quentin Blake from *How Tom Beat Captain Najork and His Hired Sportsmen* by Russell Hoban. Text copyright © 1974 by Yankee Rover, Inc. Illustrations copyright © 1974 by Quentin Blake./ Illustration by Emily Arnold McCully from *The Twenty-Elephant Restaurant* by Russell Hoban. Text copyright © 1978 by Russell Hoban. Illustrations copyright © 1978 by Emily Arnold McCully. All reprinted by permission of Atheneum Publishers.

AVON BOOKS. Cover illustration from *Marked by Fire* by Joyce Carol Thomas. Copyright © 1982 by Joyce Carol Thomas. Reprinted by permission of Avon Books.

B. T. BATSFORD LTD. Photograph and illustration from *Shadow Puppets, Shadow Theatres and Shadow Films* by Lotte Reiniger. Copyright © 1970 by Lotte Reiniger. Both reprinted by permission of B. T. Batsford Ltd.

BEHRMAN HOUSE, INC. Illustration by Lillian Fischel from *The Wise Men of Helm and Their Merry Tales* by Solomon Simon. Copyright 1945 by Solomon Simon. Reprinted by permission of Behrman House, Inc.

BRADBURY PRESS, INC. Jacket illustration by Michael Heslop from *Killer on the Track* by Douglas Rutherford. Copyright © 1973 by Douglas Rutherford. Reprinted by permission of Bradbury Press, Inc.

CAMBRIDGE UNIVERSITY PRESS. Illustration by Prue Theobalds from *Chike and the River* by Chinua Achebe. Copyright © 1966 by Cambridge University Press. Reprinted by permission of Cambridge University Press.

JONATHAN CAPE LTD. Illustration by Stuart Tresilian from *We Couldn't Leave Dinah* by Mary Treadgold./ Illustration by Nicola Bayley from *La Corona and the Tin Frog* by Russell Hoban. Text copyright © 1974 by Russell Hoban. Illustrations copyright © 1979 by Nicola Bayley. Both reprinted by permission of Jonathan Cape Ltd.

CAROLRHODA BOOKS, INC. Photograph by Gerry Zeck from *I Love to Dance* by Gerry Zeck. Copyright © 1982 by Carolrhoda Books, Inc. Reprinted by permission of Carolrhoda Books, Inc.

THE CHILD'S WORLD, INC. Illustration by Franz Altschuler from *Bobbin's Land* by Carol Cornelius. Copyright © 1978 by The Child's World, Inc. Reprinted by permission of The Child's World, Inc.

DAVID C. COOK PUBLISHING CO. Illustration from *Professor Q's Mysterious Machine* by Donna Fletcher Crow. Reprinted by permission of David C. Cook Publishing Co.

COWARD, McCANN & GEOGHEGAN, INC. Illustration by Lydia Dabcovich from *The*

Boy Who Would Be a Hero by Marjorie Lewis. Text copyright © 1982 by Marjorie Lewis. Illustrations copyright © 1982 by Lydia Dabcovich./ Illustration by Bruce Degen from *Commander Toad in Space* by Jane Yolen. Text copyright © 1980 by Jane Yolen. Illustrations copyright © 1980 by Bruce Degen. Both reprinted by permission of Coward, McCann & Geoghegan, Inc.

T. Y. CROWELL, INC. Illustration by David Palladini from *The Girl Who Cried Flowers and Other Tales* by Jane Yolen. Text copyright © 1974 by Jane Yolen. Illustrations copyright © 1974 by David Palladini./ Illustration by David Palladini from *The Moon Ribbon and Other Tales* by Jane Yolen. Text copyright © 1976 by Jane Yolen. Illustrations copyright © 1976 by David Palladini./ Illustration by David Palladini from "The Lad Who Stared Everyone Down," in *The Girl Who Cried Flowers and Other Tales* by Jane Yolen. Text copyright © 1974 by Jane Yolen. Illustrations copyright © 1974 by David Palladini./ Illustration by David Palladini from "Sans Soleil," in *The Moon Ribbon and Other Tales* by Jane Yolen. Text copyright © 1976 by Jane Yolen. Illustrations copyright © 1976 by David Palladini. All reprinted by permission of T. Y. Crowell, Inc.

DELACORTE PRESS. Illustration by Lilo Fromm from *Fourteen Cases of Dynamite* by Gina Ruck-Pauquèt. Copyright © 1962 by Annette Betz Verlag. Copyright © 1968 by Dell Publishing Co., Inc. Reprinted by permission of Delacorte Press.

DIAL BOOKS FOR YOUNG READERS. Illustration by Simms Taback from *Fishy Riddles* by Katy Hall and Lisa Eisenberg. Text copyright © 1983 by Katy Hall and Lisa Eisenberg. Illustrations copyright © 1983 by Simms Taback. Reprinted by permission of Dial Books for Young Readers.

DILLON PRESS, INC. Photograph from *Japan: Where East Meets West* by Judith Davidson. Copyright © 1983 by Dillon Press, Inc. Reprinted by permission of Dillon Press, Inc.

DODD, MEAD & CO. Illustration by Jeni Bassett from *In a Lick of a Flick of a Tongue* by Linda Hirschmann. Text copyright © 1980 by Linda Hirschmann. Illustrations copyright © 1980 by Jeni Bassett. Reprinted by permission of Dodd, Mead & Co.

DOUBLEDAY & CO., INC. Jacket illustration by R. Andrew Parker from *Girls at War and Other Stories* by Chinua Achebe. Copyright © 1972, 1973 by Chinua Achebe./ Jacket illustration by James McMullan from *The Albino Blue* by Carl L. Biemiller. Copyright © 1968 by Carl L. Biemiller./ Illustration by Daniel San Souci from *Song of Sedna: Sea-Goddess of the North,* adapted by Robert D. San Souci. Text copyright © 1981 by Robert D. San Souci. Illustrations copyright © 1981 by Daniel San Souci./ Illustration by Doug Anderson and others from *The Complete Book of Children's Theater* by Vernon Howard. Copyright © 1955, 1956, 1957, 1959, 1960, 1961, 1962, 1964, 1969 by Sterling Publishing Co. All reprinted by permission of Doubleday & Co., Inc.

E. P. DUTTON, INC. Illustration by Peter and Virginia Parnall from *Roadrunner* by Naomi John. Text copyright © 1980 by Naomi John Flack. Illustrations copyright © 1980 by Peter Parnall and Virginia Parnall./ Sidelight excerpts from *Caste and Outcast* by Dhan Gopal Mukerji. Copyright 1923 by E. P. Dutton, Inc. Copyright renewed 1951 by Mrs. Dhan Gopal Mukerji./ Illustration by Boris Artzybasheff from *Gay-Neck: The Story of a Pigeon* by Dhan Gopal Mukerji. Copyright 1927 by E. P. Dutton, Co., Inc. Copyright renewed © 1955 by Mrs. Dhan Gopal Mukerji./ Illustration by Lawrence DiFiori from *Mice on Ice* by Jane Yolen. Text copyright © 1980 by Jane Yolen. Illustrations copyright © 1980 by Lawrence DiFiori./ Illustration by Glen Rounds from *Uncle Lemon's Spring* by Jane Yolen. Text copyright © 1981 by Jane Yolen. Illustrations copyright © 1981 by Glen Rounds./ Illustration by Florence Weber from *The Master Monkey* by Dhan Gopal Mukerji. Copyright 1932 by E. P. Dutton & Co., Inc./ Illustration by Boris Artzybasheff from *Ghond, the Hunter* by Dhan Gopal Mukerji. Copyright 1928 by E. P. Dutton & Co., Inc./ Illustration by Morgan Stinemetz from *Hari, the Jungle Lad* by Dhan Gopal Mukerji. Copyright 1924 by E. P. Dutton & Co., Inc. All reprinted by permission of E. P. Dutton, Inc.

EDITIONS JEAN DUPUIS. Illustration by Peyo from *La Soupe aux Schtroumpfs* by Peyo and Yvan Delporte. Copyright © 1976 by Peyo and S. A. Editions Jean Dupuis. Reprinted by permission of S. A. Editions Jean Dupuis.

EDITIONS GLENAT. Sidelight excerpts and illustration by Peyo from "Interview with Peyo," by T. Groensteen in *Les Cahiers de la Bande Dessinee*, no. 54, September, 1983. Both reprinted by permission of Editions Glenat.

HENRI ELKAN MUSIC PUBLISHERS. Sheet music cover from the 1959 edition of "Abraham Lincoln Walks at Midnight." Reprinted by permission of Henri Elkan Music Publishers.

FABER & FABER LTD. Illustration by Ken Kiff from *The Magic Ring and Other Russian Folk Tales,* retold by Robert Chandler. Text copyright © 1979 by Robert Chandler. Illustrations copyright © 1979 by Faber & Faber Ltd. Reprinted by permission of Faber & Faber Ltd.

FOUR WINDS PRESS. Illustration by Chris Conover from *Where Did My Mother Go?* by Edna Mitchell Preston. Text copyright © 1978 by Edna Mitchell Preston. Illustrations copyright © 1978 by Chris Conover. Reprinted by permission of Four Winds Press.

GARRARD PUBLISHING CO. Paintings by Victor Mays and flags by Henri A. Fluchère from *The Story of the United States Flag* by Wyatt Blassingame. Copyright © 1969 by Wyatt Blassingame. Reprinted by permission of Garrard Publishing Co.

GROSSET & DUNLAP, INC. Illustration by Earle Goodenow from "Aladdin; or, The Wonderful Lamp," in *The Arabian Nights.* Copyright 1946 by Grosset & Dunlap, Inc. Reprinted by permission of Grosset & Dunlap, Inc.

HARCOURT BRACE JOVANOVICH, INC. Illustration by Ian Ribbons from *The Sea Gull* by Penelope Farmer. Copyright © 1966 by Penelope Farmer./ Illustration by James J. Spanfeller from *The Summer Birds* by Penelope Farmer. Copyright © 1962 by Penelope Farmer./ Illustration by James J. Spanfeller from *Emma in Winter* by Penelope Farmer. Text copyright © 1966 by Penelope Farmer. Illustrations copyright © 1966 by Harcourt Brace & World, Inc./ Illustration by Janet Stevens from "Lemonade," in *Not Like That, Armadillo* by Ida Luttrell. Text copyright © 1982 by Ida Luttrell. Illustrations copyright © 1982 by Janet Stevens./ Illustration by Fermin Rocker from *Lotte's Locket* by Virginia Sorensen. Copyright © 1964 by Virginia Sorensen./ Illustration by Karin Anckarsvärd from *Doctor's Boy* by Fermin Rocker. Copyright © 1963 by Karin Anckarsvärd. English translation copyright © 1965 by Harcourt, Brace & World, Inc. All reprinted by permission of Harcourt Brace Jovanovich, Inc.

HARPER & ROW, PUBLISHERS, INC. Photograph from *Ike: Abilene to Berlin* by Stephen E. Ambrose. Copyright © 1973 by Stephen E. Ambrose./ Illustration by David Palladini from *If You Call My Name* by Crescent Dragonwagon. Text copyright © 1981 by Crescent Dragonwagon. Illustrations copyright © 1981 by David Palladini./ Illustration by Garth Williams from *Bedtime for Frances* by Russell Hoban. Text copyright © 1960 by Russell C. Hoban. Illustrations copyright © 1960 by Garth Williams./ Illustration by Kenneth Rowell from *Falter Tom and the Water Boy* by Maurice Duggan. Copyright © 1958 by Maurice Duggan./ Illustration by Lillian Hoban from *A Baby Sister for Frances* by Russell Hoban. Text copyright © 1964 by Russell Hoban. Illustrations copyright © 1964 by Lillian Hoban./ Illustration by David Palladini from *Twenty-Six Starlings Will Fly through Your Mind* by Barbara Wersba. Text copyright © 1980 by Barbara Wersba. Illustrations copyright © 1980 by David Palladini. All reprinted by permission of Harper & Row, Publishers, Inc.

HASTINGS HOUSE, PUBLISHERS, INC. Sidelight excerpts from *The Technique of Film Animation* by John Halas and Roger Maxwell. Reprinted by permission of Hastings House, Publishers, Inc.

HOLIDAY HOUSE, INC. Illustration by Marvin Bileck from *Rain Makes Applesauce* by Julian Scheer. Reprinted by permission of Holiday House, Inc.

HOLT, RINEHART & WINSTON GENERAL BOOK. Illustrations by Angela Barrett from *The King, the Cat and the Fiddle* by Yehudi Menuhin and Christopher Hope. Text copyright © 1983 by Yehudi Menuhin and Christopher Hope. Illustrations copyright © 1983 by Angela Barrett. Both reprinted by permission of Holt, Rinehart & Winston General Book.

THE HORN BOOK, INC. Sidelight excerpts from *Illustrators of Children's Books: 1957-1966,* compiled by Lee Kingman and others. Copyright © 1968 by The Horn Book, Inc./ Sidelight excerpts from an article "Fruits from the Living Tree," by Dhan Mukerji in *Newbery Medal Books: 1922-1955,* edited by Bertha Mahony Miller and Elinor Whitney Field in *The Horn Book.* Copyright 1955 by The Horn Book, Inc./ Sidelight excerpts from an article "Children: The Inexhaustible Source of Human Energy," by Mario Salvadori in *Horn Book,* December, 1983. Copyright © 1983 by Mario Salvadori. All reprinted by permission of The Horn Book, Inc.

HOUGHTON MIFFLIN CO. Illustration by Jack Kent from *Q Is for Duck: An Alphabet Guessing Game* by Mary Elting and Michael Folsom. Text copyright © 1980 by Mary Elting and Michael Folsom. Illustrations copyright © 1980 by Jack Kent. Reprinted by permission of Houghton Mifflin Co.

JEWISH PUBLICATION SOCIETY OF AMERICA. Sidelight excerpts from *In the Thicket* by Solomon Simon./ Sidelight excerpts from *My Jewish Roots* by Solomon Simon. Both reprinted by permission of Jewish Publication Society of America.

KENT STATE UNIVERSITY PRESS. Illustration by Vachel Lindsay from "The Swan with the Crown," in *Springfield Town Is Butterfly Town and Other Poems for Children* by Vachel Lindsay. Copyright © 1969 by Pierre Dussert. Reprinted by permission of Kent State University Press.

KESTREL BOOKS. Sidelight excerpts from an article "Thoughts on Being and Writing," by Russell Hoban in *The Thorny Paradise,* edited by Edward Blishen. Reprinted by permission of Kestrel Books.

ALFRED A. KNOPF, INC. Illustration by Lucy, Joel, Joan, and John Gardner from *A Child's Bestiary* by John Gardner (with additional poems by Lucy Gardner and Eugene Rudzewicz). Copyright © 1977 by Boskydell Artists Ltd./ Sidelight excerpts from *Unfinished Journey* by Yehudi Menuhin. Copyright © 1976 by Yehudi Menuhin and Patrick Seale Books Ltd./ Jacket illustration by Rob Sauber from *Operation: Dump the Chump* by Barbara Park. Text copyright © 1982 by Barbara Park. Jacket illustration copyright © 1982 by Rob Sauber./ Illustration by Donna Diamond from *If Only I Could Tell You* by Eve Merriam. Text copyright © 1983 by Eve Merriam. Illustrations copyright © 1983 by Donna Diamond./ Illustration by Thomas O'Donohue from *Nickel Mountain* by John Gardner. Copyright © 1963, 1966, 1971, 1972, 1973 by John Gardner./ Illustration by Daniel Biamonte from *Freddy's Book* by John Gardner. Copyright © 1980 by John Gardner./ Illustration by Joe Servello from *In the Suicide Mountains* by John Gardner. Copyright © 1977 by Boskydell Artists Ltd. All reprinted by permission of Alfred A. Knopf, Inc.

LERNER PUBLICATIONS CO. Illustration by Hans Baltzer from *Behind the Circus Tent* by Allan D. Jacobs and Leland B. Jacobs. Copyright © 1967 by Lerner Publications Co. Reprinted by permission of Lerner Publications Co.

J. B. LIPPINCOTT CO. Illustration by Carol Newsom from *When the Boys Ran the House* by Joan Carris. Text copyright © 1982 by Joan Carris. Illustrations copyright © 1982 by Carol Newsom./ Illustration by Clarence F. Underwood from *Beau Brocade* by Baroness Orczy. Copyright 1906 by Ainslee Magazine Co. Copyright 1907 by J. B. Lippincott Co. Both reprinted by permission of J. B. Lippincott Co.

LITTLE, BROWN & CO. Illustration by Leonard Everett Fisher from *The Quest of Columbus,* edited and adapted by Robert Meredith and E. Brooks Smith. Copyright © 1966 by Robert K. Meredith and Edric B. Smith, Jr. Reprinted by permission of Little, Brown & Co.

LOTHROP, LEE & SHEPARD BOOKS. Illustration by Patience Brewster from *Good as New* by Barbara Douglass. Text copyright © 1982 by Barbara Douglass. Illustrations copyright © 1982 by Patience Brewster./ Illustration by Mariana from *Little Bear's Thanksgiving* by Janice. Copyright © 1967 by Lothrop, Lee & Shepard Books. Both reprinted by permission of Lothrop, Lee & Shepard Books.

MACDONALD & CO. Sidelight excerpts from *Unfinished Journey* by Yehudi Menuhin. Copyright © 1976 by Yehudi Menuhin and Patrick Seale Books Ltd. Reprinted by permission of Macdonald & Co.

MACMILLAN PUBLISHING CO. Illustration by George Richards from "Two Old Crows," in *Johnny Appleseed and Other Poems* by Vachel Lindsay. Copyright 1913, 1914, 1917, 1925, and 1928 by The Macmillan Co./ Illustration by George Richards from "The Path in the Sky," in *Johnny Appleseed and Other Poems* by Vachel Lindsay. Copyright 1913, 1914, 1917, 1925, and 1928 by The Macmillan Co./ Illustration by George M. Richards from *Every Soul Is a Circus* by Vachel Lindsay./ Illustration from *The Litany of Washington Street* by Vachel Lindsay./ Illustrations by John Falter from *The Scarlet Pimpernel* by Baroness Orczy. Illustrations copyright © 1964 by The Macmillan Co./ Jacket illustration by Stuart Tresilian from *Puck of Pooks Hill* by Rudyard Kipling. Copyright © by Rudyard Kipling. All reprinted by permission of Macmillan Publishing Co.

McGRAW-HILL BOOK CO. Jacket illustration by Rob Howard from *Come Aboard and Bring Your Dory!* by Elisabeth Ogilvie. Copyright © 1969 by Elisabeth Ogilvie. Reprinted by permission of McGraw-Hill Book Co.

W. W. NORTON & CO., INC. Illustration by Betty Maxie from *Violin: Six Lessons with Yehudi Menuhin* by Yehudi Menuhin. Copyright © 1971 by Yehudi Menuhin. Reprinted by permission of W. W. Norton & Co., Inc.

PANTHEON BOOKS, INC. Illustration by Oscar De Mejo from *The Tiny Visitor* by Oscar De Mejo. Copyright © 1982 by Oscar De Mejo./ Illustration by Victoria Chess from *The Great Frog Swap* by Ron Roy. Text copyright © 1981 by Ron Roy. Illustrations copyright © 1981 by Victoria Chess./ Illustration by Lillian Hoban from *Awful Thursday* by Ron Roy. Text copyright © 1979 by Ronald Roy. Illustrations copyright © 1979 by Lillian Hoban. All reprinted by permission of Pantheon Books, Inc.

PARENTS MAGAZINE PRESS. Illustration by Lillian Hoban from *Emmet Otter's Jug-Band Christmas* by Russell Hoban. Text copyright © 1971 by Russell Hoban. Illustrations copyright © 1971 by Lillian Hoban. Reprinted by permission of Parents Magazine Press.

THE PUTNAM PUBLISHING GROUP, INC. Illustration by Ed Young from *Yeh-Shen: A Cinderella Story from China,* retold by Ai-Ling Louie. Text copyright © 1982 by Ai-Ling Louie. Illustrations copyright © 1982 by Ed Young./ Illustration by Linda Boehm from *I Know a Dentist* by Naomi Barnett. Text copyright © 1977 by Naomi Barnett. Illustrations copyright © 1977 by Linda Boehm./ Illustration by James Marshall from "The Pythong," in *How Beastly! A Menagerie of Nonsense Poems* by Jane Yolen. Text copyright © 1980 by Jane Yolen. Illustrations copyright © 1980 by James Marshall./ Illustration by Colin McNaughton from *The Flight of Bembel Rudzuk* by Russell Hoban. Text copyright © 1982 by Russell Hoban. Illustrations copyright © 1982 by Colin McNaughton. All reprinted by permission of The Putnam Publishing Group, Inc.

RAINTREE PUBLISHERS, INC. Illustration by Thomas Buchs from *Crash in the Wilderness* by Susan Black. Copyright © 1980 by Raintree Publishers, Inc./ Illustration by Wayne Atkinson from "The Magic Bottle," in *Myths of the Orient* by Barbara Christesen. Copyright © 1977 by Contemporary Perspectives, Inc. Both reprinted by permission of Raintree Publishers, Inc.

RANDOM HOUSE, INC. Sidelight excerpts from *Pipers at the Gates of Dawn: The Wisdom of Children's Literature* by Jonathan Cott. Copyright © 1981, 1983 by Jonathan Cott./ Illustration by Peyo from "Romeo and Smurfette," in *Romeo and Smurfette and Twelve Other Smurfy Stories* by Delporte and Peyo. Copyright © 1978 by Peyo and S.E.P.P. Belgium. English text copyright © 1979 by Hodder & Stoughton Ltd. Both reprinted by permission of Random House, Inc.

THE SEABURY PRESS, INC. Illustration by Anne Dalton from *The Shadow of the Hawk and Other Stories* by Marie de France. Retold by James Reeves. Text copyright © 1975 by James Reeves. Illustrations copyright © 1975 by William Collins & Sons Co. Ltd./ Illustration by Tomie de Paola from *The Giants Go Camping* by Jane Yolen. Text copyright © 1979 by Jane Yolen. Illustrations copyright © 1979 by Tomie de Paola./ Illustration by Friso Henstra from *The Little Spotted Fish* by Jane Yolen. Text copyright © 1974, 1975 by Jane Yolen. Illustrations copyright © 1975 by Friso Henstra. All reprinted by permission of The Seabury Press, Inc.

PATRICK SEALE BOOKS LTD. Sidelight excerpts from *Unfinished Journey* by Yehudi Menuhin. Copyright © 1976 by Yehudi Menuhin and Patrick Seale Books Ltd. Reprinted by permission of Patrick Seale Books Ltd.

SIMON & SCHUSTER, INC. Illustration by Lawrence Ratzkin from *The Inner City Mother Goose* by Eve Merriam. Text copyright © 1969 by Eve Merriam. Illustrations copyright © 1969 by Lawrence Ratzkin. Reprinted by permission of Simon & Schuster, Inc.

THE THIRD PRESS. Illustration by Per Christiansen from *How the Leopard Got His Claws* by Chinua Achebe and John Iroaganachi. Copyright © 1973 by The Third Press. Reprinted by permission of The Third Press.

TUNDRA BOOKS, INC. Illustration by Araneus from *Pouf, a Moth—une Mite* by Peter Angeles. Copyright © 1976 by Tundra Books, Inc. Reprinted by permission of Tundra Books, Inc.

VAN NOSTRAND REINHOLD CO., INC. Sidelight excerpts from *Experimental Animation: An Illustrated Anthology* by Robert Russett and Cecile Starr. Reprinted by permission of Van Nostrand Reinhold Co., Inc.

FRANKLIN WATTS, INC. Illustrations by Julie Frankel from *The Whole Mirth Catalog: A Super Complete Collection of Things* by Michael Scheier and Julie Frankel. Copyright © 1978 by Michael Scheier and Julie Frankel./ Photograph by Tony Gibbs from *Sailing: A First Book* by Tony Gibbs. Copyright © 1974 by Tony Gibbs./ Photograph from *Busing* by Judith Bentley. Copyright © 1982 by Judith Bentley. All reprinted by permission of Franklin Watts, Inc.

Sidelight excerpts from *Links in the Chain of Life* by Baroness Emmuska Orczy. Reprinted by permission of Joan Orczy-Barstow./ Television still from "The Smurfs." Copyright © 1983 by Hanna-Barbera Productions, Inc. and Sepp International, S. A. Reprinted by permission of Wallace Berrie./ Sidelight excerpts from "Beginnings," by Maurice Duggan in *Landfall 80.* Reprinted by permission of Barbara Duggan./ Sidelight excerpts from *A Latch against the*

Wind by Victoria Forrester. Reprinted by permission of Victoria Forrester./ Photograph from *Vachel Lindsay: Fieldworker for the American Dream* by Ann Massa. Copyright © 1970 by Indiana University Press. Reprinted by permission of Indiana University Press./ Sidelight excerpts from an article "Learning from Disney and Dickens," by John Gardner in *New York Times,* January 30, 1983. Copyright © 1983 by The New York Times Co. Reprinted by permission of The New York Times Co./ Sidelight excerpts from an article "PW Interviews: Russell Hoban," by Barbara A. Bannon in *Publishers Weekly*, May 15, 1981. Copyright © 1981 by Xerox Corp. Reprinted by permission of *Publishers Weekly./* Illustration by Nata Kazalovski from *Robert Ventures* by Solomon Simon. Copyright 1938 by Solomon Simon. Reprinted by permission of Sholem Aleichem Folk Institute./ Sidelight excerpts from *Writing Books for Children* by Jane Yolen. Reprinted by permission of The Writer, Inc.

Appreciation also to the Performing Arts Research Center of the New York Public Library at Lincoln Center for permission to reprint the theater still "You're a Good Man, Charlie Brown."

PHOTOGRAPH CREDITS

Chinua Achebe: Archives, University Library, University of Massachusetts/Amherst; Marvin Bileck: Emily Melligan; Donna Fletcher Crow: Garrett Photography; Pierre Culliford (in a garden): Andrea J. Bernstein/*People Weekly*. Copyright © 1982 by Time, Inc.; Judith Davidson: Wes Hohlbein; Penelope Farmer: Fay Godwin; John Gardner: Gerard Malanga; Russell Hoban: Chris Stelle Perkins; Russell Hoban (at his desk): Ian Cook/*People Weekly*. Copyright © 1981 by Time, Inc.; Ida Luttrell: William P. Luttrell; Claire Mackay: Joseph Schmid; Olga Maynard: Tom Gillespie; Yehudi Menuhin: Felix Schmidt; Dhan Gopal Mukerji (1936): UPI/Bettmann News Photos; Baroness Emmuska Orczy: Culver Pictures, Inc.; Barbara Park: Bob Wilcox Studio; Dorothy Rosenberg: Grady-Jentoff Photographers; Gina Ruck-Pauquèt: Eckhard, Garmisch-Pertenkirchen; Robert D. San Souci: Catherine Hopkins; Eric Douglas Vincent: Brad "Fumble-Focus" Foster; Gerry Zeck: Pam Zeck.

something About the Author

ACHEBE, Chinua 1930-

PERSONAL: Born November 16, 1930, in Ogidi, Nigeria; son of Isaiah and Janet Achebe; married Christie Chinwe Okoli, 1961; children: Chinelo (daughter), Ikeehukwu (son), Chidi (son), Nwando (daughter). *Education:* Attended Government College, Umuahia, 1944-47; University College, Ibadan, B.A., 1953. *Home:* 305 Marguerite Cartwright Ave., Nsukka, Nigeria. *Office:* Institute of African Studies, University of Nigeria, Nsukka, Nigeria.

CAREER: Nigerian Broadcasting Corp., producer of Lagos, Nigeria, 1954-57, controller in Enugu, 1958-61, director in Lagos, 1961-66; University of Nigeria, Nsukka, senior research fellow, 1966-73, professor of English, 1973—. Visiting professor of English at University of Massachusetts-Amherst, 1972-75, and University of Connecticut, 1975-76. Member of Council, University of Lagos, 1966; chairman, Citadel Books Ltd., 1967; director of Heinemann Educational Books Ltd. (Nigeria), 1970—, and Nwankwo-Ifejika Ltd. (publisher; Nigeria), 1970—. *Member:* Contemporary Society (Lagos), Mbari Club (Ibadan), Lagos Film Society. *Awards, honors:* Margaret Wrong Memorial Prize, 1959; Nigerian National Trophy, 1960; Rockefeller travel fellowship to East and Central Africa, 1960; UNESCO travel fellowship to United States and Brazil, 1963; Jock Campbell-*New Statesman* award, 1965; D.Litt. from Dartmouth College, 1972, University of Southampton, 1975, and University of Ife (Nigeria), 1978; Commonwealth Poetry Prize, 1974; D.Univ., University of Stirling, 1975; Neil Gunn fellow, Scottish Arts Council, 1975; honorary fellow, Modern Language Association of America, 1975; Lotus Award for Afro-Asian Writers, 1975; LL.D., University of Prince Edward Island, 1976; D.H.L., University of Massachusetts-Amherst, 1977.

WRITINGS: Things Fall Apart (novel), 1958, McDowell, Obolensky, 1959, reprinted, Fawcett, 1977; *No Longer at Ease* (novel), Heinemann, 1960, Obolensky, 1961; *The Sacrificial Egg and Other Stories,* Etudo (Onitsha, Nigeria), 1962; *Arrow of God* (novel), Heinemann, 1964, John Day, 1967; *A Man of the People* (novel), John Day, 1966; *Chike and the River* (juvenile), Cambridge University Press, 1966; *Beware Soul-Brother and Other Poems,* Nwanko-Ifejika (Nigeria), 1971, Doubleday, 1972, revised edition, Heinemann, 1972; (editor) *The Insider: Stories of War and Peace from Nigeria,* Chatham Bookseller, 1971; (with John Iroaganachi) *How the Leopard Got His Claws* (juvenile; illustrated by Per Christiansen), Nwanko-Ifejika, 1972, bound with *Lament of the Deer,* by Christopher Okigbo, Third Press, 1973; *Girls at War and Other Stories* (short stories), Doubleday, 1973; *Christmas in Biafra and Other Poems,* Doubleday, 1973; *Morning Yet on Creation Day* (essays), Doubleday, 1975; *The Drum,* Fourth Dimension Publishers (Nigeria), 1977, reprinted, in *Wonders,* edited by Jonathan Cott and Mary Gimbel, Summit Books, 1980. Also author of "The Flute," a retelling of an African folktale, which is included in *Sharing Literature with Children,* edited by Francelia Butler, David McKay, 1977. Founding editor, Heinemann "African Writers" series, 1962—; editor, *Okike,* 1971—.

SIDELIGHTS: Achebe was born of Christian parents in Ogidi, in eastern Nigeria on November 16, 1930. He was raised with the values of a traditional village life, although his adult life witnessed the rapid modernization of his country. "My father, although a converted Christian, was really a member of the traditional society—he was really full grown in the traditions of Igbo life when he decided to become a Christian; so he knew all about our culture. My children, however, belong to the world culture to which American children belong. They went to school in America for several years, and liked the same kind of music that children in America and England enjoy. But I'm in between these two. And we can talk about 'transitions'— it's a cliché, of course, since every day's a transition—but I think that I'm much more a part of a transitional generation

CHINUA ACHEBE

than any other. And this is very exciting. Of course it carries its penalties, since you're in a no man's land, you're like the bat in the folktale—neither bird nor mammal—and one can get lost, not being one or the other. This is what we are, we can't do anything about it. But it does help if you have the kind of temperament I have, which tries to recover something from our past. So you have one foot in the past—my father's tradition—and also one in the present—where you try to interpret the past for the present.

"My world—the one that interests me more than any other—is the world of the village. It is one, not the only, reality, but it's the one that the Igbo, who are my people, have preferred to all others. It was as if they had a choice of creating empires or cities or large communities and they looked at them and said, 'No, we think that what is safest and best is a system in which everybody knows everybody else.' In other words, a village. So you'll find that, politically, the Igbos preferred the small community; they had nothing to do—until recently . . . with kings and kingdoms." [Jonathan Cott, *Pipers at the Gates of Dawn: The Wisdom of Children's Literature*, Random House, 1981.[1]]

As a child living in the village of Ogidi, Achebe was told folktales by his mother and older sister, as was the custom. ". . . Any child growing up at that time, unless he was particularly unlucky, would be told stories as part of his education. It doesn't happen anymore. The stories are now read in books, and very rarely is there a situation in which the mother will sit down night after night with her family and tell stories, with the young children falling asleep to them. The pace of life has

altered. . . . Our generation is unique. And I was lucky to have been part of the very tail end of that older tradition. Perhaps we may not be able to revive it, but at least we can make sure that the kind of stories our children read carry something of the aura of the tales our mothers and sisters told us."[1]

Achebe, who has devoted his adult life to language, both in his teaching and in his writing, first learned to speak in his native Igbo. At about the age of eight, he began to study English as well.

Teaching English and writing became his major professions. Achebe has been affiliated with the University of Nigeria since 1966, and was visiting professor of English in the United States from 1972 until 1976. In the United States he taught English at the University of Massachusetts from 1972 until 1975 and at the University of Connecticut from 1975 until 1976. He married and had four children. ". . . The youngest girl was just over a year old when we left Nigeria and went to America. And when she went to nursery school—she was just two—she refused to speak English, even though she was already bilingual like everybody else in the family—she had a few words of each language. She refused to talk to her teachers, and we realized that she was putting up a fight for her language. And it lasted a couple of months. Incidentally, one of the conditions she exacted from me for going to school was that I had to tell her a story in Igbo as I drove her there. And another coming back every day, too. I didn't quite know what to make of it, but I think that it reveals the importance both of language and of stories. And if a child is deprived of these things I think he or she will be unhappy. The imagination becomes stiff. A lot of cruelty, in fact, comes from a lack of imagination—I think it's all very much connected. And I really feel that stories are not just meant to make people smile, I think our life depends on them.''[1]

In 1978, the University of Massachusetts bestowed upon Achebe an honorary D.H.L. degree. About his influence on western education, he reflected: ''Whether or not the West learns anything from the African experience is a matter for the West to decide. I can only say that a major prerequisite to learning is humility; and that on present showing this virtue is extremely difficult for the West, thanks to its immense material success.''[1]

Beginning with the 1958 publication of his first novel, *Things Fall Apart*, Achebe has gained world recognition as a major contemporary novelist. Especially in his novels, he shows concern over the impact of colonialism on the individual and on society.

Achebe's first book for children was published in 1966. It was an adventure story about a young boy entitled *Chike and the River*. The prefix ''chi'' in Igbo is found in most names. ''When we talk about *chi*, we're talking about the individual spirit, and so you find the word in all kinds of combinations. Chinwe, which is my wife's name, means '*Chi* owns me'; mine is Chinua, which is a shortened form of an expression that means 'May a *chi* fight for me.' My son is named Chidi, which means '*Chi* is there.' So it's almost in everybody's name in one form or the other. Our youngest girl asked me why she didn't have *chi* in her name. She thought it was some kind of discrimination, so she took the name Chioma, which means 'Good *chi*.'

''Chike is a shortened form of Chinweike, which means '*Chi* has the strength or the power.' And that's what that frail-looking character has—he has the power.''[1]

The book was written at the advice of a friend. ''. . . It's a 'children's novel,' if you like. And it came about . . . thanks to Christopher Okigbo who really made me do it. . . . I enjoy writing for children, it's very important for me. It's a challenge I like to take on now and again because it requires a different

They sat on the exposed roots of a mango tree and began to munch their suya. ■ (From *Chike and the River* by Chinua Achebe. Illustrated by Prue Theobalds.)

(From *The Sacrificial Egg and Other Short Stories* by Chinua Achebe.)

kind of mind from me when I'm doing it—I have to get into the mind of a child totally, and I find that very rewarding. I think everybody should do that, not necessarily through writing a story, but we should return to childhood again and again. And when you write for children it's not just a matter of putting yourself in the shoes of a child—I think you have to be a child for the duration. It's not easy to begin with, and I didn't know if I could do it, it never occurred to me until Christopher Okigbo said I must do a children's story.''[1]

Achebe's short story, ''The Flute,'' was a retelling of an African folktale. ''This story is . . . really a traditional folktale, and what I've done is to retell it . . . while adding a few details—such as the one where the boy himself makes his own flute. I'm very much concerned about our consumer culture in which few people make anything themselves anymore. Our ancestors made things, and so I put this detail in the story, and I think that one is entitled and expected to do that. Of course the purist collector of folktales would say this is terrible. But my concern is that stories are not only retrieved and kept alive but also added to, just as they always were, and I think this is really what a living, traditional storyteller would do. I loved the stories my mother and elder sister told me, but there were always little changes here and there. And this was part of the entertainment—you heard a tale a hundred times, but each day there was one additional little twist, which was expected.

. . . All the animals in the forest lived as friends. ■ (From *How the Leopard Got His Claws* by Chinua Achebe and John Iroaganachi. Illustrated by Per Christiansen.)

I think that stories are the very center, the very heart of our civilization and culture. And to me it's interesting that the man who thinks he's strong wants to forbid stories. . . . So I think a writer instinctively gravitates toward that 'weakness,' if you like; he will leave the 'masculine' military strength and go for love, for gentleness. For unless we cultivate gentleness, we will be destroyed. And this is why you have poets and storytellers.''[1]

The author believes that children are far more receptive to morals in stories than are adults. ''. . . The adult is someone who has seen it all, nothing is new to him. Such a man is to be pitied. The child, on the other hand, is new in the world, and everything is possible to him. His imagination hasn't been dulled by use and experience. Therefore, when you restory the adult, what you do is you give him back some of the child's energy and optimism, that ability to be open and to expect anything. The adult has become dull and routine, mechanical, he can't be lifted. It's as if he's weighted down by his experience and his possessions, all the junk he's assembled and accumulated. And the child can still fly, you see. . . .

''. . . I think the adult sometimes loses sight of the nature of stories. But these great fundamental issues have never changed and never will. I mean, children always ask the same questions:

Who made the world? How come some people are suffering? Who made death? And to think that we have somehow moved on to more 'adult' subject matters is simply self-deception. What we do, of course, is quite often get trapped in trivia masked in high-falutin language. But the basic questions are still the same, and this is what children's stories particularly deal with.

''I think that mankind's greatest blessing is language. And this is why the storyteller is a high priest, and why he is so concerned about language and about using it with respect. Language is under great stress in the modern world—it's under siege. All kinds of people—advertisers, politicians, priests, technocrats—want to get a hold of it and use it for their own ends; these are the strong people of today; the storyteller represents the weakness we were talking about. But of course every poet is aware of this problem. . . . And this is where children come into it, too, because you can't fool around with children—you have to be honest with language in children's stories; mere cleverness won't do.''[1]

Achebe's children's story *How the Leopard Got His Claws* is an animal fable, written both to entertain and to instruct. The background to the story was the Biafran War. ''That story was made at a very difficult time politically—at the beginning of the Biafran struggle. A good friend of mine, a very fine poet named Christopher Okigbo, who was killed fighting for Biafra, had set up a publishing house. We had fled from different parts of Nigeria because our lives were in danger—he fled from Ibadan, I fled from Lagos, and we returned to Enugu. (He had been West African representative for Cambridge University Press, so he knew about publishing. . . .) So when we both arrived back in Enugu, he suggested that we set up a press. I said, 'Well, you set it up, you know about it, and I'll join.' He said, 'You'll be chairman and I'll be the managing director' [laughing], so the Citadel Press was formed: The name came from the idea of the fortress—you flee from a foreign land, in danger, and return home to your citadel. Little did we know that Enugu wasn't safe—anyway, that's another story.

"We were going to concentrate on children's books, and so we told our friends we were planning on publishing and asked for manuscripts from all the writers around. And a man named John Iroaganachi sent in a story called 'How the Dog Became Domesticated'—it was a charming, traditional type story, but it was rather weak. So I decided to edit it, and as I edited it, it grew . . . it grew until it just turned into something else, it wasn't about the dog at all anymore but rather about the leopard. And it was now a parable about Nigeria—the common house that had been torn apart.

"I was possessed by that story, which works on very many levels. Biafra was represented by the leopard . . . but let's not talk about whom the dog represents; I think a good story remains valid even beyond the events described. It is however, interesting to mention that when the city where we were working fell to the federal troops, we had that book in press. In fact, the last time I saw Christopher Okigbo was when he came to discuss it with me. That day a bomb fell on my house. And the end of it was that Enugu was sacked, and we fled and abandoned the book.

"Now, at the end of the war, we went back to the site of the publishing house, and it had been razed to the ground—it seemed to me that whoever did it didn't like publishing or at least this particular publishing house and perhaps this particular book. Fortunately, there was one proof copy that somehow survived—I think a friend of ours, a relation of Christopher Okigbo's who had a copy of the galleys, fished it out and brought it to me. And so I made a few more changes, not major ones, and it was published. Later on, one chap who was working as an intelligence officer with the federal troops said to me, 'You know, of all the things that came out of Biafra, that book was the most important.'

"Children read the book and love it. Not only in Nigeria, but also in East Africa, where they did a special edition of it. In Nigeria it sold out very quickly—it was out of print for a long time—but a Nigerian publisher has just reissued it, and it's used as a supplementary reader in schools.

"I don't believe children get all the levels—they're not supposed to—but I think they get the main point about the ingratitude and opportunism of the animals, and about the danger of not working together when they have a common problem. Of course, the villain is the dog . . . which is a problem, I understand, for readers in the West—it's very difficult for them to see a dog in the role of a villain, but I did that deliberately. John's original story had the dog as the nice guy, a wonderful fellow who became a slave. But I don't like slaves, so this is why I turned the plot around 180 degrees.

"It was a very interesting experiment. I asked Okigbo to write the lamentation of the deer—the song it sings when it's thrown out of the house by the dog. So in fact there were three people involved in making this story. Actually, four, because of the illustrations. What happened is that at the end of the war Biafra was in very bad shape, and some friends of mine in Enugu set up a publishing house. And they said that they wanted to do what I and Okigbo had tried to do before the war. They knew some Norwegian people, who in fact had shown interest in Biafra during the war—the Scandinavian countries had been very sympathetic to Biafra. So it was through that connection that a Norwegian firm decided to publish the story, and they commissioned Per Christiansen, a leading illustrator of Norwegian children's books, to do the pictures. And then the Norwegians printed the book, though it was published in Nigeria."[1]

In all of Achebe's stories, both adult and juvenile, there are moral messages. ". . . To say that a good story is weakened because it conveys a moral point of view is absurd, because in my view all the great stories do convey such a point. A tale may be fascinating, amusing—creating laughter and delight and so forth—but at its base is a sustaining morality, and I think this is very important.

"In the Igbo culture, the relationship between art and morality is very close, and there's no embarrassment at all in linking the two, as there would be in Western culture.

". . . We create these tales and fables, like God creating man in his own image. These folktales aren't just decorative things—

(Jacket illustration by R. Andrew Parker from *Girls at War and Other Stories* by Chinua Achebe.)

they tell us so much about the people who make them. And when told to children, they're intended for their safety, for their survival in the world.''¹

FOR MORE INFORMATION SEE: Nigeria Magazine, June 1964; *New Statesman,* January 29, 1965; John Press, editor, *Commonwealth Literature: Unity and Diversity in a Common Culture,* Heinemann, 1965; *Books Abroad,* summer, 1966; *Insight,* October/December, 1966; *Observer,* March 5, 1967; *Canadian Forum,* June, 1967; *Time,* November 10, 1967; *New York Times Book Review,* December 17, 1967; *Negro History Bulletin,* March, 1968; *Critique,* Volume XI, number 1, 1969; G. D. Killam, *The Novels of Chinua Achebe,* Africana Publishing, 1969; David Caroll, *Chinua Achebe,* Twayne, 1970; *Contemporary Literary Criticism,* Gale, Volume I, 1973, Volume III, 1975, Volume V, 1976, Volume VII, 1977, Volume XI, 1979; Johnathan Cott, *Pipers at the Gates of Dawn: The Wisdom of Children's Literature,* Random House, 1981.

AITKEN, Amy   1952-

BRIEF ENTRY: Born October 19, 1952. Aitken attended New College in Sarasota, Fla., and Parsons School of Design. Described by *Publishers Weekly* as a "talented author-illustrator," she has written four picture books published by Bradbury. In her first book, *Ruby!* (1979), vivacious young Ruby daydreams about her future. She decides to be a rock star, an author, an artist, a movie star, or even President. *Booklist* commented that "... Aitken's first book deserves notice for the effervescent quality of the artwork," while *School Library Journal* stated "... the attractive watercolor and pencil illustrations are energetic and warm." In *Ruby, the Red Knight* (1983), Ruby imagines herself a knight in King Arthur's court and battles against a witch, a dragon, a giant, and a wizard. Aitken also wrote *Wanda's Circus* (1985) and *Kate and Mona in the Jungle* (1981), in which two girls seated atop a concrete statue of an elephant take an imaginary trip to the jungle. Her illustrated work for others includes *I'm Not Moving* by Penelope Jones and *The One in the Middle Is a Green Kangaroo* by Judy Blume. *Residence:* New York, N.Y.

AMBROSE, Stephen E(dward)   1936-

PERSONAL: Born January 10, 1936, in Decatur, Ill.; son of Stephen Hedges (a physician) and Rosepha (Trippe) Ambrose; married former wife, Judith Dorlester, 1957; married Moira Buckley, 1968; children: Stephenie, Barry Halleck, Andrew, Grace, Hugh. *Education:* University of Wisconsin, B.S., 1957, Ph.D., 1963; Louisiana State University, M.A., 1958. *Office:* Department of History, University of New Orleans, New Orleans, La. 70122.

CAREER: Louisiana State University in New Orleans (now University of New Orleans), 1960-64, began as instructor, became associate professor of history; Johns Hopkins University, Baltimore, Md., assistant professor, 1964-66, associate professor of history, 1966-69; U.S. Naval War College, Newport, R.I., Ernest J. King Professor of Maritime History, 1969-70; Kansas State University, Manhattan, Dwight D. Eisenhower Professor of War and Peace, 1970-71; University of New Orleans, professor of history, 1971—. Visiting assistant professor, Louisiana State University, Baton Rouge, 1963-64.

Member: American Military Institute (member of board of directors), American Committee on the History of the Second World War (member of the board of directors), Lewis and Clark Heritage Trail Foundation (member of board of directors), Big Blue Athletic Association (president, 1976-77), Chi Psi.

WRITINGS: (Editor) *A Wisconsin Boy in Dixie,* University of Wisconsin Press, 1961; *Halleck: Lincoln's Chief of Staff,* Louisiana State University Press, 1962; *Upton and the Army,* Louisiana State University Press, 1964; *Duty, Honor, and Country: A History of West Point,* Johns Hopkins Press, 1966; *Eisenhower and Berlin, 1945,* Norton, 1967; (editor) *Institutions in Modern America: Innovation in Structure and Process,* Johns Hopkins Press, 1967; (associate editor) *The Papers of Dwight D. Eisenhower: The War Years,* five volumes, Johns Hopkins Press, 1970; *The Supreme Commander: Eisenhower,* Doubleday, 1970; *Rise to Globalism: American Foreign Policy, 1938-70,* Penguin, 1971, third revised edition, *Rise to Globalism: American Foreign Policy since 1938,* Penguin, 1983; (with James A. Barber, Jr.) *The Military and American Society,* Free Press, 1972; *Ike: Abilene to Berlin* (illustrated with maps and photographs), Harper, 1973; *Crazy Horse and Custer: The Parallel Lives of Two American Warriors,* Doubleday, 1975; *Ike's Spies: Eisenhower and the Espionage Establishment,* Doubleday, 1981; *Eisenhower: Soldier, General of the Army, President-Elect 1890-1952,* Simon & Schuster, 1983; (with Richard H. Immerman) *Milton S. Eisenhower: Educational Statesman,* Johns Hopkins Press, 1983. Author of television documentary, "Eisenhower: Supreme Commander," for BBC-TV, 1973. Author of bi-weekly column, *Baltimore Evening Sun,* 1968— Contributor of reviews and articles to numerous

STEPHEN E. AMBROSE

(From *Ike: Abilene to Berlin* by Stephen E. Ambrose. Photograph courtesy of the U.S. Army.)

journals and newspapers, including *American Historical Review*, *Harvard Magazine*, *American Heritage,* and *New York Times Book Review*.

WORK IN PROGRESS: A full length biography of Richard M. Nixon.

SIDELIGHTS: "My greatest joy is camping and canoeing with my wife, five children, and Labrador retriever. Together we have camped on every one of Crazy Horse's and Custer's battlefields, and on most of Eisenhower's. For the military historian, nothing compares to actually walking over the ground; for the father, nothing beats doing it with one's family."

FOR MORE INFORMATION SEE: Washington Post, October 10, 1970; *New York Review of Books,* May 6, 1971, September 2, 1971; *Times Literary Supplement,* November 5, 1971; *Contemporary Reviews,* January, 1977.

Some books are to be tasted, others to be swallowed, and some few to be chewed and digested: that is, some books are to be read only in parts, others to be read, but not curiously, and some few to be read wholly, and with diligence and attention.

—Francis Bacon

ANDERSON, Mona   1910-

PERSONAL: Born March 11, 1910, in New Brighton, New Zealand; daughter of William and Alice (Holland) Tarling; married Ronald Edward Anderson (a sheep rancher), June 15, 1940. *Education:* Educated in Canterbury, New Zealand. *Religion:* Anglican, *Home:* 15 McMillan St., Darfield, Canterbury, New Zealand.

CAREER: Operator, with husband, of sheep ranch in Rakaia Gorge, Canterbury, New Zealand. Writer. *Awards, honors:* Member of the Order of the British Empire.

WRITINGS—All published by A. H. & A. W. Reed, except as indicated: *A River Rules My Life,* 1963; *Good Logs of Algidus,* 1965; *Over the River,* 1966; *The Wonderful World at My Doorstep,* 1968; *A Letter From James,* 1972; *Marylou: A High Country Lamb* (children's book), 1975; *The Water-Joey,* 1976; *Old Duke* (children's book), 1977; *Home Is the High Country* (children's book; illustrated by David Cowe), C. E. Tuttle, 1979; *Both Sides of the River,* 1981. Contributor to *Family Doctor, Weekly Press,* and *New Zealand Herald.* Writer of radio scripts.

SIDELIGHTS: "All my life I lived in the country and was brought up in the company of boys—two brothers and four boy cousins. I was permitted to go on their bird nesting and fishing expeditions on condition that I carry the tin of worms or climb a tree with my mouth filled with bird's eggs and carry them safely to the ground. As they tickled the elusive trout or bobbed for eels, I sat on the bank of the cool stream and jotted down notes and wrote little stories about our small dog getting stuck down a rabbit burrow, or about the scent of burning gorse sticks as the boys made a fire to roast potatoes in their jackets, or about Grandfather's cat that got caught by his tail in a rabbit trap. 'Girls are such stupid creatures, always writing silly, secret notes,' they accused.

"After leaving school, music became my first love, and for a while the only notes that interested me were the notes on the stave and staff. While the boys played cricket on the big flat beside our house, I practised on the piano. Finally, I started writing again, and wrote stories for several magazines.

"When I married and went to live on an isolated high-country sheep station, I made friends with lots of little animals—hedgehogs, opossums, paradise-ducks and keas, etc. I found them so loving and fascinating that I felt I must put it all down on paper and share my experiences with children."

ANGELES, Peter A.   1931-

PERSONAL: Spelling of surname legally changed; born February 21, 1931, in Ambridge, Pa.; son of Adam Peter and Kaliope (Moschos) Angelos; married Elizabeth McConnaughy (a medical research assistant), June 7, 1951 (deceased); children: Beth (Mrs. Jon Basham), Jane, Adam. *Education:* Columbia University, B.A., 1952, M.A., 1954, Ph.D., 1956. *Politics:* Independent. *Religion:* Unitarian-Universalist. *Home:*

Peter A. Angeles (right) with illustrator Gary Kuroda.

MONA ANDERSON

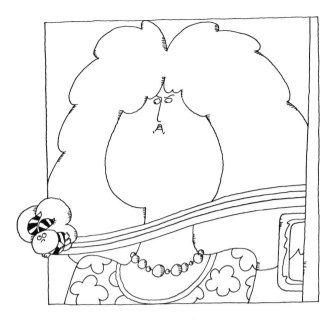

**When she sees one she says "Pouf!" . . . . Elle dit
"Pouf!" quand elle voit une mite.** ■ (From *Pouf, a
Moth—une Mite* by Peter Angeles. Illustrated by
Araneus.)

974 Cocopah Dr., Santa Barbara, Calif. 93110. *Agent:* Jose
Abarrientos, 707 Lighthouse Ave., Pacific Grove, Calif. 93950.
Office: Department of Philosophy, Santa Barbara City College,
721 Cliff Dr., Santa Barbara, Calif. 93109.

CAREER: University of Western Ontario, London, assistant
professor, 1956-63, associate professor, 1963-70; Santa Barbara City College, Santa Barbara, Calif., professor of philosophy, 1970—. Visiting professor, Albert Schweitzer College,
Vaud, Switzerland, 1966. *Member:* American Philosophical
Association, American Humanist Association. *Awards, honors:* Canada Council fellowship, 1968-69; National Endowment of the Humanities fellowship, 1973.

*WRITINGS: The Possible Dream: Toward Understanding the
Black Experience,* Friendship, 1970; *The Problem of God,* C.
E. Merrill, 1974; *Introduction to Sentential Logic,* C. E. Mer-
rill, 1976; (editor) *Critiques of God,* Prometheus Books, 1976;
Pouf, a Moth—une Mite (illustrated by Araneus), Tundra
Books, 1976; (contributor) James L. Christian, editor, *Extra
Terrestrial Intelligence: The First Encounter,* Prometheus Books,
1976; *Dictionary of Philosophy,* Barnes & Noble, 1981; *Dic-
tionary of Christian Religion and Theology,* Harper, 1985;
Dictionary of World Religions, Prometheus Books, 1986.
Contributor of technical articles, children's stories, poetry,
horoscopes, and one-act avant-garde plays to journals and
literary magazines.

WORK IN PROGRESS: Manuscripts in the fields of introduction to philosophy and the philosophy of religion.

SIDELIGHTS: "Writing children's stories and plays is my first
love, but it is difficult getting them published and I can't make
a living at it, thus I spend my time on textbooks—not that I
make a living on them but they contribute somewhat to my
academic reputation and survival. I keep living in the dream
that someday publishers will see how good my children's stories really are and buy a bundle of them."

AUBRY, Claude B.   1914-1984

OBITUARY NOTICE—See sketch in *SATA* Volume 29: Born
October 23, 1914, in Morin Heights, Quebec, Canada; died in
1984. Canadian librarian and author. Aubry served as director
of the Ottawa Public Library from 1953 to 1979. Prior to that
time, he was chief of personnel at the Montreal Civil Library.
He was also a member of the library consultants board of
Encyclopedia Canadiana and of the editorial board of *Canadian Children's Literature.* Aubry wrote several award-winning books for children, originally published in French and
later translated into English. These include *Les Iles du roi Maha
Maha II: Conte fantaisiste canadien,* or, *The King of the Thousand Islands: A Canadian Fairy Tale; Le Loup de Noel,* or,
The Christmas Wolf; and *Le Violon magique et autres legendes
du Canada francais,* or, *The Magic Fiddler and Other Legends
of French Canada.* In 1962 he was the recipient of the Association Canadienne des Bibliothecaires de Langue Francaise
award for *Les Iles du roi Maha Maha II,* as well as the Canadian
Library Association's Book of the Year Award for *Le Loup de
Noel.* Aubry was decorated with the Order of Canada in 1974;
the following year, he was appointed Officier de l'Ordre International du Bien Public. His memberships included the Canadian Authors Association, Canadian Library Association,
Alliance Francaise, and Association France-Canada.

FOR MORE INFORMATION SEE: Contemporary Authors,
Volume 106, Gale, 1982; *Canadian Who's Who: 1983,* University of Toronto Press, 1983.

BALTZER, Hans (Adolf)   1900-

PERSONAL: Born in 1900, in Berlin, Germany; son of a car-
penter. *Residence:* East Germany.

CAREER: Began career in commercial art in 1924; free-lance
illustrator of children's books, beginning about 1960. *Awards,
honors:* Silver medal, Leipzig International Book Art Exhibition.

ILLUSTRATOR—All for children: Jonathan Swift, *Gullivers
reisen,* Hoch-Verlag, c. 1960, translation published as *Gulliv-
ers Travels,* edited by Elaine Moss, Constable, 1961, Duell,
Sloan & Pearce, 1963; Gunther Feustel, *Jose: A Story of South
America,* translated from the German by Stella Humphries,
Methuen, 1966, published as *Jose: A Tale from South America,*
Dial, 1968 (originally published by Altberliner Verlag, 1963);
Allan D. Jacobs and Leland B. Jacobs, *Behind the Circus Tent,*
Lerner Publications, 1967; Gotz R. Richter, *Sado und Apii,*
Kinderbuchverlag, 1967; Wolfgang Zeiske, *Weissfleck,* Kinderbuchverlag, 1967; Zeiske, *Dolchkralle,* Kinderbuchverlag,
1968; Zeiske, *Grimbart,* Kinderbuchverlag, 1968; R. Amonov
und K. Ulug-Sade, *Die Sandelholztruhe,* Verlag Volk und Welt
Kultur und Fortschritt, 1968, translation by Katya Sheppard
published as *The Sandalwood Box: Folk Tales from Tadzhik-
istan,* Sadler, 1972, Scribner, 1975; Zeiske, *Esox: The Story
of a Pike,* Delacorte, 1970 (originally published by Kinderbuchverlag, 1964); Ernst Adler, *Ko und Ala,* Holz-Verlag,
1970; Erwin Strittmatter, *Pony Pedro,* Kinderbuchverlag, 1970;
Hanna Künzel, *Eselchen Nik,* Union Verlag, 1971, translation
and adaptation by Richard Sadler published as *Nick, the Little
Donkey,* Sadler, 1971; Kurt David, *Der Schwarze Wolf,* 1971,
translation by Anthea Bell published as *Black Wolf of the Steppes,*
Houghton, 1972; Benno Pludra, *Die Reise nach Sundevit,* Thi-
enemann, 1972. Illustrator of over seventy children's books.

(From *Behind the Circus Tent* by Allan D. Jacobs and Leland B. Jacobs. Illustrated by Hans Baltzer.)

SIDELIGHTS: Greatly influenced by Russian artist N. Carusin, Baltzer's forte lies in his lively illustrations of animals. His singular works of animals are well-known throughout Germany.

BARNETT, Naomi   1927-
(Naomi Barnett Buchheimer)

PERSONAL: Born December 14, 1927, in Cincinatti, Ohio; daughter of I. A. (a professor) and Fannie (Reisler) Barnett. *Education:* University of Cincinnati, B.A., 1946; Ohio State University, M.A. 1951; St. John's University, Jamaica, N.Y., Ed.D., 1979. *Politics:* Democrat. *Home:* 128 Woodhaven Pl., Oberlin, Ohio 44074.

CAREER Taught in elementary schools in Ohio, 1946-55; G. P. Putnam's Sons, New York, N.Y., writer, editor, 1956-78; Borough of Manhattan Community College of the City University of New York, New York, N.Y., lecturer, 1970-75, and 1979-80; Oberlin Public Schools, Oberlin, teacher in Talent Development Program, 1980-81; Lorain County Community College, Elyria, Ohio, instructor in developmental education,

1981—. Scholastic Magazines, New York, N.Y., writer, 1959-64; Hofstra University, Hempstead, N.Y., taught elementary education, 1964-65. *Member:* Phi Beta Kappa.

WRITINGS—All under name Naomi Barnett Buchheimer; juvenile; all published by Putnam: *Night Outdoors*, 1960; *I Know a Teacher*, 1967; *I Know a Ranger*, 1971; *I Know a Dentist* (illustrated by Linda Boehm), 1977.

"Let's Go" series; juvenile; all published by Putnam: *Let's Go to a Bakery*, 1956; . . . *to a Firehouse*, 1957; . . . *to a Library*, 1957; . . . *to a Post Office*, 1957, new edition, 1964; . . . *to a Candy Factory*, 1958; . . . *to a School*, 1958; . . . *to a Telephone Company*, 1958; . . . *to a Television Station*, 1958; . . . *to a Dentist*, 1959; . . . *Down the Mississippi with LaSalle*, 1962.

Other: (With Arnold Buchheimer) *Equality through Integration*, Anti-Defamation League of B'nai B'rith, 1965. Also author of teaching guides for two reading textbooks for Macmillan, and of teaching guides for two social studies textbooks for Silver Burdett. Contributor to *Scholastic Teacher* and *Elementary English Journal*. Contributing editor, Scholastic Magazines.

While we were waiting, I asked Mrs. Gold and my mother about a sign on the wall. ■ (From *I Know a Dentist* by Naomi Barnett. Illustrated by Linda Boehm.)

. . . A moonstone will lure you right into the waves and the ocean spray. ■ (From *Rockhound Trails* by Jean Bartenbach. Illustrated by the author.)

BARTENBACH, Jean 1918-

PERSONAL: Born August 12, 1918, in Brooklyn, N.Y.; daughter of Mark (a musician) and Bertha (a singer; maiden name, Cooper) Marcus; married Lou Lewis (marriage ended); married Allen Bartenbach (an actor), 1954; children: Julie Gray. *Education:* Attended Pratt Art Institute and Otis Art Institute. *Home:* Los Angeles, Calif. 90065.

CAREER: Artist and author. Has held various jobs, including waitress, assembly-line worker, fork-lift operator, longshoreman, and actress. Also established own silk screen and textile business, Los Angeles, Calif., about 1941-51. *Member:* Southern California Society of Literature for Young People and Children, The Eagle Rock Writers Panel, Pasadena Lunch Bunch.

*WRITINGS—*For children: *Rockhound Trails* (nonfiction; self-illustrated), Atheneum, 1977. Also contributor of articles to numerous periodicals for both children and adults, including *Highlights for Children, Jack and Jill, Humpty Dumpty, Children's Playmate, Good Housekeeping, Saturday Evening Post, Outdoor World, Country Beautiful,* and others.

WORK IN PROGRESS: Further research in the areas of geology, endangered animal species, and biographies of authors and illustrators.

SIDELIGHTS: "I started to write thirteen years ago and went through the learning process by taking an adult evening course. I made wonderful, lasting friendships with writers. In about three years I started to sell to magazines. Everyone encouraged me to write a book. So I did. I wrote about my hobby of rock collecting and was able to combine my talents by illustrating the book I had written. The art was as difficult to do as the writing. Nothing comes easy."

FOR MORE INFORMATION SEE: Northeast News Herald (Los Angeles, Calif.), April 6, 1977, May 6, 1978; *Valley News* (San Francisco Valley, Calif.), February 4, 1978; *Star Review* (Los Angeles, Calif.), November 22, 1980.

BATIUK, Thomas M(artin) 1947-

BRIEF ENTRY: Born March 14, 1947, in Akron, Ohio. Cartoonist. Batiuk is the creator of the comic strip "Funky Winkerbean," which first appeared in 1972 and is now in 350 U.S. newspapers. The strip follows the high school career of characters "Funky," "Les," "Bull Buska," and others, while specifically focusing on the everyday problems they face. In a *Detroit News* article, Batiuk said that all the characters are based on people he has known. One of them, "Harry L. Dinkle," is a prototype of his high school band director. "I've been glad ever since that I took band," confessed Batiuk. In the beginning, Batiuk gleaned material for the strip from his own high school days at Midview High, but now stays fresh by substituting for the school's art teacher about six or seven times a year. He otherwise returns there twice a week to sketch in the art room. Earlier in his career, Batiuk taught art at Eastern Heights Junior High School in Elyria, Ohio. Since 1979 he has collaborated with cartoonist Tom Armstrong on the syndicated comic strip "John Darling," featuring Darling, a television talk-show host who originally appeared as a character in "Funky Winkerbean." Batiuk's cartoon collections include *Funky Winkerbean* (Xerox Education Publications, 1973), *Play It Again Funky* (Tempo Books, 1975), *Funky Winkerbean, Closed Out* (Tempo Books, 1977), and *You Know You've Got Trouble When Your School Mascot Is a Scapegoat* (Fawcett, 1984). *Address:* c/o Field Newspaper Syndicate, 1703 Kaiser Ave., Irvine, Calif. 92714.

FOR MORE INFORMATION SEE: Cartoonist Profiles, June, 1974; *Contemporary Authors,* Volumes 69-72, Gale, 1978; *Who's Who in America, 1984-85,* Marquis, 1984; *Detroit News,* August 8, 1984.

BENTLEY, Judith (McBride)   1945-

PERSONAL: Born April 8, 1945, in Indianapolis, Ind.; daughter of Robert Edward (a college president) and Luella (Hart) McBride; married Allen Bentley (an attorney), June 6, 1970; children: Anne, Peter. *Education:* Oberlin College, B.A., 1967; New York University, M.A. (history of American civilization), 1969, M.A. (educational psychology), 1975. *Religion:* Congregational. *Home and Office:* 4747 132nd Ave. S.E., Bellevue, Wash. 98006.

The Court said black children could no longer be kept in separate schools and that the separate schools for blacks at that time were not equal to the schools for whites. ■ (From *Busing* by Judith Bentley. Photograph courtesy of United Press International.)

CAREER: Saturday Review, New York City, editorial assistant, 1970-71, assistant editor, 1972; Newsweek Books, New York City, copy editor, 1973-74; New York City Community College, Brooklyn, N.Y., adjunct instructor in reading skills, 1975-77; Dalton School, New York City, preceptor, 1977-79; writer and editor, 1979—. *Member:* Pacific Northwest Writers Conference.

WRITINGS—For young people: *State Government* (edited by Richard Darilek), F. Watts, 1978; *The National Health Care Controversy,* F. Watts, 1981; *American Immigration Today: Pressures, Problems, Policies,* Messner, 1981; *Busing: The Continuing Controversy,* F. Watts, 1982; *Justice O'Connor,* Messner, 1983; *The Nuclear Freeze Movement,* F. Watts, 1984. Contributor to magazines, including *Family Health* and *Seattle's Child.*

SIDELIGHTS: "Writing combines the best of work and play for me. In what other line of work can you spend hours finding out all about a subject, reading extensively, browsing and digging in libraries, and talking to people about subjects they love?

JUDITH BENTLEY

Given the chance, I would read books all the time; I have become a minor expert on many subjects. Since life must be more productive than that, I turned to writing as a means to share information rather than just absorbing it.

"Writing has been a way for me to be involved in the world, too. Growing up in Indianapolis, with deep family roots in southern Indiana, I made up my own neighborhood newspaper with a friend, wrote for the high school newspaper, then the college newspaper, and reported for Indianapolis and Cleveland newspapers as a summer intern. When I graduated from college I went to New York to find a place in publishing.

"Publishing is glamorous but low-paying and lacks a clear career ladder. In the late 1960s, women were just beginning to break through the barriers that had confined us to researching, not writing; typing, not editing; and answering the phone, not interviewing. I spent five years at Crowell, Collier, Macmillan, *Saturday Review,* and Newsweek Books, where I met other young women in similar struggles.

"The changes didn't come fast enough, so I went off to freelance editing and writing and teaching. When my two children were young I decided to stay home and write, hoping they would take long naps. Once in awhile they obliged. Now that they're in school and preschool, time comes my way more easily, but I still have just one or two carefully planned hours a day to write.

"I began writing young adult nonfiction after I answered an ad in *Publishers Weekly* for writers on a social science series. From that first book (on *State Government*) came associations with two editors at two publishers. (The first editor left and joined another publisher, leaving the book in another editor's hands.)

"Of the six books I've written, the biography of Sandra Day O'Connor was the most fun and greatest challenge because the mystery of someone's life is never completely unraveled. Research for the biography took me to Washington to interview Justice O'Connor in her Supreme Court chambers and then to Arizona to talk to lawyers and judges in Phoenix and finally to the isolated ranch on the Arizona-New Mexico border where she grew up. O'Connor was an inspiring subject. As I juggled children and home in order to work, I found reassurance in her ability to do the same.

"Writing also provides access to people you would not ordinarily meet. My book on the nuclear freeze movement introduced me to some courageous people who are refusing to ignore the threat of nuclear war and overcoming community pressures to avoid the subject.

"Ideas for books come to me from the communities I live in. When I was living in a downtown Brooklyn neighborhood, the influx of new immigrants to the United States was obvious and prompted the book on recent immigration (which was also suggested by a librarian). Living in a suburb of Seattle, I became aware of the burgeoning freeze movement and of other new peace groups, some of them reacting to the Trident submarine base on Puget Sound and the production of cruise missiles by Boeing. Nuclear war was a subject I avoided until it came to my own backyard. Once I read about it, I was motivated to write about it.

"Most of my writing has been young adult books; I haven't tried fiction yet, but it might come as a relief to be able to make up the facts."

BIEMILLER, Carl L(udwig)　1912-1979

PERSONAL: First syllable of surname is pronounced "bee"; born December 16, 1912, in Camden, N.J.; died from a stroke September 28, 1979, in Monmouth Beach, N.J.; son of Carl L. (a printer) and Charlotte (a hairdresser; maiden name, Curtis) Biemiller; married Fanonda Mulvey, April 27, 1935; children: John Bennett, Carl Ludwig III, Gary Mulvey, Eric Curtis. *Education:* Attended Charles Morris Price School of Advertising and Journalism. *Politics:* Republican. *Religion:* Presbyterian. *Residence:* Monmouth Beach, N.J. *Agent:* Louis Mercier, 342 Madison Ave., New York, N.Y. 10017.

CAREER: Philadelphia Record, Philadelphia, Pa., promotion manager, 1935-37; *Courier-Post,* Camden, N.J., assistant publisher, 1937-42; National Association of Manufacturers, New York, N.Y., speech writer, 1942-45, 1958-62; *Holiday,* Philadelphia, executive editor, 1945-57; *Philadelphia Daily News,* Philadelphia, assistant to the editor, 1957-58; author of books for young people. Public relations writer, Bell & Stanton, New York, N.Y., at intervals, 1967-79; public relations director in

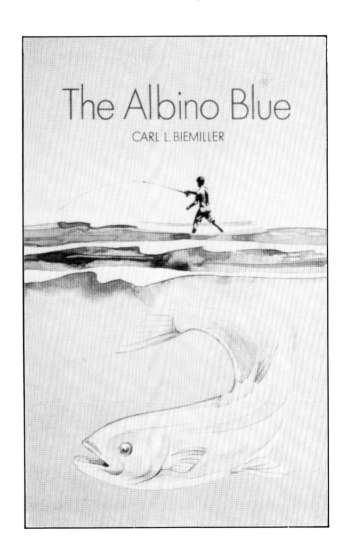

He flipped the bail on his spinning reel and snapped his surf rod through a careless arc which shot a hundred feet of nearly invisible monofilament line out past the hump-backed breakers. ■ (Jacket illustration by James McMullan from *The Albino Blue* by Carl L. Biemiller.)

Atlantic City, N.J., 1971-73; trustee, Monmouth Beach Library. *Member:* National Sports Writers Association, American Littoral Society, Atlantic City Press Club, Poor Richard Club and Pen and Pencil Club (both Philadelphia). *Awards, honors:* Award from the Atlantic City Press Club for an article that appeared in *Holiday;* knighthood from the Italian government for articles written on Italy.

WRITINGS—All for young people: *The Magic Ball from Mars* (first appeared as series "Jonny and the Space-o-Tron" in *Jack and Jill;* illustrated by Kathleen Voute), Morrow, 1953; *Starboy* (sequel to *The Magic Ball from Mars;* first appeared as series "Jonny and the Boy from Space" in *Jack and Jill;* illustrated by K. Voute), Holt, 1956; *Any Friend of Owney's* (illustrated by Charles Hawes), Putnam, 1966; *The Albino Blue,* Doubleday, 1968; *The Hydronauts,* Doubleday, 1970; *Follow the Whales: The Hydronauts Meet the Otter-People,* Doubleday, 1973; *Escape from the Crater: More Adventures of the Hydronauts,* Doubleday, 1974; *The Hydronaut Adventures* (collection), Doubleday, 1981.

Other: (With Ivan Hill) *How to Make America More Honest,* edited by Joan Hill, Ethnics Resource Center, 1974. Also contributor of over one thousand articles to newspapers and magazines.

SIDELIGHTS: "My first juvenile novel began innocently enough as a short story for *Jack and Jill,* which was once—on the eve of saturation television—a children's publication of distinction. By the time Ada Rose (the magazine's knowing and remorseless editor) was through, the short story had become a seven-part serial, a science fiction work known as *The Magic Ball from Mars.* . . .

"A second followed when *The Magic Ball* . . . spawned a sequel, *Starboy,* published by Holt. I remember thinking what a lot of effort it took to escape a simple short story.

"My third and fourth efforts in the juvenile field—*Any Friend of Owney's* and *The Albino Blue* were single books . . . amusing enough for young readers to justify bookstore shelf space. But

Carl Biemiller, about 1958.

with the fifth, *The Hydronauts,* I was back with the options and problems of serialization by a process I can describe only as planned inadvertence. . . .

"I don't know how it is with other authors but I find it hard to believe that many set out deliberately to create a string of works with the same characters and the same generic tasks and motivations. True, there are good serial books in our stores and libraries. But the big boff days of Tom Swift, the Merriwells, the Rover Boys and the Hardys and all those nurse heroines and horse heroes are supposed to be over. Aren't they?

"Still, the form persists and I keep hearing Ada Rose telling me that a child's war against insecurity is best fought from the fortress of the familiar, that children want to know and be easy with the same fictional people for as long as they may, that they want them to have new adventures; they want their story characters to be friends, and anyone knows it takes some time to make a friend. But then Ada, bless her Quaker-Meeting soul, also thought that all children were one child.

"I don't. I think they are all different and that many are smarter than others. As a man with chronic lazies, I find that young smarts give me one of my major problems, although in the creation of this current series they may also give me doctorates in marine biology, geology, metallurgy, nuclear physics, psychology, medicine, meteorology and a host of oceanography's related disciplines. Science fiction is a mind-expanding genre. Research is one of its daily calisthenics because plausibility extended into the fringes of fantasy demands a foundation of fact.

"The narrative line can be strong and sharp and the action can be absorbing, but if a fact or a hypothesis rooted in a rearrangement of fact isn't right, I am likely to hear from some sixth-grader planning to win a Nobel Prize or some girl math wizard in the eighth grade who is building a home computer.

"In *The Hydronauts,* one of my Sea Wardens is working in a kelp forest of stipes, mutated by radioactive bombardment into plants as large as great trees. He swims among spores as large as basketballs. Comes a note from a Fort Wayne twelve-year-old, stating that not all mutation produces giantism, that all life forms are mutants, and some of them may be microscopic. Further, he is the smallest boy in his class and also serves at the altar of his church. Also in *The Hydronauts,* human life is laboratory-created in a form adapted to in-sea living so that the race of man may live without land support. Why not, writes a liberated ninth-grade girl. And cites heart transplants, kidney transplants, artificial hips, total blood transfusions and cornea banks and ends by asking who needs babies.

"I used to answer all reader letters, scary or not. The postal service solved that problem by pricing me out of business. But nothing will get me out of time-consuming, albeit wonderful, chores of research.

"Fortunately, perhaps, it is easy to get into a series and out of one. It is sticky only in the middle, and that may not be as uncomfortable as it used to be, particularly if the metier is science fiction and the subject matter is as grand as all tomorrow.

"Certainly taboos are fewer in the field, although I am fussy about manners, which are fundamentally expressions of consideration for others. I see no reason why my characters can't be courtly. And when it comes to the creation of a series, there is a code in the Marine Service described in *The Hydronauts*

that says, 'Anything done for the cause of compatibility is not only condoned but required.'" [Carl L. Biemiller, "A Series Can Creep Up On You," *Publishers Weekly,* July 16, 1973.]

Biemiller died of a stroke on September 28, 1979. He was a trustee of the Monmouth Beach Library [New Jersey], and many friends donated money in his name to that institution, to be used toward the construction of the Carl L. Biemiller wing.

FOR MORE INFORMATION SEE: Carl L. Biemiller, "Make Us a Story, Daddy," *Holiday,* April, 1946, reprinted, *Reader's Digest,* May, 1946; C. L. Biemiller, "A Series Can Creep Up On You," *Publishers Weekly,* July 16, 1973; *Authors of Books for Young People,* 2nd edition supplement, Scarecrow, 1979. Obituaries: *New York Times,* October 3, 1979; *Contemporary Authors,* Volume 106, Gale, 1982.

BILECK, Marvin 1920-

PERSONAL: First syllable of surname is pronounced "Bee"; born March 2, 1920, in Passaic, N.J.; son of Louis and Lee (Rosenzweig) Bileck; married second wife Emily Nelligan (an artist). *Education:* Attended Cooper Union, 1939-46, and London School of Architecture, 1945. *Residence:* RFD 4, Old Robertsville Rd., Winsted, Conn.

MARVIN BILECK

(From *Rain Makes Applesauce* by Julian Scheer. Illustrated by Marvin Bileck.)

CAREER: Artist and illustrator of books for children. Philadelphia College of Art, Philadelphia, Pa., assistant professor of drawing, book design, and calligraphy, 1961-67; Queen's College, Flushing, N.Y., associate professor of art, 1967—. Work has been exhibited in numerous American Institute of Graphic Arts Children's Books Shows and is in the Shapiro Collection of the Portland Museum, Portland, Ore. Bileck's etchings, engravings, and woodcuts are in collections in the United States and Europe. *Military service:* U.S. Army, World War II; served in Europe, North Africa, and England. *Awards, honors:* Fulbright fellowship, 1958, for study in Paris, France; *Rain Makes Applesauce* was named one of ten best illustrated children's books of the year, 1964, by the *New York Times* and was a Caldecott Medal honor book, 1965.

WRITINGS—All self-illustrated; all for children: (With Julian Scheer) *Rain Makes Applesauce,* Holiday House, 1964; (with Beatrice S. deRegniers), *Penny,* Viking, 1966.

Illustrator; all for children, except as indicated: Alfred Kazin, *A Walker in the City* (adult memoir), Harcourt, 1951; Mildred Lawrence, *Crissy at the Wheel,* Harcourt, 1952; Anne T. White, *All about the Stars,* Random House, 1954; Louis MacNeice, *The Penny that Rolled Away,* Putnam, 1954; Fingal Rosenquist, *Nipper Shiffer's Donkey,* Harper, 1955; Johanna Johnston, *Sugarplum,* Knopf, 1955; Anne Colver, *Nobody's Birthday,* Knopf, 1961; Barbara C. Freeman, *Timi, the Tale of a Griffin,* Grosset, 1970.

WORK IN PROGRESS: By Trolley Past Thimbledon Bridge with Ashley Bryan.

SIDELIGHTS: "Childhood, as I look back on it, was an enjoyment of stories, sports, and scouting. While the comics interested me in drawing funny pictures, gradually I found that anything I drew gave me a thrill. I liked to tell stories and invent characters and loved to see people 'come alive.' Scouting introduced me to nature, which inspired a basic sense of growth.

"Artistically speaking, 'I was born' when I came to Cooper Union. Here I learned the formal substance of pictures. Architecture—my major—gave me the concept of structure. I try to make forms and build everything in the picture. Design introduced me to the flat plane, taught me to organize the elements and taught me of rhythm in drawing. Graphics brought me closer to books and printing and here within the fragrance of printer's ink, I saw the evolution of reproduced work and knew that engraving, etching and book illustration were interrelated and of meaning to me." [Lee Kingman and others, compilers, *Illustrators of Children's Books: 1957-1966,* Horn Book, 1968. Amended by Bileck.[1]]

About his book illustration Bileck commented: "I try to relate the autographic and photomechanical processes. *A Walker in the City* was an instance where the glass was lacquered, and the illustrations needled in as in etching, the copper plate resulting from this drawn negative. This made for a more direct and finer line.

"Abstract and aesthetic considerations are more intimately connected to the naturalistic and humanistic. I believe in the people and want them to be more 'real' and to exist in their imagery, while . . . years ago abstract participation was so blinding that I was decorating pages, and my people were artificial and had no depth."[1]

Bileck usually designs the books he illustrates. "I consider a body type as dynamic and functional a shapeform as any part

of the illustration. I was delighted by the imagery and excited by the thought of my pictures [in *Rain Makes Applesauce*] giving rise to such fantasies and how as they grew they implicated more and varied ramifications of these imaginings. In *Penny,* I was intrigued by the scale—that by getting way down to this low level one could see landscapes across a tablecloth and one could feel the arched-strength in wispish things such as blades of grass which almost feel like high trees."[1]

Bileck heads the graphics section of the art department at Queen's College, where he teaches drawing, etching, engraving, woodcutting, and other techniques.

FOR MORE INFORMATION SEE: Bertha E. Miller and others, compilers, *Illustrators of Children's Books: 1946-1956,* Horn Book, 1958; Diana Klemin, *The Art of Art for Children's Books,* Clarkson Potter, 1966; Lee Kingman and others, compilers, *Illustrators of Children's Books: 1957-1966,* Horn Book, 1968; Doris de Montreville and Elizabeth D. Crawford, *Fourth Book of Junior Authors and Illustrators,* H. W. Wilson, 1978.

Shoving off, she skidded over to the next one, her heart pounding when she almost missed it. ■ (From *Crash in the Wilderness* by Susan Black. Illustrated by Thomas Buchs.)

BLACK, Susan Adams 1953-

PERSONAL: Born February 17, 1953, in Cincinnati, Ohio; daughter of David Delaine Black (a planning counselor) and Margaret Stout (Reeve). *Education:* University of California, Berkeley, B.A., 1976. *Agent:* Richard Krawetz & Associates, 337 East 13th St., New York, N.Y. 10013. *Office:* 238½ S. Poinsettia Pl., Los Angeles, Calif. 90036.

CAREER: KNXT-TV, Los Angeles, Calif., production assistant, 1977-78; Talent & Booking Publishing, Inc., Hollywood, Calif., managing editor, 1978-80; Xiphias Computer Graphics, Santa Monica, Calif., graphics program documentation writer, 1979—; Damar Films, Ltd., Beverly Hills, Calif., production coordinator, 1980-84.

WRITINGS: Crash in the Wilderness (juvenile; illustrated by Tom Strobel), Raintree, 1980, new edition (illustrated by Thomas Buchs), 1982; *Louise LaBiche in Hollywood* (self-illustrated serial), Platinum Jackalopes Publishing, 1980; *This Is Pop* (self-illustrated juvenile), Overleaf Press, 1982; *The Totally Awesome Val Guide* (humor), Price, Stern, & Sloan, 1982. Editor of *Talent and Booking Directory*, 1978-80.

WORK IN PROGRESS: The Louise LaBiche Chronicles: A Study in Tension, a self-illustrated collection of stories; *Lady in a Greenhouse,* a novel; *My Dog Bitman,* a self-illustrated juvenile book.

SIDELIGHTS: ''The alienation of modern life will get you every time. Keep your sense of humor. When in doubt, shop.''

BOTKIN, B(enjamin) A(lbert) 1901-1975

PERSONAL: Born February 7, 1901, in Boston, Mass.; died July 30, 1975, in Croton-on-Hudson, N.Y.; son of Albert (a barber) and Annie (Dechinick) Botkin; married Gertrude Fritz, August 30, 1925; children: Dorothy Ann (Mrs. Jerome A. Rosenthal), Daniel Benjamin. *Education:* Harvard University, A.B. (magna cum laude), 1920; Columbia University, M.A., 1921; University of Nebraska, Ph.D., 1931. *Residence:* Croton-on-Hudson, N.Y. *Agent:* Curtis Brown Ltd., 575 Madison Ave., New York, N.Y. 10022.

CAREER: University of Oklahoma, Norman, instructor, 1921-31, assistant professor, 1931-38, associate professor of English, 1938-40; Federal Writers Project, Washington, D.C., national folklore editor, 1938-39; Library of Congress, Washington, D.C., chief editor of writers unit, Library of Congress Project, 1939-41, resident fellow in folklore, 1941-42, assistant in charge, later chief of Archive of American Folk Song (in Music Division), 1942-45; free-lance writer and editor, beginning in 1945. Visiting summer professor at University of Montana, 1932, at New Mexico Normal (now New Mexico Highlands) University, 1933. Consultant to committee on population problems, National Resources Committee, 1936; chairman of executive committee, Workshop for Cultural Democracy, 1956-58. Committee member, National Folk Festival, beginning in 1934.

MEMBER: American Folklore Society (fellow; president, 1944; delegate to American Council of Learned Societies, 1951-53), International Folk Music Council, Manuscript Society, Northeast Folklore Society, New York Folklore Society (honorary vice-president), Nebraska Folklore Society, Phi Beta Kappa.

B. A. BOTKIN

Awards, honors: Julius Rosenwald Foundation Fellow, 1937-38; honorary fellow in folklore, Library of Congress, 1942-55; Guggenheim Fellow, 1951; Litt.D., University of Nebraska, 1956; Centennial Medal of Civil War Round Table of New York, 1963; Louis M. Rabinowitz Foundation grant, 1965.

WRITINGS: The American Play-Party Song, with a Collection of Oklahoma Texts and Tunes, University of Nebraska Press, 1937, 2nd edition with new preface, Ungar, 1963.

Editor: (And contributor) *Folk-Say: A Regional Miscellany,* four volumes, University of Oklahoma Press, 1929-32; *The Southwest Scene: An Anthology of Regional Verse,* Economy Co., 1932; *A Treasury of American Folklore: Stories, Ballads, and Traditions of the People,* Crown, 1944 (published in England as *The American People, in Their Stories, Legends, Tall Tales, Traditions, Ballads, and Songs,* Pilot Press, 1946), selections re-issued as *The Sky's the Limit,* Louis Untermeyer, editor, Editions for the Armed Forces, 1944, and reissued as *A Pocket Treasury of American Folklore,* Pocket Books, 1950; *Lay My Burden Down: A Folk History of Slavery,* University of Chicago Press, 1945; *A Treasury of New England Folklore: Stories, Ballads, and Traditions of the Yankee People,* Crown, 1947, revised edition published as *A Treasury of New England Folklore: Stories, Ballads, and Traditions of the Yankee Folk,* 1965; *A Treasury of Southern Folklore: Stories, Ballads, Traditions, and Folkways of the People of the South,* Crown, 1949; *A Treasury of Western Folklore,* Crown, 1951, revised edition, 1974; (with Alvin F. Harlow) *A Treasury of Railroad Folklore: The Stories, Tall Tales, Traditions, Ballads and Songs of the American Railroad Man,* Crown, 1953; *Sidewalks of America: Folklore, Legends, Sagas, Traditions, Customs, Songs, Stories and Sayings of City Folk,* Bobbs-Merrill, 1954; *A Treasury of Mississippi River Folklore: Stories, Ballads, Traditions and Folkways of the Mid-American River Country,* Crown, 1955; *New York City Folklore: Legends, Tall Tales, Anecdotes, Stories, Sagas, Heroes and Characters, Customs, Traditions, and Sayings,* Random House, 1956; *A Treasury of American Anecdotes: Sly, Salty, Shaggy Stories of Heroes and Hellions, Beguilers and Buffoons, Spellbinders and Scapegoats, Gagsters and Gossips, from the Grassroots and Sidewalks of America,* Random House, 1957; (with Carl Withers) *The Illustrated Book of American Folklore: Stories, Legends, Tall Tales, Riddles, and Rhymes,* Grosset, 1958; *A Civil War Treasury of Tales, Legends and Folklore,* Random House, 1960.

Contributor: W. T. Couch, editor, *Folk and Folklore: Culture in the South,* University of North Carolina Press, 1934; Caroline F. Ware, editor, *The Cultural Approach to History,* Columbia University Press, 1940; *Round-up: A Nebraska Reader,* University of Nebraska Press, 1957; *Folklore in Action,* American Folklore Society, 1962; Jay Monaghan, editor, *A Sampler of Western Folklore and Songs,* Messner, 1963. Contributor of articles and introductions to other anthologies.

Editorial consultant: "Life Treasury of American Folklore," Time, Inc., 1961; (for book and two records) *The Folklore of the Badmen, the Badmen, Songs, Stories and Pictures of the Western Outlaws from Backhills to Border, 1865-1900,* Columbia Records, Inc., 1963. Consultant on games, *American College Dictionary,* 1963.

Editor, and author of notes for albums 7-10, "Folk Music of the United States from Records in the Archive of American Folk Song," Library of Congress, 1945.

Contributor to *Collier's Encyclopedia, Funk & Wagnalls Standard Dictionary of Folklore, Mythology and Legend, World Book Encyclopedia.* Contributor to *American Speech, Frontier, Negro Digest, Carleton Miscellany, New York Folklore Quarterly, Southwest Review, Trend, Vogue, Prairie Schooner,* and other journals and magazines. Contributing editor, *Southwest Review,* 1929-37, *New York Folklore Quarterly,* beginning in 1946 (columnist, beginning in 1950); editor and publisher, *Space,* 1934-35; member of publication committee, *Westerners New York Posse Brand Book,* 1954-59.

SIDELIGHTS: Botkin graduated magna cum laude from Harvard University with a B.A. degree in English, received a master's degree from Columbia University, and a doctoral degree from the University of Nebraska. In 1937 he went to Washington, D.C. as a Rosenwald Fellow, and was named a fellow in folklore at the Library of Congress.

A noted folklorist, Botkin edited numerous collections of folktales, legends, folksongs, and folk customs. He served as a folklore consultant and a contributor to encyclopedias and dictionaries. He was best known, however, for his definitive work on folklore, *A Treasury of American Folklore: Stories, Ballads, and Traditions of the People,* published in 1944 with a foreword by Carl Sandburg.

FOR MORE INFORMATION SEE: New York Post, May 4, 1944; *Nebraska Alumnus,* March, 1964; Bruce Jackson, editor, *Folklore and Society: Essays in Honor of Benjamin A. Botkin,* Folklore Associates, 1966. Obituaries: *New York Times,* July 31, 1975; *Publishers Weekly,* August 18, 1975.

BOWMAN, Kathleen (Gill)   1942-

BRIEF ENTRY: Born December 19, 1942, in Minneapolis, Minn. Bowman attended Lawrence University and received her B.S., M.A., and Ph.D. from the University of Minnesota. During her career she has worked as a junior high school teacher, a university instructor in education, a director of human relations, and an educational program consultant. In 1977 she became a research associate of the Legislative Advisory Council on the Economic Status of Women. She has also been a

member of the American Civil Liberties Union, the National Organization for Women, and the Women's Equity Action League. Her six juvenile books in the "New Women" series (all published by Creative Education in 1976) contain brief biographies of notable women in various fields. Among the women represented are dancer Martha Graham, singer Diana Ross, newscaster Barbara Walters, and psychologist Joyce Brothers. Bowman also includes information on career preparation with emphasis on the problems these professionals have faced as women in their fields. The books in the series are: *New Women in Medicine, New Women in Media, New Women in Entertainment, New Women in Social Sciences, New Women in Art and Dance,* and *New Women in Politics.* Bowman is also the author of two high-interest/low-vocabulary biographies: *On Stage: Elvis Presley* and *On Stage: Johnny Cash* (both Creative Education, 1976).

FOR MORE INFORMATION SEE: Contemporary Authors, Volumes 69-72, Gale, 1978.

BRANDT, Catharine   1905-

PERSONAL: Born January 23, 1905, in Jacksonville, Ill.; daughter of Jerome E. (a business executive) and Charlotte (Halsted) Gates; married Russell L. Brandt (a chain store manager, superintendent, and buyer), June 2, 1927 (died January 21, 1966); children: Russell L., Jr., Barbara (Mrs. Philip Weiler). *Education:* Bethel College, St. Paul, Minn., 1951-56; University of Minnesota, 1953-54. *Religion:* Protestant. *Home:* 5800 St. Croix Ave., Apt. 404, Minneapolis, Minn. 55422.

CAREER: Writer, 1953—. Member of faculty at North Central Bible College, Minneapolis, Minn., and Decision School of Christian Writing. Also worked as private secretary. Volunteer worker at nursing home. *Member:* American Bell Association, National League of American Pen Women, Minnesota Christian Writers Guild (past president).

WRITINGS: A Woman's Money: How to Protect and Increase It in the Stock Market, Parker Publishing, 1970; *The Story of Christmas for Children,* Augsburg, 1974; *Praise God for This New Day: Second Thoughts for Busy Women* (illustrated by Audrey Teeple), Augsburg, 1975; *We Light the Candles* (booklet), Augsburg, 1976; *You're Only Old Once* (illustrated by A. Teeple), Augsburg, 1977; *Flowers for the Living,* Augsburg, 1977; *God Bless Grandparents: The Adventures of Being a Grandparent,* Augsburg, 1978; *Forgotten People,* Moody, 1978; *Still Time to Sing: Prayers and Praise for Late in Life,* Augsburg, 1980; *Still Time to Pray,* Augsburg, 1983; (with Irma Stoll) *The Sparrow's Song,* Tyndale, 1984.

Author of "Talking with Teens," a weekly column for teenagers in Union Gospel Press's *My Delight,* 1969-73. Contributor of more than seven hundred articles and stories to magazines.

WORK IN PROGRESS: A juvenile novel; a devotional book for people on the verge of retirement.

SIDELIGHTS: "When I was ten or eleven I wrote plays for our neighborhood bunch, and we acted them out for our mothers and younger children.

"As a young person I was unable to go to college. In 1952, with my son in college and my daughter in high school, I began a series of college and university courses with a view toward writing. I write a great deal on the subject of old age. An editor of a Baptist Sunday school take-home paper, for whom I once wrote, suggested that I do an article on how young people can help the elderly. I've been writing on that subject ever since.

"Most of my writing, but not all, has been for religious markets. While not top-paying, they represent a wide readership. My articles and prayers printed in *Decision* magazine reach a potential three million readers. I write because I'd rather be writing than doing anything else. Also, I can explain to readers what it means to me to be a Christian and how I feel about God.

"A small critique group meets monthly at my home. So far we have had published numerous articles and thirty-five books. The group is still going strong.

"I support young people today in every way I can. The ones I know are bright and knowledgeable, eager to accomplish what the older generation has sometimes failed to do. All of us, including teens, are living under a great stress today and all of us need encouragement. I see my writing as that—encouragement wherever possible.

"For youngsters who want to write I say, 'Walk away from TV and read—classics, current events, newspapers. Ask your teachers or librarian for suggestions. Many gifted writers are publishing fascinating books for young people. READ.'"

CATHARINE BRANDT

nine fishermen
going fishing
in a very small boat
on the rough and windy sea.

(From *One, Two, Three, Going to Sea: An Adding and Subtracting Book* by Alain. Illustrated by the author.)

Squirrel dropped a nut on Little Bear's nose. But Little Bear kept right on sleeping. ■ (From *Little Bear's Thanksgiving* by Janice. Illustrated by Mariana.)

BRUSTLEIN, Daniel 1904-
(Alain)

PERSONAL: Born September 11, 1904, in Mulhouse, Alsace, France; naturalized U.S. citizen, 1933; married Janice Tworkov (author of children's books), 1941; *Education:* École des Arts, Geneva, Switzerland, certificate of capacity. *Home:* 8 rue de General Bertrand, Paris 75007, France.

CAREER: Worked as interior decorator and printed-silk designer in Paris, France, and New York, N.Y.; free-lance cartoonist, illustrator, and author, 1940—. Work has been shown in exhibitions, including those at Stable Annual, New York City, 1952, 1953; Corcoran Gallery Annual, Washington, D.C., 1958; École de Paris, Galerie Charpentier, 1961, 1962; National Institute of Arts and Letters, 1967; Patricia Learmonth Gallery, New York City, 1977; American Painters in the French National Collections, Centre Beaubourg, Paris, 1977; A. M.

Sachs Gallery, New York City, 1978; La Famille des Portraits, Musee des Arts Decoratifs with Musee de Louvre, Paris, 1979-80. Work is represented in collections of the Pompidou and Louvre museums, both in Paris, France. *Awards, honors:* Premiere Selection du Prix P. L. Weiller, Musee Marmottan, Paris, 1971.

WRITINGS—All under pseudonym Alain; all self-illustrated: *Petite histoire de la guerre en caricatures,* Atar, 1919; *The Elephant and the Flea* (juvenile), McGraw, 1956; *Alain's Steeplechase,* Simon & Schuster, 1956; *Yoga for Perfect Health,* Associated Books, 1957; *The Magic Stones* (juvenile), Whittlesey House, 1957; *One, Two, Three, Going to Sea: An Adding and Subtracting Book* (juvenile), Young Scott Books, 1964; *Alain on Happiness,* translated from the French by Robert D. Cottrell and Jane E. Cottrell, Ungar, 1973; *The Gods,* translated by Richard Pevear, New Directions, 1974.

Illustrator; under the pseudonym Alain: Lee Strout White, *Farewell to Model T,* Putnam, 1936; Ernest Mortenson, *You Be the Judge,* Longmans, 1940; written by wife, Janice Brustlein, *It's Spring! It's Spring!* (juvenile), Lothrop, 1956; J. Brustlein, *Minette* (juvenile), Whittlesey House, 1959; Harrison Kinney, *Kangaroo in the Attic* (juvenile), McGraw, 1960; Dale Fife, *A Stork for the Bell Tower* (juvenile), Coward, 1964; Fife, *A Dog Called Dunkel* (juvenile), Coward, 1966.

Contributor of cartoons to periodicals, including *New Yorker, Collier's* and *Saturday Evening Post.*

FOR MORE INFORMATION SEE: Lee Kingman and others, compilers, *Illustrators of Children's Books: 1957-1966,* Horn Book, 1968.

BRUSTLEIN, Janice Tworkov (Janice)

PERSONAL: Married Daniel Brustlein (an artist), 1941. *Home:* 8 rue de General Bertrand, Paris 75007, France.

CAREER: Writer of books for children. *Awards, honors: Mr. and Mrs. Button's Wonderful Watchdogs* was named a "Children's Choice" by the International Reading Association, 1979.

WRITINGS—All juvenile; all under name Janice: *It's Spring! It's Spring!* (illustrated by husband, Daniel Brustlein, under pseudonym, Alain), Lothrop, 1956; *The Lonely Little Lady and Her Garden,* Lothrop, 1958; *Little Bear's Sunday Breakfast,* Lothrop, 1958; *Minette* (illustrated by Alain), Whittlesey House, 1959.

Little Bear's Pancake Party (illustrated by Maria Curtis Foster, under pseudonym, Mariana), Lothrop, 1960; *Angélique* (illustrated by Roger Duvoisin), Whittlesey House, 1960; *Little Bear's Christmas* (illustrated by Mariana), Lothrop, 1964; *Little Bear's Thanksgiving* (illustrated by Mariana), Lothrop, 1967; *Little Bear Marches in the St. Patrick's Day Parade* (illustrated by Mariana), Lothrop, 1967; *Little Bear Learns to Read the Cookbook* (illustrated by Mariana), Lothrop, 1969.

Little Bear's New Year's Party (illustrated by Mariana), Lothrop, 1973; *Mr. and Mrs. Button's Wonderful Watchdogs* (illustrated by R. Duvoisin), Lothrop, 1979.

BURMAN, Ben Lucien   1896-1984

OBITUARY NOTICE—See sketch in *SATA* Volume 6: Born December 12, 1896, in Covington, Ky.; died of a cerebral hemorrhage, November 12, 1984, in New York, N.Y. Author. Burman wrote over twenty books throughout his lifetime, both adult novels and stories for children. He is best remembered as a writer of the rural South, particularly life on the Mississippi River. A Harvard graduate, Burman began his writing career in the 1920s as a reporter/editor for newspapers like the *Boston Herald* and *New York Sunday World.* During World War II, he served as war correspondent for The Reader's Digest and the Newspaper Enterprise Association, traveling to Africa and the Middle East. In 1947 he was awarded the French Legion of Honor for his reports from Africa on the Free French forces. Burman's first successful novel was *Steamboat Round the Bend,* published in 1933 and later made into a motion picture starring Will Rogers. Other novels followed, including *Blow for a Landing, Rooster Crows for Day,* and *The Sign of the Praying Tiger.*

For children, Burman wrote a series of books based on the mythical Louisiana town of Catfish Bend. Inhabited by an amusing group of anthropomorphic animals, Catfish Bend was the setting for over six books in which Burman humorously parodied the foibles of man. The series spans over thirty years in publication dates, beginning with *High Water at Catfish Bend* in 1952 and ending with *Thunderbolt at Catfish Bend* in 1983, Burman's last completed work. Accompanied with illustrations by his wife, Alice Caddy, the books have sold over 16 million copies in eleven languages. In addition to numerous awards for his writings, Burman was honored in 1983 by the designation of October 8 as Ben Lucien Burman Day by the states of Louisiana and Kentucky. Also designated by the governor of Louisiana was the town of Port Hudson as Catfish Bend.

FOR MORE INFORMATION SEE: Contemporary Authors, New Revision Series, Volume 8, Gale, 1983; *Twentieth-Century Children's Literature,* 2nd edition, St. Martin's, 1983. *Obituaries: New York Times,* November 13, 1984; *Publishers Weekly,* November 30, 1984.

BURSTEIN, John   1949- (Slim Goodbody)

BRIEF ENTRY: Born December 25, 1949, in Mineola, N.Y. Entertainer, author, and television personality. The star of a one-man act called "The Inside Story," Burstein has appeared as "Mr. Slim Goodbody" before over half a million school children and on television since 1974. Wearing a flesh-colored body suit displaying pictures of bones, muscles, and internal organs in their proper places, Burstein sings and performs in an effort to inform children about how their bodies function. He believes "it is vitally important that children learn to appreciate their bodies and love themselves." As an author of juvenile books, Burstein has written *Slim Goodbody: What Can Go Wrong and How to Be Strong* (McGraw, 1978) and *Slim Goodbody's Healthy Days Diary: Activity Book* (Caedmon, 1983). Under the name Slim Goodbody he wrote *Lucky You!* (McGraw, 1980), *The Force Inside You* (Coward, 1983), *The*

Healthy Habits Handbook (Coward, 1983), and a story entitled *The Get-Well Hotel* (McGraw, 1980). His filmstrips, released by the Society for Visual Education, include: "Slim Goodbody and Your Body," 1978, "Slim Goodbody's World of Animals and Plants," 1981, and "Slim Goodbody's World of Weather and Climate," 1983. In 1978 Burstein received the New Jersey Institute of Technology's New Jersey Authors Award for *Slim Goodbody, the Inside Story* (McGraw, 1977).

FOR MORE INFORMATION SEE: Newsweek, May 12, 1975: *Contemporary Authors,* Volume 69-72, Gale, 1978.

CAREW, Jan (Rynveld) 1925-

BRIEF ENTRY: Born September 24, 1925, in Agricola, Guyana. Novelist, poet, playwright, artist, educator, and author of stories for children. Since 1972 Carew has served as professor and chairman of the department of African-American studies at Northwestern University in Evanston, Ill. Prior to that time, he held a variety of positions such as customs officer in the British Colonial Civil Service, 1940-43, price control officer for the government of Trinidad, 1943-44, director of culture and advisor to the prime minister of British Guyana, 1962, advisor to the publicity secretariat of the government of Ghana, 1965-66, and lecturer in Afro-American studies at Princeton University, 1969-72. From 1950 to 1951 he spent his time as an artist and writer in Paris and Amsterdam; the following year, he toured as an actor with the Laurence Olivier Company. In the late 1960s, he was commissioned as an artist and writer by the Canadian Broadcasting Co. to do numerous programs in Toronto.

Carew's first adult novel, *Black Midas,* was published in 1958. Others followed, like *The Last Barbarian* and *Moscow Is Not My Mecca.* His first book for children appeared in 1974 under the title *The Third Gift.* It is an African tale that tells the story of a tribe of people who receive the gifts of work, beauty, and imagination. "Rich, melodic prose . . . , " observed *Booklist,* "retains the lilting phraseologies that emphasize the tale's ethnicity. . . ." Carew's second juvenile book, *Children of the Sun* (Little, Brown, 1978), also contains elements of folklore. In this tale of twin brothers begotten by the sun and a woman of the earth, *Publishers Weekly* took note of "the ritualistic feelings of legends in the controlled, stately prose. . . ." Carew is also the author of seven books in Longman's "Knockouts" series, designed for slow-learning adolescents. His short stories and poetry appear in several anthologies, and he has written numerous plays for stage, television, and radio. In addition to his writing and teaching, Carew has served as co-chairman of the Third World Energy Institute since 1978. *Office:* Department of African-American Studies, Northwestern University, 2003 Sheridan Rd., Evanston, Ill. 60201.

FOR MORE INFORMATION SEE: Contemporary Authors, Volumes 77-80, Gale, 1979; *The Writers Directory: 1984-86,* St. James Press, 1983.

CARMICHAEL, Carrie (Harriet Carmichael)

PERSONAL: Born in Plainfield, N.J.; daughter of William and Harriet (a teacher; maiden name, Wentlandt) Carmichael; married Jeff Greenfield (a writer and broadcaster), May 11, 1968; children: Casey (daughter), David. *Education:* Muhlenberg College, B.A., 1966; New York University, M.A., 1968. *Home:*

322 West 72nd St., Apt. 11B, New York, N.Y. 10023. *Agent:* Pat Berens, Sterling Lord Agency Inc., 660 Madison Ave., New York, N.Y. 10021.

CAREER: Author, reporter, and broadcaster. United Press International, New York, N.Y., financial reporter (under pseudonym Harriet Carmichael), 1967-1968; NBC Radio Network, New York City, broadcaster of daily radio program "Workplace," 1978—. Member of board of directors, Rheedlan Foundation, 1982. *Awards, honors:* Broadcast award from the National Commission on Working Women, 1982; first prize from the Odyssey Foundation for radio series, "When a Child Is Missing," 1984.

WRITINGS—Nonfiction: Non-Sexist Childraising (adult), Beacon, 1977; *Bigfoot: Man, Monster, or Myth?* (juvenile), Raintree, 1977; *Secrets of the Great Magicians* (juvenile), Raintree, 1977; (with Marcia L. Storch) *How to Relieve Cramps and Other Menstrual Problems* (adult), Workman Publishing, 1982; (with Ruby Wright) *Mama Ruby's Book of Baby Knowledge,* Bantam, 1984.

CHANDLER, Robert 1953-

PERSONAL: Born February 3, 1953, in Germany; son of Roger (a British Army Officer) and Catherine (Quirk) Chandler. *Education:* Attended Winchester College, 1966-70; Leeds University, B.A. (with honors), 1975; Oxford University, graduate study, 1976-77. *Residence:* London, England. *Agent:* Curtis Brown, Ltd., 1 Craven Hill, London W2, England.

CAREER: Poet, translator, and author. Also employed as a teacher of astrology and folktale interpretation.

ROBERT CHANDLER

She walked more than a day, more than two days, more than three days—no one knows how many. ▪ (From *The Magic Ring and Other Russian Folk Tales*, retold by Robert Chandler. Illustrated by Ken Kiff.)

WRITINGS—For children: (Reteller) *The Magic Ring, and Other Russian Folk Tales* (illustrated by Ken Kiff), Faber, 1979; (translator) Alexander Afanasyev, compiler, *Russian Folk Tales* (illustrated by Ivan Bilibin), Random House, 1980. Contributor of poems, articles, and translations to various journals, including *London Magazine*, *Poetry Nation Review* and *Modern Poetry in Translation*.

WORK IN PROGRESS: Translation from the Russian, *Life and Fate* by Vassily Grossman; *The Story of Stories*, a book for children; a volume of poetry; translations of poetical works by Pablo Neruda and Guilleric.

SIDELIGHTS: "I am deeply interested in the areas of mythology, comparative religion, folklore, and astrology. The psychology of Carl Jung has been a necessary guide to me in these bewildering areas. I have been teaching astrology for several years. I also teach courses on the interpretation of folktales from the perspective of Jungian psychology.

"I see the great collections of European folktales—Grimm, Afanasyev, Asbjörnsen, etc.—as books of wisdom, our legacy from the rich and varied culture of peasant Europe. Like any other compendium of collective wisdom—the I-Ching or the Bible—they draw on deep springs that are beyond the reach of any individual.

"Storytelling is one of the most ancient activities. It is an art that is sadly lost in our culture. Even the most basic sense of the meaning of 'story' is almost lost to us—most of us are cut off from any real sense of history, whether that of our family, our town or village, or our country.

"What I write myself must inevitably spring from my own personal concerns and problems, and those of the collapsing culture I have been born into. It is not for me to hope to attain the profound objectivity of the greatest of folktales. Nevertheless, I do feel that most modern prose is over sophisticated; I do feel a sense of kinship with the anonymous storytellers of the past, and I do hope to allow my own writing to nourish itself from their rich traditions.

"Linked to my love of story is my love of language and etymology, the story of words. I speak fluent Russian and Spanish (I have lived for a year in both Russia and Spain), and I have a reading knowledge of French, Spanish, Italian and Romanian. I am at present teaching myself German by reading a complete edition of the Brothers Grimm in both German and English.

"The widespread physical and psychic ill-health of our society appears to be rooted in our alienation from many of man's most fundamental instinctual activities. We have forgotten how to cook, how to eat, how to walk, how to dream. . . . I have spent much of the last five years studying cooking and nutrition from the perspective of macrobiotics, posture and relaxation with the help of the Alexander technique, and learning, with the help of a Jungian analyst, to understand my dreams and acquire a deeper sense of my own life story. All of this has had a profound effect on both the manner and matter of my writing."

CHRISTESEN, Barbara 1940-

PERSONAL: Surname is pronounced Kriss-tessen; born March 7, 1940, in New York, N.Y.; daughter of Stanley (a grocery store manager) and Florence (Schultz) Suchy; married John Denis Christesen (a college professor), November 16, 1963. *Education:* Hunter College (now of the City University of New York), B.A., 1960. *Religion:* Roman Catholic. *Home and office:* Waccabuc Rd., Goldens Bridge, N.Y. 10526.

CAREER: Educational Development Laboratories, Huntington, N.Y., editor and writer, 1965-68; free-lance writer of educational materials, 1969—. President of Westchester Editorial Services. Co-editor of *Road Four* (a community newsletter), 1974-78.

WRITINGS—All for children: *Folktales of the World*, Simon & Schuster, 1970; *The Magic and Meaning of Voodoo*, Contemporary Perspectives, 1977; *Myths of the Orient*, Contemporary Perspectives, 1977; *The First Olympic Games*, Contemporary Perspectives, 1978; *Introduction to Business*, Prentice-Hall, 1981; *Prehistoric "Monsters" that Still Walk the Earth*, Contemporary Perspectives, 1981. Also author of *Baroque New York*. Contributor of instructional materials and audio-visual teaching aids to such companies as Scholastic Publications, Inc., Reader's Digest Educational Division, Educational Enrichment Materials, and Team Productions.

WORK IN PROGRESS: The First Civil War, a study of the Seminole wars with the U.S. Government.

The two sat down and dined on the choicest of meats, the most delicate of fish, the rarest of fruits and cakes. ■ (From "The Magic Bottle," in *Myths of the Orient* by Barbara Christesen. Illustrated by Wayne Atkinson.)

SIDELIGHTS: "I have wanted to be a writer ever since I was a child, but I entered the field of educational writing quite by accident. While job-hunting in 1965, I answered an ad for an editorial assistant at a Long Island company. The company turned out to be Educational Developmental Laboratories which, I soon learned, produced audio-visual materials, most of which were aimed at improving reading skills. In the three years that I worked in the EDL offices, I literally 'learned the business' from the bottom up. I advanced to the position of associate editor, writing and overseeing a number of highly diversified programs.

"Since becoming a free-lancer in 1969 I have written just about every type of instructional material. My favorite type of writing—and the type which brings out my most creative talents—is humor geared to the thinking of teens and pre-teens.

"Whenever I get the opportunity to write pure fiction I usually try to give my stories a humorous tone—I love writing comedy and satire. Several years ago I worked on a *Reader's Digest*

program for which I wrote twenty audio scripts in the style of the old radio comedies. I consider them to be the best work I've ever done. I was present at one of the recording sessions, and when I saw professional actors standing at microphones reading the lines I had written it was one of the biggest thrills of my career. I think script writing is the type of work I do best, and it's also my favorite. I'd love to have the opportunity to write a script for television someday. The fact that I'm too shy to speak in front of an audience is probably one reason why I get so much pleasure from hearing other people read my words. I love writing speeches for people, and when I'm lucky enough to hear the speech delivered, it's like hearing myself thinking aloud.

"One of the best things about the writing field is the opportunity for learning which it provides me. Every time I do research for a book or an article, I feel that I not only broaden my knowledge, but widen my interests, as well. After writing a book on voodoo which required me to read a great deal of material on the subject, I found myself eager to learn more and more about it. In the same way I became interested in oriental mythology, the Seminole Indians in Florida, prehistoric life, and scores of other topics which I had never explored before.

"With regard to the Seminole Indians, one of my greatest ambitions as a writer is to tell the story of how the Seminoles were the first people to help black slaves escape to freedom, and how the wars which they fought with the government were the first conflicts over slavery in this country—a kind of 'first Civil War.'"

HOBBIES AND OTHER INTERESTS: "I love to travel and have been to France and Mexico several times. My French is quite adequate, especially since my husband and I have very dear French friends whom we visit as often as we can. (My Spanish was good at one time, but is now quite rusty; a writing assignment in Mexico or Spain would do wonders for it!) My other major interests are music (all types) and cooking. I am considered a gourmet cook and love to cook and bake for large parties."

COLLOMS, Brenda 1919-

PERSONAL: Born January 14, 1919, in London, England; daughter of Henry James and Jessie (Ward) Stenning; married Albert Lionel Colloms (a lawyer), August 5, 1961; children: Adrian, Martin. *Education:* University of London, B.A. (with honors), 1956; University of Liverpool, M.A., 1958. *Home:* 123 Gloucester Ave., Primrose Hill, London NW1 8LB, England.

CAREER: Writer. Has worked as publisher's reader, translator, story adviser for a film company, and journalist. Lecturer for adult education classes. *Member:* Society of Authors, Working Men's College (honorary librarian).

WRITINGS: Certificate History, four volumes, Dent, 1966-70; *Israel,* Hart-Davis, 1971, John Day, 1972; *The Mayflower Pilgrims,* Wayland, 1973, St. Martin's, 1977; *Charles Kingsley,* Constable, 1975; *Victorian Country Parsons,* Constable, 1977; *Victorian Visionaries,* Constable, 1982. Editor of journal of Working Men's College.

WORK IN PROGRESS: Fox and the Sisters, a book on "romantic radicals of the early nineteenth century, with especial emphasis on the attempts of women to win civil liberties, achieve divorce reform, and be recognised as individuals in their own right."

SIDELIGHTS: "I became sidetracked in Victorian studies quite by accident about ten years ago and have found them endlessly fascinating. My publisher suggested I write a collective biography, and I embarked on the project without realizing its complexity. The author has to keep many different strands of the story going at the same time whilst managing to avoid repetition. The reward for the writer—and one hopes for the reader, too—is that one makes friends with an entire circle of characters.

"Collective biographies seem inevitably to involve a great deal of research, and the author becomes resigned to the fact that much of this research has to be its own reward as it can never be confined in only one volume.

"As for suggestions to any would-be writers—anyone can start a book; it just takes discipline to finish one!"

CAROL CORNELIUS

CORNELIUS, Carol 1942-

PERSONAL: Born November 18, 1942, in St. Joseph, Mo.; daughter of James J. (a security officer) and Dorothy (a homemaker; maiden name, Norene) Bokay; married Ronald D. Cornelius (a dairy farmer), December 16, 1966; children: Richard D., Ronda A. *Education:* Attended Benedictine College, 1961-62; Missouri State College, 1981—. *Address:* P.O. Box 62, Easton, Mo. 64443.

CAREER: Author of books for children. *Member:* Missouri Writers Guild (St. Joseph).

WRITINGS—All for children; "Concept Books" series; all published by Child's World: *Polka Dots, Checks, and Stripes* (illustrated by Diana Magnuson), 1978; *Bobbin's Land* (illustrated by Franz Altschuler), 1978; *Isabella Wooly Bear Tiger Moth* (illustrated by F. Altschuler), 1978; *Hyla (Peep) Crucifer: The Story of the Spring Peeper Frog* (illustrated by F. Altschuler), 1978.

WORK IN PROGRESS: "A traditional fairytale, a perception book on similarities, and an adult mystery."

SIDELIGHTS: "My interest in reading and its offshoot writing can be directly attributed to the fact that my parents, grandparents, aunts and uncles took the time to sing to me, to tell me stories and, very importantly, to teach me nursery rhymes. My head is still full of nursery rhymes."

Between the dark and the daylight,
   When the night is beginning to lower,
Comes a pause in the day's occupations,
   That is known as the Children's Hour.
      —Henry Wadsworth Longfellow

Now Bobbin didn't have time to sing. Every time he looked at his five chicks, he saw five wide-open, empty mouths. ■ (From *Bobbin's Land* by Carol Cornelius. Illustrated by Franz Altschuler.)

COSGROVE, Stephen E(dward)   1945-

BRIEF ENTRY: Born July 26, 1945, in Spokane, Wash. Cosgrove is the author of over fifty children's books and the founder of a publishing company. Prior to writing for children, he was an assistant manager for C-Star Concrete and a vice-president for Fleet Investment. His writing career began after he and his wife decided to have children. In a *Seattle Post-Intelligence* article, he emphasized how he was dissatisfied with the children's books he saw for his future offspring and ''. . . decided to do something that would build a child's imagination.'' Cosgrove founded his own publishing company, Serendipity Communications Ltd. (now Serendipity Press). He started the venture on his belief that it was possible to create inexpensive fantasy books for children without sacrificing the quality of their production. His low-priced books are represented in various series, among them ''Bugg Books'' and ''Bear Board Books,'' and many of them have been illustrated by Robin James.

Among Cosgrove's fantasies is *The Gnome from Nome* in which a gnome and an otter living at the North Pole try to find out the human's secret of staying warm. In *Leo the Lop,* a bunny whose ears don't stand upright becomes the laughingstock of his fellow rabbits. Leo tries hard to conform until a possum teaches all the rabbits a lesson about what is normal. Cos-

grove's other books include: *In Search of the Saveopotomas, The Muffin Muncher, Wheedle on the Needle, Little Mouse on the Prairie, Trapper, Grampa Lop, Lord and Lady Bugg, The Bugglar Brothers, Bumble B. Bear: A Gift for the Giving,* and *Crick-ette.* Several of his books have been adapted into filmstrips and one, *Creole,* was made into a motion picture and a video cassette.

FOR MORE INFORMATION SEE: Seattle Post-Intelligencer, November 24, 1974; *Authors in the News,* Volume 1, Gale, 1976; *Contemporary Authors,* Volumes 69-72, Gale, 1978.

CROW, Donna Fletcher   1941-
(Elizabeth Paul)

PERSONAL: Born November 15, 1941, in Nampa, Idaho; daughter of Leonard S. (a real estate investor) and Reta (a teacher; maiden name, Book) Fletcher; married Stanley D. Crow (an attorney), December 14, 1963; children: Stanley D., Jr., Preston, John, Elizabeth Pauline. *Education:* Attended Pasadena College, 1960-62; Northwest Nazarene College, B.A. (summa cum laude), 1964. *Politics:* Republican. *Religion:* Nazarene. *Home:* 3776 La Fontana Way, Boise, Idaho 83702. *Agent:* Teal & Watt Literary Agency, 2036 Vista Del Rosa, Fullerton, Calif. 92631.

CAREER: English and drama teacher at Nampa High School, Nampa, Idaho, 1963-64 and Lexington Christian Academy, Lexington, Mass., 1965-66; Boise High School, Boise, Idaho, teacher of English, 1967-68. Director of local Nazarene drama ministry, 1974—; patron of Boise Philharmonic Association. *Member:* Romance Writers of America, Oregon Shakespearean Festival Association, Boise Gourmet Club, Phi Delta Lambda.

WRITINGS: Recipes for the Protein Diet, Gold Quill Publishers, 1972; (contributor) Robert D. Troutman and Evelyn Beals, editors, *Leading Children in Worship,* Aldersgate, 1980; (contributor) Jane Allen, editor, *Mountain Tops,* Faith for Today, 1982; *Frantic Mother Cookbook,* Harvest House, 1982; *Professor Q's Mysterious Machine* (juvenile), David Cook, 1983; *C Is for Christmas* (children's activity book), Green Baron, 1983; *Dr. Zarnof's Evil Plot* (juvenile), David Cook, 1983; (under pseudonym Elizabeth Paul) *Greengold Autumn* (adult romance novel), Zondervan, 1984; *Mr. Xanthus' Golden Scheme* (juvenile), David Cook, 1985; *The Desires of Your Heart* (adult romance novel), Zondervan, 1985; *Love Unmerited* (adult romance novel), Zondervan, 1985.

Plays: *Called Unto Holiness* (eleven scenes), first produced in Boise, Idaho, at First Church of the Nazarene, November 3, 1978, excerpts published, Lillenas, 1982 and 1983; *A Rumor of Resurrection* (five scenes), first produced at First Church of the Nazarene, April 20, 1980, Lillenas, 1983; *An Upper Room Experience* (one-act), first produced at First Church of the Nazarene, May 23, 1982, Lillenas, 1983; *Puppets on Parade* (a collection), first produced in Nampa, Idaho, at Northwest Nazarene College, October 16, 1981, Lillenas, 1985; *Because You Ask Not* (five scenes), first produced at First Church of the Nazarene, November 19, 1982, Standard Publishing, 1985.

(From *Professor Q's Mysterious Machine* by Donna Fletcher Crow.)

DONNA FLETCHER CROW

Contributor to magazines, including *Virtue, Family Life Today, Plastercraft, Living with Children, Arkenstone, Modern Liturgy, Herald of Holiness, The Christian Writer, Come Ye Apart,* and *Preacher's Magazine.*

WORK IN PROGRESS: Adult romance novels—*Brandley's Search, A Woman's Place, But the Greatest of These, The Flame Burns On, Roses for the Bride;* "Balance Due," a modern Faustus play; *General Knute's Battle Stratagem,* a juvenile book; *Love on Horseback,* a juvenile romance to be published by Zondervan; *Seekers of the Caves,* a juvenile fantasy novel.

SIDELIGHTS: "I am probably one of the luckiest people in the world because I have had three dreams in my life and they have all come true. From my earliest memory I wanted to be a rodeo queen, to have a family, and to be a writer.

"I was five years old when I first saw a Snake River Stampede parade with the queen riding at the head of it. I decided right then that someday I would do that. When I was in the third grade my uncle, who was foreman of a cattle ranch, gave me a big gentle gray horse. He said if I was going to break my neck on a horse I might as well do it on a gentle one. I named my horse Smokey and rode him everyday. I rode bareback because my daddy said I'd be a better rider if I learned without a saddle first. It was also safer that way—no danger of getting dragged in a stirrup if I fell off.

"I loved Smokey but I could never win a parade ribbon on him because he was really very ugly. So when I was in the sixth grade my uncle found a beautiful sorrel Arabian stallion for me. I won lots of ribbons on Duke (really Duhki Rababbi—but it was too hard to say, 'Whoa, Duhki Rababbi!' when I wanted a sliding stop) and began immediately training him for the difficult maneuvers of the queen contest. The summer I taught Duke to do a clover leaf pattern around three barrels was also the summer I took swimming lessons. I appeared every day at the city pool with enormous black and blue bruises on my legs from hitting the barrels when Duke came too close to them.

"When I was sixteen I was chosen by my saddle club to be a princess in the queen's court. The next year my first dream came true when I won the Snake River Stampede Queen contest over thirty-five other contestants. I had a wonderful summer riding in parades, appearing at rodeos, and doing publicity work for the rodeo on radio, TV, and personal appearances.

"The next year I became Miss Rodeo Idaho and at the Miss Rodeo America contest in Las Vegas, Nevada, I was chosen runner-up.

"My second dream began coming true when I met Stanley Dean Crow at a college debate tournament. That night we dated each others' debate partners, but pretty soon we got it right and we were married at Christmastime of our senior year in college. Then we moved to Cambridge, Massachusetts, where my husband attended Harvard Law School and I taught high school English and drama. Our third year in Cambridge our first son, Stanley, Jr., was born.

"We moved back to Boise, Idaho, where my husband began practicing law and I taught school one more year. Then our second son, Preston Fletcher, was born. Four years later, we had our third son, John Downing. But I had to wait longer yet for my dream to be really complete. We had been married sixteen years when our daughter, Elizabeth Pauline, was born. But she was worth waiting for.

"I began writing when I was six years old. At least I tried. I wanted to write a play of 'The Three Little Pigs,' but I was severely hampered by the fact that I couldn't write yet. So instead I marshalled the neighborhood children into a set-building crew. We cut the first little pig's house out of cardboard and stuck straw on with maple syrup. When the maple syrup ran out we gave up.

"When I was in grade school I loved to lie in the grass under a big cottonwood tree or in the middle of an alfalfa field where no one could see me and write poetry with illustrations. Both the poems and the pictures were awful.

"When I was in the sixth grade I wrote scripts for TV westerns, always casting myself as the heroine. I loved the parts where the hero rescued the heroine, but I never could write very good fight scenes. I also designed a series of novels for young readers and wrote most of the first two.

"But again, I had to wait a long time for a dream to come true. I became a professional writer only five years ago. I write plays, cookbooks, magazine articles, and novels. I especially enjoy writing for young people because I get my inspirations from my own children.

"*Professor Q's Mysterious Machine* was born when Preston came home from school waving two Choose Your Own Adventure books. 'None of these books ever stays in the library overnight and I got *two* of them!' he yelled. He dropped down on a stool at the kitchen counter and began reading. Stanley came in from junior high and picked up the other one. Two hours later I couldn't get either of them to come to the dinner table—and we were having chocolate cake for dessert!

"'There *has* to be some way to apply this technique to Bible study,' I thought. *Professor Q's Mysterious Machine* was the result, in which Professor Q's time machine takes readers to Bible lands where they are confronted with the same choices biblical characters faced.

"My fantasy/adventure novel, *Seekers of the Caves of Geolu*, came from ideas I got hearing my boys play Dungeons and Dragons with their friends. My book of puppet scripts, *Puppets on Parade*, came from watching 'Sesame Street' with my younger children and because Preston is in a puppet troupe. *The Frantic Mother Cookbook* is all about my family and the things we like to eat. And *Love on Horseback* is based on my experience as a rodeo queen—although I didn't have any romances then, I was far too busy with my horse.

"So I guess that if my first two dreams hadn't come true my third one couldn't have. Sometimes one has to wait a long time and work very hard, but dreams *can* come true."

FOR MORE INFORMATION SEE: Jennie F. Downing Crow, compiler, *Johnston, Stapp, and Allied Families,* privately printed, [North Platte, Neb.], 1979; *Contemporary Authors,* Volume 108, Gale, 1983.

CULLIFORD, Pierre   1928-
(Peyo)

PERSONAL: Born June 25, 1928, in Brussells, Belgium; married wife, Nine, about 1951; children: Thierry (son), Veronique. *Residence:* Brussels, Belgium.

CAREER: Author and illustrator of books for children; creator of the cartoon characters, the "Smurfs."

WRITINGS—All for children; all written under pseudonym Peyo; all self-illustrated; "Smurfs" series, in English translation; all titles originally published in French by Dupuis (Paris): *The Smurfette,* Hodder & Stoughton, 1978; (with Yvan Delporte) *The Smurfs and the Egg* [*and*] *The Hundredth Smurf,* Hodder & Stoughton, 1978, also published as *The Hundredth Smurf,* Random House, 1982; (with Y. Delporte) *Smurphony in C* [*and*] *The Flying Smurf,* Hodder & Stoughton, 1978, also published separately as *The Flying Smurf,* Random House, 1982, and *Smurphony in C,* Random House, 1982; *The Smurfs and the Magic Flute,* adapted by Y. Delporte, translated by Anthea Bell, Hodder & Stoughton, 1979, Random House, 1983; (with Y. Delporte and Gos) *The Weather Smurfing Machine* [*and*] *Smurf Stories,* translated by A. Bell and Derek Hockridge, Hodder & Stoughton, 1979, also published as *The Weather-Smurfing Machine,* Random House, 1982; *The Smurfs and the Howlibird,* translated by A. Bell and D. Hockridge, Hodder & Stoughton, 1980, Random House, 1983; (with Y. Delporte) *The Smurfic Games* [*and*] *Smurf of One and Smurf a Dozen of the Other,* translated by A. Bell and D. Hockridge, Hodder & Stoughton, 1980, Random House, 1984.

Peyo in a garden of Smurfs.

Smurf Cake, Random House, 1981; *A Smurf in the Air*, Random House, 1981; *The Fake Smurf* (based on original story by Y. Delporte), Random House, 1981; *The Wandering Smurf*, Random House, 1981; *The Astrosmurf*, Random House, 1982; *Baker Smurf's Sniffy Book*, Random House, 1982; *The Smurf Punch-Out Book*, Random House, 1982; *King Smurf*, Random House, 1982; *A Little Smurf Bedtime Story*, Random House, 1982; *Rainy Day: A Smurf Book of Feelings*, Random House, 1982; *The Wonderful World of Smurfs*, Random House, 1982; *The Smurf-Catching Trap*, Random House, 1982; *Smurf on the Grow*, Random House, 1982; *A Smurf Picnic*, Random House, 1982; *The Smurf's Apprentice*, Random House, 1982; *Coloring Magic with Painter Smurf*, Random House, 1983; (with Y. Delporte) *Romeo and Smurfette and Twelve Other Smurfy Stories*, Random House, 1983; *Smurf Water Fun*, Random House, 1983; *The Smurf Activity Book*, translated by A. Bell and D. Hockridge, Random House, 1983; *The Smurf Year-Round Coloring Book*, Random House, 1983; *The Smurfs and Their Woodland Friends*, Random House, 1983; *Through the Seasons with Smurfette*, Random House, 1983; *The Smurf ABC Book*, Random House, 1983; *What Do Smurfs Do All Day?*, Random House, 1983; *Baby Smurf's First Words*, Random House, 1984; (with Michel Matagne) *The Smurfs and the Miller*, Random House, 1984; (with M. Matagne) *The Smurfs and the Toyshop*, Random House, 1984.

Other "Smurf" books; all self-illustrated, except as indicated: all published by Dupuis: *Le Chatiment de Basenhau*, 1954; *Le Maitre de Roucybeuf*, 1955; *Le Lutin du bois aux roches*, 1956; *La Pierre de lune*, 1957; *Le Serment des Vikings*, 1958; *La Source des dieux*, 1958; *La Fleche noire*, 1959; *Le Sire de Montresor*, 1960; *La Guerre des sept fontaines*, 1962; *L'Anneau de Castellac*, 1963; *Le Pays maudit*, 1964; *Les Schtroumpfs noires*, 1964; *Les Schtroumpfs et les jouets* (illustrated by M. Matagne), 1969; *Les Schtroumpfs et le cracoucass*, 1969; *Le Sortilege de Maltrochu*, 1970; *Une Fete chez shtroumpfs*, 1976; *La Flute a six schtroumpfs*, 19(?).

"Brisefer" series; all written with Francois Walthery; all published by Dupuis: *Les Taxis rouges*, 1963; *Madame Adolphine*, 1966; *Les Douze Travaux de Benoit Brisefer*, 1968; *Tonton placide*, 1969; *Le Cirque Bodoni*, 1971; *Lady d'Olphine*, 197(?).

Other works: *Ca, c'est poussy*, Dupuis, 1976; *Pour faire une flute*, Dupuis, 1976.

ADAPTATIONS—Television: "The Smurfs" (special), NBC-TV, November 29, 1981; "The Smurfs Springtime Special," NBC-TV, April 8, 1982; "The Smurfs Christmas Special," NBC-TV, December 13, 1982; "The Smurfs," NBC-TV, weekly one-hour animated series, produced by Hanna-Barbera Productions; "Evil Wizard Smurf-erized" (special), NBC-TV, 1982; "My Smurfy Valentine" (special), NBC-TV, February 13, 1983; "Smurfing in Sign Language," NBC-TV, December 24, 1983; "Hefty and Wheelsmurfer," NBC-TV, October 13, 1984; "The Smurfic Games," NBC-TV, May 20, 1984; "Smurfily Ever After," NBC-TV, February 13, 1985.

Animated film: "The Smurfs and the Magic Flute," Belvision, 1975 (produced in France as "La Flute a six schtroumpfs").

The evolution of the Smurfs. ■ (From an "Interview with Peyo," by T. Groensteen in *Les Cahiers de la Bande Dessinée,* no. 54, Sept., 1983.)

A vivid model sheet which captures the essence of Smurfette, the only female Smurf.

SIDELIGHTS: "I was born in Brussells on **June 25, 1928** of a Belgian mother and of an English father who later became a naturalized Belgian. My father was a stockbroker, and if he hadn't died when I was only eight years old I would most likely have followed his example and gone into the brokerage business myself. Since I have no natural gift whatsoever for mathematics, I would have made a terrible stockbroker." [*Cahiers de la Bande Dessinée,* no. 54, (Belgium), 1983.[1]]

"I still have my father's picture at home in my study. I would have liked very much to know him. . . . My memory of him is one of a very gentle man, 'a good man' as they say. I still miss him today, to such an extent that I still go and spend some time at his grave. We talk to each other. Well, I talk to him and tell him: 'Daddy I hope you are proud of me. . . .' I don't really expect an answer, but I feel like there is a kind of communication between us. I really regret not having known him better." [*Spirou* Magazine, (Belgium), 1984.[2]]

"My mother played the piano, and above all she had a passion for the theater. Passion which I inherited. At The Institut Saint Louis where I went to school, it was traditional to put on a play for the occasion of the annual school awards. As for me, I was much more interested in the forthcoming performance than in my grades."[1]

An unremarkable student, Culliford admitted: "I'd be lying if I told you that I was a brilliant pupil. As is the rule for a cartoonist, I spent my school years illustrating the margins of my exercise books. I was particularly fond of the Latin course where we were using notebooks with very wide margins, therefore less confining. . . ."[1]

"But I never told myself like Franquin or Roba: 'Some day I'll be a cartoonist.'" [*Cahiers de la Bande Dessinée,* no. 12, (Belgium), 1971.[3]]

". . . I spent three months at the School of Fine Arts. Just enough time for me to copy several plaster busts and carry on several flirtations with the numerous girls who came to school hoping to find a boyfriend, if not a husband. Since I was mostly interested in caricatures and cartoons, the kind of education I received from the Fine Arts school didn't really meet my expectations. . . ."[1]

Soon after, Culliford went to work in an animation studio. "I was seventeen years old when I saw an ad for a job in an animation studio."[3] "Two possible positions caught my atten-

Peyo at work.

(From "The Smurfs and the Magic Flute," the first full-length animated motion picture starring the famous blue dwarfs. Music scored by Michel Legrand. Released by Belvision, 1975.)

tion: assistant dental mechanic, and draughtsman in an animation studio. I went after the first position because it was closer to where I lived, but the job had already been taken. The second position was still free and I was hired as a 'washperson.' That's it for my 'debut.'"[2]

"... Working in that studio was the big chance of my life; there, I met Franquin, Morris, and Paape who were already working as animators. Unfortunately, my experience was very brief: the studio soon went bankrupt, mainly because of the swarm of American animated cartoons distributed all over Europe. I lost sight of Franquin and the others at the very time they were first appearing in the comics. As for me, I went into advertising. I was working for several agencies, but at the same time I got the opportunity to publish one of my cartoons in *La Derniere Heure* ["The Last Hour", a Belgian daily newspaper]."[1]

"Johan" was Culliford's first cartoon character. It was at this time that Culliford selected the pseudonym "Peyo." "My real name, Culliford, seemed far too long, and also it's beginning sound is not the best: my schoolmates already called me 'Cuckoo!'. . . . Peyo comes from my Christian name Pierre. As a kid I was called Pierrot and one of my cousins who could not yet pronounce the r, used to say Peyooot. . . ."[1]

Creator of the Smurfs, Culliford related the birth of their name. "Twenty-five years ago, I was spending some time at the seaside with Franquin, and in the course of a meal I asked him: 'Pass me the. . . . "schtroumpf."' The name of what I wanted had momentarily escaped me and I simply made up a substitute for 'stuff' or 'whatchamacallit' etc. . . . Franquin thought that the word was very amusing and we kept including it in our conversation during the next several days. A month later, I had to give a name to the little creatures I'd just drawn and 'schtroumpf' spontaneously came to mind. . . ."[1] Smurf became the anglicized version of "schtroumpf."

"... Yvan Delporte, then the Chief Editor of *Spirou* . . . had the idea of issuing . . . 'mini-stories,' and because of their size, the Smurfs fitted that format perfectly. So, I decided to go ahead and try to give them a life of their own, independent from the 'Johan' stories. It was an immediate success. I had noticed that 'The Flute and the Six Smurfs' was doing much better than any other stories. I simply redrew the episodes published in the 'mini-stories' and adapted them to a regular book format. Francis helped me with the job of reproduction which was a little fastidious, since the pleasure of creation wasn't there anymore. . . ."[1]

Romeo and Smurfette

(From "Romeo and Smurfette," in *Romeo and Smurfette and Twelve Other Smurfy Stories* by Yvan Delporte and Peyo. Illustrated by Peyo.)

(From *La Soupe aux Schtroumpfs* by Peyo and Yvan Delporte. Illustrated by Peyo.)

When the Smurfs find an Easter egg in the forest, the baby duck that hatches from it adopts Smurfette as its mother. ∎ (From "The Smurf's Springtime Special." First presented on NBC-TV, April 8, 1982.)

With the advent of the Smurfs, Culliford abandoned his other characters "Johan" and "Pirlouit." "I'm the first to regret it! I still have a very special feeling of tenderness for those two characters, but it's true that I'm a prisoner of the Smurfs' success. It's for them and not for 'Pirlouit' that the readers and the publishers are asking. . . . Success dictated it! . . . Of course the day the Smurfs stop amusing me, I'll stop drawing them. But that day is yet to come. The Smurfs make up a sufficiently diversified community for me to create infinite possibilities of interesting situations."[1]

Although the Smurfs became very successful characters, they weren't received without criticism. "It has been said that children stopped learning to read because of the Smurfs! . . . Also many parents complained about not understanding their children anymore because they were using the Smurf language between themselves. But those reactions are part of a larger contempt for comic strips and onomatopoeia in general . . . etc.

". . . The episode where the Smurfette was born was hardly out when a great many critics accused me of misogyny, phallicism, etc. . . . Honestly, I don't think of myself as a misogynist. On the contrary. The Smurfette is a caricature, without

malice, of the feminine nature with its good and bad qualities. I especially wanted to show how women hold us by appealing to our feelings; that willfully or not, they exert a real power over men by means of emotions. Jacques Brel, whom I admired very much, explains it very well in his song 'The Doe.' And look around you, you'll see for yourself that in most married couples, it's the woman who wears the trousers."[1]

The first animated cartoon with the Smurfs was made in 1959. "Dupuis had just opened an animation studio with Eddy Russack as director. This studio had already made ten or a dozen short animated films with the Smurfs, but they were only half-animated and the adaptation had been done without me. In 1975, television produced 'The Flute and the Six Smurfs' which I supervised very closely. I dedicated two years of my life to that project, and I learned all the techniques of animation. I must say I was not unhappy with the results, especially with the drawings and the quality of the animation."[1]

The movie brought the Smurfs to the attention of advertising agencies and toy manufacturers.

The studio of Hanna-Barbera is in charge of producing the American Smurfs. ". . . Their studios are based in Los Angeles where I go every six months to supervise the work. There are more than a thousand people working full time on my little Smurfs! It's unbelievable! It's stupendous! The means they have at their disposal cannot in any way be compared with what we have here. I'm aware of the unique opportunity which has been offered to me. The only thing I insisted on from the start was that the Smurfs not chew gum and not drink Coca-Cola. I didn't want my little characters to be Americanized.

"I won on that point although from time to time I am still surprised by a detail here and there. For example, I wrote a script with no other instruction than: 'The Smurfs are playing ball.' Well, I was blown away when I saw the screening; they had adapted 'playing with a ball' to all the gestures of American baseball!"'[1]

Culliford writes part of the television script "... in collaboration with Yvan Delporte, and the Americans also send us some proposals. I have the right to refuse any scripts I don't like, but the final decision comes from NBC. In this connection I'd like to underline one thing. The United States is always being touted as the land of freedom, and yet I was amazed by the fact that everyone there seemed to live in fear of what their neighbours were going to say or think. At NBC, self-censorship goes to the extreme because they know that the slightest tasteless mistake will immediately be exposed and blown out of proportion by the two other competitive networks ABC and CBS. So, you have to be extremely cautious with regard to violence, drugs, racism, the portrayal of women, etc. . . .

"Let me give you two examples. First, the Smurf wearing glasses is a perpetual pain in the neck with his incessant lectures. So, I was planning on having him regularly knocked out with a sledge-hammer by another Smurf. Well, the heads of NBC thought it was much too violent for television. They claimed this might give American kids the notion of taking daddy's hammer and beating their little sisters over the head. Now, on the other hand, I could use an anvil for the same purpose because it's rare and unusual to possess one at home. Second, they wouldn't allow the Great Smurf to use philters and powders for fear that the viewers might associate it with drugs. Potions in the cartoons are not to be smelled, drunk or eaten. The Great Smurf just settles for throwing around golden powder. So, you see how far it can go! . . ."'[1]

(From the one-hour weekly animated series "The Smurfs," first broadcast on NBC-TV, September 12, 1981. Copyright © 1983 by Hanna-Barbera Productions, Inc. and Sepp International, S.A.)

Papa Smurf, more than 500 years old, introduces Baby Smurf to the ancient Greek tradition of lighting the torch. ■ (From the animated television special "The Smurfic Games." Presented on NBC-TV, May 20, 1984.)

Besides drawing and writing, Culliford oversees the business details of his projects. "... I refuse to entrust my business to professionals who would either sell me a bill of goods, or neglect the quality for a larger profit. And on no account will I accept that. I want to supervise everything so that my little characters stay attractive and the same as they've always been. Schultz did the same thing with his 'Peanuts,' and he was right. You know, I was asked several times to hire a team of cartoonists who would produce Smurfs in continuous succession. I've always refused."[1]

"... I have to keep an eye on everything. Anyway, I have that impression. My son Thierry often tells me 'Listen, Daddy, hand over some of your work to others; for Christ's sake, enjoy life while you still can.' To which I answer 'Okay, you're absolutely right! By the way—you see that drawing over there? Well, the movement of the hands has to be corrected. It doesn't quite work yet.' You see I have this need to control everything where my work is concerned. It may be a weakness, but it's also a strength in my opinion. In my case, I'm incapable of behaving any other way. I need to be 100% involved in what I'm doing, no 200%.... "

"I've always remembered my brother's advice: 'What deserves to be done, deserves to be done well.' This became engraved in my memory and in a way became an aim in my life. The satisfaction of a job well done is a reward in itself. It has happened that I've finished a drawing quicker than I wished to, without giving it the last touch. When I see one of those drawings today I must admit that I quickly turn the page. If I had to give any advice today, it would be my brother's: 'What deserves to be done, deserves to be done well.... '"

With a busy work schedule, Culliford has little free time, "... not even for my own family. In the past I enjoyed playing tennis and taking walks in the forest and watching television.... Now, I don't do those things anymore. I've also always loved to travel, it's a way of meeting new people and establishing new relationships. Today my trips are strictly business ones, and I regret that very much. Apart from Hanna-Barbera Studio, I know nothing of Los Angeles. I would add that if I appreciate tremendously the American business spirit, I also find it extremely difficult to talk to them about anything else."[1]

FOR MORE INFORMATION SEE: People, September 27, 1982; *Cahiers de la Bande Dessinée,* no. 12, [Belgium], 1971, no. 54, 1984; *Spirou* Magazine, [Belgium], 1984.

Children have neither past nor future; they enjoy the present, which very few of us do.
—Jean de La Bruyère

Twinkle, twinkle, little bat!
How I wonder what you're at!
Up above the world you fly!
Like a teatray in the sky.
—Lewis Carroll
(pseudonym of Charles Lutwidge Dodgson)

DALTON, Anne 1948-

PERSONAL: Born December 5, 1948, in London, England; married Andrew F. Stimson (a zoologist), June 29, 1974; children: Matthew Charles. *Education:* Attended Camberwell School of Arts and Crafts and Hornsey School of Art. *Home and office:* 18 Brenda Rd., London S.W. 17 (7DB), England. *Agent:* Laura Cecil, 27 Alwyne Villas, London N1 2HG, England.

CAREER: Part-time teacher and illustrator of children's books. *Awards, honors:* The *Times* Educational Supplement "Junior Information Book Award," 1978, for *Tournaments.*

ILLUSTRATOR—All for young people: Penelope Lively, *Boy without a Name,* Parnassus, 1975; Hilary Seton, *The Stonemason's Boy,* Heinemann, 1975; James Reeves, reteller, *The Shadow of the Hawk, and Other Stories by Marie de France,* Collins, 1975, Seabury, 1977; Ruth Marris, *The Virgin and the Angel,* Heinemann, 1977; Richard Barber, *Tournaments,* Penguin, 1978; Maurice Baring, *The Blue Rose,* Kaye & Ward, 1982.

WORK IN PROGRESS: Text and illustrations for *Prince Star,* publication by Kaye & Ward.

ANNE DALTON

As if in a dream, Marec went on, not stopping to ask herself where the track was leading her nor what she would find at the end of it. ■ (From *The Shadow of the Hawk and Other Stories* by Marie de France. Retold by James Reeves. Illustrated by Anne Dalton.)

DAVES, Michael   1938-

PERSONAL: Surname is pronounced ''Dave's''; born March 4, 1938, in Wichita Falls, Tex; son of Floyd Lee and Johnnie (Dunn) Daves; married Patricia McLean (a teacher), August 29, 1958; children: Paul Lee, Donna Michelle. *Education:* Midwestern University, B.A., 1959; Southern Methodist University, Th.M., 1963; Southwestern College, D.Hum., 1972. *Politics:* Democrat. *Home:* 3629 Green Hollow Dr., Grand Prairie, Tex. 75051. *Office:* First United Methodist Church, P.O. Box 128, 400 South Avenue C, Duncanville, Tex. 75116.

CAREER: Minister, North Texas Conference, United Methodist Church, serving churches in Wichita Falls, Tex., 1957-59, Addison, Tex., 1959-62, Plano, Tex., 1962-63, Holliday, Tex., 1963-66; minister, Prairie Heights United Methodist Church, Grand Prairie, Tex., 1966-72; minister to society, 1972-76; minister, Memorial United Methodist Church, Dallas, Tex., 1977-78; associate minister, Preston Hollow United Methodist Church, Dallas, Tex., 1978-81, and First United Methodist Church, Duncanville, Tex., 1981—. Vice-chairman, North Texas Conference, Commission on Worship, 1963-70. *Member:* Duncanville Ministerial Association, American Association of Pastoral Counselors. *Awards, honors:* Steck-Vaughn Award, Texas Institute of Letters, 1968, for *Young Reader's Book of Christian Symbolism.*

WRITINGS: Devotional Talks for Children, Baker Book, 1961, 2nd edition, 1967; *Sermon Outlines on Romans,* Revell, 1962; *Famous Hymns and Their Writers,* Revell, 1962; *George Matheson: The Free Captive* (booklet), Upper Room, 1962; *Meditations on Early Christian Symbols,* Abingdon, 1964; *Come with Faith,* Abingdon, 1965; *Young Reader's Book of Christian Symbolism* (illustrated by Gordon Laite), Abingdon, 1967; *The Service of Marriage* (booklet), T-M Press, 1968; *Advent: A Calender of Devotion,* Abingdon, 1971.

Regular contributor of columns in *Texas Methodist* and *Grand Prairie Daily News.* Contributor of articles and sermons to religious magazines and journals, including *Pulpit, Pulpit Preaching, Pulpit Digest, Together, Christian Century, Motive, Upper Room, Christian Advocate, Church School, Music Ministry,* and *Methodist Story.*

SIDELIGHTS: ''One of the side benefits of writing is the great people you meet. I've had letters from all over the world. The writers want to say thank you for something I've written that they've found helpful.

''I've been interested in Christian symbolism ever since I was a teenager growing up in Wichita Falls, Texas, and wondering what the symbols in stained glass windows meant. When I graduated from seminary, I found that not many adults or children knew what the symbols were saying. So two of my books were born from an early interest in symbols. The stories behind them are rich, indeed, and help us learn more about the Bible and Christian history.

''Since my book for children has been recommended for use in church schools by the United Methodist Church, I've talked

. . . Patti answered, "It means that Jesus cares for his children like a shepherd cares for his sheep." She was right. ■ (From *Young Reader's Book of Christian Symbolism* by Michael Daves. Illustrated by Gordon Laite.)

with many church school teachers who have used it in their classes. Children have used the sketches to help them with ideas for posters and banners. The book has also found a ready audience with adults. This doesn't really surprise me because a good children's book has something for all ages.

"The book is an art form. For me, part of the excitement of writing is to see your typewritten manuscript set in type, illustrated and bound. In this, the writer becomes a partner with the editors, illustrators, and printers.

"Travel has been an important part of my life lately. My family and I were involved in a pastor trade to Deal, Kent, England, in 1980. An English pastor and his wife came to our church and we went to theirs in a pulpit exchange. We were only ten miles from Canterbury and spent many wonderful hours exploring historic Canterbury Cathedral.

"In 1983 we toured Belgium and Holland. We also went to Germany for a week and toured the sites which Martin Luther, the Protestant Reformer, has made famous. This was the year of the 500th anniversary of his birth.

"My wife teaches fourth grade at Austin Elementary School in Grand Prairie. My daughter, Michelle, is in high school. My son, Paul, is an art major at Southern Methodist University. Grand Prairie, where I live, and Duncanville, where I work, are both suburbs of Dallas."

HOBBIES AND OTHER INTERESTS: Reading novels and plays, swimming, tennis, hiking, racquetball, travel.

JUDITH DAVIDSON

DAVIDSON, Judith 1953-

PERSONAL: Born September 21, 1953, in Portland, Ore.; daughter of Evan (a jazz musician) and Pamela (a poet; maiden name, Parrish) Porter. *Education:* Attended University of Oregon, 1979; Antioch University, B.A., 1982; graduate study, Bank Street College of Education, 1982—, Also studied at Kyoto Japanese Language School and Tezukayama Women's College. *Residence:* New York.

CAREER: Author. Has been employed in a variety of jobs, including Japanese consulate and teacher of English in Japan. Member of Children's Writers Workshop, Bank Street College of Education, New York, N.Y.; chairwoman, Friends of the Library Committee, Jerome Park Branch Library, New York, N.Y. *Member:* Japan Society.

WRITINGS: Japan: Where East Meets West (juvenile), edited by Terry Hopkins, Dillon, 1983. Translator into English of *Night of the Milky Way Railroad* and *Crossing the Snow.* Also contributor of articles to newspapers and periodicals, including *Publishers Weekly* and the *Oregonian.*

WORK IN PROGRESS: "I have just finished a novel for middle school children. I want to try detective fiction next."

SIDELIGHTS: "America is a country of many cultures. We need to understand our own roots as well as the roots of friends and neighbors in our communities.

"I have five younger brothers and sisters. The crazy warmth of a big family will always, I hope, be a part of my work."

MICHAEL DAVES

The Japanese Alps, located on the island of Honshu, attract thousands of mountain climbers and skiers. ■ (From *Japan: Where East Meets West* by Judith Davidson. Photograph courtesy of the Consulates General of Japan.)

OSCAR De MEJO

De MEJO, Oscar   1911-

PERSONAL: Surname is pronounced "De Mayo"; born August 22, 1911, in Trieste, Austro-Hungarian Empire (now Italy); came to the United States, January 1, 1947; naturalized U.S. citizen, 1952; son of Guido (in business) and Enrica (Dollenz) De Mejo; married Alida Valli Altenburger (an actress), March, 1944 (divorced, 1967); married Dorothy Graham (a dancer), December 27, 1967; children: (first marriage) Carlo, Lawrence. *Education:* Received law degree from University of Siena, 1935; received degree in political and social sciences from University of Padua, 1937. *Religion:* Catholic. *Home:* 322 West 57th St., Apt. 10M, New York, N.Y. 10019. *Agent:* Gloria Safier, 244 East 53rd St., New York, N.Y. 10022.

CAREER: Worked for an insurance company in Trieste and Rome, Italy, 1938-41, and as an analyst of film reviews for an Italian film distributor, 1941-43; artist, 1949—. Worked in public relations, 1960-69. Affiliated with Aberbach Fine Art. Commissioned works include series of oil paintings for Irving Allen's film "New Mexico," 1949; series of sixteen paintings on the American Revolution, commissioned by Paul Foley of Interpublic Group Companies, 1973, and shown at New World Pavilion, Hall of Presidents, Jamestown, Va., at Botetourt Gallery, College of William and Mary, Williamsburg, Va., both 1975, and at the Whitney Museum of American Art and at the Davlyn Gallery, New York, both 1976; series of twelve paintings on the history of Italian Unification, commissioned by Mondadori Editore, 1973; series of five paintings titled "Five Great Moments in American History," commissioned by Graphic Press, 1974; series of eight paintings, commissioned by Carlo Amato of Old World Gallery for Merck Sharpe & Dohme, Belgium, 1974; series of twenty-five paintings on

the history of America, commissioned by Bob Guccione, 1974; series of eight paintings on sports during the American Revolutionary period, commissioned by *Sports Illustrated,* 1975; series of fourteen paintings on Harlem Globetrotters, commissioned by Amato for Metromedia, 1976; two lithographs, commissioned by George Caspari, 1976; series of paintings on the Kentucky Derby, commissioned by *Sports Illustrated,* 1977.

EXHIBITIONS: One-man shows include those at Cowie Galleries, Los Angeles, Calif., at Santa Barbara Museum of Art, Calif., at Palace of Legion of Honor, San Francisco, Calif., at Sagittarius Gallery, New York, at Romi Gallery, Paris, France, at Stendhal Gallery, Milan, Italy, 1951-60, and at Graham Gallery, New York, 1975.

Group shows include Biennale of Art Naif at the Lugano Museum, Switzerland, 1972; "La Grande Domenica" at the Museo La Rotonda di Via Besana, Milan, 1974; "Die Kunst der Naiven" at Museum of Munich, 1974, and at Kunsthaus, Zurich, 1975; "Adam & Eve" at Portal Gallery, London, 1977; two exhibitions at Musee d'Art Naif de l'Ile de France, 1978 and 1981; "Patriotic Folk Art" at Yorktown Victory Center, Va., 1979-80; "Into the '80's Collection" at Alex Rosenberg Gallery, New York, 1979-80; "Twentieth Century Images of George Washington" at Fraunces Tavern Museum, New York, 1982; "La Genie des Naifs" at Grand Palais de Champs-Elysees, Paris, 1982.

Works also exhibited in shows at Taylor Galleries, Beverly Hills, Calif., 1949, at Carlebach Gallery, New York, 1950, at Levi Gallery, Milan, 1971, and at Galleria d'Arte dei Bibliofili, Milan, 1972. De Mejo's *The Inauguration of George Washington* was shown by the Virginia Independence Bicentennial Commission at Yorktown Victory Center, 1977. Lublin Graphics presented four of his lithographs at the New York Expo, 1980. His *The Red House* was featured in Europe on UNICEF greeting cards, 1980.

AWARDS, HONORS: Medal "Ambrogino d'Argento" from the city of Milan, 1973; *New York Times* selected *The Tiny Visitor* as one of the ten best illustrated children's books of 1982.

WRITINGS: Diary of a Nun (novel), Pyramid, 1955, 3rd edition, 1964; *Fresh Views of the American Revolution* (paintings; notes and comments by Paul Foley), Rizzoli International, 1976; *The Tiny Visitor* (juvenile; self-illustrated), Pantheon, 1982; *There's a Hand in the Sky* (juvenile; self-illustrated), Pantheon, 1983; *My America* (paintings and text), introduction by Selden Rodman, foreword by Gillo Dorfles, Abrams, 1983; *The Forty-Niner,* Harper, 1985.

SIDELIGHTS: De Mejo is an internationally-known artist, famous for his primitive style that blends symbols with realism. He exhibits this "naive" style in his series of sixteen Revolutionary War paintings—reproduced in *Fresh Views of the American Revolution* and in *My America*—and in his children's book *The Tiny Visitor,* all of which met with critical acclaim.

"My main interest is painting, though I also like to write and illustrate children's books."

FOR MORE INFORMATION SEE: Publishers Weekly, April 26, 1976, September 3, 1982; *Washington Post Book World,* August 8, 1976, November 7, 1982; *Art News,* December, 1976; *Parents' Choice,* fall, 1982; *New York Times Book Review,* November 24, 1982, November 20, 1983, December 4, 1983.

(From *The Tiny Visitor* by Oscar De Mejo. Illustrated by the author.)

DENGLER, Sandy 1939-

BRIEF ENTRY: Born June 8, 1939, in Newark, Ohio. A graduate of Bowling Green State University, Dengler received her M.S. from Arizona State University. In addition to her career as a writer, which began in 1972, she has been a volunteer worker at places like Death Valley, Yosemite National Park, and the Grand Canyon since 1965. Describing herself as a "non-sectarian Christian," Dengler is the author of eight juvenile historical novels that promote Christian values as part of Moody's "Pioneer Family Adventure" series. *The Horse Who Loved Picnics* (1980) describes the lessons learned by a young boy living on a Texas homestead during the nineteenth century, including ways to apply the Bible to his daily life. In *Rescue in the Desert* (1981), Daniel attempts to save his friend Carrie from the Indians while struggling with an inward rebellion toward God over his father's death. Other books in the series are: *Summer of the Wild Pig* (1979), *Arizona Longhorn Adventure* (1980), *The Melon Hound* (1980), and *Mystery at McGeehan Ranch* (1982). Dengler also wrote *Soeorro Island Treasure* (1983) and *The Chain Five Mystery* (1984), both of Moody's "Daniel Tremain Adventures" series. Among her other works are the puzzle books *Beasts of the Field* (Moody, 1979) and *Birds of the Air* (Moody, 1981), and the romance novels, *Song of the Nereids* and *Summer Snow* (both Zondervan, 1984). Dengler is currently working on a third historical romance novel for Zondervan. *Office:* Tahoma Woods, Star Route, Ashford, Wash. 98304.

FOR MORE INFORMATION SEE: Contemporary Authors, Volume 112, Gale, 1985.

DODSON, Susan 1941-

BRIEF ENTRY: Born January 19, 1941, in Pittsburgh, Pa. A free-lance textile artist and author of novels for young adults, Dodson studied at California State College and the Art Institute of Pittsburgh. Remembering her own difficult years as an adolescent, Dodson writes for young adults "possibly to help . . . and hopefully to entertain them." The protagonists in her three novels find themselves embroiled in situations which, although not commonplace, exhibit the shared emotions and fears of adolescence. In *The Creep* (Four Winds, 1979), a fifteen-year-old babysitter becomes the police decoy for a psychotic child rapist. *Bulletin of the Center for Children's Books* described it as "a story filled with suspense and danger . . . [with] smoothly integrated . . . romance . . . and some material about acquiring new friends." The dangerous and oftentimes sordid life of runaway teens is the focus in *Have You Seen This Girl?* (Four Winds, 1982). "This vivid portrait of alienated youth," noted *School Library Journal,* "is populated with intriguing characters, neatly captured through dialogue and description . . . [and] a sense of harsh realism." Dodson's latest novel, *Shadows across the Sand* (Lothrop, 1983), is a mystery that features a teenage heroine whose life becomes intertwined with an odd assortment of retired showpeople. *Residence:* New York, N.Y.

FOR MORE INFORMATION SEE: Contemporary Authors, Volumes 97-100, Gale, 1981.

There was a long silence
and Grandpa looked kind of sad.
"It's *better* than new!" I shouted, laughing.
And I gave him my best bear hug.

(From *Good as New* by Barbara Douglass. Illustrated by Patience Brewster.)

(From the film "A Different Kind of Winning," based on the book *Skateboard Scramble* by Barbara Douglass. Released by Learning Corporation of America, 1980.)

DOUGLASS, Barbara   1930-

PERSONAL: Born April 27, 1930, in Wilmar, Calif.; daughter of Allen and Phyllis (Seymour) Gaunt; married Robert Douglass (an engineer), January 26, 1949; children: Suzanne, Dana, Robert, Mrs. Dorothy Hunt, Dale. *Education:* Cosumnes River College, 1982-84; currently attending Sacramento City College. *Residence:* Elk Grove, Calif.

CAREER: Author of books for children. Has been variously employed as a greenhouse assistant, secretary, police clerk, reporter, and chimney sweeper. *Member:* Society of Children's Book Writers, California Writers Club (Sacramento branch, secretary, 1982-84). *Awards, honors: Good as New* was selected as one of *Booklist*'s "Literary Landmarks" in children's books, 1982.

WRITINGS—All for children; all fiction, except as indicated: *Skateboard Scramble* (illustrated by Alex Stein), Westminster, 1979; (with Shirley Parenteau) *A Space Age Cook Book for Kids* (nonfiction; illustrated by Laura Maestro), Prentice-Hall, 1979; *Sizzle Wheels* (illustrated by James McLaughlin), Westminster, 1981; *Good as New* (illustrated by Patience Brewster; Junior Literary Guild selection), Lothrop, 1982; *The Great Town and Country Bicycle Balloon Chase* (illustrated by Carol Newsom), Lothrop, 1984. Also author of weekly sports column "Running Around Town" in *Elk Grove (Calif.) Citizen.*

ADAPTATIONS: "Skateboard Scramble" (film), Learning Corp., 1980; "Skateboard Scramble" (cassette), Talking Books, 1982.

WORK IN PROGRESS: The Chocolate Chip Cookie Contest, publication expected by Lothrop.

BARBARA DOUGLASS

SIDELIGHTS: "As an only child in a mobile family, I attended elementary schools in Monterey Park, San Gabriel, Baldwin Park, Rosemead, and other locations in southern California; high schools in Alhambra, California, and Juneau, Alaska. But although I was an only child, I never was a lonely child, for I always had books, and the wonderful characters within them to keep me company.

"My earliest memories are of books, first an ABC scrapbook my grandfather made, with lettering in his own elegant script and pictures cut from magazines, later a small copy of Robert Louis Stevenson's *A Child's Garden of Verses*. Books were my favorite gifts, and when I discovered libraries I was sure I had discovered Utopia. Each patron was limited to six books at a time then. It took a deliciously long time to select just six books and usually I began reading the most irresistible one while walking home."

Despite the great influence reading had on her as a child, Douglass did not consider writing professionally until 1976 when she entered a bicentennial essay contest. Articles and short stories soon followed, and she eventually turned her efforts toward writing books for children.

DUGGAN, Maurice (Noel)   1922-1974

PERSONAL: Born November 25, 1922, in Auckland, New Zealand; died December 11, 1974, in Auckland, New Zealand; married Barbara Platts, 1946; children: one. *Education:* Attended University of Auckland. *Residence:* Auckland, New Zealand.

CAREER: Worked in advertising, beginning 1961; J. Inglis Wright Advertising Ltd., Auckland, New Zealand, staff member, 1965-72; writer. *Awards, honors:* Hubert Church Memorial Prose Award, 1957; New Zealand Library Association Esther Glenn Award, 1959, for *Falter Tom and the Water Boy;* Katherine Mansfield Memorial Short Story Award, 1959; Robert Burns Fellow at Otago University, 1960; New Zealand Literary Fund scholarship, 1966; Freda Buckland Award, 1970, for his advancement of New Zealand literature.

WRITINGS: Immanuel's Land (short stories), Pilgrim Press, 1956; *Falter Tom and the Water Boy* (juvenile; illustrated by Kenneth Rowell), Blackwood & Janet Paul, 1957, Criterion, 1958; (with others) *New Authors: Short Stories 1,* Hutchinson, 1961; *Summer in the Gravel Pit: Stories,* Blackwood & Janet Paul, 1965; *O'Leary's Orchard and Other Stories,* Caxton Press, 1970; *The Fabulous McFanes, and Other Children's Stories* (juvenile; illustrated by Richard Kennedy), International Publications Service, 1974; *Collected Stories,* edited and introduced by C. K. Stead, Auckland University Press, 1981. Contributor to anthologies, including *New Zealand Short Stories,* edited by D. M. Davin, Oxford University Press, 1953; *Landfall Country,* edited by Charles Brasch, Caxton Press, 1962; *A Book of New Zealand,* edited by J. C. Reid, Collins (Auckland), 1964, revised edition, Peter Cape, 1979.

SIDELIGHTS: **November 25, 1922.** Born in Auckland, New Zealand. Duggan's parents were Irish Catholics who had immigrated to New Zealand. "Beginnings . . . lying on my stomach, in an unused room, in a city that was not and is not a city, in a soft flooding of light through ancient, wooden venetian blinds, having discovered fathoms down under the forgotten accumulations of the bow-fronted china-cabinet—pink coral, bone china, Beleek ware, a crucifix containing a splinter of the Holy Cross (Cairo)—a book by Jules Verne.

"Only the title remains with me. And a sense of mystery and solitude, and of curious light filtered through bars of green.

"In a house where remote relatives, aged and ill, lived remotely in huge rooms, permitting me this sanctuary and cups of tea and tram fares, on my free Sunday from Catholic boarding-school. Free between the brackets of morning Mass and evening Benediction, whose tediums and inconsequence disturbed but whose umbers and golds sometimes entranced.

"I was thirteen: I left school that year." [Maurice Duggan, "Beginnings," *Landfall 80,* New Zealand Publishers, 1966.[1]]

Duggan's relationship with his family was very poor—he was constantly running away from home. By the time he was fifteen, he had left home permanently. "As a first generation New Zealander this was a large part of the environment in which I grew up; the sad Irish bravura; the drear Irish Catholicism; the Irish syndrome—booze, melancholy and guilt; the pointless, loud pride—for what had they to be proud of, each man a Joseph in his coat of bright verbs?; the intolerance; the low superstition; the peculiarly Irish deceit. (What in God's name would it be like to be a Scot?)

"Books were rare in the house and the small shelf was a static collection; no one to my memory bought books. Pen and paper

Maurice Duggan in Wellington, New Zealand, 1960. Photograph courtesy of Alexander Turnbull Library, John Reece Cole Collection, Wellington, New Zealand.

had to be stalked. Each man spoke from his private text, so that I longed to speak to a non-Catholic, an Irishman without the mad maggot, which in his better moments my father consented to be, protestant and puzzled.''[1]

1939. Lost a leg to osteomyelitis, an infection of the bone. ''. . . It took a long time before the messages stopped coming in from the outpost; and my dreams were entirely physical, so that by day I led one sort of life and at night went haring up mountains, charging across fields. Until the running stopped.''[1]

The tragic amputation was probably a factor in Duggan's decision to start writing at the age of nineteen. ''. . . I'd time on my hands and whole libraries through my head, or so it seemed, and I'd better make some fist of dealing with what was, after all, no great tragedy. Up the hill to night-school, across the slope to the public library, feeling like a fool, standing by the empty seats in the tram, because I couldn't master the me-

chanics of the knee-bend—until I learned the insouciance of the platform-rider, cigarette for excuse. My beginnings as a heavy smoker.

''. . . I was nineteen and the story covered nineteen pages of foolscap; and we looked at each other in profound suspicion. This was going to be more complicated than the knee-mechanism, or anything else, and I wouldn't even be walking here, yet a while. Supposing it were more than a goofy optimism.''[1]

1943. ''I was living at this time with two of my sisters in a roomy old house in Mount Eden, and I hated going out. Anyone I'd ever known, or so it seemed, was making or preparing for the journey to a war. I received a white feather through the post and another, quite openly given, as I stood on the tram-platform smoking my cigarette.

''Then I was 'manpowered' into essential industry, stamping

Falter Tom would tell them a salty tale, wink at them, then shoo them off as though they were tame birds. ■ (From *Falter Tom and the Water Boy* by Maurice Duggan. Illustrated by Kenneth Rowell.)

out metal chassis for radio transceivers for American troops in the Pacific. It was a heavy, tough job; but I felt I was proving something. The firm's contract was negotiated on a cost-plus-ten-percent basis, with a piece-rate bonus for the men on the presses and an extra bonus for setting up your own power-press from the templates. My pockets were filled with coins and duty-free Bourbon and black-market Camels.''[1]

1945. "... My first publication, in *Anvil,* a little magazine that ran to only two issues. And in the same year publication in *Speaking for Ourselves* which Frank Sargeson edited, and Bob Lowry printed, for the Caxton Press.

"I knew much encouragement in these years but held stolidly to my inflated style, a sedulous apecraft, and sweated through Auckland summers, now working part-time in the radio factory. I wound wire onto radiator bars and packed transformers, tapping in the plates with a neat hammer; and in the afternoons, with a view to the harbour, I wrote—in a flat on Takapuna beach.''[1] That same year Duggan married Barbara Platts.

1947. Although he had left school in his early teens, Duggan was able to gain provisional admission to Auckland University College. While attending the university, he wrote for the literary annual, *Kiwi,* and, in 1948, edited it. By this time he was recognized as a promising young writer. "At this time, too, I wrote [the short story] 'Six Place Names and a Girl.' It was perhaps less a story than a prose celebration of a topography and a time that, in rediscovery and re-creation, moved me strongly enough to force me away from what had become

a habit of rhetoric. If it was to be strong, it had to be simple; the language must be a focusing glass and not, as had up to now been the case, a sort of bejewelled and empty casket. I learned to murder my darlings; and have mostly benefited, in my writing, by continuing the painful slaughter, ever since. Though bits of bombast do get by, of course, to my shame.

"The title 'Six Place Names and a Girl' was supplied by Frank Sargeson [another New Zealand author and Duggan's mentor]: I thought it, and still think it, a good one. And *Landfall* published it.''[1]

At the close of the forties' decade, Duggan went to Europe—his first trip out of New Zealand. "... In three years in London I wrote most of the stories in *Immanuel's Land* (the epigraph I treasured for the irony it gathered in this context: the book from which it came I can only deplore), living, happily enough, on extremely short commons in a crumbling house off Haverstock Hill, visiting friends in Cambridge and Oxford and crossing the channel whenever this was possible. Some of this I tried to set down in a short travel journal, 'Voyage.' ''[1]

In Spain Duggan contracted tuberculosis, which left him a semi-invalid for much of the fifties' decade. "In Spain I brightly and voluminously coughed. And the doctor said, 'No essmoking,' and the *practicante,* the man the Spaniards called 'the picador,' rode up the hill on his bicycle with his lance of streptomycin ('Mush bettaire?') and beyond the small window three men transformed a dead olive tree into a meticulous stack of neat cords of wood.

Duggan in 1963. Photograph courtesy of Alexander Turnbull Library, John Reece Cole Collection, Wellington, New Zealand.

"I owe the doctor a debt, Doctor Severa of Palma de Mallorca, because the cost of the antibiotic was enormous and he did not charge us. The big box of fine cigars sent from London was more gesture than recompense. . . .

"And at Greenlane, at a rather later date, the doctor shook hands and said, 'Report back once a year.'"[1]

1957. ". . . I was thirty-five. And through Cornwall Park as I elatedly walked it was spring, bright oaks, dark olives, yes, by the stone wall and the prefab Scouts' Den, with silver under their leaves, and I had the feeling of having passed a barrier as I crossed the cattle stops—that were for sheep. I had read myself almost blind: I had written a little; and I was abroad again.

"About this time I finally abandoned the writing of a novel which I had tentatively named *Along the Poisoned River*—the same river as 'Flood.' I turned away from this novel because I saw it as eating up what Maugham has called the 'imaginative capital' at one great gulp. There was too much in it; and too little. I ceased to be subject, in that sense, from then on. . . .

"I began, as a way of making a little money until I was fit enough for the market place, to write for School Publications. I began with *Falter Tom and the Water Boy* because this was a story I had been telling the children of friends, and my own son, over the years. Later it was published in Great Britain and in America and if the financial return from it was not great it at least bettered by far anything I have earned from writing for adults; but then the cases, as I recognize, are different. One would not agree to tailor one's writing in the manner required (wrongly?) for children."[1]

1960. Awarded the Burns fellowship at Otago University. ". . . The conditions were wonderful; and it seemed the most natural thing in the world to sit in a room and write. It was a good climate for working. I wrote 'Blues for Miss Laverty,' 'Riley's Handbook,' a short novel, and the first draft of 'Along Rideout Road that Summer.' I also wrote much verse of a rather undistinguished kind. And wished the year would never end."[1]

1961. Went into advertising, which he hated, but was successful at. "I earn my living in the market place, as an advertising copywriter: the crying of wares is, at the least, an ancient trade.

"It is normal to give away a little of one's life in order not to lose it all. Six or eight hours a day so as not to die of starvation. And then—there is profit in all things for anyone really in search of it.

"But I confess that this (from Camus) doesn't make me feel entirely comfortable."[1]

1966. Awarded the Government Scholarship in London. ". . . I have raised often enough with myself the question of whether, given other conditions, without that first illness I would have turned to writing. I do not know. Certainly there was no moment when I ever, consciously, wanted to be a writer. Perhaps the years of omnivorous, even feverish, reading urged a direction; but not every such reader turns writer. Two years at University undoubtedly did a great deal to discipline and direct the raw autodidact: my marks did not shame me, and I looked far more critically at what I wrote. My friendship with Frank Sargeson and Greville Texidor, especially in those early years, opened doors and expanded vistas. But looking now from the centre of the fabric (my father was a draper) there seems no point at which warp and weft do not continuously interrupt each other.

"If I have placed too much emphasis on the merely physical aspects it is because I see this as inseparable, if I am to speak at all, from the larger question. If one sort of life becomes, in some aspects, impossible then another must be devised. (In fact many of the difficulties in that sense have disappeared with the passing of time.) I see it as an aspect of beginnings, as I hope I have shown: though something other than illness might have brought that light to a similar focus."[1]

December 11, 1974. Died of cancer. "I look in vain for big books, the decent output. I work too slowly, and too irregularly. (There is no substitute for will.) The output has been small, and I must take what confidence I can from what seem to me small successful things. . . . "[1]

FOR MORE INFORMATION SEE: Maurice Duggan, "Beginnings," *Landfall 80,* New Zealand Publishers, 1966; (obituary) *AB Bookman's Weekly,* February 3, 1975; *Contemporary Novelists,* St. Martin's Press, 1976; *Twentieth Century Children's Writers,* St. Martin's Press, 1978; Maurice Duggan, *Collected Stories,* edited and introduction by C. K. Stead, Auckland University Press, 1981.

PENELOPE FARMER

The images were much more dangerous and more frightening than Miss Hallibutt had been, though they looked quite hazy images, only half alive. ■ (From _Emma in Winter_ by Penelope Farmer. Illustrated by James J. Spanfeller.)

FARMER, Penelope (Jane) 1939-

PERSONAL: Born June 14, 1939, in Westerham, Kent, England; daughter of Hugh Robert MacDonald and Penelope (Boothby) Farmer; married Michael John Mockridge (a lawyer), August 16, 1962 (divorced, 1977); married Simon Shorvon (a neurologist), January 20, 1984; children: (first marriage) Clare Penelope, Thomas. _Education:_ St. Anne's College, Oxford, Degree in History (with second-class honors), 1960; Bedford College, London, Diploma in Social Studies, 1962. _Politics:_ ''Left-wing.'' _Home:_ 15 Stamford Brook Rd., London W.6, England. _Agent:_ Deborah Owen, 78 Narrow St., London E14, England.

CAREER: Writer. Teacher for London County Council Education Department, London, England, 1961-63. _Member:_ Society of Authors. _Awards, honors: The Summer Birds_ received a Carnegie Medal commendation, 1963.

WRITINGS—Children's books, except as indicated: _The China People_ (illustrated by Pearl Falconer), Hutchinson, 1960; _The Summer Birds_ (illustrated by James J. Spanfeller), Harcourt, 1962, revised edition, Dell, 1985; _The Magic Stone_ (illustrated by John Kaufmann), Harcourt, 1964; _The Saturday Shillings_

(illustrated by Prudence Seward), Hamish Hamilton, 1965; _Emma in Winter_ (illustrated by J. J. Spanfeller), Harcourt, 1966; _The Sea Gull_ (illustrated by Ian Ribbons), Harcourt, 1966; _Charlotte Sometimes_ (illustrated by Chris Connor), Harcourt, 1969, revised edition, Dell, 1985.

Daedalus and Icarus (picture book; illustrated by C. Connor), Harcourt, 1971; _Dragonfly Summer_ (illustrated by Tessa Jordan), Hamish Hamilton, 1971, Scholastic Book Services, 1974; _The Serpent's Teeth: The Story of Cadmus_ (picture book; illustrated by C. Conner), Collins (London), 1971, Harcourt, 1972; _A Castle of Bone_, Atheneum, 1972; _The Story of Persephone_ (picture book; illustrated by Graham McCallum), Collins (London), 1972, Morrow, 1973; _William and Mary: A Story_, Atheneum, 1974; _Heracles_ (illustrated by G. McCallum), Collins (London), 1975; _August the Fourth_ (illustrated by Jael Jordan), Heinemann, 1975, Parnassus, 1976; _Year King_ (young adult novel), Atheneum, 1977; _The Coal Train_ (illustrated by W. Bird), Heinemann, 1977; (compiler) _Beginnings: Creation Myths of the World_ (illustrated by Antonio Fransconi), Chatto & Windus, 1978, Atheneum, 1979; _Saturday by Seven_, Penguin, 1978; (translator) Amos Oz, _Soumchi_ (illustrated by William Papas), Harper, 1980; _The Runaway Train_ (illustrated by W. Bird), Heinemann, 1980;

. . . He was such a strange boy . . . . ■ (From _The Summer Birds_ by Penelope Farmer. Illustrated by James J. Spanfeller.)

Standing in the Shadow (adult novel), Gollancz, 1984; *Eve: Her Story* (adult novel), Gollancz, 1985. Also author of short stories and of television and radio scripts, including "The Suburb Cuckoo," 1961.

WORK IN PROGRESS: Adult novel.

SIDELIGHTS: "I live in London now, but I grew up in the country in Kent on the North Downs, and we often went to the South Downs. I've a great feel for this country. It's very bare and bony and old, and I love it. The settings of *The Summer Birds* and *Emma in Winter* are in this area. The settings were built up from elements in different places but aren't one specific place. *Sea Gull* is set in Wiltshire, another part of the south of England which is a lot different. They're inland downs as opposed to downs by the sea. That is the one book which is based in a very, very specific area—you know, the topography and all that. It's one place that I love very much. We used to go and stay with friends who had a house there. I liked this and I wanted to use it for a setting, and I did. The house is still there. It's been taken over by someone who doesn't really have any feeling for the character of the house at all but fills the garden with very fat plastic gnomes. We still go and look at it, and the countryside is lovely just the same. I'd like perhaps someday to set another book there, but this hasn't so

far happened." [Cornelia Jones and Olivia R. Way, *British Children's Authors: Interviews at Home,* American Library Association, 1976.[1]]

As a child, Farmer enjoyed reading and writing stories. "I started writing for children because I was asked to. I wrote a book of short stories when I was very young and still at school. They were published in England, and they were neither for adults nor for children. They were a collection of sort of fairy stories. Margaret McElderry of Harcourt, Brace read them. She didn't think she could find a market for it in the States but said they would like to commission me to do a children's book. I started from there really."[1]

Farmer, who writes fantasy for children, comments about her writing. "I don't write for any particular age group. I have to occasionally because there is a series of books in this country which I have written for, and occasionally I write for radio for a specific age range. But when I sit down and write a long novel, one of the things I really start entirely because I want to do it, not because anyone asks me to do it, then I just write it as it comes and let the publishers decide. I don't write a book for children, I write a book; and this is a big distinction, I think. If you start off saying, 'Well, an eight-year-old might take that, but I don't think he'd take that,' then you'd just

. . . Stephen, the greatest gull-trainer in the world. ■ (From *The Sea Gull* by Penelope Farmer. Illustrated by Ian Ribbons.)

write a bad book in any terms. I do think you've got to set up a sort of scale of age in your mind. You do a little thing in the back of your brain, saying, 'No, leave it out. That's too much. That's too sophisticated.' But it's not a very conscious thing. It's there in the background, but you forget about it totally. Once you start writing, you find that once you've created a style of writing, the thing goes on from there. You know, the thing has its own coherence, its own form. You somehow don't exceed the limits that you've set yourself.

"Up to a point . . . I do plan a book in detail. I think you have to. I have to make up an outline from the point of view of publishing it, for the mechanics and that sort of thing. I have to make up a synopsis to send to the publisher, anyway. This, I find, is a very useful discipline, but I don't necessarily stick to the synopsis. It's there, giving me a kind of kicking-off point. Very often you find the whole plot changes. Things happen in the plot which could never have happened before you've actually written a part of it. In some instances the plot naturally springs from what you've written, where it probably wouldn't have occurred to you before. It comes spontaneously, all at once. You get an idea, and it is just a little silly thing, and it might sound very insignificant and unimportant. It grows gradually bit by bit. You walk down the street and you see something that gives you another idea. You add it in, or you may not. You may find you want to add it in but it doesn't quite fit, and you fiddle around with it and you fiddle around with it. Finally, somehow, it slides into place in the plot, or it doesn't and you chuck it out. You must always allow for this; you must allow for things developing. Sometimes the things that develop are much better than the original, sort of mechanical, setting-out of the plot.

"I don't know how I create my characters. You have sometimes preconceptions about a character as somebody you know whom you want to use, or anyway start off with. But very often the character just grows in the course of writing a book. You bring a character in. Sometimes you're consciously developing a character. Sometimes they sort of develop themselves, and sometimes the development is part of the structure of the book. The book may need a certain kind of character to balance the others. This is self-conscious, even though to a large extent the character is developing unconsciously, subconsciously. This is something you feel. It is sort of a feeling of balance and contrast.

"Practically any character is difficult to write about. Probably you only understand them inasmuch as they have certain elements of you in them. So you're starting with different facets of your own character and using them to build up someone separate, distinct. I think the most difficult characters are always the ones you're looking at from the outside all the time. Sometimes it's much easier; you can set a character with a couple of sentences, and it works very well. But I think one of my most difficult characters was Bobby Fumpkins, the fat boy in *Emma in Winter*. This had to be a creation in a sense. The other characters I was thinking through all the time, but he had to build up. He started off as a subsidiary character, and I sort of built him up to round him out. I had difficulties. To what extent I succeeded I still don't know. I didn't always feel that I'd perhaps rounded him out well enough, because he was more deliberately created, in a way, than the other characters.

"Charlotte and Emma are very much based on my mother and her sister as little girls. They were rather in the same situation, with no parents and having to be everything to each other. One of them was very much the responsible one and protected her sister, who was rather difficult. Emma and Charlotte have grown in their own ways and aren't exactly based on my mother and her sister now, but this is where it started.

"I have another book about Charlotte, the older of the two sisters in *The Summer Birds*. It's called *Charlotte Sometimes*. It's a completely different setting. It's in a boarding school which is set very near where I live in London. It's a very complicated plot, and it's rather difficult to explain it in the abstract. She lands back in time, in the same school, but in 1918 during the First World War. It goes backwards and forwards between the two periods. Anyway, that's the beginning of the germ of the plot.

"I find it very difficult to talk about any book which I am currently involved with. I can look at *The Summer Birds* and say it was about so and so, and this happened and that happened, because that was a long time ago. But with a book that I've only just finished, I find that a synopsis sounds very bare and bald and stupid. If you've been living with it for a long time, it's so familiar to you and you know it so well that it sounds completely unoriginal and completely boring, and you have no confidence in it. But once a book's been out and everyone's seen it and knows the main idea as well as you do, you're not so embarrassed about talking about it.

"When you are a writer, you work very much by yourself, shut up in a little room. You get very inward-looking and depressed by what you're doing, and it's all totally related to yourself. Being a writer can be incredibly lonely sometimes. But I balance it . . . [with other] kind[s] of project[s]. . . ."[1]

HOBBIES AND OTHER INTERESTS: Reading, walking, travelling, cinema, listening to music, playing the piano, opera.

FOR MORE INFORMATION SEE: Elementary English, September, 1974; Penelope Farmer, "Patterns on a Wall," *Horn Book,* October, 1974; Hugh Crago, "Penelope Farmer's Novels," *Signal 17,* May, 1975; Edward Blishen, editor, *The Thorny Paradise: Writers on Writing for Children,* Kestrel, 1975; Cornelia Jones and Olivia R. Way, *British Children's Authors: Interviews at Home,* American Library Association, 1976; David Rees, "The Marble in the Water: The Real World in Penelope Farmer's Novels," *Horn Book,* October, 1976; D. L. Kirkpatrick, *Twentieth-Century Children's Writers,* St. Martin's, 1978; *Children's Literature in Education,* vol. 14, no. 3, 1983.

FLACK, Naomi John (White) (Naomi John, Naomi John Sellers)

PERSONAL: Born in Oklahoma; daughter of John Marion (a professor) and Annie (Rice) White; married Elbert Eugene Sellers, 1949 (deceased); married John Edmund Flack (an artist), 1976; children: (stepdaughter) Jenny Flack (Mrs. Philip Harriman). *Education:* University of Oklahoma, A.B. and M.A. *Residence:* San Mateo, Calif.

CAREER: Full-time writer. Muskogee High School, Muskogee, Okla., teacher of English; Oklahoma Agricultural and Mechanical College (now Oklahoma State University), Stillwater, instructor in English; Burlingame High School, Burlingame, Calif., teacher of English. *Wartime service:* U.S. Navy, WAVES instructor, 1941-45. *Member:* Authors League of America, American Association of University Women, Delta Kappa Gamma, Phi Delta Theta, Alpha Chi Omega.

NAOMI JOHN FLACK

WRITINGS—All published under name Naomi John Sellers, except as indicated; all for children, except as indicated: *Cross My Heart* (young adult romance), Doubleday, 1953; *Charley's Clan* (fiction; illustrated by Unada), A. Whitman, 1973; *The Little Elephant Who Liked to Play* (fiction; illustrated by Yoko Mitsuhashi), Ginn, 1974; (under name Naomi John) *Roadrun-ner* (nonfiction; illustrated by Peter Parnall and Virginia Parnall; Junior Literary Guild selection), Dutton, 1980.

Also contributor of over seventy short stories to periodicals, including *Ladies Home Journal, Cosmopolitan, Woman's Day, Country Gentleman, Collier's, Seventeen, Canadian Home Journal,* and others.

WORK IN PROGRESS: Currently researching a book about a coyote.

SIDELIGHTS: ''Ever since I was five years old and printed my name in a copy of *Alice in Wonderland,* I have wanted to write. I first wrote a neighborhood gossip sheet, then I wrote for the high school newspaper and then for the university paper. After that, I wrote short stories. My first book was a young adult love story, *Cross My Heart*.

''At present I am writing books for children, although I occasionally stop to write a short story. I write from the subconscious entirely; then I check facts with research work in the library, for I want everything to be not only believable, but authentic.

''I grew up in Oklahoma and taught school there. I wrote for the teachers' magazine, a column that was syndicated in several other state teachers' magazines. In California, I met and married another Oklahoman, who is an artist.

''He paints in his studio and I write in mine. We each understand the necessity of working alone and then sharing our interests which are music and traveling.

''Unlike many writers, I really like to write. And when some editor likes what I write, I feel that I am being paid for breathing.''

Each time, the roadrunner pressed himself closer into the notch of the saguaro cactus. ■ (From *Roadrunner* by Naomi John. Illustrated by Peter and Virginia Parnall.)

. . . The solid red field of the British flag was now divided into thirteen red and white stripes, for the thirteen united colonies. ■ (From *The Story of the United States Flag* by Wyatt Blassingame. Painting by Victor Mays. Flags by Henri A. Fluchère.)

FLUCHÈRE, Henri A(ndré) 1914-

PERSONAL: Born July 31, 1914, in France; came to the United States, 1925; became naturalized citizen, 1935; son of Armand H. (a draftsman) and Emma (Aubanel) Fluchère; married Ruth Allen, 1944 (divorced, January, 1946); married Maud Elliot Hall (a musician), September 4, 1946; children: Peter, Michael, Marion. *Education:* Attended Brooklyn College (now of the City University of New York), 1933-35, City College (now of the City University of New York), 1935-36, and Columbia University, 1946-48. *Politics:* Democrat. *Religion:* Episcopalian. *Home and office:* 21 Oak St., Irvington, N.Y. 10533.

CAREER: Free-lance writer, 1950—. Art director for McGraw's Technical Writing Service, 1950-53. Irvington village trustee, 1958-60, police commissioner, 1958-60, and acting mayor, 1959-60. Consultant on wines and gastronomy. *Military service:* U.S. Army, Intelligence, 1942-46; became master sergeant; received Purple Heart. *Member:* American Wine Society.

WRITINGS: (With John Musacchia and M. J. Grainger) *Airbrush Techniques,* Reinhold, 1953; (with J. Musacchia and M. J. Grainger) *Course in Beginning Watercolor,* Reinhold, 1956; *Wines,* Western Publishing, 1973, enlarged edition, 1974. Also author of "The Westchester Winetaster," a weekly column in Westchester newspapers. Editor of *Consumer Wineletter,* 1973—

Illustrator; of interest to young readers; nonfiction: Leo Schneider, *You and Your Cells,* Harcourt, 1964; L. Schneider, *Microbes in Your Life,* Harcourt, 1966; Michael Chester, *Relativity: An Introduction for Young Readers,* Norton, 1967; L. Schneider, *Long Life to You: Modern Medicine at Work,* Harcourt, 1968; (with Victor Mays) Wyatt Blassingame, *The Story of the United States Flag,* Garrard, 1969; Barry J. Schiff, *Flying,* Golden Press, 1971.

Michael Folsom and wife, Marcia.

FOLEY, (Mary) Louise Munro 1933-

BRIEF ENTRY: Born October 22, 1933, in Toronto, Ontario, Canada. Editor, author, and lecturer. During the 1950s Foley worked as a copy editor at various radio and television stations in Ontario, Canada and the western United States. She also has been employed as a copy chief for retail stores and as a columnist for the *News-Argus* in Goldsboro, N.C. In 1976 Foley received her B.A. with honors from California State University at Sacramento and was editor at that same university's Institute for Human Management until 1980. Among her works of fiction for children are *The Caper Club* (Random House, 1969), *Sammy's Sister* (Western Publishing, 1970), and *Tackle 22* (Delacorte, 1978). She has written several books in Bantam's "Choose Your Own Adventure" series—*The Lost Tribe, The Mystery of the Highland Crest* (both 1984)—and Scholastic Inc.'s similar "Twistaplot Books" series—*The Train of Terror* (1982), *The Sinister Studios of KESP-TV* (1983). Foley is also the editor of *Stand Close to the Door,* a collection of material taken from workshops on social work for the aged, and *Women in Skilled Labor.*

FOR MORE INFORMATION SEE: Contemporary Authors, Volumes 37-40, revised, Gale, 1979; *The Writers Directory: 1984-1986,* St. James Press, 1983.

FOLSOM, Michael (Brewster) 1938-

PERSONAL: Born in 1938; son of Franklin Brewster (an author of books for children) and Mary (an author of books for children; maiden name, Elting) Folsom; married Marcia McClintock (a college instructor). *Education:* Graduated from Antioch College; Rutgers University, M.A.; graduate study, University of California, Berkeley; also studied at Leeds University.

CAREER: Author of books for children. Has also been employed as an instructor at Massachusetts Institute of Technology.

WRITINGS—All for children; all nonfiction; all written with mother, Mary Elting: *The Secret Story of Pueblo Bonito* (illustrated by Kathleen Elgin), Harvey House, 1963; *The Mysterious Grain: Science in Search of the Origin of Corn* (illustrated by Frank Cieciorka), M. Evans, 1967; *Q Is for Duck: An Alphabet Guessing Game* (illustrated by Jack Kent; Junior Literary Guild selection), Clarion Books, 1980.

Other: (Editor, with Steven D. Lubar) *The Philosophy of Manufactures: Early Debates over Industrialization in the United States,* MIT Press, 1981.

Because a Cat Naps

(From *Q Is for Duck: An Alphabet Guessing Game* by Mary Elting and Michael Folsom. Illustrated by Jack Kent.)

FORRESTER, Victoria   1940-

PERSONAL: Born March 18, 1940, in Pasadena, Calif.; daughter of Victor (a psychiatrist) and Leslie (Wadsworth) Parkin; foster mother, Sheila Clark Ueberroth; married Alan Forrester, June 14, 1960; children: Chad. *Education:* University of California, Los Angeles, B.A., 1961, M.L.S., 1963, M.A., 1970. *Religion:* Christian. *Home:* One Owlswood Dr., Larkspur, Calif. 94939. *Office:* Saint Mark's School, 375 Blackstone Dr., San Rafael, Calif. 94903.

CAREER: Santa Monica Public Library, Santa Monica, Calif., reference librarian, 1963-68, children's librarian, 1969-71; Saint Mark's School, San Rafael, Calif., librarian, 1980—. *Member:* American Library Association, Society of Children's Book Writers. *Awards, honors: Oddward* was selected for Children's Book Council-American Book Sellers Association Book Exhibit, 1983; Parent's Choice Award for illustration, 1983, for *The Magnificent Moo.*

WRITINGS—Juvenile; all self-illustrated, except as noted; all published by Atheneum: *Oddward* (picture book), 1982; *Bears and Theirs: A Book for Bear Lovers* (puns), 1982; *The Touch Said Hello* (picture book), 1982; *The Magnificent Moo* (picture book), 1983; *Words to Keep against the Night* (poetry), 1983; *The Candlemaker and Other Tales* (illustrated by Susan Seddon Boulet), 1984; *A Latch against the Wind,* 1985.

WORK IN PROGRESS: Poor Gabriella: A Christmas Story, with illustrations by Susan Boulet.

VICTORIA FORRESTER

SIDELIGHTS: "I live with my husband and our son in a town that lies between Mount Tamalpais and the San Francisco Bay. The windows of our home look out into a grove of redwood trees, and our doors admit a beloved company of cats and dogs. We live in a part of the country where it rains most of the winter, and the seasons are distinct and beautiful.

"For as long as I can remember, I've looked at both writing and drawing as a way of knowing. I've written nothing longer than a tale, and the writing that I most enjoy is poetry.

"When I was a girl of perhaps fifteen, I began to realize that liking to write poetry made one a bit different. I was as 'horse crazy' as any girl my age; the difference was that my horse had wings and couldn't be saddled except in my imagination.

"A few years later, at the university, I majored in English. Most of the classes were interesting but a bit dry. Not so the course taught by Frances Clarke Sayers. In it we read fantasy and fables, folk tales and fairy tales, and I was drawn to them as to a starry night. I sensed that they grazed in the same pasture as my horse.

"I wondered if I would ever be lucky enough to make up a tale myself. What I learned in the years that followed was that nobody can 'make up' a tale, that only if you are very ready will a good story allow you to catch it. And what does it mean to 'be ready?' Perhaps it means to wait with nothing but pure expectation and to listen for the sound of wings.

"*The Candlemaker and Other Tales* is a collection of four original tales that came to me at different times in my life: 'The Candlemaker,' 1970; 'The Butterfly with No Keys,' 1977; 'The Crocodile with the Roller-Coaster Smile,' 1979; and 'The Two Bowls of Water,' 1982. Always, the stories took me by surprise. I saw each as a whole and only half sensed the import, or the symbolic meaning, of the visual imagery. But it was because I knew that the imagery had meaning that I told the stories. My task as a writer was simply to trust the traditional rhythms of the storyteller and to allow the tales to unfold themselves in the telling. I am drawn to poetry for a similar reason: one begins with imagery that takes one by surprise and ends in a new place of understanding.

"In 1970 I sent a single tale to Jean Karl at Atheneum Publishers, and she replied with a note of encouragement. For the next eleven years I sent nothing to anyone. In 1981 I again sent work to Jean Karl. As it happened, everything I sent was to be published in the next three years.

"The materials that have been published are very different from one another. *Bears and Theirs,* a collection of graphic puns, was designed when I was a graduate student. *The Touch Said Hello,* a picture book about an old tree coming into springtime, was also designed and illustrated while I was working for my M.A. in art (U.C.L.A., 1970).

"In 1971 our son, Chad, was born. My two picture books for young children grew out of the atmosphere of his early childhood and our shared delight. I am a librarian, and in telling these stories to other children I hear his laughter again.

"*Words to Keep against the Night* is a collection of seventeen small poems each illustrated with a single print.

"*A Latch against the Wind* is a collection of poetry written between 1981 and 1984 and illustrated with line drawing. I designed the book and printed the first copies by hand on a Vandercook #3 proof press. The 'Fog' is part of the collection."

> "The fog like a white stag appeared—
> As sudden to the eye.
> It formed itself as legends form—
> Made antler out of sky.

> Nor was it without chronicle;
> Long sentences of sea,
> In cadence like an ancient rhyme,
> Ascribed it poetry."

[Victoria Forrester, *A Latch against the Wind,* Atheneum, 1985.]

"In 1984 I wrote *Poor Gabriella: A Christmas Story*. The idea for the book came to me in the words of a dream. I woke remembering them and wrote the story in the first hours of the morning. The book is illustrated by Susan Boulet in oil pastel and colored pencil. I've seen the first pictures, and, as with everything Susan does, I am in awe of her gift."

So they traded sounds, and the cow went back to the meadow meowing happily to herself, while the cat went on down the road saying, "MOO!" just as loudly as possible. ■ (From *The Magnificent Moo* by Victoria Forrester. Illustrated by the author.)

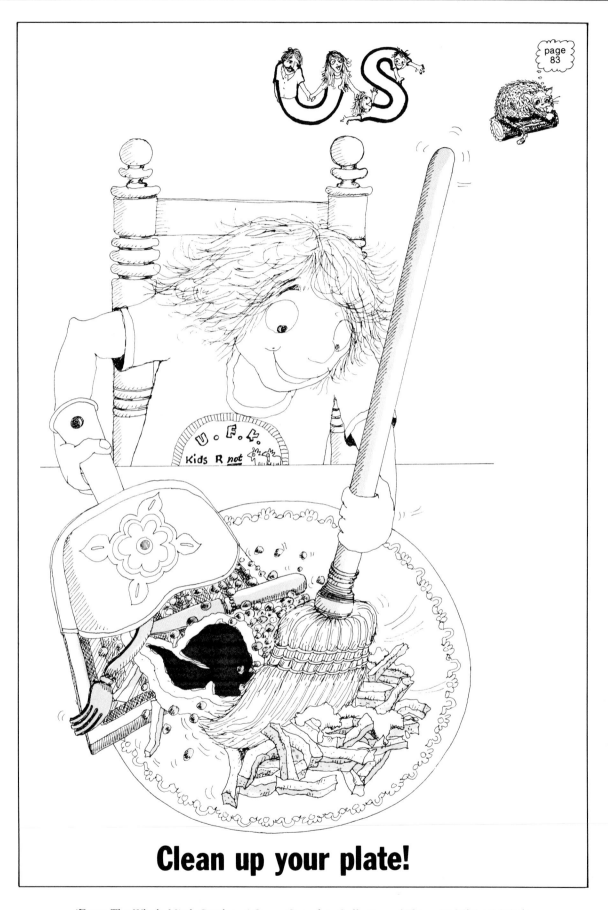

Clean up your plate!

(From *The Whole Mirth Catalog: A Super Complete Collection of Things* by Michael Scheier and Julie Frankel. Illustrated by Julie Frankel.)

Julie Frankel's interpretation of herself and husband, Michael Scheier.

FRANKEL, Julie   1947-

PERSONAL: Born June 24, 1947, in Los Angeles, Calif.; married Michael Scheier (a teacher and author), 1977. *Education:* Attended Art Students League, 1956-64; Carnegie-Mellon University, B.F.A. (honors), 1968. *Residence:* Putnam Valley, N.Y. *Address:* P.O. Box 694, Putnam Valley, N.Y. 10579.

CAREER: Author and illustrator of children's books. Has also worked as a teacher trainee in an elementary school and a creator of jigsaw puzzles. *Member:* Graphic Artists Guild, Cartoonists Guild (chairman of market and promotions committee), Society of Children's Book Writers. *Awards, honors:* Readers' Choice Award, for *My Autograph Book,* for *Ridiculous World Records,* and for *Digging for My Roots;* Children's Choice Award, International Reading Association, 1979, for *The Whole Mirth Catalog: A Super Complete Collection of Things.*

WRITINGS: My Autograph Book (juvenile), Scholastic Book Services, 1975.

With husband, Michael Scheier; all juvenile: *Ridiculous World Records,* Scholastic Book Services, 1976; *Digging for My Roots,* Scholastic Book Services, 1977; *The Whole Mirth Catalog: A Super Complete Collection of Things* (illustrated by J. Frankel), F. Watts, 1978; *What to Do with the Rocks in Your Head: Things to Make and Do Alone, with Friends, with Family, Inside, and Outside,* F. Watts, 1980; *Me by Me,* Scholastic Book Services, 1982; *More Ridiculous World Records,* Scholastic Book Services, 1983; *The Wildlife Romance Fill-In-Book,* Scholastic Book Services, 1984. Also contributor of cartoons to *Animals, Animals, Animals* (cartoon collection), edited by George Booth, and others, Harper, 1979, and to the periodicals *Cosmopolitan, Audubon Magazine,* and *The Runner Magazine.*

WORK IN PROGRESS: "Books relating to puns, imaginative activities, fill-in formats, adoption, and humor relating to birds, plants, and wildlife, all with elaborate illustrations."

SIDELIGHTS: "I grew up in Manhattan and was educated at Hunter Elementary School, Columbia Grammar School, the High School of Music & Art, and the Art Students League. I received a bachelor of fine arts degree with honors from Carnegie-Mellon University.

"I met Michael Scheier in 1968 and we started a working relationship as teacher-teacher trainee, sharing a third-grade classroom on the lower east side of New York City. For a time we lived in Berkeley, California, where we made and sold finely crafted imaginative jig-saw puzzles.

"Upon returning East, we embarked on a collaborative effort in publishing.

"I have lived in many neighborhoods in New York, but find real fulfillment in our Putnam Valley home nestled in over ten acres of woods with a small stream, a cat, and a working vegetable garden, still an easy drive to the city."

GARDNER, John (Champlin, Jr.)
1933-1982

PERSONAL: Born July 21, 1933, in Batavia, N.Y.; died in a motorcycle accident, September 14, 1982, in Susquehanna, Pa.; son of John Champlin (a farmer) and Priscilla (an English teacher; maiden name, Jones) Gardner; married Joan Louise Patterson (a composer), June 6, 1953 (divorced); married Liz M. Rosenberg (a writer; divorced); children: (first marriage) Joel, Lucy. *Education:* Attended De Pauw University, 1951-53; Washington University, St. Louis, A.B., 1955; State University of Iowa, M.A., 1956, Ph.D., 1958.

CAREER: Oberlin College, Oberlin, Ohio, instructor, 1958-59; Chico State College (now California State University), Chico, Calif., instructor, 1952-62; San Francisco State College (now San Francisco State University), San Francisco, Calif., assistant professor of English, 1962-65; Southern Illinois University, Carbondale, professor of English, 1965-76; State University of New York, Binghamton, professor of English, 1978-82. *MSS* (small literary magazine), founder and editor. Distinguished visiting professor, University of Detroit, 1970-71; visiting professor, Northwestern University, 1973, and Ben-

JOHN GARDNER

nington College, 1975. *Member:* Modern Language Association of America, American Association of University Professors. *Awards, honors:* Woodrow Wilson fellowship, 1955-56; Danforth fellowship, 1970-73; Guggenheim fellowship, 1973-74; National Education Association award, 1972; *Grendel* was named one of best fiction books of 1971 by *Time* and *Newsweek; October Light* was named one of ten best books of 1976 by *Time* and *New York Times;* National Book Critic's Circle award for fiction, 1976, for *October Light; Dragon, Dragon and Other Timeless Tales* was chosen Outstanding Book of the Year, 1975, by *New York Times Book Review;* recipient of Armstrong Prize for the radio play "The Temptation Game."

WRITINGS—Juvenile; fairytales, except as noted: *Dragon, Dragon, and Other Timeless Tales* (illustrated by Charles Shields), Knopf, 1975; *Gudgekin, the Thistle Girl, and Other Tales* (illustrated by Michael Sporn; Junior Literary Guild selection), Knopf, 1976; *In the Suicide Mountains* (illustrated by Joe Servello), Knopf, 1977; *A Child's Bestiary* (poetry collection [includes additional poems by Lucy Gardner and Eugene Rudzewicz]; self-illustrated with Lucy, Joel, and Joan

Gardner), Knopf, 1977; *The King of the Hummingbirds, and Other Tales* (illustrated by M. Sporn), Knopf, 1977; *The Art of Fiction: Notes on Crafts for Young Writers,* Random House, 1984.

Adult; novels, except as noted: *The Resurrection,* New American Library, 1966; *The Wreckage of Agathon,* Harper, 1970; *Grendel,* Knopf, 1971; *The Sunlight Dialogues,* Knopf, 1972; *Jason and Medeia* (epic poem), Knopf, 1973; *Nickel Mountain: A Pastoral Novel,* Knopf, 1973; *The King's Indian: Stories and Tales,* Knopf, 1974; *October Light,* Knopf, 1976; *Poems,* Lord John Press, 1978; *Vlemk, the Box-Painter,* Lord John Press, 1979; *Freddy's Book,* Knopf, 1980; *The Art of Living, and Other Stories,* Knopf, 1981; *Mickelsson's Ghosts,* Knopf, 1982.

Nonfiction: *The Construction of the Wakefield Cycle,* Southern Illinois University Press, 1974; *The Construction of Christian Poetry in Old English,* Southern Illinois University Press, 1975; (contributor) Matthew Bruccoli and C. E. Frazer, Jr., editors, *Pages,* Volume 1, Gale, 1976; *The Poetry of Chaucer,* Southern Illinois University Press, 1976; *The Life and Times of Chaucer,* Knopf, 1977; *On Moral Fiction,* Basic Books, 1978; *On Becoming a Novelist,* Harper, 1983.

Plays; all published by New London Press: *Death and the Maiden,* 1979; *Rumpelstiltskin* (libretto), 1979; *William Wilson* (libretto), 1979; *Frankenstein* (libretto), 1979; *The Temptation Game* (radio play), 1980.

Editor: (With Lennis Dunlop) *The Forms of Fiction,* Random House, 1961; (and author of introduction) *The Complete Works of the Gawain-Poet* (modern English version), University of Chicago Press, 1965; (and author of notes) *The Gawain-Poet: Notes on "Pearl" and "Sir Gawain and the Green Knight",* Cliff's Notes, 1967; (and author of notes) *Le Morte D'Arthur: Notes,* Cliff's Notes, 1967; (with Nicholas Joost) *Papers on the Art and Age of Geoffrey Chaucer,* Southern Illinois University Press, 1967; (and author of notes) *"The Alliterative Morte Arthure," "The Owl and the Nightingale" and Five Other Middle English Poems* (modern English versions), Southern Illinois University Press, 1971; (with L. M. Rosenberg) *MSS: A Retrospective,* New London Press, 1980; (with Shannon Ravenal, and author of introduction) *The Best American Short Stories: 1982,* Houghton, 1982.

Also author of plays "The Latest Word from Delphi," 1978, "Helen at Home," 1978, "Samson and the Witch" (libretto), 1978, "The Pied Piper of Hamlin" (libretto), 1978, "The Waterhorse" (radio play), 1978, and "The Angel" (radio play), 1978. Contributor of short stories to *Southern Review, Quarterly Review of Literature,* and *Perspective;* of poetry to *Kenyon Review, Hudson Review,* and other literary quarterlies; and of articles to *Esquire, Saturday Evening Post, New York Times, Reader's Digest, Redbook,* and other magazines and newspapers.

ADAPTATIONS: "Grendel, Grendel, Grendel" (animated film), with the voice of Peter Ustinov, Animation Australia Pty. Ltd., 1981.

SIDELIGHTS: ". . . I grew up in a family where literary influence was everywhere, including under the bridge on our dirt road, where I kept my comic books. My father is a memorizer of poetry and scripture, a magnificent performer in the old reciter tradition. . . . He did readings of everything from Edgar Guest to Shakespeare and The Book of Job at the monthly Grange meetings, in schools, churches, hospitals. While he milked the cows, my mother (who'd once been his high school

English teacher) would read Shakespeare's plays aloud to him from her three-legged stool behind the gutter, and he would take, yelling from the cow's flank, whatever part he'd decided on that night—Macbeth, King Lear, Hamlet and so on.

"My mother was a well-known performer too, except that she mainly sang. She had one of those honey-sweet Welsh soprano voices and sang everything from anthems to the spirituals she'd learned from an old black woman who took care of her during her childhood in Missouri. Often my mother performed in blackface, with a red bandana, a practice that may sound distasteful unless you understand that she wasn't kidding; she was authentic, flatting, quarter-toning, belting it out: She was amazing. They frequently worked together, my mother and father,

and were known all over western New York. Sometimes they were in plays—my mother often directed—and wherever they went, riding around in the beat-up farm truck or just sitting in the kitchen, they sang, always in harmony, like crazy people.

"The house was full of books, very few of them books that would now be thought fashionable aside from the Shakespeare and Dickens. My parents read aloud a lot—the narrative poems of Scott, miles of Longfellow, spooky stories by Edgar Allan Poe, the poems of Tennyson and Browning, also rather goofy religious writers (I loved them; what did I know?) like Lloyd C. Douglas and some woman whose name escapes me now, who wrote Jesus-filled love stories with titles like 'A Patch of Blue.' My grandmother, who was bedridden through much of

The Elephant

**When the Elephant blows
His nose,
Everything goes!**

■ (From *A Child's Bestiary* by John Gardner, with additional poems by Lucy Gardner and Eugene Rudzewicz. Illustrated by Lucy, Joel, Joan, and John Gardner.)

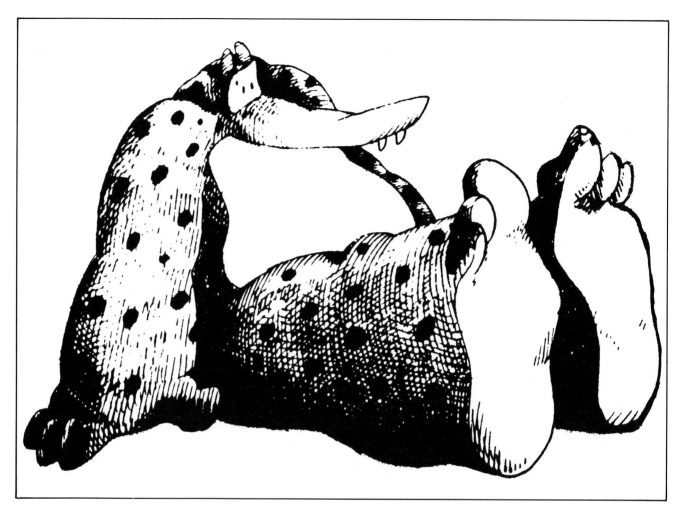

Character sketch of Grendel for the animated film "Grendel, Grendel, Grendel," starring the voice of Peter Ustinov. Produced by Animation Australia Pty. Ltd., 1981.

my childhood, was especially fond of this religious lady, and one of my more pleasant chores was to read her these tender little novels. The climax was always the moment the boy shyly touched the girl's hand. . . .

"My favorite authors, at least when I was between the ages of 8 and 18, were in what might be described as the nonrealistic tradition: God, Dickens and Disney. One of my less pleasant chores when I was young was to read the Bible from one end to the other. Reading the Bible straight through is at least 70 percent discipline, like learning Latin. But the good parts are, of course, simply amazing. God is an extremely uneven writer, but when He's good, nobody can touch him. I learned to find the good parts easily . . . and both the poetry and the storytelling had a powerful effect on what I think good fiction ought to be!

"Dickens I ran into when I was in my early teens, when I began to find the Hardy Boys tiresome and unconvincing. I never liked realism much, but the irrealism of two boys having long conversations while riding on motorcycles (I was big on motorcycles myself) was more than I could put up with. Running across Dickens was like finding a secret door. I read book after book, and when I'd finished the last one I remember feeling a kind of horror, as if suddenly the color had gone out of the world; then luckily I discovered that when you went

back to one of the ones you had read first, you couldn't remember half of it, you could read it again and find it even better, so life wasn't quite as disappointing as for a moment I'd thought.

"For me at that time Disney and Dickens were practically indistinguishable. Both created wonderful cartoon images, told stories as direct as fairy tales, knew the value of broad comedy spiced up with a little weeping. I have since learned that Dickens is occasionally profound, as Disney never deigns to be; but that was never why I valued Dickens or have, now, a bust of him in my study to keep me honest. Unconsciously—without ever hearing the term, in fact—I learned about symbolism from Dickens and Disney, with the result that I would never learn to appreciate, as I suppose one should, those realistic writers who give you life data without resonance, things merely as they are. Dickens's symbolism may never be very deep—the disguised witches and fairy princesses, Uriah Heep and his mother flapping around like buzzards, or all the self-conscious folderol of *A Tale of Two Cities*—but in my experience, anyway, it spoils you forever for books that never go oo-boom.

"There were other important influences during this period of my life, probably the most important of which was opera. The Eastman School of Music presented operas fairly often (and of course played host to traveling opera companies, including the Met). From Dickens and Disney (not to mention God) it took no adjustment to become opera-addicted. The plots of most operas (not all, heaven knows) are gloriously simple-minded or, to put it more favorably, elemental; the stage is nothing if not a grand cartoon (Wagner's mountainscapes and gnomes, Mozart's crazies, Humperdinck's angels, the weirdness and clowning that show up everywhere from 'La Bohème' to 'The Tales of Hoffmann'). I was by this time playing French horn, and of course I'd always been around singing. So I got hooked at once—hence my special fondness now for writing librettos.

"By the time I reached college my taste was, I'm afraid, hopelessly set. Predictably I was ravished by Melville—all those splendid cartoon images, for instance Ahab and the Chinese coolies he's kept hidden until the first time he needs to lower away after whale—and of course by Milton, who must be considered one of the all-time great cartoonists. . . . I'm afraid the embarrassing truth is that the whole literary tradition opened out, for me, from Disney and his kind. I got caught up in the mighty cartoons of Homer and Dante, (much later Virgil and Apollonius), the less realistic 18th- and 19th-century novelists (Fielding, Smollett, Collins and the rest), the glorious mad Russians (Tolstoy, Dostoyevsky, Bely), and those kinds of poets who fill one's head with strange, intense visions, like Blake, Coleridge and Keats.

"For me the whole world of literature was at this time one of grand cartoons. I thought of myself mainly as a chemistry major and took courses in English just for fun. I guess I thought literature was unserious, like going to the movies or playing in a dance band, even an orchestra. It did not seem to me that one ought to spend one's life on mere pleasure, like a butterfly or cricket. Beethoven, Shakespeare, Richard Strauss, Conan Doyle might be a delight, but to fritter away one's life in the arts seemed, well, not quite honest. Then I came across the New Criticism.

"At the first college I went to (for two years) I'd read nearly all of the Modern Library, partly for fun, partly because I felt ignorant around my fellow students, people who could talk with seeming wisdom about Camus and Proust, Nietzsche and Plato—I soon discovered they hadn't really read what they claimed to have read, they'd just come from the right part of town—but I'd never in any serious sense 'studied' literature. . . . But when I moved to Washington University in St. Louis I got a whole new vision of what literature was for— that is, the vision of the New Criticism. Like the fanatic I've always been, I fell to analyzing fiction, digging out symbols and structural subtleties, learning about 'levels' and so on.

"I don't say this was a foolish activity—in fact I think the New Critics were basically right: It's much more interesting and rewarding to talk about how literature 'works' than to read biographies of the writer, which is mainly what the New Criticism replaced. Working with the famous books by Cleanth Brooks and Robert Penn Warren, I began to love things in fiction and poetry that I'd never before noticed, things like meaning and design, and, like all my generation, I made the great discovery that literature is worthwhile, not a thing to be scorned by serious puritans but a thing to be embraced and turned cunningly to advantage. I learned that literature is Good for you; and that writers who are not deeply philosophical should be scorned. I began to read realists—two of whom, Jane Austen and James Joyce, I actually liked—and I began to write 'serious' fiction; that is, instead of writing pleasant jingles or stories I desperately hoped would be published in *The Saturday Evening Post* or maybe *Manhunt*, I began shyly eyeing *The Kenyon Review*. With a sigh of relief (though I'd

enjoyed them, in a way) I quit math and science and signed up, instead, for courses in philosophy and sociology and psychology, which I knew would make me a better person and perhaps a famous writer so brilliant and difficult that to get through my books you would need a teacher.

"This period lasted longer than I care to admit. On the basis of my earnestness and a more or less astonishing misreading of Nietzsche (I was convinced that he was saying that only fiction can be truly philosophical) I won a Woodrow Wilson Fellowship to the University of Iowa, where I meant to study in the famous Writers' Workshop but soon ended up taking medieval languages and literature, the literature God had been nudging me toward all along: 'Beowulf,' 'The Divine Comedy,' the Gawain poet and Chaucer. The scales fell from my eyes. My New Critical compulsion to figure out exactly how everything works, how every nuance plays against every other, had suddenly an immense field to plow. I continued to read and think about other literature—I went through a Thomas Mann phase, a Henry James phase and so on—but I found myself spending more and more time trying to figure out medieval works.

(From *Nickel Mountain* by John Gardner. Illustrated by Thomas O'Donohue.)

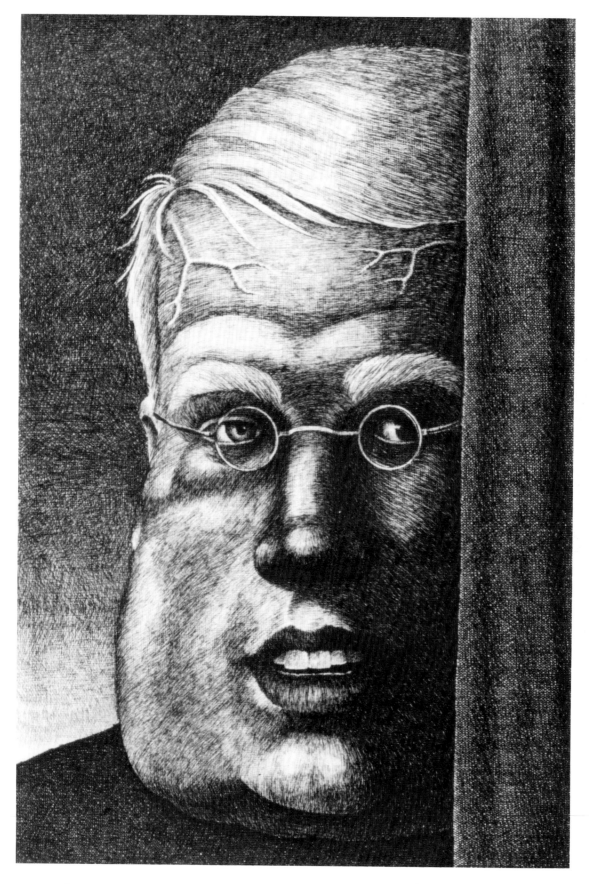

The professor drew his head back outside the curtain now and, whether or not with his son's permission, reached up and snatched the curtain open. ■ (From *Freddy's Book* by John Gardner. Illustrated by Daniel Biamonte.)

"It seems to me that when I began working on medieval literature, in the late 50's and early 60's, scholars knew very little about even the greatest works in that literature. No one had really figured out the structure of the works of the Gawain poet, not to mention 'Beowulf' or the poetry of Chaucer. People were still arguing about whether or not 'Beowulf' is a Christian poem; people were still trying to shuffle around *The Canterbury Tales*. The usual New Critical method, which is to stare and stare at the work until it comes clear, was useless on the material, because again and again you found yourself staring at something that felt like a symbol or an allusion, or felt that maybe it ought to be some kind of joke but you couldn't see the humor. To figure out the poem you had to figure out the world it came from—read the books the poets knew, try to understand esthetic principles abandoned and forgotten centuries ago. One had no choice but to become a sort of scholar.

In a certain kingdom, in a certain land, there lived . . . . ▪ (From *In the Suicide Mountains* by John Gardner. Illustrated by Joe Servello.)

Gardner, 1982. Photograph by Joel Gardner.

"I found in medieval culture and art, in other words, exactly what I needed as an instrument for looking at my own time and place. I of course never became for a moment a medieval Christian believer, but medieval ideas and attitudes gave me a means of triangulating, a place to stand. And, needless to say, medieval literature had built into it everything I'd liked best from the beginning, back in the days of God, Dickens and Disney, of grotesques (cartoon people and places), noble feeling, humor (God was perhaps a little short on humor) and real storytelling.

"... When I think back now over the influences which have helped to shape the way I write, I notice, with a touch of dismay that they were as much bad influences as good ones. I won't criticize God (anyway, He's almost certainly been misquoted), but clearly the influence of Dickens and Disney was not all to the good. Both of them incline one toward stylized gestures.... A writer like me, seduced by cartoon vision, tends to go again and again for the same gestural gimmicks, a consistent pattern of caricature (compare the way doors in Dostoyevsky are forever flying open or slamming).

"I look over my fiction of 20 years and see it as one long frenzy of tics—endlessly repeated words like *merely* and *grotesque,* a disproportionate number of people with wooden fingers and a dreary penchant for frowning thoughtfully or darting their eyes around like maniacs. I seem incapable of writing a story in which people do not babble philosophically, not really because they're saying things I want to get said but because earnest babbling is one of the ways I habitually give vitality to my short-legged, overweight, twitching cartoon creations. And needless to say, from artists like Dickens and Disney I get my morbid habit of trying to make the reader fall into tender weeping.

"The whole New Critical period I went through, and the scholarly period that followed it, betrayed me, I think, into an excessive concern with significance. It's probably the case that novels and stories are more interesting if, in some sense or another, they mean something. But it has begun to dawn on me that—in fiction, as in all the arts—a little meaning goes a long way...." [John Gardner, "Learning from Disney and Dickens," *New York Times Book Review,* January 30, 1983.[1]]

About his work habits with his own writing, Gardner once explained: "I write as much as I can. I get up early in the morning, stay up late at night, and write all the time. When I have nothing else to do, I write. Luckily, because of my university, sometimes I can go someplace far away where I'm protected from my own weaknesses. Not that I consider writing a duty—but since I have a family of whom I am very fond, and we have friends who visit us, I often don't get much writing time in. When I go somewhere I don't know, it takes us two or three months to build up a circle of friends and thus interrupt my work.

"I work from rhythms more than anything else—the way a sentence sounds in terms of rhythmical structure and the words you choose because of that structure...." [Joe David Bellamy, *The New Fiction: Interviews with Innovative American Writers,* University of Illinois Press, 1974.[2]]

FOR MORE INFORMATION SEE—Books: Joe David Bellamy, editor, *The New Fiction: Interviews with Innovative American Writers,* University of Illinois Press, 1974; *Contemporary Literary Criticism,* Gale, Volume II, 1974, Volume III, 1975, Volume V, 1976; *Dictionary of Literary Biography,* Gale, Volume 2, 1978, *Yearbook: 1982,* 1983; Martha E. Ward and Dorothy A. Marquardt, *Authors of Books for Young Peo-*

"Literary detective work is always fun, for a certain kind of mind at least, but the work I did on medieval literature, then on later classical literature, was for me the most exciting detective work I've ever done or heard of. The thing was, not only did you solve interesting puzzles, but when you got them solved you found you'd restored something magnificent, a work of art—in the case of 'Beowulf' or 'The Canterbury Tales'—supremely beautiful and noble. One unearthed tricks of the craft that nobody'd known or used for a long, long time—tricks one could turn on one's own work, making it different from anybody else's and yet not crazy, not merely novel.

"I think every writer wants to sound like him or herself; that's the main reason one sees so many experimental novels. And of course the risk in the pursuit of newness is that, in refusing to do what the so-called tradition does, one ends up doing exactly the same thing everybody else trying to get outside the tradition does. For better or worse (I'm no longer much concerned about whether it's better or worse), I joined up with an alternative tradition, one with which I felt almost eerily comfortable. My church-filled childhood delighted in discovering a Christianity distant enough—in fact, for all practical purposes, *dead* enough—to satisfy nostalgia without stirring embarrassment and annoyance, as modern Christianity does....

ple, 2nd edition, Scarecrow, 1979; Joyce Renwick and Howard Smith, *John Gardner: An Interview,* New London Press, 1980; Robert A. Morace and Kathryn Van Spanckeven, editors, *John Gardner: Critical Perspectives,* afterword by Gardner, Southern Illinois University Press, 1982; David Cowart, *Arches and Lights: The Fiction of John Gardner,* Southern Illinois University Press, 1983; Sally Holmes Holtze, editor, *Fifth Book of Junior Authors and Illustrators,* H. W. Wilson, 1983; Gregory L. Morris, *A World of Order and Light: The Fiction of John Gardner,* University of Georgia Press, 1984.

Periodicals and newspapers: *Esquire,* January, 1971; *Book World,* December 24, 1972; *Time,* January 1, 1973, December 20, 1976; *Newsweek,* December 24, 1973; John Askins, "Conversations with John Gardner on Writers and Writing," *Detroit Free Press,* March 23, 1975; *New York Times,* November 14, 1976, December 26, 1976, January 2, 1977; *New York Times Book Review,* January 30, 1983.

Obituaries: *New York Times,* September 15, 1982; *Chicago Tribune,* September 16, 1982; *Times* (London), September 18, 1982; *Chronicle of Higher Education,* September 22, 1982; *Macleans,* September 27, 1982; *Newsweek,* September 27, 1982; *Times,* September 27, 1982; *Publishers Weekly,* October 1, 1982; *Current Biography,* November, 1982; *School Library Journal,* November, 1982; *America,* December 25, 1982.

GESNER, Clark 1938-
(John Gordon)

PERSONAL: Born March 27, 1938, in Augusta, Me.; son of Herbert (a Unitarian Minister) and Eleanor (a retired teacher; maiden name, Clark) Gesner. *Education:* Princeton University, B.A., 1960. *Home:* 87 Remsen St., Brooklyn, N.Y. 11201. *Agent:* Leo Bookman, William Morris Agency, 1350 Ave. of the Americas, New York, N.Y. 10019.

CAREER: Writer for theater and television and free-lance composer, filmmaker, and director. Columbia Broadcasting System, Inc., New York, N.Y., staff writer and composer for "Captain Kangaroo" and "Mister Mayor," 1963-66; The Children's Television Workshop, New York, N.Y., contributing writer and composer for "Sesame Street" and "Electric Company," 1968—. *Military service:* U.S. Army Special Services, 1961-63. *Member:* American Society of Composers, Authors, and Publishers (ASCAP), The Dramatist Guild, Writer's Guild of America, East. *Awards, honors:* Recipient of a New York Park Association award for the song, "Ode to a Park"; LaSalle (college) Music Theatre award for "You're a Good Man, Charlie Brown"; Princeton University Triangle Club.

WRITINGS: Finnerty Flynn and the Singing City (juvenile; illustrated by Ferd A. Sondern), Lancelot Press, 1969; (under pseudonym John Gordon) *Stuff, Etc.: A Collection,* Lippincott, 1970.

Plays: (Composer, lyricist, librettist; written under pseudonym John Gordon) *You're a Good Man, Charlie Brown* (musical based on the comic strip "Peanuts" by Charles M. Schulz; first produced Off-Broadway at Theatre 80 St. Marks, March 7, 1967; produced on Broadway at John Golden Theatre, June 1, 1971), Random House, 1967; (composer and lyricist; written with Nagle Jackson) *The Utter Glory of Morrissey Hall* (musical comedy; first produced in Santa Maria, Calif., at Pacific

Conservatory of the Performing Arts, summer, 1976; produced on Broadway at Mark Hellinger Theatre, May 13, 1979), Samuel French, 1981; "To Build on the Heights, the Story of Brooklyn Heights," first produced in Brooklyn, N.Y., 1983. Also author of "The Ransom of Red Chief" (musical for children), 1981; and "Treasure Island" (musical for children), 1982.

Composer of numerous songs, including "Fourteen Hours and Thirty-Seven Minutes," "A Funny Way to Spend the Day," "The Peanut Butter Affair," "Ode to a Park," and "Societus Magnificat." Composer for shows, including Julius Monk reviews, "Baker's Dozen," "Bits and Pieces," and Leonard Stillman's "New Faces of 1968." Also writer for television shows "That Was the Week That Was," and PBS's "Great American Dream Machine" and "The Fifty-First State."

ADAPTATIONS—Recordings: "A Musical Visit to Captain Kangaroo's Treasure House," Peter Pan Records, 1962; "You're a Good Man Charlie Brown," with Orson Bean, Leo the Lion Records, 1966, original Broadway cast, MGM Records, 1967, original television cast, Atlantic Records, 1972; "The Utter Glory of Morrissey Hall," Original Cast Records, 1979.

WORK IN PROGRESS: Books, music, and lyrics for a musical based on Betty Boop.

SIDELIGHTS: "I write now for the same reason I have always written. It's what I like to do. A certain idea comes to mind and I know right away that it's one I would like to get down

CLARK GESNER

(From the off-Broadway stage production of the musical "You're a Good Man, Charlie Brown," written and composed by John Gordon. It opened at the Theatre 80 St. Marks, March 7, 1967.)

on paper. It may take a while, but, in general, the idea won't let go until I've gotten it out.'' [Tom Slear, ''The Writing Life,'' *Writer's Digest,* November, 1983.]

FOR MORE INFORMATION SEE: Washington Post Book World, June 2, 1968; *New York Times,* June 2, 1971, May 14, 1979; *Times* (Santa Maria, Calif.), July 28, 1976; *Valley's News* (Santa Barbara, Calif.), July 29, 1976; *Santa Ynez Valley News* (Calif.), July 29, 1976; *Lompoc Record* (Calif.), July 29, 1976; *Santa Barbara News and Review,* August 13, 1976; *San Luis Obispo Telegram,* August 17, 1976; *Los Angeles Times,* August 27, 1976; *New Yorker,* May 21, 1979; *Writer's Digest,* November, 1983.

Who often reads will sometimes wish to write.
                                              —George Crabbe

GIBBS, Wolcott, Jr. 1935-
(Tony Gibbs)

PERSONAL: Born April 5, 1935, in New York, N.Y.; son of Wolcott (a writer) and Elinor (a writer; maiden name, Sherwin) Gibbs; married Elizabeth Villa, January 4, 1958 (divorced); married Elaine St. James (a real estate investor), April 22, 1978; children: William, Eric. *Education:* Princeton University, B.A., 1957. *Office:* The New Yorker, 25 West 43rd St., New York, N.Y. 10036.

CAREER: Doubleday & Co., Inc., New York, N.Y., publicity manager, 1958-63, editorial assistant, 1963-64; J. B. Lippincott Co., New York, N.Y., editor, 1966-68; *Motor Boating,* New York, N.Y., book editor, 1968-75; *Motor Boating and Sailing,* New York, N.Y., executive editor, 1975; *Yachting,* New York, N.Y., editor, 1975-81; *The New Yorker,* New York, N.Y., executive editor, 1981—. Member of Rules of the Road Advisory Commission. *Military service:* U.S. Army National Guard, 1957-63; U.S. Coast Guard Auxiliary. *Awards, honors:*

The mast is now ready to be stepped, and unless it's a very short one or you're very large, you'll need a helper. ▪ (From *Sailing: A First Book* by Tony Gibbs. Photograph by the author.)

Powerboating was chosen one of New York Public Library's Books for the Teenager, 1980.

WRITINGS—Under name Tony Gibbs: *Practical Sailing* (adult), Hearst Books, 1971; *Pilot's Work Book* (adult), Seven-Seas Press, 1972; *Pilot's Log Book* (adult), Seven-Seas Press, 1972; *Powerboating* (adult), Lippincott, 1973; *Sailing: A First Book* (juvenile; illustrated by Gary L. Falkenstern), F. Watts, 1974; *Backpacking* (juvenile; illustrated by Linda Burnett), F. Watts, 1975; *Navigation: Finding Your Way on Sea and Land* (juvenile), F. Watts, 1975; *Advanced Sailing* (adult), St. Martin's, 1975; *The Coastal Cruiser: A Complete Guide* (adult), Norton, 1981; (editor) *The Coastal Navigator's Notebook* (adult), International Marine Publishing, 1982 (contains revised editions of *Pilot's Work Book* and *Pilot's Log Book*); *Cruising in a Nutshell: The Art and Science of Enjoyable Voyaging in Small Auxiliary Yachts* (adult), Norton, 1984.

Also author of editor's page and of "Rough Log," a column, in *Yachting*, 1976-78. Contributor to boating magazines and to *The New Yorker*.

GOODE, Stephen   1943-

BRIEF ENTRY: Born March 5, 1943, in Elkins, W.Va. Author of nonfiction for young adults. A former lecturer in history at Rutgers University, Goode has been a full-time writer since 1972. Critics have noted his concise, objective, and thorough approach to writing in sixteen books that cover controversial political topics of interest to the modern-day American reader. As an historian, Goode realizes the importance of what he terms the "long-range, historic point of view." He firmly establishes the origins of his subject matter before presenting any conflicting theories that may exist as well as an overview of possible solutions or outcomes. As an author, Goode strives to achieve ". . . clarity and the ability to distill a great deal of information into a readable and interesting book." His titles reflect the concern he shares with many over situations and events that are causing major upheaval in the mainstream of American society: *Guerilla Warfare and Terrorism* (F. Watts, 1977), *The National Defense System* (F. Watts, 1977), *The Nuclear Energy Controversy* (F. Watts, 1980), *The End of Detente?: U.S.-Soviet Relations* (F. Watts, 1981), *Reaganomics: Reagan's Economic Program,* (F. Watts, 1982) and *Violence in America* (Messner, 1983). He has also written on such timely issues as *Assassination!: Kennedy, King, Kennedy* (F. Watts, 1978) and *The Right to Privacy* (Messner, 1983). *Home:* 5860 North 14th St., Arlington, Va. 22205.

FOR MORE INFORMATION SEE: Contemporary Authors, Volume 105, Gale, 1982.

GOODENOW, Earle   1913-

PERSONAL: Born July 13, 1913, in Chicago, Ill.; children: Ariane, Nadine. *Education:* Attended School of the Art Institute of Chicago, National Academy of Design, and Art Students League. *Home:* New York, N.Y.

CAREER: Painter and book illustrator; has also worked in advertising. Work exhibited in one-man shows, including those in New York and Paris, and in group shows, including the

EARLE GOODENOW

West Virginia Biennial, "Directions in American Painting" in Pittsburgh, Penn., and the Corcoran Biennial.

WRITINGS—All for children; all self-illustrated: *Cow Concert,* Knopf, 1951: *The Cow Voyage,* Knopf, 1953; *The Lazy Llama,* Follett, 1954; *Angelo Goes to the Carnival,* Knopf, 1955; *The Peevish Penguin,* Follett, 1955; *Angelo Goes to Switzerland,* Knopf, 1956; *The Bashful Bear,* Follett, 1956; *The Careless Kangaroo,* Walck, 1959; *The Last Camel,* Walck, 1968; *The Owl Who Hated the Dark,* Walck, 1969.

Illustrator; for children: *The Arabian Nights: Tales from the Thousand and One Nights,* Grosset, 1946; Stanley A. Widney, *Elevator to the Moon,* Follett, 1955; Frances Toor, *Made in Italy,* Knopf, 1957.

SIDELIGHTS: Goodenow studied to be a painter, but worked in advertising instead. After his first child was born, he started writing and illustrating children's books.

His work has been exhibited in one-man shows and in group shows. He is included in the Kerlan Collection at the University of Minnesota.

FOR MORE INFORMATION SEE: Bertha Mahony Miller and others, compilers, *Illustrators of Children's Books: 1946-1956,* Horn Book, 1958.

Books are a guide in youth and entertainment for age.
—Jeremy Collier

*The magician never doubted
but this was the lamp he wanted*

(From "Aladdin; or, The Wonderful Lamp," in *The Arabian Nights.* Illustrated by Earle Goodenow.)

JAMES E. HAAS

HAAS, James E(dward)   1943-

PERSONAL: Born January 17, 1943, in New York, N.Y.; son of William Joseph (a butcher) and Ellen (Hulser) Haas; married Lynne Flannery (a teacher), March 22, 1969; children: James E., Jr., Daniel Brian. *Education:* St. John's University, Jamaica, N.Y., B.A., 1965; St. Mary's Seminary and University, Baltimore, Md., M.A., 1972. *Religion:* Roman Catholic. *Residence:* Severna Park, Md. *Office:* 650 Kensington Ave., Severna Park, Md. 21146.

CAREER: High school English and French teacher in Towson, Md., 1965-67; director of religious education in Roman Catholic church in Baltimore, Md., 1968-74; Twenty-Third Publications, Mystic, Conn., assistant editor, 1974-78; Time Consultants, Severna Park, Md., religious education consultant, 1974-79; currently Maryland representative, Beckley Cardy Co., Mt. Laurel, N.J. Member of faculty at St. Mary's Seminary and University, 1972—; program director of Archdiocese of Baltimore's Congress on Liturgy; program coordinator of East Coast Conference for Religious Education. Chairman of Ann Arundel County, Md. school board nominating convention committee, 1981-82.

WRITINGS: Shout Hooray (juvenile), Morehouse, 1972; (with wife, Lynne Haas) *Make a Joyful Noise* (juvenile), Morehouse, 1973; *Praise the Lord* (juvenile), Morehouse, 1974; (author of study and activity guides) Marie McIntyre, *Communion between Parent and Child,* Twenty-Third Publication, 1974;

Rainbow Songs: Musical Selections for Children, Morehouse, 1975; (with William Freburger) *The Eucharistic Prayers for Children,* Ave Maria Press, 1976; (with W. Freburger) *The Forgiving Christ,* Ave Maria Press, 1977; *Liturgies for the Gift of Life,* Sadlier, 1977; *Liturgies for the Gift of Peace and Jesus Forgives,* Sadlier, 1977.

Author of "Holydays and Holidays," a film strip series, Twenty-Third Publications, 1974—. Contributor of articles to a wide variety of publications, including newspapers, journals, and church magazines. Associate editor, *Religion Teacher's Journal,* 1974; editor, *Kensington Crier,* 1982.

SIDELIGHTS: "My books relate to worship for children but are directed toward teachers and ministers on an ecumenical basis."

WORK IN PROGRESS: A book on using audiovisual aids.

HOBBIES AND OTHER INTERESTS: Swimming, tennis, skiing, playing guitar, writing music, international travel, running (has participated in a marathon).

HELLER, Linda   1944-

BRIEF ENTRY: Born September 14, 1944, in New York, N.Y. A free-lance illustrator, Heller attended the Rhode Island School of Design and has received awards for her work as an animated filmmaker. She is the author and illustrator of five books for children, all published by Macmillan. Each book creates a different mood in text and illustrations, leading *Publishers Weekly* to label her "uncommonly inventive and versatile." Her first book, *Lily at the Table* (1979), features the surrealistic adventure of a small girl bored with the plateful of food set before her. The same magazine took note of its "stratospherically imaginative, funny and skillful pictures that need no words." Heller shrinks Lily down to a minute size and follows her through a variety of antics, such as fishing in a bowl of cereal, skateboarding down a wedge of cheese, and beaming like a cherry from atop a cupcake. In *Alexis and the Golden Ring* (1980), Heller effectively evokes images of Russian folklore in the story of a young man on his way to be married who stops to help an old woman. He is rewarded with a magical gold ring which, in turn, aids him as he encounters difficult passage through the countryside. *Booklist* observed: "Set against stark white backgrounds and tinged with pale, icy tones of blue and yellow, the illustrations reflect a world of snow and ice rich in fantastical happenings."

Heller's three other books—*Horace Morris* (1980), *Trouble at Goodewoode Manor* (1981), and *The Castle on Hester Street* (1982)—were also well-received by critics. *Publishers Weekly* called *Horace Morris* "another original, twisty tale brimful of fun" and described *The Castle on Hester Street* as a book that "gladdens hearts again . . . rich in color and detail." The amusing recollections of two grandparents' arrival in the United States as immigrants from Russia, *The Castle on Hester Street* received the Parents' Choice Award in 1982 as well as the 1983 Children's Book Award from the Association of Jewish Libraries. In addition to her own books, Heller has provided the illustrations for three books written by David A. Adler that focus on Jewish holidays, Howard Schwartz's *Elijah's Violin and Other Jewish Fairy Tales,* and Mirra Ginsburg's *The Magic Stove. Home:* 7 East 86th St., New York, N.Y. 10028.

FOR MORE INFORMATION SEE: Contemporary Authors, Volume 108, Gale, 1983.

HIRSCHMANN, Linda (Ann) 1941-

PERSONAL: Born September 14, 1941, in Charleston, S.C.; daughter of L. A. (an accountant) and J. (Berkman) Hirschmann. *Education:* University of South Carolina, B.A., 1962; Columbia University, M.A., 1965; also attended Harvard University and San Carlos Universidad. *Home and office:* 1610 Peace St., Durham, N.C. 27701.

CAREER: Elementary school teacher in Charleston, S.C., 1962-64; teacher of emotionally disturbed and mentally retarded in Spring Valley, N.Y., 1965-66 and in San Francisco, Calif., 1968-69; *Scholastic* (magazine), New York, editor and staff writer, 1966-67; art gallery hostess in Cambridge, Mass., private detective trainee in Boston, Mass., apartment rental agent in New York, and bookkeeper in California, 1966-75; Macmillan Publishing Co., New York City, editor, 1967-68; Model

**A whale swims along with its mouth open wide,
And scoops plants, water, shrimp, and fishes inside.**

■ (From *In a Lick of a Flick of a Tongue* by Linda Hirschmann. Illustrated by Jeni Bassett.)

Cities of U.S. Department of Housing and Urban Development, Atlanta, Ga., public affairs and information officer, 1970-71; tour leader and assistant manager of pension in Guatemala City, Guatemala, 1975-76; Durham Technical Institute, Durham, N.C., teacher of intellectual stimulation courses at rest homes and of writing courses at Arts Council, 1977-78; Continuing Education Division of Duke University, Durham, teacher of writing for children, 1981—.

WRITINGS—Juvenile; nonfiction: *Adventures in South Carolina,* Sandlapper Magazine Press, 1970; *In a Lick of a Flick of a Tongue* (illustrated by Jeni Bassett), Dodd, 1980.

Author of short stories (fiction and biographies) for seven basal readers, published by Macmillan, Allyn & Bacon, and Houghton Mifflin, c.1970-83. For Model Cities Atlanta, 1970-71, wrote and produced four television scripts, founded and wrote interagency newsletter, wrote pamphlets, and edited U.S. Department of Housing and Urban Development (HUD) submittals. Author of teaching guides for Croft-Nei, 1975-76. Contributor of articles and book reviews to newspapers and periodicals, including *Boston Globe* and *Durham Herald.*

WORK IN PROGRESS: Heart of the Jaguars, a juvenile quest novel based on Guatemalan experiences; picture books, both fiction and nonfiction.

SIDELIGHTS: ''Writing was neither a dream nor a faint interest of mine. After I left teaching, I stumbled by happenstance into a variety of jobs that demanded writing skills. Forced to develop mine, I fell in love with the challenge and now am addicted to the profession, especially writing for children.

''My travels include a six-month hitchhike through the United States and Canada and numerous extensive trips through Europe and Central and South America. The catastrophic Guate earthquake of 1976 guided me into a wonder-filled awareness of our interconnectedness with each other and with the universe. Writing has become one avenue for sharing and expanding this realization.

''Writing is paradoxical in that by shutting myself, pen, and paper off from the world I simultaneously move closer to everyone in it. For example, to write fictionalized or personalized history accurately, I am required to understand feelings as well as facts. Why does someone risk her life? What is fear? To move beyond fear how much concern/love must we feel? Why do we? What's that involvement based on? I find that writing the seemingly simplest of stories unites me with people, forces me to grow, not only as a person who writes but also as one who cares.

''When I began to write, I thought *the* goal was to order pretty words. I've since discovered honesty. How I say something matters only after I've found something to say. What scares me? Reassures me? Matters to me? No story can be about only its character. It is also about its author—and its reader as well.

''Some people live on Earth; others, in books. A believable character in my stories or in those of other authors is no less real to me than are my friends next door. Each keeps me company, makes a new experience or emotion accessible to me, compliments my life.''

HOBAN, Russell C(onwell) 1925-

PERSONAL: Born February 4, 1925, in Lansdale, Pa.; son of Abram T. (an advertising manager for the *Jewish Daily Forward*) and Jeanette (a store owner; maiden name, Dimmerman) Hoban; married Lillian Aberman (an illustrator), January 31, 1944 (divorced, 1975), married Gundula Ahl (a bookseller), 1975; children: (first marriage) Phoebe, Abrom, Esmé, Julia, (second marriage) Jachin Boaz, Wieland, Benjamin. *Education:* Philadelphia Museum School of Industrial Art, student, 1941-43. *Home:* Fulham, London, England. *Office:* c/o David Higham Associates Ltd., 5-8 Lower John St., London W1R 4HA, England.

CAREER: Artist and illustrator for magazine and advertising studios, New York, N.Y., 1945-51; Fletcher Smith Film Studio, New York, N.Y., story board artist and character designer, 1951; Batten, Barton, Durstine & Osborn, Inc., New York, N.Y., television art director, 1952-57; J. Walter Thompson Co., New York, N.Y., television art director, 1956. Worked as a free-lance illustrator for advertising agencies and magazines, including *Time, Life, Fortune, Saturday Evening Post, True,* and also worked as an art instructor at the Famous Artists Schools, Westport, Conn. and at the School of Visual Arts, New York, N.Y. *Military service:* U.S. Army, Infantry, 1943-45; served in Italian campaign; received Bronze Star. *Member:* Authors Guild, Society of Authors, P.E.N. *Awards, honors: Bread and Jam for Frances* was chosen one of Library of Congress' Children's Books, 1964; Boys' Club Junior Book Award, 1968, for *Charlie the Tramp; Emmet Otter's Jug-Band Christmas* was chosen one of *School Library Journal's* Best Books, 1971, received the Lewis Carroll Shelf Award, and The Christopher Award, children's book category, both 1972; Whitbread Literary Award, 1974, and International Board on Books for Young People honor list, 1976, both for *How Tom Beat Captain Najork and His Hired Sportsmen; A Near Thing for Captain Najork* was chosen one of *New York Times* Best Illustrated Children's Books of the Year, 1976; Recognition of Merit from the George G. Stone Center for Children's Books, 1982, for his contributions to books for younger children.

LINDA HIRSCHMANN

Hoban calls his desk "my only place of business." His wife calls it "a health risk."

WRITINGS—Juvenile, except as noted: *What Does It Do and How Does It Work* (self-illustrated), Harper, 1959; *The Atomic Submarine* (self-illustrated), Harper, 1960; *Bedtime for Frances* (illustrated by Garth Williams; ALA Notable Book), Harper, 1960; *The Story of Hester Mouse, Who Became a Writer and Saved Most of Her Sisters and Brothers and Some of Her Aunts and Uncles from the Owl,* Norton, 1965; *Goodnight,* Norton, 1966.

The Sea-Thing Child (illustrated by Abrom Hoban), Harper, 1972; *Letitia Rabbit's String Song* (illustrated by Mary Chalmers; Junior Literary Guild selection), Coward, 1973; *The Lion of Boaz-Jachin and Jachin-Boaz* (adult novel), Stein and Day, 1973; *How Tom Beat Captain Najork and His Hired Sportsmen* (illustrated by Quentin Blake; ALA Notable Book), Atheneum, 1974; *Kleinzeit* (adult novel), Viking, 1974; (with Sylvie Selig) *Ten What?: A Mystery Counting Book* (illustrated by S. Selig), Scribner, 1975; *Dinner at Alberta's* (illustrated by James Marshall; ALA Notable Book; Junior Literary Guild selection), Crowell, 1975; *Turtle Diary* (adult novel), J. Cape, 1975, Random House, 1976; (with S. Selig) *Crocodile and Pierrot* (illustrated by S. Selig), J. Cape, 1975, Scribner, 1977; *A Near Thing for Captain Najork* (illustrated by Q. Blake), Atheneum, 1976; *Arthur's New Power* (illustrated by Byron Barton), Crowell, 1978; (with Emily Arnold McCully) *The Twenty-Elephant Restaurant* (illustrated by E. A. McCully), Atheneum, 1978, published in England with illustrations by Q. Blake, J. Cape, 1980; *La Corona and the Tin Frog* (illustrated

by Nicola Bayley; originally published in *Puffin Annual,* 1974), J. Cape, 1978, Merrimack Book Services, 1981; *The Dancing Tigers* (illustrated by David Gentleman), J. Cape, 1979, Merrimack Book Services, 1981.

Flat Cat (illustrated by Clive Scruton), Philomel, 1980; *Ace Dragon Ltd.* (illustrated by Q. Blake), J. Cape, 1980, Merrimack Book Services, 1981; *Riddley Walker* (adult novel), J. Cape, 1980, Summit Books, 1981; *They Came from Aargh!* (illustrated by Colin McNaughton), Philomel, 1981; *The Serpent Tower* (illustrated by D. Scott), Methuen/Walker, 1981; *The Great Gumdrop Robbery* (illustrated by C. McNaughton), Philomel, 1982; *The Battle of Zormia* (illustrated by C. McNaughton), Philomel, 1982; *The Flight of Bembel Rudzok* (illustrated by C. McNaughton), Philomel, 1982; *Pilgermann* (novel), Summit Books, 1983; *Jim Frog* (illustrated by Martin Baynton), Holt, 1984; *Lavinia Bat* (illustrated by Martin Baynton), Holt, 1984; *Charlie Meadows* (illustrated by Martin Baynton), Holt, 1984.

All illustrated by Lillian Hoban: *Herman the Loser,* Harper, 1961; *The Song in My Drum,* Harper, 1961; *London Men and English Men,* Harper, 1962; *Some Snow Said Hello,* Harper, 1963; *The Sorely Trying Day* (ALA Notable Book), Harper, 1964; *A Baby Sister for Frances,* Harper, 1964; *Nothing to Do,* Harper, 1964; *Bread and Jam for Frances,* Harper, 1964, (book and record) Scholastic Book Services, 1969; *Tom and the Two Handles,* Harper, 1965; *What Happened When Jack* _and Daisy Tried to Fool the Tooth Fairies,_ Four Winds Press, 1966; _Henry and the Monstrous Din,_ Harper, 1966; _The Little Brute Family,_ Macmillan, 1966; _Save My Place,_ Norton, 1967; _Charlie the Tramp,_ Four Winds Press, 1967, (book and record) Scholastic Book Services, 1970; _The Mouse and His Child_ (novel; ALA Notable Book), Harper, 1967; _A Birthday for Frances,_ Harper, 1968; _The Pedaling Man and Other Poems,_ Norton, 1968; _The Stone Doll of Sister Brute,_ Macmillan, 1968; _Harvey's Hideout,_ Parents Magazine Press, 1969; _Best Friends for Frances,_ Harper, 1969; _Ugly Bird,_ Macmillan, 1969; _The Mole Family's Christmas,_ Parents Magazine Press, 1969; _A Bargain for Frances,_ Harper, 1970; _Emmet Otter's Jug-Band_

Christmas, Parents Magazine Press, 1971; _Egg Thoughts and Other Frances Songs,_ Harper, 1972.

Illustrator: Edgar Allan Poe, _Tales and Poems of Edgar Allan Poe,_ Macmillan, 1967.

Contributor of articles to _Holiday_ and _Family Circle._ Has written material for British Broadcasting Corporation's children's radio programs. Contributor of illustrations to _Sports Illustrated._

ADAPTATIONS—Movies and filmstrips: ''The Little Brute

(From the ABC-TV Children's Special "Emmet Otter's Jug-Band Christmas," starring Jim Henson's Muppets. Adapted from the book by Russell and Lillian Hoban, it was first presented on December 15, 1980.)

They collected admissions and they sold hot dogs . . . . ■ (From *The Twenty-Elephant Restaurant* by Russell Hoban. Illustrated by Emily Arnold McCully.)

"This is very good indeed," she said. "We'll run it in the next issue." ■ (From *La Corona and the Tin Frog* by Russell Hoban. Illustrated by Nicola Bayley.)

Emmet rowed up and down the river, from Turtle Bend to Osprey Point, picking up the laundry that Ma's customers left on their boat landings, and he delivered it when it was done. ■ (From *Emmet Otter's Jug-Band Christmas* by Russell Hoban. Illustrated by Lillian Hoban.)

Family'' (filmstrip with record or cassette), Miller-Brody, 197(?); ''Frances Series'' (filmstrip with record or cassette; includes ''Bedtime for Frances,'' ''A Baby Sister for Frances,'' ''Bread and Jam for Frances,'' ''A Birthday for Frances,'' ''Best Friends for Frances''), BFA Educational Media, 1974; ''The Mouse and His Child'' (feature film), de Faria-Lockhart-Sanrio Productions, 1977; ''Emmet Otter's Jug-Band Christmas,'' Henson Associates, broadcast on HBO, December, 1978.

Recordings: ''Bedtime for Frances, A Baby Sister for Frances, Bread and Jam for Frances, A Birthday for Frances,'' read by Glynis Johns, music by Don Heckman, Caedmon, 1977; ''A Bargain for Frances and Other Stories,'' read by G. Johns, music by D. Heckman, Caedmon, 1977; ''The Mouse and His Child,'' read by Peter Ustinov, Caedmon, 1977.

SIDELIGHTS: Hoban was born on February 4, 1925, in Lansdale, Pennsylvania into an artistic family. To stimulate the development of his children, Hoban's father rewarded them with nickels for witty remarks, exceptional drawings, and such. His father, an advertising manager of the ''Jewish Daily Forward'' in Philadelphia, directed amateur productions of plays, and was a strong supporter of union leader Norman Thomas. ''The first two rules of etiquette I learned were never to cross a picket line and always to eat the union label on the rye bread for good luck.''

From the age of five Hoban drew and sketched as much as possible. His older sister, a successful illustrator whose work included covers for *Saturday Evening Post,* was a strong influence on Hoban's art. When Hoban was eleven his father died, and his mother opened a store to support the family.

Graduating from high school at the age of sixteen, Hoban entered Temple University, but dropped out after five weeks. He attended the Philadelphia Museum School of Industrial Art for a year and a half, describing himself as a non-conformist in school.

Hoban married fellow artist Lillian Aberman in 1944, and a year later was discharged from the Army. For the next ten years he held a variety of jobs, including freight handler, shipping clerk, messenger for Western Union, and electroplating assistant. In his spare time Hoban freelanced as a designer for silk screen shops. A six-month stint as an art director for Printers Ink taught Hoban much about printing and reproduction. He also worked for two years as an illustrator for the Wexton Company. Hoban's art ability was put to use in art studios, animation studios, and on several small magazines. For five years he was a television art director for a large advertising agency.

In 1956 Hoban left the advertising agency to freelance. His ambition had always been to become a painter, so he resolved to use his spare time painting New York scenes. Soon his lunch hours were spent painting the boxers at Stillman's Gym, the famous training gym for would-be prize fighters. *Sports Illustrated* asked him to do a series on Stillman's, which launched his career as a sports illustrator. ''There was a time . . . when I used to spend most of my . . . hours at Stillman's Gym in New York City, and all of my evenings drawing and painting the people I had seen there. As many sedentary persons, I enjoyed the aura . . . that surrounds boxing. . . .'' [Russell Hoban, ''Meaning for a Middleweight,'' *Holiday,* November, 1964.[1]]

An interest in machinery of all kinds led to the publication of Hoban's first book for children in 1959. *What Does It Do and How Does It Work* was written and self-illustrated by Hoban and published by Harper. Beginning in 1961 with publication of *Herman the Loser,* his wife, Lillian, became his illustrator. With a family of four, most of the ideas for the Hobans' books came from daily family situations. About his early children's books, Hoban said: ''There was always a child less than three-feet high around, and that is the point of view I've generally written from. I write the stories to be read aloud, and I try for a good sound, for an easy reading rhythm for the reader and a comfortable intake rhythm for the listener. All of the stories depend on carefully observed detail. They are mostly about ordinary domestic problems, so I have to pay close attention to what is going on in the house, looking for whatever humor may be in the situation and the resolution of it; and the resolution has to be one that really works. I do a lot of revising,

"Kiss me again," said Frances. ■ (From *Bedtime for Frances* by Russell Hoban. Illustrated by Garth Williams.)

Mother and Father tucked her in . . . . ■ (From *A Baby Sister for Frances* by Russell Hoban. Illustrated by Lillian Hoban.)

"He's right," said Bembel Rudzuk, and sawed off another piece of cheesecake. ■ (From *The Flight of Bembel Rudzuk* by Russell Hoban. Illustrated by Colin McNaughton.)

and even when a first draft comes quickly it usually gets worked over many times.''

Until 1969 Hoban, his wife, and their four children lived in Wilton, Connecticut, where the husband-and-wife team collaborated on more than twenty books, including the minor classic *The Mouse and His Child*, an ALA Notable Book of 1967. ''*The Mouse and His Child* was my first novel-length book, and I worked on it, continuing picture books meanwhile, over a period of three years. For two of those years I had a full-time job as an advertising copywriter. The whole story went through four complete rewrites, and within each rewrite every page was rewritten several times. . . . It's slow work, because I have to feel my way along—I have ideas to get the books started, but I don't know where the story will take me. I have to find out about the characters and the circumstances as they develop. Often I get stuck and can't make any forward progress for a while. Then I content myself with what I call lateral progress—I write notes to help me find out more about my material: what is likely to happen and why. Or I research the factual elements of the story to get the hard specifics that limit and influence what can happen. Sometimes I can't even

do that, so I just talk to myself on the typewriter to keep words coming out of the machine until things begin to move again.

''My working rule is just to try to keep going—to do a little if I can't do a lot, and to keep looking and listening for the story that wants to be written.''

About his work habits during those years, Hoban wrote: ''My schedule is not a very rigid one: I get up as early as I can and run two miles every morning. After breakfast I sit down at the typewriter—if I let anything else come first the day is lost. I work as far into the day as I can, with a nap in the afternoon if possible. My hours are long or short depending on whether I'm making real headway on a book or just trying to figure out where I am; when things are really moving I work in the evenings too. And of course there are days when nothing gets done at all.''

Hoban and his family moved to London, England in 1969, where he concentrated on writing rather than art work. His marriage broke up the next year, and the family, excluding Hoban, returned stateside. After writing over thirty-one chil-

"Very well," said Aunt Fidget Wonkham-Strong at table in her iron hat. "Eat your greasy bloaters." ■ (From *How Tom Beat Captain Najork and His Hired Sportsmen* by Russell Hoban. Illustrated by Quentin Blake.)

dren's books, Hoban began writing adult novels at the age of forty-six. ''It was Ferdinand Monjo who helped me make the transition from children's books to adult. I would send him each chapter I wrote of *The Mouse and His Child,* and he would give me his comments. Without knowing it I wanted to get into adult fiction, to use all of myself and my experience. Only after my wife and I separated did I feel free.

''*The Lion of Boaz-Jachin and Jachin-Boaz* is the most autobiographical novel I've written. I saw a lion relief from Nineveh in the British Museum, and I began to think of a supernatural story about lions, but I could not get it together until after my family had broken up. Then I thought of a frustrated father leaving his wife and son and the rage of the son evoking a lion, the lion literally coming into being because of forces operating within the father and the son.'' [Barbara A. Bannon, ''PW Interviews: Russell Hoban,'' *Publishers Weekly,* May 15, 1981.[2]]

In 1975 Hoban married Gundula Ahl, a German-born bookseller. He has three sons by his second marriage. ''In the last few years I've gotten to be good friends with my head. I see my psychiatrist daily, and I read him what I write. I think it probably works another way with other people than the way it works with me. There always seems to be something in my mind waiting to put something together with some primary thought I will encounter. It's like looking out of the window and listening to the radio at the same time. I am committed to what comes to me, however it links up.''[2]

Hoban lives with his second family in Fulham, England, where he has recently received accolades for his adult writings. According to the author, it is the loss of his first marriage and the resulting estrangement from his children that had a tremendous impact on his adult fiction. '' 'The poet must surrender himself as he is at the moment to something which is more valuable,' says Eliot. 'The progress of the artist is a continual self-sacrifice, a continual extinction of personality.' Well, it takes a real high-flying intellectual to come up with something that elementary. What else, really, could the progress of an artist possibly be? Art, like babies, is one of the things life makes us make, and the strongest, most passionate

(From the full-length animated movie "The Mouse and His Child," starring the voices of Peter Ustinov, Cloris Leachman, and Andy Devine. Based on the novel by Russell Hoban. Produced by de Faria-Lockhart-Sanrio Productions, 1977.)

affirmation of the self is necessarily the losing of the self in that continuous stream of being in which we change the past and the past changes us. The babies don't belong to us and neither does the art, because what can the most powerful integration of self with life be but the dropping of what precious fussy little identity that we wear like morning dress and a bowler hat? For goodness' sake forget it. And once it's forgotten, time and the light are now. And the next moment and the moment after that.

"... Life continues its changing balance of war and peace, famine and plenty, hope and despair, and the devaluation of currencies and people. Are writers moving forward towards time and the light? Are they achieving that affirmative extinction of personality, that necessary symbiosis with the past? Some are, I think, particularly those who write for children and young people.

"I don't read many contemporary novels, but sometimes I talk to people who do. It seems to me and some of my friends that more and more adult novels are not essentially literary. Many of them simply communicate experience, and that of itself is not art. . . . There are empty spaces now in literature, vacated by the so-called adult novel, and some of those spaces now become new territory for children's writers.

"As we move forward in this stretto of time the distinctions between children and adults blur and fade: today's children do not live in an expurgated world. With their elders they must endure sudden deaths and slow ones, bombs and fire falling from the sky, the poisoning of peaceful air and the threatened extinction of this green jewel of Earth. They must endure the reality of mortal man. Like Mr. Fast in Leon Garfield's book we have sold the self that must at all costs be preserved and not betrayed. New selves arise each moment, and we must offer them a friendly hand of innocence and encouragement." [Russell Hoban, "Thoughts on Being and Writing," *The Thorny Paradise,* edited by Edward Blishen, Kestrel, 1975.[3]]

Hoban's adult novel *Riddley Walker* [J. Cape, 1980] took five and a half years and fourteen drafts to complete. In it, he imagined life several millenniums after a nuclear holocaust and then invented the debased, fragmented language that survivors might use to rebuild their civilization. Since words are heard rather than read spelling follows pronunciation, multisyllabic forms are broken and prose rhythm echoes those of speech. "Russell Hoban has transformed what might have been just another fantasy of the future into a novel of exceptional depth and originality," states the *New York Times Book Review.* "He has created a hero who, deprived of all other references, reads the worlds through his instincts, his imagination, his unconscious, without losing touch with his own reality, or becoming either more or less then he is: a twelve-year-old who has become a man and is fighting to maintain his clarity and independence in a devastated land. He is also an orphan haunted by an unspecified sense of grief; the Iron Age he lives in is made even more desolate by the vague memory of what has been lost and will never be recovered. . . . He survives by looking at what is in front of him and seeing it as though for the first time: 'Looking at that black leaders eyes they myndit me of gulls eyes. Eyes so fearce they cudnt even be sorry for the naminal they wer in. Like a gull I seen 1 time with a broakin wing and dad kilt it. Them yeller eyes staret scareless to the las. The jus happent to be in the gull but they dint care nothing for it.'"

Hoban's works are included in the Kerlan Collection at the University of Minnesota.

FOR MORE INFORMATION SEE: Frederic Whitaker, "The Unusual Career of Painter-Illustrator Russell Hoban," *American Artists,* October, 1961; *Wilton Bulletin* (Wilton, Conn.), September 26, 1962; Walt Reed, editor, *The Illustrator in America: 1900-1960's,* Reinhold, 1966; Doris de Montreville and Donna Hill, editors, *Third Book of Junior Authors,* H. W. Wilson, 1972; Russell Hoban, "Thoughts on Being and Writing," *The Thorny Paradise,* edited by Edward Blishen, Kestrel, 1975; John Rowe Townsend, "A Second Look: *The Mouse and His Child,*" *Horn Book,* October, 1975; *Time,* February 16, 1976, June 22, 1981; Barbara A. Bannon, "PW Interviews: Russell Hoban," *Publishers Weekly,* May 15, 1981; Fred Hauptfuhrer, "After the Apocalypse the Language Riddle in the Bleak New World of Russell Hoban," *People,* August 10, 1981; *Time,* May 16, 1983.

HOWARD, Vernon (Linwood) 1918-
(Paul Castle, Don Jordan)

PERSONAL: Born in 1918; married; children: three. *Residence:* 303 Ridge Rd., Boulder City, Nev. 89005.

CAREER: Author. Lecturer and teacher of self-improvement and mysticism courses, Boulder City, Nev.

WRITINGS—For children: *Steve Scott and the Hidden City* (fiction), Moody, 1943; *Children's Missionary Library* (biography series; illustrated by J. L. Craig), twelve volumes, Revell, 1949-51; *The Mystery of the Six Clues* (fiction), Van

VERNON HOWARD

Kampen Press, 1952; *Handbook of Bible Games for All Ages*, Zondervan, 1953; *Short Plays for All-Boy Casts*, Plays, 1954; *Humorous Monologues* (illustrated by Doug Anderson), Sterling, 1955, revised edition (illustrated by Audrey Witchern), 1973; *Holiday Monologues* (illustrated by D. Anderson), Sterling, 1956; (under pseudonym Paul Castle) *101 Funny Things to Make and Do* (illustrated by D. Anderson), Sterling, 1956; (under pseudonym Don Jordan) *Party Stunts for All*, Zondervan, 1957; *Monologues for Boys and Girls* (illustrated by Margaret), Sterling, 1957; *Monologues for Teens* (illustrated by Patt Willen), Sterling, 1957; *Easy Plays for Church and School*, Zondervan, 1957; *500 Games for Boys and Girls*, Zondervan, 1958; *Pantomines, Charades, and Skits* (illustrated by D. Anderson), Sterling, 1959, revised edition (illustrated by Shizu), 1974; *Quick Comedy Skits*, Zondervan, 1959.

Short Plays from the Great Classics (illustrated by Shizu), Sterling, 1960; *More Charades and Pantomimes* (illustrated by D. Anderson), Sterling, 1961; *Puppet and Pantomime Plays* (illustrated by D. Anderson), Sterling, 1962; *Talking to an Audience* (illustrated by D. Anderson), Sterling, 1963; *Acts for Comedy Shows: How to Perform and Write Them* (illustrated by D. Anderson), Sterling, 1964; *Getting Started as an Author* (illustrated by D. Anderson), Sterling, 1965; (editor) *The Complete Book of Children's Theater* (illustrated by D. Anderson and others), Doubleday, 1969; *Fun Games for Boys and Girls*, Zondervan, 1974; *One Hundred Games for Boys and Girls*, Zondervan, 1974.

Adult nonfiction: *Work Power: Talk Your Way to Life Leadership*, Prentice-Hall, 1958; *Time Power for Personal Success*, Prentice-Hall, 1960; *Success Through the Magic of Personal Power*, Prentice-Hall, 1961; *Your Magic Power to Persuade and Command People*, Prentice-Hall, 1962; *Action Power: The Miracle Way to a Successful New Life*, Prentice-Hall, 1963; *The Richer You: Ten Magic Steps that Change Your Life Quickly*, Brewster, 1963; *Secrets of Mental Magic: How to Use Your Full Power of Mind*, Prentice-Hall, 1964; *Psycho-Pictography: The New Way to Use the Miracle Power of Your Mind*, Parker Publishing, 1965; *The Mystic Path to Cosmic Power*, Parker Publishing, 1967; *The Power of Your Supermind*, Parker Publishing, 1968; *Pathways to Perfect Living*, Parker Publishing, 1969; *Esoteric Mind-Power: Secrets for New Success and Happiness*, CSA Press, 1973; *Inspire Yourself*, CSA Press, 1975; *There Is a Way Out!*, CSA Press, 1975; *The Esoteric Encyclopedia of Eternal Knowledge*, Thorson, 1976; *Esoteric Mind Power*, De Vorss, 1980.

Plays; first published in *Plays:* "Blue Serge Suit," October, 1953; "Turkey for All," November, 1953; "Paloma, Princess of Pluto," January, 1954; "Valentine Box," February, 1954; "Valley Forge Was Never Like This," February, 1954; "Danger: Pixies at Work," May, 1955; "Bird Court," November, 1955; "Lazy Fox," January, 1956; "Vegetable Salad," February, 1956; "Happy Poet," February, 1956; "Singing Shark," May, 1957.

Also author of *The Mystic Masters Speak* and *1,500 Ways to Escape the Human Jungle*.

FOR MORE INFORMATION SEE: *Human Behavior*, March, 1979.

My fondest affection, Lady Dulcinea. ■ (From *The Complete Book of Children's Theater* by Vernon Howard. Illustrated by Doug Anderson and others.)

JOHNSON, Dorothy M(arie) 1905-1984

OBITUARY NOTICE—See sketch in *SATA* Volume 6: Born December 19, 1905, in McGregor, Iowa; died of Parkinson's disease, November 11, 1984, in Missoula, Mont. Short story writer, editor, and educator. The author of numerous western short stories for adults, Johnson also wrote nearly a dozen books for children. Her best known western stories were published in two collections during the 1950s, *Indian Country* and *The Hanging Tree*. It was from these two books that several popular motion picture adaptations emerged, namely, "The Hanging Tree," "The Man Who Shot Liberty Valance," and "A Man Called Horse." Through her stories, Johnson gained a reputation for historical accuracy, brevity of style, and themes dealing with the courage and strength of ordinary people. When the short story market suffered a decline in the late 1950s, she turned to juvenile writing. Most of her books for children also focus on the American West, such as *Famous Lawmen of the Old West, Some Went West,* and *Montana;* however, she produced *Greece: Wonderland of the Past and Present* and *Farewell to Troy,* books which reflect her love for a land she had visited several times. In addition to her writing career, Johnson worked as a managing editor for several publishing companies in New York from 1935 to 1950. She served as assistant professor of journalism at the University of Montana for fifteen years, beginning in 1952. Among the awards she received are the Spur Award from Western Writers of America, the Levi Strauss Golden Saddleman Award, and the Western Heritage Wrangler Award.

FOR MORE INFORMATION SEE: Judy Alter, *Dorothy M. Johnson*, Boise State University, 1980; *Contemporary Authors, New Revision Series*, Volume 6, Gale, 1982; *Fifty Western Writers: A Bio-Bibliographical Sourcebook*, Greenwood Press, 1982; *The Writers Directory: 1984-1986*, St. James Press, 1983. *Obituaries: Newsweek*, November 11, 1984; *New York Times*, November 13, 1984.

LAIKEN, Deirdre S(usan)   1948-

BRIEF ENTRY: Born January 21, 1948, in New York, N.Y. Editor, free-lance writer, and part-time educator. Laiken graduated from State University of New York College at Buffalo in 1969 and received her M.S.Ed. from the same institution the following year. For the next four years she was employed as a teacher of English in Buffalo, N.Y. public schools. Since 1974 she has been an editor for *Scholastic* magazine and is also a part-time teacher of creative writing. In addition to several books for adults, Laiken has written four nonfiction works for young adults. Her first, *Mind/Body/Spirit* (Messner, 1978), was followed by *Listen to Me, I'm Angry* (Lothrop, 1980). The latter, written with her husband/psychotherapist Alan J. Schneider, is a survey of how young people can deal with the complex emotion of anger. *Bulletin of the Center for Children's Books* described it as "straightforward . . . and direct. . . . A sensible book [that] can help adolescents understand their own and other people's anger. . . ."

Another young adult book Laiken wrote with her husband is *The Sweet Dreams Love Book: Understanding Your Feelings* (Bantam, 1983). Like *Listen to Me, School Library Journal* noted that this book contains "sensible, straightforward advice without a trace of preaching. . . ." *Voice of Youth Advocates* agreed, commending the authors' use of case histories and questionnaires in "an excellent job of working through the dilemmas of adolescence." Laiken's books for adults include *Daughters of Divorce* (Morrow, 1981), a study of the effects of parental divorce on women, and *Lovestrong: A Woman Doctor's True Story of Marriage and Medicine* (Times Books, 1984). *Home and office:* 1036 Garden St., Hoboken, N.J. 07030.

FOR MORE INFORMATION SEE: Contemporary Authors, Volume 104, Gale, 1982.

LEGG, Sarah Martha Ross Bruggeman (?)-1982

OBITUARY NOTICE: Died August 29, 1982. Legg was the founder of The Magic Fishbone, a well-known and innovative children's bookshop located in Carmel, Calif. Dedicated to the principle of excellence in children's literature, Legg opened the doors of her bookshop in 1963 with a few hundred titles in stock; by 1972 the shop had expanded to larger quarters and virtually thousands of books. Through professional study, Legg carefully selected the titles available in The Magic Fishbone for a clientele that included readers ranging from preschoolers to young adults, students of children's literature, parents, and teachers. Her love of children's books was instilled throughout her ever-growing enterprise, evidenced in special personal touches such as the gift-wrapping of books, teas for grandmothers, popcorn-popping story times for children, and an individual book-of-the-month selection based on a particular

child's needs and interests. Formerly an elementary schoolteacher for ten years, Legg also conducted sessions for parents on the selection of quality reading for their children. As The Magic Fishbone grew in reputation, so did the demand for Legg as a speaker on children's books. Her lecture circuit included cooperative nursery schools and workshops for Montessori and learning disabilities teachers.

FOR MORE INFORMATION SEE: Horn Book, April, 1977. *Obituaries: Horn Book,* December, 1982.

LEONARD, Constance (Brink)   1923-

BRIEF ENTRY: Born April 27, 1923, in Pottsville, Pa. Author of juvenile and adult mystery novels. A 1944 graduate of Wellesley College, Leonard wrote stories, poetry, and other pieces for years although she never intended them for publication. Her first book appeared in 1971, a children's story entitled *The Great Pumpkin Mystery.* "As a longtime mystery addict," confessed Leonard, "I thought it would be fun to try writing one, and then another, and another." She is now the author of nearly ten mysteries, all published by Dodd. Of the four novels she has written for young adults, three are part of the "Tracy James Mysteries" series. In *The Marina Mystery* (1981), young Tracy is attracted to marina dockmaster Peter Sturtevant whom she follows to the Florida Keys where he is working. While there she uncovers a dope-smuggling operation and solves the murder of one of the boaters. In *Stowaway* (1983), the amateur sleuth joins with Sturtevant and his wealthy cruise clients as they all attempt to rescue a young girl from an illegal alien smuggling operation. Leonard's latest book, *Aground* (1984), follows Tracy as she travels to her parents' summer home in Maine and encounters unsettling happenings in a cult commune. In *Shadow of a Ghost* (1978) another heroine, Kathy, finds herself in the midst of gypsy curses and ghosts while on a trip to England. Leonard's adult mysteries include *The Other Maritha* (1972), *Steps to Nowhere* (1974), and *Hostage in Illyria* (1976). *Address:* Box 226, Francestown, N.H. 03043.

FOR MORE INFORMATION SEE: Contemporary Authors, Volumes 49-52, Gale, 1975.

LEWIN, Hugh (Francis)   1939-

BRIEF ENTRY: Born December 3, 1939, in Lydenburg, Transvaal, South Africa. Journalist and author. Lewin spent seven years as a political prisoner in his native land—the result of his opposition to apartheid. Those years are chronicled in his adult book, *Bandiet: Seven Years in a South African Prison* (Barrie & Jenkins, 1974). Upon his release, he moved to England where he worked as an editor. Filled with memories of the years he spent as a child in South Africa, Lewin realized that his own small daughters had no such recollections. The desire to teach them about the homeland they never knew led him to produce a series of picture books featuring "Jafta," a little black boy about four or five years old. Originally published in England, the series has been made available in the United States by Carolrhoda.

In a review of *Jafta, Jafta and the Wedding, Jafta's Father,* and *Jafta's Mother* (all Carolrhoda, 1983), *School Library*

Journal observed: "These four stories . . . are lighted by the affection of an author born in South Africa . . . and are as warm as their gold and brown coloring." In *Jafta,* the young boy's feelings are liberally expressed in metaphors as he purrs "like a lion cub," jumps "like an impala," or dances "like a zebra." Although his adventures are universal childhood experiences, Jafta's environment is completely African. Lewin opens some of the books with "There are some words in this story that might be new to you . . . ," thereby ensuring explanation of vocabulary that may be unknown to young Western readers. *Language Arts* took note of Lisa Kopper's accompanying illustrations, especially "the copper-tinted images of the boy" and the "warm hues [that] adroitly hint of the dry earth tones present in the . . . dusty environment." The latest books in the series are *Jafta: The Town* and *Jafta: The Journey* (both 1984). *Residence:* Harare, Zimbabwe.

FOR MORE INFORMATION SEE: Hugh Lewin, *Bandiet: Seven Years in a South African Prison* (autobiographical), Barrie & Jenkins, 1974.

LEWIS, Marjorie   1929-

PERSONAL: Born May 3, 1929, in New York, N.Y.; daughter of Leon (a designer of menswear) and Julie (a teacher; maiden name, Rudomin) Schwartz; married Philip Lewis (a producer of documentary television films), September 12, 1954; children: Victoria Laura, David, James. *Education:* Russell Sage College, B.A., 1949; Rutgers University, M.L.S., 1970. *Politics:* Democrat. *Religion:* Jewish. *Home:* 13 Hubbard Dr., White Plains, N.Y. 10605. *Office:* Scarsdale Junior High School, Scarsdale, N.Y. 10583.

CAREER: CBS-TV, New York City, film production assistant, 1951-55; American Red Cross, New York City, press information officer, 1955-56; Compton Advertising, New York City, supervisor of film production for the East Coast, 1956-58; Brookside School, Montclair, N.J., school librarian, 1965-71; American School, London, England, substitute teacher of English and history, 1971-74; Scarsdale Public Library, Scarsdale, N.Y., children's librarian, 1974-76; Scarsdale Junior High School, Scarsdale, school librarian, 1976—. *Member:* American Library Association, Storytellers Guild of Westchester, Beta Phi Mu, National Writer's Union.

WRITINGS—For children: *The Boy Who Would Be a Hero* (illustrated by Lydia Dabcovich), Coward, 1982; *Ernie and the Mile-Long Muffler* (illustrated by Margot Apple), Coward, 1982; *Wrongway Applebaum,* Coward, 1984. Contributor of reviews to *School Library Journal* and an article entitled, "Charlie's Garden," to *Ms. Magazine.*

WORK IN PROGRESS: A novel for young adults; a poetry anthology for young adults.

SIDELIGHTS: "I suppose I always wanted to write a book. Who doesn't? It wasn't until my own children were growing up, however, that I learned to respect children's books for the artistry that goes into them. And, at the same time, I learned to respect children for their unique needs and their taste that is not *less* than adult stuff—only different.

"I consider myself unbelievably fortunate to be able to still enjoy children and young adult books even though my own children are grown. As a librarian and book reviewer, I get to

MARJORIE LEWIS

see quite a lot of new books—and, because children are in my charge, I feel an enormous responsibility to be critical of what I read.

"I believe in stories—in giving children delight. I believe in the power of words to create music, laughter, and tears. I believe that books can lighten our lives; illuminate our society; deepen our sensitivity. I believe that we, as authors, owe children an attention to beautifully produced work that marries excellent writing to excellent design. I believe that books are a form of magic. I want to give children that magic—through my own writing as well as through my work as a librarian.

"I have tried in my own books to have a verbal 'lilt' to the text that makes them easy to read aloud; so many books that would be fun to read aloud lack that special oral rhythm. I think children should have the pleasure of listening to big words, too. I believe, as you can surmise, that children should be read to forever! Librarians, parents and teachers should not stop reading aloud just because a child has learned to read.

"The search for quality that is worth both the reader's and the audience's time is a difficult quest, but such quality is there. To find it means becoming familiar with literature, and it is here that librarians exhibit their particular expertise. It is a *trust* to be the ones to introduce children and story to each other. Storytelling, story reading—that's where it's at."

"I am now working in a junior high school and have discovered that the twelve to fourteen age group is my favorite all-time great span! They are affectionate, funny, passionate, uncertain, swaggering, insecure, and lonely. Their very self-centeredness

Well . . . in a time that was not now, in a place that was not here, there was a boy who lived with his old mother in a small village. ■ (From *The Boy Who Would Be a Hero* by Marjorie Lewis. Illustrated by Lydia Dabcovich.)

is countered by their willingness to be your friend. Nobody has been quite as thrilled over the publication of my first two books than my own students. They are proud and admiring. And critical, too. 'You should have. . . .' 'Why didn't you . . .?'

"I wrote *The Boy Who Would Be a Hero* because I wanted to write a story that would read aloud gracefully and have delicious words to introduce to young readers. I wrote *Ernie* because, well, I'm not sure there was any great reason. He just grew into a sturdy kid who coped. Also, he knew when to stop, which is a lesson we all have to learn. Especially mothers who are always telling children to finish what they start, even when the product is not nearly as much fun as the doing it was, or when more was bitten off than could be comfortably chewed. I would like to continue writing books that I think children will like. I will continue, as a librarian, to give them the gift of books by fine authors whose works I admire. What more wonderful present can I give to my students?"

LINDSAY, (Nicholas) Vachel   1879-1931

PERSONAL: Born November 10, 1879, in Springfield, Ill.; died by his own hand, December 5, 1931, in Springfield, Ill.; son of Vachel Thomas (a doctor) and Esther Catharine (Frazee) Lindsay; married Elizabeth Conner (a teacher), May 19, 1925; children: Susan Doniphan, Nicholas Cave. *Education:* Attended Hiram College, 1897-1900, Art Institute of Chicago, 1900-03, New York School of Art, 1904-05. *Politics:* Democrat. *Religion:* Campbellite. *Residence:* Springfield, Ill.

CAREER: Poet and author. While attending art school, worked for Marshall Field's (department store), Chicago, Ill., 1901-03, and as a museum guide at the Metropolitan Museum of Art in New York, N.Y.; lectured in art at the Y.M.C.A., New York City, winters, 1905-08; went on a walking tour through the southern United States distributing copies of his poem ''The Tree of Laughing Bells'' in exchange for food and lodging, spring, 1906; went on his second walking tour, traveling through New Jersey, Pennsylvania, and Ohio, 1908; lectured at the Y.M.C.A., Springfield, Ill., winter, 1908-09; lectured for the Anti-Saloon League, central Illinois, 1909-10; went on third walking tour from Illinois to New Mexico, bringing with him copies of his poetry and speaking on ''the gospel of beauty,'' summer, 1912; following the publication of his first two volumes of poetry, in 1913 and 1914, he became known for his chanting verse and toured the country giving recitals at universities, schools and clubs, until about 1922; poet-in-residence, Gulfport Junior College, Gulfport, Miss., 1923-24.

MEMBER: National Institute of Arts and Letters, Poetry Society of America, Author's League of America, Author's Guild of Author's League of America, Authors and Composers (Great Britain), Incorporated Society of Playwrights, English Speaking Union, Phi Beta Kappa, Chapter Alpha (honorary member, 1922), Cliff Dwellers (Chicago), Players (New York), Author's Club (London). *Awards, honors:* Helen H. Levinson Prize, *Poetry* magazine, 1915, for poem ''The Chinese Nightingale''; first American poet invited by Oxford University to recite his poems, 1920; Award of Honor, *Poetry,* 1928, for genius and originality; honorary degrees from Baylor University, 1920, and Hiram College, 1930.

WRITINGS—Of special interest to young readers: *Johnny Appleseed and Other Poems* (illustrated by George Richards), Macmillan, 1928, new edition, 1961, reprinted, Buccaneer, 1981; *Springfield Town Is Butterfly Town, and Other Poems for Children* (self-illustrated), preface by Louis Untermeyer, Kent State University Press, 1969.

Selected poetry: *The Tramp's Excuse and Other Poems* (pamphlet; no. 4 of ''War Bulletin''), [Springfield, Ill.], 1909; *Rhymes to Be Traded for Bread,* [Springfield?], ca. 1912; *General William Booth Enters into Heaven, and Other Poems,* M. Kennerley, 1913; *The Congo, and Other Poems,* introduction by Harriet Monroe, Macmillan, 1914, reissued, 1933; *The Chinese Nightingale, and Other Poems,* Macmillan, 1917; *The Daniel Jazz and Other Poems,* G. Bell & Sons (London), 1920; *The Golden Whales of California and Other Rhymes in the American Language,* Macmillan, 1920; *Going-to-the-Sun,* D. Appleton, 1923; *Babylon* (originally published in *New York Evening Post*), Mrs. Dicken's Book Shop (Memphis, Tenn.), 1923; *Going-to-the-Stars,* D. Appleton, 1926; *The Candle in the Cabin: A Weaving Together of Script and Singing,* D. Appleton, 1926; *Every Soul Is a Circus,* Macmillan, 1929; *Rigmarole, Rigmarole* (pamphlet), Random House, 1929.

Prose: *War Bulletin,* numbers 1-3, and 5 (pamphlets; no. 4 issued as ''The Tramp's Excuse''), [Springfield], 1909; *The Village Magazine* (self-illustrated), [Springfield], 1910, 4th imprint, enlarged, Jeffersons Printing, 1925; *A Letter about My Four Programmes, for Committees in Correspondence,* [Springfield?], 1910; *Adventures While Preaching the Gospel of Beauty,* M. Kennerley, 1914; *The Art of the Moving Picture,* Macmillan, 1915, revised edition, 1922, reprinted (with an introduction by Stanley Kauffmann), Liveright, 1970; *A Handy Guide for Beggars, Especially Those of the Poetic Fraternity,* Macmillan, 1916; *The Golden Book of Springfield,* Macmillan, 1920; *The Litany of Washington Street* (essays), Macmillan, 1929; *A Letter of Vachel Lindsay on the ''Movies'',* privately printed, 1945.

Collections: *Collected Poems,* Macmillan, 1923, revised edition, 1925, reissued, 1959; *Selected Poems of Vachel Lindsay,* edited with an introduction by Hazelton Spencer, Macmillan, 1931; *Letters of Nicholas Vachel Lindsay to A. Joseph Armstrong,* edited by A. Joseph Armstrong, Baylor University Press,

1940; *Selected Poems,* edited by Mark Harris, Macmillan, 1963; *Adventures, Rhymes, and Designs* (with an essay by Robert F. Sayre), Eakins, 1968; *The Western Illinois Poets: The Early Poetry of Vachel Lindsay, Edgar Lee Masters, and Carl Sandburg,* edited by John E. Hallwas, Western Illinois University, 1975; *Letters of Vachel Lindsay,* edited by Marc Chenetier, B. Franklin, 1979; *Collected Poems,* Volume I, edited by Dennis Camp, Spoon River Poetry Press, 1983.

ADAPTATIONS—Recordings: ''The Congo,'' read by the author, National Council of Teachers of English, Columbia University Press, 1931; ''The Flower-Fed Buffaloes, The Chinese Nightingale, The Mysterious Cat, General William Booth Enters into Heaven, [and] The Moon's the North Wind's Cooky'' (three records), read by the author, National Council of Teachers of English, Columbia University Press, 1931, rereleased as ''Vachel Lindsay Reading The Congo, Chinese Nightingale, and Other Poems,'' Caedmon, 195(?); ''The Santa Fe Trail [and] The Congo,'' Michigan State Normal College, 195(?); ''Abraham Lincoln Walks at Midnight,'' sung by Neil Tangeman, music by Roy Harris, M-G-M Records, 1955; ''Poetry,'' read by son, Nicholas C. Lindsay, Caedmon, 1967; ''General William Booth's Entrance into Heaven,'' music by Charles E. Ives, Composers Recordings, 1978.

Sheet music: ''The Daniel Jazz,'' music by Louis Gruenberg, R. St. Hoffman, 1925, another adaptation, music by Herbert Chappell, Novello, 1963; ''General William Booth Enters into Heaven,'' music by Sydney Homer, G. Schirmer, 1926, an-

VACHEL LINDSAY

My little lake. It was the moon.... ■ (From "The Path in the Sky," in *Johnny Appleseed and Other Poems* by Vachel Lindsay. Illustrated by George Richards.)

other adaptation, music by Philip James, Witmark, 1933; "Abraham Lincoln Walks at Midnight," music by Elie Siegmeister, Arrow Music Press, 1939, another adaptation, music by R. Harris, Associated Music Publishers, 1962; "The Congo," music by Maynard Klein, Ditson, 1941, another adaptation, music by Jacques Wolfe, C. Fischer, 1948, adaptation for children by Paul Paviour published as "The Congo Jive," Boosey & Hawkes Music Publishers, 1974; "In Praise of Johnny Appleseed," music by Eunice Kettering, [Ashland?, Ohio], 1957, another adaptation, music by Gail T. Kubik, F. Colombo, 1962; "Samson and the Gates of Gaza," music by Elizabeth Maconchy, Chappell, 1968.

Other musical adaptations include "The Congo," music by Arthur Bergh, 1918; "Animals and Insects," music by L. Gruenberg, 1925; "Daniel," music by Harvey Enders, 1925; "Two Old Crows: An Exercise in Stuttering for Male Voices," music by H. Enders, 1932; and "To a Golden Haired Girl," music by George F. McKay, 1936.

SIDELIGHTS: **November 10, 1879.** Born in Springfield, Illinois. Lindsay's mother taught him at home because he was a sickly child. When he grew stronger, he was sent to Stuart Grammar School.

1893. Entered Springfield High School. A teacher, Susan Wilcox, was a major influence. Lindsay acknowledged his gratitude to her in a letter written years later: "I do not think the world would be monotonous if there were a few more in it like you.... Really, it would be such a pleasure to talk things over. You helped me so much to sustain a mood that I myself desire to keep. What I am with you, is what I consider it my business to be all the time. The plane on which we thought and talked is one in which I am so very much more comfortable than most any other.

"... I owe you an inestimable debt for the mere kindness of your heart and the readiness of your mind.... It was plainly

as good a time to you as to me, which is the best part of the memory, and therefore I do not have to thank you too much." [Marc Chenetier, editor, *Letters of Vachel Lindsay*, Franklin, 1979.[1]]

September, 1897. Entered Hiram College with his sister, Olive.

November, 1899. Decided, despite his parents' wishes, that his future was not as a doctor. "At last I am attending my choice of a college, it is organized within myself. I want to read all the great books and think over the great thoughts and wrestle with them as Jacob wrestled with the angel.... Every inch of my will up to thirty-one years goes to the evolution of myself.... I have a world to save, and must prepare, prepare, prepare.

"My life is empty when I try to enjoy what the uncreative enjoy, it is empty when I try to find in myself the motives that they have. To hold anything, and appropriate it, I must be in the creative mood, and I am *always* in some sort of a creative mood....

"No one can teach me, and nothing can discipline my mind but the pride of the artist. Nothing so well, at least. Let me try.

"Never in all my life have I had an unfettered chance to try with all the soul within me, with my mind free, my conscience free, with no other responsibility and no other duty—to do the only things I ever will be able to learn to do well—draw—and write, and speak." [Eleanor Ruggles, *The West—Going Home: A Life of Vachel Lindsay*, Norton, 1959.[2]]

January, 1900. Entered the Art Institute of Chicago. In September, 1901, Lindsay returned to Springfield intending to visit, but remained there for three months working at a department store. "*Just* such a position as I imagined would be best, manual labor, mainly.... I mustn't think for a minute that I am going to be a failure. I must be both an artistic and a financial success. Every man of my station in a civilized land should. Those who love him have no right to be happy if he is not a success."[2]

January, 1902. Returned to the Art Institute, where he began to develop an artistic philosophy: "Find the absolutely native American painters. Study, study, study them, and on this choose to live and die. It will be your own field, your own, for no one else has attempted such a synthesis. One little thing done from the spirit of the soil is worth a thousand great things done abroad.

"It certainly does not pay to be anything but one's self, giving it the highest, most complete artistic expression. Write as we will, there is only one set of people that an earnest soul can vitally move—those are souls that are forever akin.

"The way to strike home most thoroughly and permanently to the largest number is just to be thoroughly true to one's highest—never fearing it will be too exclusive, too personal, too exceptional, too aristocratic, to be understood."[2]

Summer, 1903. Began to experience what he called, "visions." "It is plausible, I think, that for one who had so long coordinated drawings and poems for drawings, his religious experiences should paint themselves before him in the air. Being taught by that admirable practical but unimaginative master William M. Chase never to draw a thing till I saw it on the blank paper before me, it was only the terrible power and blaze of the pictures that came that made them unusual."[2]

In September, Lindsay became engaged to Ruth Wheeler of Akron, Ohio, and left for New York City to study at the New York School of Art, under William Chase.

1904. First published poem, ''The Queen of Bubbles'' appeared in *The Critic*.

1905. Employed as a teacher and lecturer at the YMCA. Began reciting and trying to sell his poetry on the street. Decided to pursue solely the writing of poetry and give up painting. ''But I have plans in the matter of Art. I have had a great struggle with myself in this matter, unimportant to other folks, for it has no outward showing—the question of which one had the best right to my heart of hearts devotion—Art or letters. For a time at least I see the thing now settled, and I frankly conceive that I have more to say in poetry than art. And it took all the art courage out of me for a while. But now my fingers begin to tingle again to be doing, and I have some rather definite plans of some little picture books I shall make, possibly by hand, with wood-blocks, using little bits of color, and printing in editions of ten or twenty.

''There is only one plan I have, however I may seem to twist and turn to superficial observers. I want to earn leisure and solitude, that I may do the highest honor possible to the dreams that beset me. *I have only one duty—to give them form and setting, putting my whole strength into them.*''[1]

Terminated his engagement to Ruth Wheeler. ''To perfectly satisfy the Wheeler family, I must abstain from all ideas that are new, all points of view not fully expounded in the *Ladies' Home Journal*. I must confine my restless mind to saying my prayers, dressing my manly form in style and making money. *Nothing* based on deep reading, personal observation, or a study of the real masters on any line is understandable. These three, prayers, money and style, are the whole gauntlet of human endeavor.

''. . . The appearance is the thing. The soul and the dreaming and the life that go behind these things is absurd. It never entered the Wheeler imagination. Now—Ruth is a modified Wheeler. She makes all kinds of effort to follow and enjoy these things, but with several states between us, with nothing but Wheelers around her, how can we live together in spirit?''[2]

1906. Sailed to Florida with his friend Edward Broderick, then hiked from Jacksonville to Grass Springs, Kentucky, where he visited his Aunt Eudora Lindsay South. ''All my dreams and ideas of Kentucky turn on my beautiful talks with Aunt Eudora . . . her very motherly way and her deep sympathy with my struggle to make a place for my songs. It was, indeed, timely, I had had very little response anywhere and very little understanding. No one cared for my pictures, no one cared for my verse, and I turned beggar in sheer desperation. Many people try to gloss this over now and make out it was a merry little spring excursion and I didn't really mean it. They are dead wrong. It was a life and death struggle, nothing less. I was entirely prepared to die for my work, if necessary, by the side of the road, and was almost on the point of it at times. I would not be surprised if the invitation to go to Europe with my father and mother was the result of my Aunt Eudora's letters to Springfield. They were certainly at this time intensely hostile to everything I did, said, wrote, thought or drew. Things were in a state where it was infinitely easier to beg from door to door than to go home, or even die by the ditch on the highway. Aunt Dora took care of me for a month and peppered the folks at home with letters, and hence the trip to Europe. It was certainly not my idea. I did not want to go home and if they asked me home it was probably through her plain speaking.

''I will never forget the easy, dreaming Kentucky and the droning bees in the blue grass, and the walks with Cousin Eudora and Aunt Eudora, and the queer feeling of being the family disgrace somewhat straightened out when I stood up to read 'The Tree of Laughing Bells' to the school. As far as I know, I read it in my beggar's raiment. I am sure I felt that way, and it was the kind hearts around me in that particular spot that made me want to live.

''Aunt Dora was a spring like the church at Grassy Springs. I can remember visiting many people in Kentucky who spoke to me of her with the greatest gravity as a sage, a sibyl, a person to whom they were indebted, in the deepest sense. Whoever she taught, she taught by hand, one at a time, not by any machine or wholesale process. She kept her hand on them forever, and they knew it. No thundering herds ever poured through her school. The children were instructed one at a time and each had his claim forever.''[1]

After a family reconciliation, Lindsay sailed for Europe with his parents and his sister, Joy.

1908. Traveled from New York to Springfield, Illinois on foot. The adventure began at the Salvation Army Hotel in Newark, New Jersey. ''Forty-four beds in the room. Most of the men slept naked, some in underwear. Kept running to washroom. A goodly number snored. More snorted and spat spat spat on the floor. About three, half drunk, talked till midnight. Finally the fat one rolled off his bed, falling about eight feet, naked, and almost breaking his head. That shut them up. He boasted

Vachel Lindsay as a young man.

he had had fifty beers yesterday. The sheets were filthy. Mine had blood on them. The pillow cases were well oiled. . . .''[2]

Wrote to Richard Gilder, editor of *The Century Magazine*. "The printed matter I send gives you some notion of what I have been about these last years, at the New York West Side Y.M.C.A. in the Winter months. If you telephone to the *Religious Department* you will be informed as to my ability to interest pious young men in Art, Poetry and the Metropolitan Museum.

"I and a bunch of young Art students have given successful picture-shows there, and we have also decorated our rendezvous near by—the Pig and the Goose Restaurant, 355 West 58th Street. If you are at all interested in my progress as a decorator, and an influence among other decorators, you might send a trusty deputy to look the place over. If you are interested in my one other appearance in magazine print, read 'The Man Under the Yoke' in the *Outlook,* June 1, 1907. If you are interested in my capacity to make musical verse, read the 'Last Song of Lucifer' which I send. If you are interested in my

THE SWAN

A swan
Upside down,
Swimming down the Sangamon river,
Dressed in feathers, snowy and pale.

■ (From "The Swan with the Crown," in *Springfield Town Is Butterfly Town and Other Poems for Children* by Vachel Lindsay. Illustrated by the author.)

ability to condense the *Encyclopaedia Britannica* into twenty-eight stanzas, for the benefit of my Y.M.C.A. class in History, read '*God Help Us All to Be Brave,*' which I send.

"I propose that you assist me to publish a volume of poems, with my own decorations and embellishments, leading off with the historical poem I send, and using it for the title poem. *The Heroes of Time* might be a better title for it. I have already a design for every stanza. The Y.M.C.A. will certify to the popular quality of the designs."[1]

1912. ". . . I have debated most seriously in my mind a long two years mendicant tour in the West—Texas—South and North California—Washington—and then at last back home here. I seem to be a natural beggar. I have had a better time and made more friends at that than any other sort of work. I would carry the *Village* Magazine and the *Tramp's Excuse* in Waterproof covers—having already bound them for that purpose—and read to those who cared to hear. And having made two years of it—I might have a lifetime of it. But I generally anticipate coming back . . . at the end of two years and take up writing

again—especially along the line of the *Village* Magazine Philosophy—or as I sometimes call it—the New Localism. I have notes enough on my shelf—for possible theories—sketches—stories and poems to keep me writing ten years.

"For almost a year now I have for the first time been writing in a steady professional way. It is the first time in my life—and I feel I can keep it up indefinitely and forego all drawing and speaking—and be a penman only—if it is best. But I am always haunted by the call of the road—, I have America—East and South pretty well in my hand. I have lectured all over New England and begged in most of the other states—the typical ones—Florida—Georgia—North Carolina—Tennessee—Kentucky—Ohio—Pennsylvania and New Jersey. And if I walk over the West—if I have nothing else—I will have a certain grip on America—and matter to think on, that will keep me years in fathoming."[1]

Lindsay worked as a harvester along the way, and mostly depended upon the generosity of strangers who became friends and inspirations for his poetry. "It may interest you to know

Two old crows sat on a fence rail,
Thinking of effect and cause, . . .

■ (From "Two Old Crows," in *Johnny Appleseed and Other Poems* by Vachel Lindsay. Illustrated by George Richards.)

that so far my trip has been prosperous, and though I have been indeed God's fool and cut something of a harlequin figure, I learned a heap for my pains, which is the main point. So far I am in excellent health and spirits, and have material for a thousand poems, of which I may write ten, sometime. 'Tis a long lane from here to back again, and I find my route shifts with the days. But in the main I keep to the same general track toward the Pacific coast, which coast I hope to see from end to end and then return, perhaps walking through Chicago. That is as may be. I am in general keeping to my rules, though they are not cast-iron. I have had no freight-rides or train rides, have walked or been driven all the way, have stuck to the farms and villages, have made many friends and no enemies, have paid for my meals either reciting or with my pamphlets or splitting kindling, cutting weeds, hoeing corn, hoeing garden or picking cherries. Near Newton, Kansas I harvested for four days and a half and earned just enough to completely renovate my apparel, new corduroys—shoes, hat, etc.''[1]

Ended his walking tour on September 12th, in New Mexico. ''When people ask me straight out, why I quit walking in New Mexico, I tell them straight out I lost my nerve. I might say to you that suddenly—in Central New Mexico, when all was going merrily, my spiritual house burned down, and I am home for repairs. I want to rebuild it before I go again. I certainly learned a great deal. The trip was of immense though very grave profit, I had all the adventures to be expected, have gained about ten pounds in weight being now 142—and adventures enough to keep me writing several years, if I choose to write them. My Gospel was as well received as I could

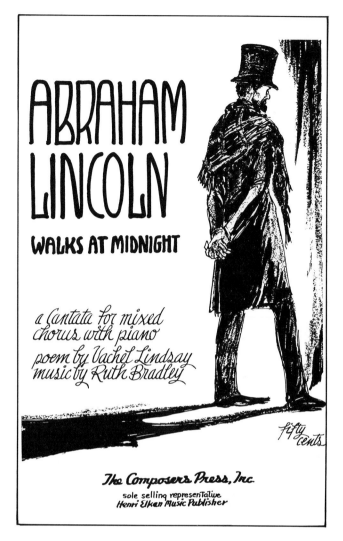

(Sheet music cover from the 1959 edition of "Abraham Lincoln Walks at Midnight.")

ask.—it was generally accepted, I mean *listened to* two or three times a day with all proper gravity—often with the most charming expressions of good-will. The thing that stands out plainest in my mind is the sixteen days of harvesting in Central Kansas, and I only wish I was strong enough physically to harvest forever. There is nothing like it—as long as a man can stand it. This appetite for ink is worse than the Demon Rum, when it keeps us from such pleasures.

''One of my minor disasters was the loss of my principal notebook—my diary in fact—in California, and what appears to be the loss of my letters home, at least they haven't turned up. But I am not especially vexed—since the principal good of the trip is the chastened ripened point of view.''[1]

1915. *The Art of the Moving Picture* was published. On the early silent film epics, Lindsay reflected: ''Not yet has the producer learned that the feeling of the crowd is patriarchal, splendid. He imagines the people want nothing but a silly lark. . . . But now a light is blazing. We can build the American soul broad-based from the foundations. We can begin with dreams the veriest stoneclub warrior can understand and lead him in fancy through every phase of life to the apocalyptic splendors.''[2]

Lindsay was well known for his recitals of chanting verse on tours throughout the United States.

... **All year through composing**
classical symphonies!
The cutest played—"Higgledy,
piggledy, rilly-ra-loo,"
On a flute of crystal, bird-like tone.

■ (From *Every Soul Is a Circus* by Vachel Lindsay.
Illustrated by George M. Richards.)

1917. When the United States entered World War I, Lindsay reluctantly registered for the draft. "My heart is very sad tonight about the war. I have not the heart to challenge Wilson. I voted for him and cannot regret it—yet Jane Addams' dauntless fight for peace goes home to my soul. I feel with her—and with him—and am all torn inside. Certainly I have no sympathy for the fire-eaters. It is so easy to get killed for a cause; but it is a bitter thing to think of killing other people. I would a hundred times rather get killed than kill anybody. I feel as guilty as if I had done it all tonight—or had a hand in it."[2]

1919. Wrote "In Praise of Johnny Appleseed," based on the story of John Chapman, who had wandered from New England to Ohio planting appleseeds wherever he went. "... The nearest to Buddha and St. Francis and Tolstoy of all West-going pioneers.... He is the West-going heart, never returning, yet with civilization always near enough to keep his heart tender for mankind. My God is the God of Johnny Appleseed, and some day I shall find Him."[2]

1920. Traveled to England with his mother. "... These English just drive me mad. The Grave digger was right in Hamlet. They are all mad here. He also might have added they are a deaf and dumb asylum as well. England seems frantically imitating Boston....

"I am simply too United States for this place, and I could lean up against the British Museum and cry. I certainly would not lean on any of these whispering English...."[1]

1921. Went East to recite and to lecture. Although he was nationally acclaimed for his writing and reciting, praise did not satisfy him. "I do not want to be the slave of past performances or habits, I cannot endure to be such a slave, *I care not what the apparent praise or reward*. I am a dead man in my own eyes, and the only resurrection is in the new vista."[2]

Went on a hiking trip to Glacier National Park with his friend Stephen Graham. "I realize that it is freedom I am seeking, and amusing adventure, more than out-doors for its mystical world meaning. So I am trying, hypothetically, to think out how a person more out of doors than myself, can get to that part of America whose soul is in the out of doors. I believe I

Johnny Appleseed's apple trees marched straight west, past his grave at Fort Wayne, Indiana, through the best apple country of Illinois, to the Pacific .... ■
(From *The Litany of Washington Street* by Vachel Lindsay.)

am more for door-steps than out of doors, more for roads than wildernesses. . . . I am vastly more geographical than ever before in my life, and since Glacier Park I remain geographical, eliminating imaginary trailless mountains. . . .''[1]

February 1, 1922. Mother died. ''It seems utterly impossible to go on without her. . . . My life is most desolate without Mama, and nothing seems worth doing without her to report to. Joy is quite determined I shall marry and live in the old house, . . . but I have no girl and no income to take care of such a place. The only way I can live and keep ahead is to travel.''[2]

January, 1923. While touring, Lindsay collapsed in Gulfport, Mississippi. ''I am sick. My lungs are sore to the bottom. I have an earache and a toothache not to speak of several other afflictions, and I have to wait till tomorrow for the dentist. . . . There is a hereditary curse knocking mighty hard at the door, . . . and knocking with an increasing frequency I assure you. You see me at the height of energy and get reports of my unending energy and be sure I pay for every pound of extra steam in this hereditary curse. If I am to live, *I must go slow.* If I want to stand still and get the people to come to me it is because I no longer think it in any way safe to go to them.''[1]

1925. Married Elizabeth Conner. ''. . . I was married May 19, here in my room to Elizabeth Conner, whose name I have changed to Elizabeth Locust-Blossom Conner, because on our walk the next day we found nothing but locust trees in full flower, the town bursting with them. We were not engaged, but married by spontaneous combustion the minute we got acquainted which was somewhere around May 18, though we had of course met a good many times in a decidedly pleasant way before. . . . We start life with a clean slate, with no heavy obligations, no unpaid debts or no promises, and the future is indeed the future. We are both in excellent health, both fond of hiking, both walk fast and hard, but she is one jump ahead of me in adoring a Latin Poet called Catullus, and I can't pass on his merits, not being able to read Latin.''[1]

May 28, 1926. Daughter, Susan Doniphan, was born.

September 16, 1927. Son born. ''. . . NICHOLAS CAVE LINDSAY. Here I sit in our little flat above guarding our little Susan Doniphan, the big sister a year and a half older who is going to help us rear him. . . . I am forty-eight years old in November—and now—out of the blue as one might say comes a son and how the world changes! The Nicholas is for my old Grandfather Nicholas Lindsay and the Cave for his dear wife of beautiful memory—Martha Cave Lindsay. It is through the Cave family that the legend of Indian blood is in our house— maybe it is only a legend.''[1]

1931. Lindsay's health and mental stability deteriorated, with a disease he did not understand, and he felt more and more depressed. ''You will have to wait till you are all of fifty-one before you know what it means to be doomed to sit in the attic with your dustiest poetry and feel your creative force thwarted every day, and youth making its last desperate despairing cry for new children within your very marrow. It's the feeling of having the door of the artistic future slammed in my face forever, the whole creative side of my future, when I used to create *new* things daily. . . .''[2]

December 5, 1931. Committed suicide by swallowing a bottle of Lysol. His death was officially attributed to heart failure. ''I will *not* be a *slave* to my yesterdays. I will *not.* I was born a *creator* not a parrot. . . .''[1]

FOR MORE INFORMATION SEE—Juvenile: Laura Benet, *Famous American Poets,* Dodd, 1950; Frances Helmstadter, *Picture Book of American Authors,* Sterling, 1962; L. Benet, *Famous Poets for Young People,* Dodd, 1964; L. Edmond Leipold, *Famous American Poets,* Denison, 1969.

Adult: Vachel Lindsay, *Adventures While Preaching the Gospel of Beauty,* M. Kennerley, 1914; V. Lindsay, *A Handy Guide for Beggars, Especially Those of the Poetic Fraternity,* Macmillan, 1916; Stephen Graham, *Tramping with a Poet in the Rockies,* D. Appleton, 1922; Edward Davison, ''Nicholas Vachel Lindsay,'' in his *Some Modern Poets and Other Critical Essays,* Harper & Brothers, 1928, reprinted, Ayer, 1968; Albert E. Trombly, *Vachel Lindsay, Adventurer,* Lucas Brothers, 1929; Edgar L. Masters, *Vachel Lindsay: A Poet in America,* Scribner, 1935, reprinted, Biblio & Tannen, 1969; Mark Harris, *City of Discontent: An Interpretive Biography of Vachel Lindsay, Being Also the Story of Springfield, Illinois, U.S.A.,* Bobbs-Merrill, 1952, reprinted, October, 1975; Eleanor Ruggles, *The West Going Heart: A Life of Vachel Lindsay,* Norton, 1959.

Ralph L. Schroeder, *Where a Lad Is: An Account of Vachel Lindsay,* Syracuse University Press, 1962; Ann Massa, *Vachel Lindsay: Fieldworker for the American Dream,* Indiana University Press, 1970; J. T. Flanagan, editor, *Profile of Vachel Lindsay,* C. E. Merrill, 1970; Glenn J. Wolfe, *Vachel Lindsay: The Poet as Film Theorist,* Arno, 1973; M. Chenetier, editor,

Vachel Lindsay in 1927.

Letters of Vachel Lindsay, Franklin, 1979; Jay R. Balderson, "Vachel Lindsay," in *American Writers,* edited by Leonard Unger, Supplement I, Part 2, Scribner, 1979; *Crisis,* August/September, 1979.

Motion pictures: "Three from Illinois," WMAQ-TV (Chicago), 1969.

Obituaries: *Nation,* December 16, 1931; *Saturday Review of Literature,* December 19, 1931; *Commonweal,* December 23, 1931.

LINFIELD, Esther

PERSONAL: Born in Cape Town, South Africa. *Education:* Received B.A. from University of Cape Town. *Residence:* San Francisco, Calif.

CAREER: Statistical worker on social survey conducted by University of Cape Town, Cape Town, South Africa; employed as a probation officer by the South African Government; served as a vocational guidance officer for the Organization for Rehabilitation Through Training, Cape Town. *Awards, honors: The Lion of the Kalahari* was named a children's book of the year, 1976, by Child Study Association.

ESTHER LINFIELD

WRITINGS: (Adapter and translator from the Afrikaans) Sam B. Hobson and George Carey Hobson, *The Lion of the Kalahari,* Greenwillow, 1976.

WORK IN PROGRESS: A children's book, based on the customs of the Xhosa-speaking peoples of southern Africa.

SIDELIGHTS: "I am rooted in the deserts and bush regions of southern Africa and have strong feelings of kinship with its indigenous people. I will be haunted, forever I suppose, by the sounds and accents of my native land. It is of the old Africa that I write, the old customs and traditions that are dying out. This is the background for my fiction."

LOEWENSTEIN, Bernice

BRIEF ENTRY: Born in New York, N.Y. Illustrator of books for children. A graduate of Bryn Mawr College, Loewenstein also attended the Art Students League. Her career has included work in the children's book departments of various publishing firms. Her first illustrated book was Elizabeth Coatsworth's *Bess and the Sphinx,* published in 1967. Since that time Loewenstein has provided illustrations for seven additional books, including Bob Wells's *The Horse on the Roof* (Lippincott, 1970), *The Cat and the Captain* (Macmillan, 1974), also by Coatsworth, Ellen Conford's *The Luck of Pokey Bloom* (Little, Brown, 1975), and Molly Cone's *Call Me Moose* (Houghton, 1978). Her latest work is Daniel Beekman's *Forest, Village, Town, City* (Crowell, 1982), an historical study of the development of the American city. In a review of the book, *Booklist* described her drawings as "evocative pencil illustrations . . . distinctive, with some rich in detail while others are shadowy as though seen through the mists of time."

LOUIE, Ai-Ling 1949-

PERSONAL: First syllable of given name sounds like "eye"; born July 18, 1949, in New York, N.Y.; daughter of Dung Ock Peter (an industrial supervisor) and Lillian (an elementary school teacher; maiden name, Dong) Louie; married Patrick Arthur Miller (a physicist and systems engineer), September 5, 1971; children: Melanie. *Education:* Sarah Lawrence College, B.A., 1971; Wheelock College, M.A., 1976. *Residence:* Middletown, N.J. *Agent:* McIntosh & Otis, Inc., 475 5th Ave., New York, N.Y. 10017.

CAREER: Teacher at elementary school in Wilmington, Ma., 1971-73, and Brookline, Ma., 1973-77; full-time writer, 1977—. *Awards, honors:* Writing Recognition Award, Council on Interracial Books for Children, 1978, for "The Truth about Uncle."

WRITINGS: (Reteller) *Yeh-Shen: A Cinderella Story from China* (juvenile; ALA Notable Book; illustrated by Ed Young), Philomel, 1982. Also contributor of poems, articles, and reviews to periodicals, professional journals, and newspapers such as *Horn Book, Bridge: Asian-American Perspective,* and *The Home News* (New Brunswick, N.J.).

WORK IN PROGRESS: Currently working on a book about a Chinese-American child.

SIDELIGHTS: "When I was a girl, it seemed I always had my nose in a book. I remember walking down the crowded, noisy hallway of my junior high school and reading all the

while. I could even climb three flights of stairs and never miss a word. I would have become a librarian, except that my mother is an elementary schoolteacher and encouraged me to be the

Her stepmother was jealous of all this beauty and goodness, for her own daughter was not pretty at all. ■ (From *Yeh-Shen: A Cinderella Story from China,* retold by Ai-Ling Louie. Illustrated by Ed Young.)

AI-LING LOUIE

same. I can't remember a time when I didn't like to write. Not long ago I came across a second grade report card of mine, on which my teacher had written a comment about 'creative' stories I had written. One of the stories, I seem to recall, was about a squirrel who came in my window and bit me. My desire to be a writer didn't come into full bloom until I became an elementary schoolteacher. I found myself fascinated by the books my schoolchildren were reading. I used to love to write stories to tell the children. *Yeh-Shen* was written for my class to hear.''

Yeh-Shen originated from ancient China, hundreds of years before the familiar Western version ever existed. In the old oral tradition of storytelling, Louie first heard the tale from her mother who had, likewise, learned it from *her* mother, who had brought the story with her to America as an emigrant from southern China.

HOBBIES AND OTHER INTERESTS: Storytelling, gardening, tennis, birdwatching, photography.

FOR MORE INFORMATION SEE: The Home News (New Brunswick, N.J.), December 5, 1982; *New York Times/New Jersey Weekly,* January 2, 1983.

Come, my best friends, my books, and lead me on.
—Abraham Cowley

LUTTRELL, Ida (Alleene) 1934-

PERSONAL: Born April 18, 1934, in Laredo, Tex.: daughter of Pelton B. (a rancher) and Helen (a teacher and rancher; maiden name, Sewell) Harbison; married William S. Luttrell (an insurance agent), January 20, 1959; children: Robert, Anne, William, Richard. *Education:* University of Texas, B.A., 1955; attended Houston Baptist University, 1969, 1970. *Religion:* Protestant. *Home:* 12211 Beauregard, Houston, Tex. 77024.

CAREER: Texas Children's Hospital, Houston, Tex., bacteriologist, 1955-63; writer. *Member:* Authors Unlimited of Houston.

WRITINGS: (Contributor) Phyllis S. Prokop, *Three-Ingredient Cookbook,* Broadman, 1981; *Not Like That, Armadillo* (juvenile; short stories; illustrated by Janet Stevens), Harcourt, 1982; *Lonesome Lester* (juvenile; Junior Literary Guild selection; illustrated by Megan Lloyd), Harper, 1984; *One Day at School* (juvenile; illustrated by Jared D. Lee), Harcourt, 1984. Also contributor of articles to periodicals such as *Antique Trader, Spinning Wheel,* and *Collectible Glass.*

WORK IN PROGRESS: Tillie and Mert, a juvenile easy-to-read book for Harper; *Be Nice to Marilyn,* a juvenile picture book for Crown.

SIDELIGHTS: ''I was raised on a small ranch in south Texas by a mother who is a great storyteller and a father who loved

IDA LUTTRELL

"But I do not want the first glass of lemonade," Armadillo said. "Your sign says, 'Lemonade 5¢. Refills 2¢.' All I have is two cents. I just want the refill." ■ (From "Lemonade," in *Not Like That, Armadillo* by Ida Luttrell. Illustrated by Janet Stevens.)

animals. Because we were so isolated, I spent my summers pestering my brother and sisters, caring for a multitude of animals—once we had eighteen cats—and reading lots of books. A favorite memory is of stepping out of the hot glare of a fierce Texas sun into the cool world of the county library where I found fun, adventure, fantasy, and romance on the pages of those wonderful books that filled the shelves.

"After I graduated from the University of Texas, I moved to Houston where I worked eight years as a bacteriologist for Texas Children's Hospital, a fulfilling job that I enjoyed. During that time I met my husband. When I had children of my own, I became interested in children's books again, especially picture books. I discovered that reading to my children when they were small gave us a special time together. It fostered a closeness between us and gave us a common interest we still share. So, books have always been associated with fun for me and I hope children find my books fun to read.

"A real concern I have is about the violence all around us and the effect it is having on today's child. It is my opinion that, now more than ever before, children need quality time from caring parents who can give them solid values to help them survive."

HOBBIES AND OTHER INTERESTS: "Besides books and reading, I enjoy gardening, plays, working in the school library, family get togethers, and sharing an interest in antique and contemporary art glass with my husband."

FOR MORE INFORMATION SEE: Jacque Goettsche and Phyllis Prokop, *A Kind of Splendor*, Broadman, 1980.

CLAIRE MACKAY

MACKAY, Claire 1930-

PERSONAL: Born December 21, 1930, in Toronto, Ontario, Canada; daughter of Grant McLaren (an accountant) and Bernice (a secretary and bereavement counselor; maiden name, Arland) Bacchus; married Jackson Mackay (an economist, engineer, and jazz musician), September 12, 1952; children: Ian, Scott, Grant. *Education:* University of Toronto, B.A. (with honors), 1952; University of British Columbia, M.S.W., 1969; University of Manitoba, Certificate in Rehabilitation Counseling, 1971. *Home and office:* 6 Frank Cres., Toronto, Ontario, Canada M6G 3K5.

CAREER: Polysar Corp., Sarnia, Ontario, library assistant in research department, 1952-55; Plains Hospital, Regina, Saskatchewan, medical social worker, 1969-71; Steelworkers' Union, Toronto, Ontario, research librarian, 1972-78; freelance researcher and writer, 1978—. *Member:* Canadian Authors Association, Writers Union of Canada, Canadian Society of Children's Authors, Illustrators, and Performers (secretary, 1977-78; president, 1979-81), Ontario Federation of Naturalists. *Awards, honors:* Grant from Ontario Arts Council, 1980, 1983, 1984; second prize from *Toronto Star* short story contest, 1980, for "Important Message: Please Read"; honorable mention from Canada Council Children's Literature Prize, 1981, and Ruth Schwartz Foundation Children's Book Award, 1982, both for *One Proud Summer;* Vicky Metcalf Award, 1983, for body of work.

WRITINGS—Juvenile: *Mini-Bike Hero*, Scholastic Book Services, 1974, revised edition, 1984; *Mini-Bike Racer* (illustrated by Merle Smith), Scholastic Book Services, 1976, revised edi-

tion, 1979; *Exit Barney McGee* (illustrated by David Simpson), Scholastic Book Services, 1979; (with Marsha Hewitt), *One Proud Summer* (historical novel), Women's Educational Press, 1981; *Mini-Bike Rescue*, Scholastic Book Services, 1982; *The Minerva Program*, James Lorimer, 1984.

Author of "Women's Words," a monthly feminist column in *Steel Labour*, 1975-78. Contributor to *Canadian Writers Guide*. Contributor of poems, short stories and articles to magazines, including *Branching Out, Canadian Women's Studies, Chatelaine, Ontario New Democrat, Toronto Star, Academy of Canadian Writers' News, Canadian Author and Bookman, Poetry Toronto,* and *Our Family*. Editor of *Canadian Society of Children's Authors, Illustrators, and Performers News,* 1978-83, associate editor, 1983—.

WORK IN PROGRESS: An adult comic novel; stories and essays; an historical novel for young adults; a nonfiction work for children on unions to be published by Kids Can Press.

SIDELIGHTS: "My entry into the field of writing (though a secret dream for years) came about largely by fluke. My youngest son nagged me into writing the book, *Mini-Bike Hero*. It altered my life profoundly. I'm still in a bemused state, but now thoroughly hooked on writing.

"One of the great—and occasionally the only—rewards in writing for children is the fan mail from kids to whom you're the best writer who ever lived. I've accumulated many letters, answered all, and find them a powerful antidote to a bad review!

I regard each letter as an honor greater than any prize awarded by adult peers and judges and as a gift of confidence when my own has wavered badly. Someday I hope to write that one excellent book that will merit that honor and that gift.''

Mini-Bike Hero and *One Proud Summer* have been published in French.

HOBBIES AND OTHER INTERESTS: Birdwatching, collecting dictionaries, philately.

MANES, Stephen   1949-

BRIEF ENTRY: Born January 8, 1949, in Pittsburgh, Pa. Writer. A graduate of the University of Southern California, Manes has written over a dozen books for children and young adults as well as several screenplays. In his books for children, he displays a humorous and nonsensical writing style that was described by a *Booklist* reviewer as ''reminiscent of Daniel Pinkwater's . . . topped by a dash of Kurt Vonnegut.'' Titles like *The Boy Who Turned into a TV Set* (Coward, 1979), *The Hooples' Haunted House* (Delacorte, 1981), and *Be a Perfect Person in Just Three Days* (Clarion Books, 1982) feature a variety of characters who cavort their way through oftentimes outlandish adventures. Manes also delves into subjects easily identifiable with young readers, such as the video craze in *That Game from Outer Space: The First Strange Thing That Happened to Oscar Noodleman* (Dutton, 1983) and its sequel, *The Oscar J. Noodleman Television Network* (Dutton, 1984). In 1983 *Be a Perfect Person in Just Three Days* was selected as a CRABbery Award honor book.

Manes reveals his serious side as a writer in *I'll Live* (Avon/Flare, 1982), a young adult novel about a high school senior who must come to terms with his father's imminent death. *Horn Book* called it a ''candid novel. . . . [that] forthrightly expresses, particularly in dialogue, the tremendous impact of terminal illness on a family. . . .'' Also for older readers is *Video War* (Avon/Flare, 1983), described by *School Library Journal* as ''a wonderfully plotted book. . . . [with] some of the most likable characters to appear in a YA novel for a long time. . . .'' Manes's latest works include several children's books written with Paul Somerson as part of Scholastic's ''K-Power Computer Books'' series. *Agent:* Dorothy Markinko, McIntosh & Otis, 475 Fifth Ave., New York, N.Y. 10017.

FOR MORE INFORMATION SEE: Contemporary Authors, Volumes 97-100, Gale, 1981.

MARTIN, William Ivan   1916-
(Bill Martin, Jr.)

BRIEF ENTRY: Born in 1916. Author, editor, folksinger, storyteller, and instructor. Martin graduated from Kansas State Teachers College and received both his M.A. and Ph.D. from Northwestern University. Co-creator of Holt, Rinehart, & Winston's ''Sounds of Language Program,'' he has lectured throughout the United States on the concept of relating sounds to printed words for beginning and slow readers. Once a high school teacher of journalism, drama, and English, Martin was also the principal of Crow Island Elementary School in Win-

netka, Ill. He joined the staff of Holt, Rinehart, & Winston during the 1960s and in collaboration with Peggy Brogan compiled the ''Sounds of Language Readers,'' a set of thirteen books with cassette tapes.

Under the name Bill Martin, Jr., Martin has produced about 200 books in eleven series for children. Among these are: *Brown Bear, Brown Bear, What Do you See?* and *Which Do You Choose?* (both Holt, 1967) of the ''Kin/Der Owl Books'' series; *Adam's Balm* and *It's America for Me* (both Bowmar, 1970) of the ''Freedom Books'' series; and *The Eagle Has Landed, I Paint the Joy of a Flower,* and *Monday, Monday, I Like Monday* (all Holt, 1970) of the ''Instant Readers'' series. Martin's other series include: ''Little Nature Books'' (1975), ''Little Woodland Books'' (1978) and ''Little Seashore Books'' (1982), all published by Encyclopedia Britannica Educational Corp. Martin has also produced tapes, records, and films including the motion-pictures ''America I Know You,'' ''I am Freedom's Child,'' and ''Reach Out'' (all released by Trend Films Corp., 1971).

FOR MORE INFORMATION SEE: Publishers Weekly, February 25, 1974; *Language Arts,* May, 1982.

MAYNARD, Olga   1920-

PERSONAL: Born January 16, 1920, in Belem, Brazil; came to United States, 1942; became naturalized citizen, 1957; daughter of Frederick and Jeanne Marie de la Borde (maiden name, de Pampellonne) Percy-Morton-Gittens; married E. R. Maynard, March, 1943; children: Hugo M., Ralph D., Stephen

OLGA MAYNARD

F., Patrick L., Antoinette I., Russell C. *Education:* "Educated by private tutor in the English system of liberal arts education to the level of a university doctorate in the arts." *Politics:* Democrat. *Religion:* Christian. *Agent:* McIntosh & Otis, Inc., 475 Fifth Ave., New York, N.Y. 10017. *Office:* School of Fine Arts, University of California, Irvine, Calif. 92717.

CAREER: University of California, Irvine, Calif., professor of dance history and research, 1969—. Lecturer in dance, Banff Centre, summers, 1973-75, Ballet West-Aspen-Snowmass Summer Dance School, 1979-80, Academy of Arts of the German Democratic Republic, 1979-80, 11th Finnish Music and Dance Festival, 1980; member of academic senate, University of California, Berkeley; documentarian, Ballet Bulgaria Pedogogic Seminars, 1977, 1979; head of department of dance history and research, School for the Training of Professional Dancers, National Institute of Fine Arts, Mexico, 1979. *Member:* International Theatre Institute (member of governing board for dance committee), United Nations Educational, Scientific and Cultural Organization (UNESCO). *Awards, honors:* Recipient of grant from Ford Foundation, 1969-70, National Foundation for the Arts, 1971, University of California, Berkeley, 1971, University of California, 1977, and others; Distinguished Award from University of California, 1981, for work in dance history research and writing.

WRITINGS—Nonfiction, of interest to young people: *The Ballet Companion*, foreword by Agnes de Mille, Macrae Smith, 1957; *The American Ballet*, Macrae Smith, 1959; *American Modern Dancers: The Pioneers*, Little, Brown, 1965; *Enjoying Opera*, Scribner, 1966.

Other: *Bird of Fire: The Story of Maria Tallchief*, Dodd, 1961; *Children and Dance and Music*, Scribner, 1968; (contributor) William Como, editor, *Nureyev*, Danaid Publishing, 1973; *Judith Jamison: Aspects of a Dancer*, Doubleday, 1982. Also senior editor and contributor of articles, essays, and monographs, *Dance Magazine;* contributor of articles, *Macmillan Yearbook*, 1973-77.

WORK IN PROGRESS: History of Ballet in America, and *Russian Dancers in the West.*

McCONNELL, James Douglas (Rutherford) 1915-
(Douglas Rutherford; Paul Temple, a joint pseudonym)

PERSONAL: Born October 14, 1915, in Kilkenny, Ireland; son of James and Edith (Cooney) McConnell; married Margaret Laura Goodwin (an author's consultant), 1953; children: Mike. *Education:* Attended Sedbergh School; Clare College, Cambridge, M.A., 1937; University of Reading, M.Phil., 1977. *Home and office:* Hal's Croft, Monxton, Andover, Hampshire SP11 8AS, England. *Agent:* Richard Scott Simon, 32 College Cross, London N11 PR, England.

CAREER: Eton College, Windsor, England, language teacher and housemaster, 1946-73. *Military service:* British Army, Intelligence Corps, 1940-46; served in North Africa and Italy; mentioned dispatches, 1944. *Member:* Crime Writers Association, Detection Club, Tidworth Golf Club.

WRITINGS: Learn Italian Quickly, MacGibbon & Kee, 1960; *Learn Spanish Quickly*, MacGibbon & Kee, 1961, Citadel,

JAMES DOUGLAS McCONNELL

1963; *Learn French Quickly*, MacGibbon & Kee, 1966; *Eton: How It Works*, Faber, 1967, Humanities, 1968; *Eton Repointed: The New Structures of an Ancient Foundation*, Faber, 1970; (editor) *Treasures of Eton*, Chatto & Windus, 1976; *Early Learning Foundation*, Four Seasons Publications, 1979; *The Benedictine Commando*, Hamish Hamilton, 1981.

With Francis Durbridge; all published by Hodder & Stoughton: (Under joint pseudonym Paul Temple) *The Tyler Mystery*, 1957; (Under joint pseudonym Paul Temple) *East of Algiers*, 1959; *The Pig-Tail Murder*, 1969; *A Man Called Harry Brent*, 1970; *Bat out of Hell*, 1972; *A Game of Murder*, 1975; *The Passenger*, 1977; *Tim Frazer Gets the Message*, 1980; *Breakaway*, 1981; *The Doll*, 1982.

Under name Douglas Rutherford; published by Collins, except as indicated: *Comes the Blind Fury*, Faber, 1950; *Meet a Body*, Faber, 1951; *Flight into Peril*, Dodd, 1952 (published in England as *Telling of Murder*, Faber, 1952); *Grand Prix Murder*, 1955; *The Perilous Sky*, 1955; *The Chequered Flag*, 1956; *The Long Echo*, 1957, Abelard, 1958; *A Shriek of Tyres*, 1958, published as *On the Track of Death*, Abelard, 1959.

Murder Is Incidental, 1961; *The Creeping Flesh*, 1963, Walker & Co., 1965; (editor) *Best Motor Racing Stories*, Faber, 1965; *The Black Leather Murders*, Walker & Co., 1966; *Skin for Skin*, Walker & Co., 1968; (editor and author of introduction) *Best Underworld Stories*, Faber, 1969; *The Gilt-Edged Cockpit*, 1969, Doubleday, 1971.

Clear the Fast Lane, 1971, Holt, 1972; *The Gunshot Grand Prix*, 1972, Bradbury, 1974; *Killer on the Track*, 1973, Brad-

The three cars screamed past the pits almost neck and neck. On the narrow road their wheels were within an inch of touching. ■ (Jacket illustration by Michael Heslop from *Killer on the Track* by Douglas Rutherford.)

bury, 1974; *Kick Start,* 1973, Walker & Co., 1974; *Rally to the Death,* 1974, Bradbury, 1975; *Mystery Tour,* 1975, Walker & Co., 1976; *Race against the Sun,* 1975; *Return Load,* Walker & Co., 1977; *Collision Course,* Macmillan, 1978, large print edition, Lythway Press, 1980; *Turbo,* Macmillan, 1980; *Porcupine Basin,* 1981; *Stop at Nothing,* Walker, 1983.

WORK IN PROGRESS: Research for a book on fast cars; plans for a novel set in Italy in 1944; book about the English public schools.

SIDELIGHTS: "I wanted to be a writer from boyhood. Intelligence work in World War II gave me a background. During two decades as a master at Eton College, getting the background material for suspense stories provided the variety I needed in a rather routine kind of job. Writing was and remains a pastime as much as work. I like change and excitement. Now a full-time writer, I have been writing theses on education, novels for young teenagers, learning systems for the under five-year-olds, suspense novels, and serious historical novel. I am approaching my half-century in published works.

"I now live in a thatched cottage in a Hampshire village. I have visited the United States and Africa and travel Europe often. When on a book, I work four hours mornings and sometimes two hours evenings. My books have been translated into many languages. I reckon they have been read by a number equal to the population of greater London. I want to live long enough to write another fifty books.

"My advice to aspiring authors? The first and final requirement is to want to see your work in print ardently enough to endure the labour and torment of writing and submitting a book."

HOBBIES AND OTHER INTERESTS: Golf, music, glamorous cars, travel.

FOR MORE INFORMATION SEE: New Statesman, March 10, 1967; *Times Literary Supplement,* April 13, 1967; *New York Times Book Review,* February 9, 1969, January 4, 1981; *Spectator,* November 22, 1969; *Best Sellers,* April 1, 1971.

McLENIGHAN, Valjean 1947-

BRIEF ENTRY: Born December 28, 1947, in Chicago, Ill. A free-lance writer, producer, and editorial consultant since 1977, McLenighan began her career as an editor with Reilly & Lee Books in 1970. She later went to Follett Publishing where she was an associate editorial director in the children's book department. It was there that she decided to write her own children's books. "... [I] knew," she stated, "that I could write better manuscripts than those I was being paid to edit." Overall she has written nearly twenty children's books, among them several stories based on traditional folk and fairy tales. *School Library Journal* described the retellings as "... comically slangy, pared-down versions ... told largely through dialogue that snaps right along. ..." All published by Follett, the books include *You Are What You Are* (1977), *You Can Go Jump* (1977), *Know When to Stop* (1980), and *Turtle and Rabbit* (1981).

In a different genre is McLenighan's *China: A History to 1949* (Childrens Press, 1983). *Booklist* called it "... an exceptionally well balanced treatment ...," stating that "... the author traces not just successive ruling dynasties but also intellectual and artistic trends. ..." Her other books include: three biographical books published by Raintree, *Women Who Dared* (1979), *Women and Science* (1979), and *Diana: Alone against the Sea* (1980); a book on antonyms, *Stop-Go, Fast-Slow* (Childrens Press, 1982); and another on homonyms, *One Whole Doughnut ... One Doughnut Hole* (Childrens Press, 1982). She has also produced several videotapes, including "Election Day, 1976," "Busia and Cioc," and "The Aces." Among McLenighan's anticipated works are *Greece,* for Childrens Press, and a script for the pilot of a children's television series. *Home and office:* 1907 North Bissell St., Chicago, Ill. 60614.

FOR MORE INFORMATION SEE: Contemporary Authors, Volume 108, Gale, 1983.

YEHUDI MENUHIN

MENUHIN, Yehudi   1916-

PERSONAL: Born April 22, 1916, in New York, N.Y.; son of Russian parents, Moshe (a teacher and inspector of schools) and Marutha (Sher) Menuhin; married Nola Ruby Nicholas, May 26, 1938 (divorced, 1947); married Diana Rosamond Gould (a dancer and actress), October 19, 1947; children: (first marriage) Zamira, Krov; (second marriage) Gerard, Jeremy. *Education:* Educated under private tutors in United States and Europe; studied music under Louis Persinger and Sigmund Anker in San Francisco, Georges Enesco in Rumania and Paris, and Adolph Busch in Switzerland. *Residence:* Alma, Calif.; London, England; and Gstaad, Switzerland. *Agent:* Columbia, Artists Management, Inc., 165 West 57th St., New York, N.Y. 10019; and Harold Holt Ltd., 31 Sinclair Rd., London W14 0NS, England.

CAREER: Began violin lessons at age of five in San Francisco, appeared as soloist with San Francisco Orchestra at age of seven, and recitalist at Manhattan Opera House at age of eight; made Carnegie Hall debut with New York Symphony Orchestra in 1926 and European debut with Berlin Philharmonic in 1929; following his successes in Europe, began performing with his sister, Hephzibah, presenting piano-violin sonata evenings; played more than one hundred concert engagements on world tour, 1935, then retired to his mountain estate in California for two years; subsequently soloist with orchestras under Toscanini, Stokowski, Beecham, Furtwaengler, Paray, and other famous conductors, and concert violinist on tours throughout the world, including three in India where he raised $74,000 for the Famine Fund, 1952; has introduced works by Bartok, Bloch, Enesco, Finney, Vaughan Williams, and other contemporary composers, and brought Indian and Russian music and musicians to the West. Founder of Bath Festival Orchestra (now Menuhin Festival Orchestra) which accompanies him on world tour; artistic director of Yehudi Menuhin Festival in Gstaad, Switzerland, 1957—, Bath Festival, 1959-68, and Festival of Windsor, 1969-71; has conducted three Mozart operas, recorded all nine Schubert symphonies with Bath Festival Orchestra, and played in films and on television. Founder of Yehudi Menuhin School (for young musicians), Surrey, England, 1963; president of UNESCO International Music Council, 1969-73, and president and honorary fellow of Trinity College of Music, 1971—; member of council, Arts Educational Trust, England. *Wartime activity:* Gave more than four hundred troop concerts on both sides of the Atlantic during World War II; followed liberators into France, where he reopened Paris Opera House; gave numerous concerts in Belgium and England for war charities.

MEMBER: World Academy of Art and Science (Israel, fellow), Royal Society of Arts (fellow), Royal Academy of Music (honorary member), Royal College of Music (fellow), Royal College of Art (fellow), Royal Northern College of Music (fellow), Guildhall School of Music (honorary member), American Federation of Musicians (member of advisory board), Incorporated Society of Musicians (England; president, 1965), National Trusts Concert Society (England; president), American Friends of India (member of board of directors), American Guild of Musical Artists, Society for Asian Music, Indian Council for Cultural Relations (fellow), British Society of Aesthetics (founder member), American Society for Eastern Arts, Society of Herbalists (England; member of council); officer, member, or honorary member of well over one hundred other organizations and associations in United States, England, Belgium, France, Germany, Switzerland, Italy, Netherlands, Israel, India; Century Association (New York), Athenaeum Club and Garrick Club (both London).

AWARDS, HONORS: Grand Prix du Disque (France), 1932, for recordings made with sister, Hephzibah; Gold Medal of Royal Philharmonic Society, 1962; Mozart Medal, 1965; honorary Knight Commander, Order of the British Empire, 1965; 30th Anniversary Medal of Israel Philharmonic Orchestra, 1967; Gold Medal of Société d'Encouragement au Progrès, 1967; Jawaharlal Nehru Award for fostering peace and international understanding, 1968 (presented, 1970); honorary Swiss citizen, 1970; honorary fellow, St. Catharine's College, Cambridge University, 1970; Sonning Music Prize (Denmark), 1972; Rosenberger Medal of University of Chicago, 1975; Gold Medal of Canadian Music Council, Quebec, 1975; Handel Medal of City of New York, 1976; City of Jerusalem Medal, 1976; Wolf Trap Recognition Medal, 1976; Peace Prize, Börsenverein des Deutschen Buchhandels, 1979; George Washington Award of American Hungarian Foundation, 1980; Albert Medal, Royal Society of Arts, 1981; Grand Prix du Disque, Sorbonne, Paris, 1981; Award of Merit from California Association of Teachers of English, 1981; Queens College Medal, 1982; National Music Council USA Award, 1982; International Public Relations Association President's Award, 1982; Italian National Prize, Una Vita Nella Musica, 1983. Other honors include: Legion d'honneur, Croix de Lorraine, and Ordre des Arts et des Lettres (France); Order of Leopold and Ordre de la Couronne (Belgium); Order of Merit (West German Republic); Royal Order of the Phoenix (Greece); Cobbett Medal of Worshipful Company of Musicians; and honorary degrees from universities, including D. Mus. from Oxford University, 1962, Queen's University of Belfast, 1965, University of Leicester, 1965, University of London, 1969, Cambridge University, 1970, University of California, 1972, University of Surrey, 1973, University of Ottawa, 1975, Sorbonne University, 1975, LL.D. from University of St. Andrews, 1963, University of Sussex, 1966, University of Warwick, 1968, University of Bath, 1969, D. Humane Letters from University of Maryland, European Division, 1976. Honored with freedom of the cities of Edinburgh and Bath, 1965 and 1966, respectively.

WRITINGS: Violin: Six Lessons with Yehudi Menuhin, Faber, 1971, Viking, 1972; *Theme and Variations,* Stein & Day, 1972; *Violin and Viola,* Macmillan, 1976; *Unfinished Journey* (autobiography), Knopf, 1977; (editor) *My Favorite Music Stories,* Lutterworth, 1977; (with Curtis W. Davis) *The Music of Man,* Methuen, 1979; (with Christopher Hope) *The King, the Cat, and the Fiddle* (illustrated by Angela Barrett), Holt, 1983. Contributor to journals and magazines in the United States and England.

SIDELIGHTS: **April 22, 1916.** Born in New York City of Russian-Jewish parents. "Both my parents were linguists, Imma [Menuhin's mother] notably so, and both spoke English before coming to the United States. Until I was three, however, they did not speak English to me; our family unity was expressed in a family language. I am only sorry that English was introduced before I had a chance to master reading and writing in Hebrew. Its sound is still in my ears and I have, for instance, broadcast in Hebrew, but only with a script written in phonetic letters and the proper emphases indicated. The early fluency is lost, and the words I recall tend to cluster round the physiological interests of a three-year-old, such words as *regel,* 'leg,' or *beten,* 'stomach,' probably much used in connection with aches and bruises as excuses for getting attention. After the transfer to English, Hebrew remained a household code for instructions to do this or that or be quiet and mind one's manners which outsiders were not meant to understand. Neither of my sisters had my Hebrew opportunities, but thereafter in our pursuit of languages—of which there were to be several—we all three hunted together. Indeed, they went further than I." [Yehudi Menuhin, *Unfinished Journey,* Knopf, 1977.[1]]

Menuhin on his first voyage to Europe, 1926.

Shortly after Menuhin's birth his parents moved to San Francisco where his father taught Hebrew. "In 1918, when I was two, my parents smuggled me into a matinee concert of the San Francisco Symphony Orchestra, and no misadventure occurring to dissuade them, regularly continued the contraband operation until I was old enough to have a ticket on my own account. In after years Imma let it be known that Aba [Menuhin's father] and she had taken me with them because they couldn't afford a baby-sitter. No doubt baby-sitters were a luxury in their struggling young lives, but this granted, I have my reservations about the story. It was characteristic of her to puncture myth with a deft injection of matter of fact. It was no less characteristic to hold that the earlier an experience, the more valuable. When my sisters were expected, I remember her conviction that the life she led, the music she heard, the thoughts she had, were part and parcel of the environment of the coming baby, a subject now for theses by learned doctors, but to her simply a truth. So much the more forcibly must she have believed that as soon as I could be trusted not to disgrace myself, I should be allowed to share what she and Aba delighted in. In view of my future connection with concerts, it might justly be argued that it was rather I who took them; but my own interpretation of the facts concealed by the high cost of baby-sitters is based on the happiness of my early years. . . ."[1]

1921. At the age of five began studying the violin with Louis Persinger, a renowned violinist and teacher. Menuhin had five lessons a week, supplemented by lessons from his parents and later private tutors in literature, history, mathematics, French, German, Italian, Spanish, and Hebrew. ''I went to school for precisely one day, at the age of six, by which time I could read quite well and write and calculate a little. Tremendous discussions preceded the experiment, whose brevity suggests that my parents thankfully accepted the first token of its unwisdom to return to their basic convictions. My one day was not unhappy but bewildered. Very quietly I sat in the class, the teacher stood at the front and said incomprehensible things for a long time, and my attention eventually wandered to the window, through which I could see a tree. The tree was the only detail I remembered clearly enough to report at home that afternoon and that was the end of my schooling. Some time afterward Hephzibah [Menuhin's younger sister] attended, this same school for a whole five days, at the end of which the superintendent asked for a private interview with my parents to tell them their daughter was backward; where upon Hephzibah too was whisked home and within the year fluently read and wrote. After two failures, a third experiment for Yaltah [Menuhin's youngest sister] was never even thought of.

''So we were educated at home. What did we lose thereby? Most obviously we lost acquaintance with other children. By the time I was ten I was used to adults taking me seriously but was only on tentative speaking terms with boys and girls of my own age. The academic gains and losses of the system are harder to weigh. If we didn't take mathematics beyond the beginnings of algebra and geometry, nor even study physics or chemistry, nor learn Latin and Greek, I believe that the languages and literature we did concentrate on were taken be-

Menuhin with sisters Hephzibah and Yaltah.

Menuhin at work.

yond the levels offered by most schools. I was thirteen and my sisters nine and seven when a holiday at Osperdaletti was celebrated by daily readings from *The Divine Comedy* in the original.

''To raise a gifted child is not unlike raising a cretin, I imagine. The exorbitant demands it makes can neither be ignored nor be reduced to normal measure, and the special concentration it attracts necessarily overturns ordinary priorities. There is no doubt that I shaped my parents' lives as much as they shaped mine, sending them traveling back the way they had come, drawing them into my career, leaving them without employment when in the end I left home. But for all that, I believe my sisters and I would have been the objects of no less care and organization had we never played a note. What I supplied was the framework, and perhaps the excuse, for their acting according to principle. Both Aba and Imma had very definite views on the upbringing of children and neither under any circumstances would have been greatly tempted to entrust the task to others. Fortunately in the 1920s the laws of California did not oblige them to do so.''[1]

February 29, 1924. Formal concert debut. ''The various 'firsts' that launched my career have left small mark on my memory. My formal debut . . . when I was seven, consisted of a performance, accompanied by Louis Persinger at the piano, of de Bériot's 'Scène de Ballet,' inserted into a program given at the Oakland Auditorium by the San Francisco Symphony Orchestra; which, if I am not mistaken, was repeated in San Francisco itself a few days afterward. Apart from the excitement of these appearances, I remember little about them. . . . The next year

saw my first appearance with orchestra, in a performance of Lalo's *Symphonie Espagnole,* at the end of which the conductor, Alfred Hertz, lifted me off my feet with his embrace, pressing my face into his beard, which felt like a moist whisk broom. Then, on **25 March 1925,** a month before my ninth birthday, the Scottish Rite Hall in San Francisco was engaged for a first full-length recital.

''Thus gradually I became known in my home town, met my first audiences, received their acclaim, and absorbed the experience into a life scarcely altered by it. Approaching the question in their different ways, my parents met in a united refusal to exploit their children. First of all, the family was sacrosanct. Secondly, we had our routine, which was different from other people's. Thirdly, children were not objects, not possessions, but their own flesh and blood, welded with them into a unit, no part of which could be exhibited without the whole suffering from the publicity. Aba had further motive in his disgust at the thought of exploiting a child's earning power. Concerts were necessary, at first as a test of achievement, later as a means of support, but at no time in my youth were they allowed to challenge the emphasis on family life and on the children's primary duty to study and to learn. As hitherto, time remained too valuable to be wasted on the idle curiosity of the outside world. Hence there were no interviews with newspapers; hence requests to play privately for some society's special occasion or in some rich lady's salon were equally refused; and hence we grew up naturally, shielded from the world of inquiry which would have turned us into self-regarding freaks if it could. I can't thank my parents enough for having had the common sense to regard us as normal children and the strength

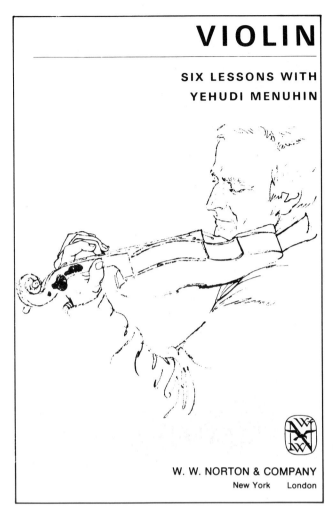

VIOLIN

SIX LESSONS WITH
YEHUDI MENUHIN

W. W. NORTON & COMPANY
New York   London

(From *Violin: Six Lessons with Yehudi Menuhin* by
Yehudi Menuhin. Illustrated by Betty Maxie.)

to resist contrary pressures.''[1]

January 17, 1926. New York debut. ''Music, having brought
us to New York, was not neglected when we got there. Apart
from practice and lessons, a new venture was tried. For some
six or seven Thursdays, I attended sightreading classes at the
Institute of Musical Art (later rebaptized Juilliard). One faculty
member, Dorothy Crowthers, was apt to describe me in later
years as having stood foremost among my older classmates,
but I think she had an indulgent memory, for my ear, which
did very likely distinguish itself in solfeggio, proved stone-
deaf to the nomenclature of harmony. Then, as now, I trusted
music and viewed language askance, and a siege force could
not have driven home those terms. I felt uncomfortably self-
conscious in the anonymity of the classroom—too great a contrast, no doubt, to home, where the very clarity of our identities
made it unnecessary to think about them.''[1]

Between the ages of ten and thirteen Menuhin was to make
New York, Paris, Berlin, and London debuts. In Paris, Menuhin met and began studying with Georges Enesco. ''Enesco
wasn't just a teacher; indeed he never so described himself.
He was the sustaining hand of providence, the inspiration that
bore me aloft. . . . To be sure, I knew Enesco hardly at all—
of his inner life I knew only what the violin could tell me, and
of his face what I had discerned from afar; but the earthy vital
tone, the shaggy crown of black hair, the Turkish cast, the

aristocratic bearing, his penetrating blue eyes, the Rumanian
Rhapsodies . . . were fragments enough for me to assemble a
Byzantine mosaic of . . . folk hero. The fact that playing the
violin represented time stolen from his 'real' work—composing—made him triumphantly Cherkessian in my eyes.

''Enesco gave me lessons whenever his concert schedule allowed, perhaps five in five successive days, then none for a
fortnight, but each one lasting an entire afternoon as if to make
amends for their irregularity. A lesson was an inspiration, not
a stage reached in a course of instruction. It was the making
of music, much as if I were his orchestra, playing under his
direction, or his apprentice-soloist and he both conductor and
orchestra, for while he accompanied me at the piano he also
sang the different voices of the score. There were few inter-
ruptions. . . .

''Above all, Enesco carried me on the wave of his conception
of the music. For years and years afterward I could hear his
voice, sometimes in words, mostly in music, telling me about
what I was playing, and as my experience grew these remembered counsels gained validity. Nothing he said was wrong,
nothing he pointed to misleading. . . . I know that everything
I do carries his imprint yet.''[1]

November 25, 1927. Carnegie Hall debut. The following year
(1928) twelve-year-old Menuhin made his first record and,
accompanied by his father, went on his first concert tour. ''. . .
It was decided that on this first tour I should play once a week,
for fifteen weeks or so, starting in San Francisco and moving
east to finish in New York. Although I have since covered the
same ground many times, I recall the towns visited then with

Yehudi Menuhin. Photograph by David Farrell.

Before long the palace had its own Royal Philharmonic Orchestra composed entirely of accountants. ■ (From *The King, the Cat and the Fiddle* by Yehudi Menuhin and Christopher Hope. Illustrated by Angela Barrett.)

Of Joachim there was no sign. The King searched for him in all his favorite places . . . . ■ (From *The King, The Cat and the Fiddle* by Yehudi Menuhin and Christopher Hope. Illustrated by Angela Barrett.)

some clarity: Los Angeles and the immense Shriners' Auditorium; Chicago, whose auditorium declined later into a sports arena, then served as a United Nations center, before being rehabilitated for music some few years ago; Pittsburgh, where I first performed the Brahms Concerto; Minneapolis, where the conductor, Henri Verbrughen, invited me home after the concert to play chamber music. . . .''[1]

1929. On his second trip to Europe, thirteen-year-old Menuhin staged a concert in Berlin, thus beginning his ''adult'' career. ''The concert was crucial because Berlin was then the musical capital of the 'civilized' world, its prestige founded on the music of the past and flourishing still in great orchestras and conductors, not to mention the most informed audiences to be found anywhere. It was a tremendous event for me.''[1]

1931. Received the first of many honors—an honorary award of the Primer Prix, first prize of the Paris Conservatoire. Menuhin's talented sister Hephzibah began to accompany him on the piano. ''. . . Her trust—in herself, in the music, and in me—was so natural that it survived public appearance and indeed embraced the audience. It was the reverse of arrogance: although she was sure of herself and her performance, her

assurance came from service to the music, so that she performed with simplicity, humility, almost naïveté, and certainly without exhibitionism or self-indulgence—virtues which were to make her particularly loved in England and France. . . .

''For Hephzibah music was a natural means of expression, a further bond between us, a happy duty. She never accompanied me in small brilliant pieces designed to show off the violinist's virtuosity. Together we played sonatas, equal voices in dialogue with one another; and being so close, needing to make no effort to bend and blend our personalities, we played them with a natural unity of conception and approach. . . .''[1]

1936. Menuhin and his family took a year off from concerts and commitments of any kind. The ''year off'' in California became known amongst the family as ''Mother's Year.'' ''. . . Although we did not know it then, this break in routine closed a chapter in our history. Before we emerged into public life again, in late 1937, I would be twenty-one; before a further twelve months had passed, Hephzibah, Yaltah and myself would be married, almost literally all together, and my parents suddenly bereft of the purpose which had shaped half their lives.''[1]

"I delighted in being president of the Puffin Club, which encourages young people to write poetry . . . ." ■ (From *Conversations with Menuhin* by Robin Daniels. Photograph by Sandra Lousada.)

May 26, 1938. Married Nola Ruby Nicholas. This first marriage resulted in the births of a daughter and a son. "By 1944 it had become clear that Nola and I were hopelessly at odds. So often physically apart, we had grown ever further apart in emotion, but had the circumstances been different, the outcome would have been the same—a truth which she was ready to acknowledge sooner than I was: on an early holiday, before the wartime commitments began, she suggested we hadn't enough in common to build a marriage on. For my part, I could not imagine that a wife could be any less permanent than a parent or a sister, or any less ideal. Each of us had married an illusion, she as well as I, for the life a virtuoso leads can appear totally glamorous only in the eyes of the beholder. Our relationship was dislocated in time: had it been a more youthful or a more mature encounter, it would not have done the damage or caused the anguish that it did. It was half dream, half sadness. . . . In retrospect my first marriage seems a stepping stone, which was hardly how I imagined it then. Perhaps it is a lesson in humility to find one can so misinterpret oneself; but equally the misinterpretation may offer a lesson in the need for maintaining illusions. Perhaps one should not spend one's life doubting the validity of impulse, but just live with intensity and conviction at whatever cost. Such consolation by hindsight could not help me then, as my marriage fell apart. . . .''[1]

Three years later, in 1947, the marriage was legally terminated, and Menuhin subsequently married Diana Rosamond Gould. This second marriage resulted in the births of two sons.

1952. Raised $74,000 for the Famine Fund following a concert tour in India. Menuhin has been very involved in international causes. "Of the many causes to which I am committed, four are closest to my heart. One is Amnesty International's work for prisoners of conscience. The others concern education in its widest sense.

"First is the Puffin Club. . . . I am very devoted to the Puffins, a hundred thousand children in Britain who draw, paint, write poetry, design machinery, collect money to buy an island off the Scottish coast where puffins may live in safety and do many other wonderful things. The second is the college at West Dean in Sussex which alone in the country offers training in conservation crafts, such as furniture and clock repair, bookbinding, tapestry and so on, in an attempt to reverse the decline of craftsmanship and preserve a nation's heritage from the past. . . . I not only supported the college's aims but saw in it scope for much I was interested in, including windmills to supply electricity at low cost and the conversion of its farm to organic methods—objectives yet to be realized. Thirdly, and most importantly, there is my own school."[1]

In 1963 Menuhin founded a boarding school in Surrey, England, the Yehudi Menuhin School, to facilitate the problems of the very young, musically-talented child and to combine scholastic education with his instrumental learning. "Not all children have two devoted Jewish parents as I did, and a psychologist might suspect that my school is primarily an attempt to fill that sad gap. More deliberately, it expresses my sense of obligation to life and to the society I live in. It is, after my own musical experience, the nearest I have come to molding reality into utopian shapes, a healthy, happy community of the young, not an elite but an example to others. To me it is a constant and increasing satisfaction, not least because its origin lies in the difficulties of my adult pilgrimage to comprehension of the violin. Having made the pilgrimage, I wanted to guide others; having learned, I wanted to pass my findings on. So my school crowns my life and will be, I hope, a lasting legacy.

"In a sense, my career as a musical mentor began during my boyhood, in the years when Hephzibah and I played together in the music room at Ville d'Avray. Even earlier I had been obliged to be articulate in formulating my ideas to my accompanists—an experience which stood me in good stead: today, in front of an orchestra, I can convey by saying or singing the sounds I want produced. But making music with Hephzibah marked the real start of my teaching history, and the marvelous aspect of this start was its growing out of our relationship and family circumstances as easily and naturally as bread rising under the influence of yeast.

"Even then, I am happy to recall, I kept a balance between technique and interpretation. Interpretation was the point of these practice sessions with my sister, but I could puzzle my way toward my imaged sounds only in terms of what our four hands were doing to our two instruments. I have never put much faith in injunctions to play 'more gaily' or 'more sadly,' descriptions of achievement, not of method, but given the gaiety or sadness of the music, there were deductions to be made about tempo, emphasis, balance. All clarification starts in the dark and these were groping beginnings. One thing hampered me: such was Hephzibah's sensitivity that she did not need many words. She was an extraordinary instrument, almost an extension of myself. It was as if we did not bring our instruments together, but both played the-piano-and-the-violin. Later experience continued to spoil me: performing with musicians whom I knew and understood—Kentner, Casals, Toscanini, and many others—speech was not required."[1]

In 1973 the Ministry of Education and Science granted the school the same governmental status as the Royal Ballet School.

1979. After a concert tour of China, Menuhin invited four Chinese students to his schools. The result was so successful that the government of China invited his students to return to China in 1982, where the students gave concerts in Peking and Shanghai. ". . . I have learned that my childish dream of bringing peace to mankind was both too vast—for it failed to take into account that peace and happiness for everybody were not necessarily compatible; and too narrow—for in the manner of the urban Jew I restricted my ambitions to human society. Today I realize that it is to life I owe my allegiance. I am no less an idealist for being more of a realist than I once was. I still look to music to bind and heal; I still think the musician can be a trusted object offering his fellowmen solace but also a reminder of human excellence; I believe as strongly as ever that our finite world turns on finite individual efforts to embody an ideal.

"Perhaps more modest stages give me some achievement to claim. Violinistically I can point to an understanding of my instrument which has grown day by day, year by year. I knew the pinnacles of mastery very early, although I could not always sustain my knowledge, nor analyze nor teach it. Today I can do these things. Musically too, the violin repertoire which in childhood I experienced directly I now experience consciously, in every part of my anatomy. Conducting has stretched mind and imagination, balancing the miniature perfection of finger joints upon fingerboard with the large communal interpretation of great scores.''[1]

In addition to being a great violinist, Menuhin has been a deeply committed humanitarian. He has attacked countless injustices, including industrial pollution and Soviet repression of dissidents. He has promoted music and the cultural exchange of musicians as a means of reducing international tensions.

Menuhin regrets that he did not have the time to be a conven-

In 1976 students from Menuhin's school played at the British Embassy in Washington, D.C. at Queen Elizabeth's request.

tional parent. ''My life, the habit of traveling, made it impossible. The children [were] involved on their own but with a lot of parental concern.'' [*People*, April 15, 1985.[2]]

Zamira and Jeremy are concert pianists. Gerard has published his first novel. ''Now we talk the same language. We are more or less the same age. I am a young 68, they are in their 30s, 40s. It is fine.''[2]

Son Krov is an underwater photographer who has since 1972 filmed nine one-hour specials. His latest adventure has resulted in a four-part documentary, ''South Seas Voyage.'' For Krov's 1978 film, ''The Reef at Ras Muhammad,'' shot off the Sinai, his father performed the background music. ''I believe in nepotism, but I wouldn't have asked him to do it,'' says Krov. ''But when he saw it, he asked to do the music, which he then had specially composed by Edwin Roxburgh.''[2] Father and son would like to collaborate on another film linking movements of animals underwater with music. ''I never had the chance to be like Krov,'' says Menuhin. ''I was brought up by an overcautious father who always insisted on having his socks on before he got out of bed in the morning. I started [my career] very early and whatever talent I had was readily recognized. I never had to fight my way or worry about the competition—that would be very frustrating.''[2]

Among his writings are the ''Menuhin Music Guides,'' and his autobiography *Unfinished Journey*, for which he received

''Many other cities I love, but I love London most of all. *My life* **is here.''** ■ (From *Conversations with Menuhin* by Robin Daniels. Photograph by Maurice Broomfield.)

the prestigious Peace Prize of the German Book Trade Federation. In 1983 he wrote, in collaboration with Christopher Hope, the children's book, *The King, the Cat, and the Fiddle*.

FOR MORE INFORMATION SEE: New York Times, November 26, 1927, November 27, 1966, May 25, 1977; *Life*, May 20, 1966; Robert Magidoff, *Yehudi Menuhin: The Story of the Man and the Musician*, Doubleday, 1955, 2nd edition, R. Hale, 1973; *New York Times Book Review*, April 17, 1977, November 11, 1979; *Commentary*, July, 1977; Yehudi Menuhin, *Unfinished Journey*, Knopf, 1977; Lionel M. Rolfe, *The Menuhins: A Family Odyssey*, Panjandrum, 1978; Robin Daniels, *Conversations with Menuhin*, St. Martin's, 1980; *Christian Science Monitor*, Feburary 11, 1980; *People*, April 15, 1985.

MERRIAM, Eve 1916-

PERSONAL: Born July 19, 1916, in Philadelphia, Pennsylvania; children: Guy and Dee (sons). *Education:* Cornell University, student; University of Pennsylvania, A.B., 1937; graduate studies at University of Wisconsin and Columbia University. *Home:* 101 W. 12th St., New York, N.Y. 10011. *Agent:* Patricia Ayres, 169 W. 88th St., New York, N.Y. 10024.

CAREER: Author, poet, playwright. Copywriter, 1939-42; radio writer, mainly of documentaries and scripts in verse for Columbia Broadcasting System and other networks, and conductor of weekly program on modern poetry for station WQXR, New York, N.Y., 1942-46; *PM*, New York, N.Y. daily verse column, 1945; *Deb*, feature editor, 1946; *Glamour*, fashion copy editor, 1947-48; free-lance magazine and book writer, 1949—; taught courses in creative writing at City College of the City University of New York, 1965-69. Bank Street College of Education, attached to field project staff, 1958-60. Public lecturer, 1956—. *Member:* Authors Guild, Dramatists Guild Council. *Awards, honors:* Yale Younger Poets Prize, 1946, for *Family Circle; Collier's* Star Fiction Award for ''Make Something Happen,'' 1949; William Newman Poetry Award, 1957; grant to write poetic drama, Columbia Broadcasting System, 1959; Obie Award, 1976, for playwriting; National Council of Teachers of English Award, 1981, for excellence in poetry for children.

WRITINGS—Poetry; juvenile: *There Is No Rhyme for Silver* (illustrated by Joseph Schindelman; Junior Literary Guild selection), Atheneum, 1962; *It Doesn't Always Have to Rhyme* (illustrated by Malcolm Spooner), Atheneum, 1964; *Catch a Little Rhyme* (illustrated by Imero Gobbato), Atheneum, 1966; *Independent Voices* (illustrated by Arvis Stewart), Atheneum, 1968; *Finding a Poem* (illustrated by Seymour Chwast; Junior Literary Guild selection), Atheneum, 1970; *I Am a Man: Ode to Martin Luther King, Jr.* (illustrated by Suzanne Verrier), Doubleday, 1971; *Out Loud* (illustrated by Harriet Sherman), Atheneum, 1973; *Rainbow Writing*, Atheneum, 1976; *A Word or Two with You: New Rhymes for Young Readers* (illustrated by John Nez), Atheneum, 1981; *If Only I Could Tell You* (illustrated by Donna Diamond), Knopf, 1984; *Jamboree: Rhymes for All Times*, Dell, 1984; *Blackberry Ink* (illustrated by Hans Wilhelm), Morrow, 1985.

Poetry; adult: *Family Circle*, Yale University Press, 1946; *Tomorrow Morning*, Twayne, 1953; *Montgomery Alabama: Money, Mississippi and Other Places* (pamphlet in poetry), Cameron, 1957; *The Double Bed: From the Feminine Side*, Cameron,

. . . This ounce can bounce,
this ounce can pounce.

■ (From *It Doesn't Always Have to Rhyme* by Eve Merriam. Illustrated by Malcolm Spooner.)

1958, M. Evans, 1972; *The Trouble with Love,* Macmillan, 1960; *The Inner City Mother Goose* (photographs by Lawrence Ratzkin), Simon & Schuster, 1969; *The Nixon Poems,* Atheneum, 1970.

Other books; juvenile: *The Real Book about Franklin D. Roosevelt,* Garden City, 1952, revised edition, Dobson, 1961; *The Real Book about Amazing Birds,* Garden City, 1954, revised edition, Dobson, 1960; *A Gaggle of Geese* (illustrated by Paul Galdone), Knopf, 1960; *Mommies at Work* (illustrated by Beni Montresor), Knopf, 1961; *The Voice of Liberty: The Story of Emma Lazarus,* Jewish Publication Society, 1963; *Funny Town,* Macmillan, 1963; *What's in the Middle of a Riddle?,* Collier, 1963; *What Can You Do with a Pocket?* (illustrated by Harriet Simon), Knopf, 1964; *Small Fry* (illustrated by Garry MacKenzie), Knopf, 1965; *Don't Think about a White Bear* (illustrated by M. Tinkelman), Putnam, 1965; *The Story of Benjamin Franklin* (illustrated by Brinton Turkle), Four Winds Press, 1965; *Do You Want to See Something?,* Scholastic Books, 1965; *Miss Tibbett's Typewriter* (illustrated by Rick Schreiter), Knopf, 1966; *Andy All Year Round* (illustrated by M. Hoff), Funk & Wagnalls, 1968; *Epaminondas* (illustrated by Trina S. Hyman), Follett, 1968, published as *That Noodle-Head Epaminondas* (illustrated by T. S. Hyman), Scholastic Book Services, 1972; *Project One-Two-Three* (illustrated by H. Sherman), McGraw, 1971; (translator) Hana DosKocilova, *Animal Tales* (illustrated by Mirko Hanak), Doubleday, 1971; *Bam! Zam! Boom!: High Rise Going Up* (illustrated by William Lightfoot), Walker, 1972; *Boys and Girls, Girls and Boys* (illustrated by H. Sherman), Holt, 1972; *Ab to Zogg* (illustrated by Albert Lorenz), Atheneum, 1977; *The Birthday Cow* (illustrated by Guy Michel), Knopf, 1978; *Unhurry Harry* (illustrated by Gail Owens), Four Winds Press, 1978; *Good Night*

to Annie (illustrated by John Wallner), Four Winds Press, 1979; *The Christmas Box* (picture book; illustrated by David Small), Morrow, 1985.

Adult: *Woman with a Torch* (biography of Emma Lazarus), Citadel, 1956; *Figleaf: The Business of Being in Fashion* (nonfiction), Lippincott, 1960; *Basics: An I-Can-Read-Book for Grownups,* Macmillan, 1962; *After Nora Slammed the Door: American Women in the 1960's, the Unfinished Revolution,* World Publishing, 1964; *Growing Up Female in America: Ten Lives,* Doubleday, 1971; (editor with Nancy Larrick) *Male and Female under Eighteen,* Avon, 1973; *A Husband's Notes about Her,* Macmillan, 1976.

Plays; all published by Samuel French: *The Club,* 1976; *Out of Our Father's House,* 1975; *At Her Age,* 1979; *Dialogue for Lovers,* 1981; *And I Ain't Finished Yet,* 1982.

Contributor; juvenile anthologies: *Believe and Make-Believe,* Dutton, 1957; *Let's Read More Stories,* Garden City, 1960. Also contributor to magazines, including *Nation, New Republic, Saturday Evening Post, Ladies' Home Journal, True, Sat-*

"I thought that 'The Club' would be a tiny little feminist work that would never get beyond a small feminist audience. But it's still going on all over the world," says Eve Merriam. ■ (Photograph is of a promotional poster for the play "The Club.")

Taxi Man

Taxi man, taxi man,
Quick drive me home!
My house is on fire
And my children all—!

Sorry, lady,
Even in an emergency
Cabs don't go to Harlem.

(From *The Inner City Mother Goose* by Eve Merriam. Visuals by Lawrence Ratzkin.)

urday Review, Reader's Digest, New York Times Magazine, Diplomat, New York Magazine, Ms., Washington Post, Village Voice.

ADAPTATIONS: ''Inner City'' (musical play), based on *The Inner City Mother Goose,* opened on Broadway at the Ethel Barrymore Theatre, December 12, 1971, music by Helen Miller, lyrics by Merriam.

WORK IN PROGRESS: A book of wishes.

SIDELIGHTS: **July 19, 1916.** Born in Philadelphia, Pennsylvania. ''Both my parents came to this country from Russia when they were very young. My mother was two and my father five. They grew up in small towns in Pennsylvania where I was born and reared until I went away to college.

''My parents owned a chain of women's dress shops. I had two older sisters, and an older brother. The joke in the family was that they decided to go into the women's-wear business

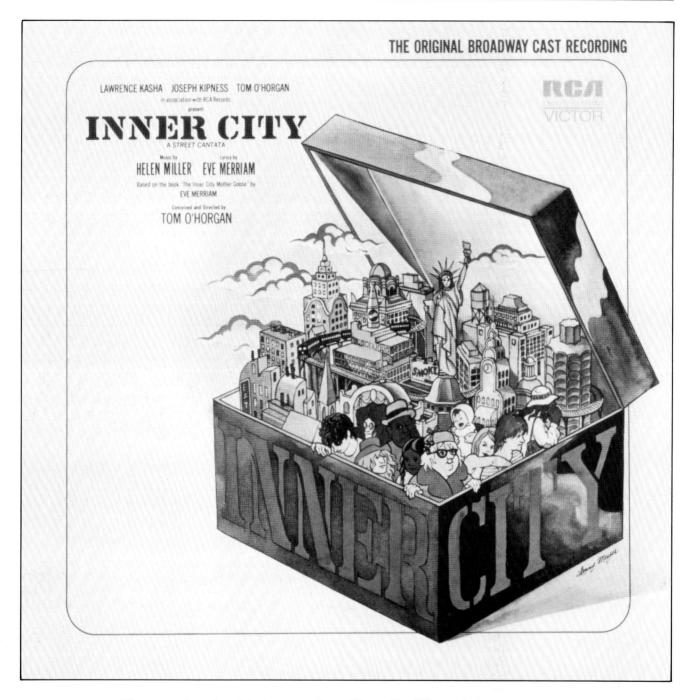

Album cover from the original cast recording of "Inner City." The musical opened at the Ethel Barrymore Theatre, December 12, 1971.

so they'd be able to afford clothing for all the girls. So I grew up with fashion, and it has always been an interest of mine.''

Books and reading were other family interests. ''My father wrote love poems to my mother before they were married. We were very thrilled to discover those poems later in life. Growing up, my brother and I were taken to Gilbert and Sullivan and I used to chant all of those tongue-twisting verses of Gilbert's. The local column of the *Philadelphia Bulletin* used to print light verse, and my brother and I would read aloud such great, declaiming things like *Ghunga Din* or *The Highway Man*. I can still remember some of the terrible verses that we learned:

'I eat my peas with honey
I've done it all my life
They do taste kind of funny
It keeps them on the knife.'

''We thought, 'Oh, gosh . . . imagine those terrible table manners of putting peas on a knife!' We thought it hilarious.

''My sisters were a half a generation older, so it was my brother and I who were thrown together. We used to make little toy airplanes out of balsa wood. When they put an oil burner in our house, they had to dig up the front yard leaving a depression

Linda Hopkins, who appeared in the musical "Inner City," adapted from *The Inner City Mother Goose* by Eve Merriam. Hopkins won a Tony award for her performance in 1972.

there. My brother and I used to pour water into it to form our own little skating pond. I was a terrible skater, but in my imagination, I was superb—the Baryshnikov of ice skating!''

Merriam enjoyed the classic children's stories during her youth. ''As a child, *Swiss Family Robinson* was one of my favorite books. The fact that the family was shipwrecked, and the mother was able to magically take out of a bag everything the family needed to survive was very thrilling. I adored all kinds of fairy tales, including Andersen's, Brothers Grimm's, the English and the Irish tales, as well as Greek, Roman and Norse mythology. In *Alice in Wonderland*, I don't remember paying much attention to illustrations. I was much more concerned with the pictures that the words were able to convey.

''Looking back on things, there are books that I certainly enjoyed as a youngster that I would consider sexist today, or even racist. I re-wrote the story *Epaminondas* because the language was racist. But the heroes and heroines remain the marvelous, adventurous spirits who as doers refused to accept the world as it was.

''I started to devour poetry of all kinds at an early age, par-

ticularly light verse, narrative and dramatic poems. I remember being enthralled by the sound of words, by their musicality and by the fact that you could have alliteration, and if you said 'Peter Peter Pumpkin Eater,' it was very funny. Or if you recited something like: 'The Highway man came riding up to the old inn door,' it was exciting because you could hear a whole orchestra with your voice.

''And, of course, there is a special magic about rhyme, the chime that rings in time. It's like the little bell at the end of the typewriter line. When you're very young, you love that bouncy-bouncing quality you get from a rhyme. Of course, not all poems have to rhyme, it's kind of an extra thing when they do. But even without rhyme, there is assonance, or alliteration, or onomatopoeia. Whatever it is, there is some kind of repetition and musicality in a poem that I don't think any other form of literature can equal.

''I also started to write when I was quite young. I was writing poems when I was about seven or eight. One of my first was about a birch tree that grew outside my bedroom window. It was a very sanctimonious, very pure poem. I remember that one line went: 'May my life be like the birch tree reaching upward to the sky.'

''By the time I got into high school I was writing serious poems for the high school magazine, as well as political and light verse for the weekly newspaper at the school. It never occurred to me that someday I might like to *be* a writer. I just wrote. I think one is chosen to be a poet. You write poems because you must write them; because you can't live your life without writing them.

''At school I had one English teacher who was encouraging, and one very irascible, difficult, tendentious old Latin teacher who made me realize the rich roots of the English language. To go back to find the root of a word, to see its origins in another language and to see how it grew and developed helped me discover both the richness and the ambiguity of words. I also became a very good speller.''

In **1946** Merriam received the Yale Younger Poets Prize. ''At that time the contest was for a book of poems awarded to someone under thirty years old. The first time I entered, I didn't win. I tried again and again for four more years until I won it. The year that I won it, Archibald MacLeish was the judge. He had been my hero. When I went away to college, I slept with a copy of his 'Conquistador' under my pillow so that no one could steal it. He wrote a poem, 'Arts Poetica' (The Art of Poetry), which began, 'Poems should be palpable and mute, like a globed fruit.' At first his idea that 'a poem should be mute' seemed ridiculous to me, because a poem uses words. Then I realized—it's true—by 'mute' he meant one should use the fewest words possible and press the unspoken. I remember being absolutely thrilled. I was very excited by his work.''

In her approach to writing poetry, Merriam admits: ''I've sometimes spent weeks looking for precisely the right word. It's like having a tiny marble in your pocket, you can just feel it. Sometimes you find a word and say, 'No, I don't think this is it. . . .' Then you discard it, and take another and another until you get it right. I do think poetry is great fun. That's what I'd like to stress more than anything else: the joy of the sound of language.

''Both the reading and writing of poetry can inevitably lead to a deepening of our profound feelings—feelings of anger, shame, rage, sadness, fear, joy—all of the things that we can feel can be shared once we come to poetry.''

Besides poetry, Merriam has written numerous fiction and non-fiction books for children and adults. ''I hate writing prose. It's very difficult. I've written a lot of prose in my time because I've had to make a living. Because I am a natural poet and the word, per se, and the sound of the word is so important to me, I agonize; I can spend two days over an introductory paragraph.

''I find that my natural tendency is to write witty things in prose if I can. But I get impatient with the explanations. I could never be a daily journalist.

''I think different people have a different cast of mind, and I finally realized that it was just *wrong* for me. A few years ago, I decided: no more book reviews, no more magazine articles. Now I only write poetry and for the theater because those are the two places where my heart is.

''Poetry is different from playwriting and prose because there is no middle person. When there aren't any characters, you're dealing directly with emotions. It's easier because you don't have to build a plot, but every word is so freighted. Every word is significant, so you have to be sure each one is a jewel. You have to watch out for ugly syllables; too many 's' sounds come out very serpentine. Too many consonants get very 'gooky,' like peanut butter sticking to the roof of your mouth. And you have to be aware of punctuation and the amount of space between lines. A poem is like a painting where the color and

Y D R E D

**Ydred (EE-dred) [ydates yunclyr.]
Ydred the Red (Claimant of Deeds)
and Ydred the Ded (Willer of Deeds)
both descended from Dred the Naught,
but the true lineage remains in doubt,
since which is the steptoe son and
which the stepheel has never been resolved....**

■ (From *Ab to Zogg* by Eve Merriam. Illustrated by Al Lorenz.)

**Autumn leaves tumble down,
Autumn leaves crumble down,
Autumn leaves bumble down. . . .**

■ (From *There Is No Rhyme for Silver* by Eve Merriam. Illustrated by Joseph Schindelman.)

space relationships are very important on the canvas. I think poetry is closer to painting than to any other form of literature.''

Merriam is also the author of several plays. ''I wrote plays when I was in college, but I didn't have any produced. Poems of mine were set to music, and often things were done as little theatrical sketches and revues. It wasn't until 1971 that the musical 'Inner City' was adapted directly from *The Inner City Mother Goose*. It ran on Broadway in 1971-72. During the past decade of my life I have been completely involved in the theatre.

''While you deal with dialogue in a play, you're not really saying the thing directly. Even in poetry, one so often says things in a roundabout way. There is symbolism and ambiguity, and I think they are part of playwriting. People think of playwriting as being all dialogue, often there is a gesture, or a look, or just a turning away or turning toward without dialogue, which is infinitely more meaningful than if the person had said something. I think that's like poetry, a very selective process, much more so than the novel.

"It's not accidental that I came to the theater by way of my poetry or that someone like Ntozake Shange, who is also a poet, came into the theatre by way of poetry. I think we are more and more aware of the theatricality of poetry and the poetry of the theatre.

"In some ways, the first play, 'Inner City,' may have meant the most to me. Going to Broadway was so exciting. To see my name in lights on Broadway and to hear the audience laughing at my jokes, or clapping for something serious—there's no thrill beyond that.

"I love the rehearsal process and the social aspect of it. I find that I do a fair amount of re-writing during rehearsals, and I

**. . . But let your voice
respond to mine:
then the knots untangle
and everything's fine.**

■ (From "The Line," in *If Only I Could Tell You* by Eve Merriam. Illustrated by Donna Diamond.)

New Presence in the Museum · House of Genius
Justice James Wilson · My Daughter the What?

The Pennsylvania Gazette

April, 1978

Found:
Eve Merriam

This 1978 University of Pennsylvania alumni magazine cover featured Eve Merriam.
Photograph courtesy of Francesco Scavullo.

work extremely well under that kind of pressure. There used to be a joke about me: 'Eve Merriam, the fastest pen in the East.' I do work very quickly.

"On opening night I feel terrified; sick. I can't eat. I usually sit as far in the back as possible with the composer and/or the director, with somebody connected with the show, never with someone close to me. It's very nerve wracking, very scary, very upsetting. Even if I think I'm being calm, I'll hear my voice getting tense and I'll snap at somebody for something ridiculous.''

Of her work habits Merriam admits to be "more of a day person. If I'm working intensely on something, I may go late into the night. But for me, there is a danger in working very late at night because I tend to get somewhat slap-happy. There comes a certain point when I just go over and over things, rewriting the same sentence or the same line.

"Mornings are always an exciting time because the world is made anew every day. I like to get up, read the morning paper, and breakfast on hot cereal, grapefruit and strong coffee before going on my walk.

"I don't walk every day. I very often take weekends off unless I have a deadline. I tend to work late mornings. Usually it's not until about ten o'clock that I get going, but if I work intensely for a couple of hours, I get a lot done. Then I may go back and work some more in the middle of the afternoon.

"I like to finish things, although I always have a number of cycles of poetry going. I have several that have been in the works for quite a few years. I work on more than one project at a time. I crave novelty and I like to do things quickly. I like to go from one thing to another.

"If I have a book that I'm keen on, then I will stay with it. For instance, with this book of love poems for teenagers that I've finished, I knew from the beginning the approximate number of poems that I was going to do. I took little notes. I didn't have time to work for quite a few months because I was involved in another project, so I got a folder, and whenever I got a notion or an idea, I'd just throw it into the folder. When my time came months later, I took out those notes. Some of them made sense, some didn't, but then I was able to write the book fairly rapidly. In *The Inner City Mother Goose* I knew just how many poems I was going to do, so I said, 'I'm going to try to write two or three a day,' which I did. That's difficult. I think that when you're writing poetry the idea comes, but then you *really* have to work at it. You mustn't give up. You go over and over it, again and again. I can almost always find ways to cut and fill up baskets with lots of crumpled paper. I never re-write poems after they've been in print. Auden said, 'A poem is never finished, it's just abandoned.'''

A major interest has been the women's rights movement. Merriam has written several influential books on feminism. "I agree with Auden who said that books don't change things. Some books do—certainly there have been landmark books in the world that have made changes. I think the Civil Rights situation, certainly the race situation is better than it was. Psychologically, it's improved. People are aware, and while there still may be only tokenism in some fields, you do see Blacks, Asian, and all sorts of people in situations you wouldn't have before. Although I still think there is a great way to go, I don't think we will ever go back to the kinds of chauvinism we had in an earlier period.

"When I was a young woman growing up, people would say, 'Oh, I hear you're a feminist,' and that was an epitaph. I used to have to hide the fact that I was a poet and a feminist otherwise, I wouldn't be popular. It was very lonely. I had no one to discuss my ideas with. I would sit and just write down dialogues with myself. That's why I love the women's movement because it's brought me comradeship. No one could be happier than I at the proliferation of the women's movement and women's writing.

"As far as my own work is concerned, I know that certain works of mine have had an influence because I have been told that *The Inner City Mother Goose* was at one time the second most banned book in the country. I didn't write it for children. It was never intended to be a children's book. But it has percolated down, certainly to high school and junior high school.

"To grow up in a world where there is much more equality and much less hypocrisy between the sexes, where there is openness and frankness is good.

"My advice to young people who want to write? Don't be discouraged.''

FOR MORE INFORMATION SEE: The Nation, January 31, 1959, March 21, 1959, June 23, 1962, December 14, 1964, June 7, 1965, October 7, 1968; *The New Republic*, November 16, 1959; *Newsweek*, July 2, 1962, August 2, 1976; *New York Times*, December 22, 1963, July 23, 1976, May 30, 1980; Brian Doyle, *The Who's Who of Children's Literature*, Schocken Books, 1968; Haviland and Smith, *Children and Poetry*, Library of Congress, 1969; *New York Times Book Review*, March 2, 1969, June 25, 1972; *Christian Science Monitor*, January 8, 1970, March 15, 1970; *Library Journal*, September, 1970, May 15, 1971; *Horn Book*, October, 1970; *New York Times Magazine*, May 2, 1971; Nancy Larrick, editor, *Somebody Turned on a Tap in These Kids*, Delacorte, 1971; Doris de Montreville and Donna Hill, editors, *Third Book of Junior Authors*, H. W. Wilson, 1972; *Dramatists Guild Quarterly*, Autumn, 1982.

MICHEL, Anna   1943-

BRIEF ENTRY: Born December 12, 1943, in Mishawaka, Ind. Author of books for children and educator. A 1967 graduate of Indiana University, Michel received her M.S. from Bank Street College in 1975. Since 1970 she has taught at various schools in New York City, including several years spent as a volunteer teacher of American Sign Language (ASL) at Columbia University. Michel's pupil at Columbia was part of an innovative research project conducted by psychologist Herbert S. Terrace on the communicative abilities of apes. For this study, a chimpanzee was raised from infancy as a human child would be and instructed in ASL. Named Nim Chimpsky, the chimpanzee eventually acquired a vocabulary of 125 signs. Michel chronicled Nim's training years in a book for intermediate readers entitled *The Story of Nim: The Chimp Who Learned Language* (Knopf, 1980). Accompanied with photographs by Dr. Terrace and Susan Kuklin, the book reveals both the "human" and simian sides of this precedent-setting primate. *School Library Journal* called Michel's record of Nim's achievements ". . . a peek at the exciting possibilities of shared thoughts and feelings with another species," while *New York Times Book Review* took note of the "uncomplicated text. . . . written with charm and enthusiasm. . . .''

Prior to *The Story of Nim,* Michel wrote three books in Pantheon's "I Am Reading" series. Aimed at the beginning independent reader, these books also deal with the growth and development of animals; however, unlike Nim, the animals are presented in their wildlife environments. The titles are: *Little Wild Chimpanzee* (1978), *Little Wild Elephant* (1979), and *Little Wild Lion Cub* (1980). Michel believes that "it is important for children to realize that animals are not the property of human beings.... If life on earth is to survive, children must grow into responsible adults who respect all life."

FOR MORE INFORMATION SEE: Contemporary Authors, Volumes 85-88, Gale, 1980.

MOCHÉ, Dinah (Rachel) L(evine)   1936-

BRIEF ENTRY: Born October 24, 1936, in New York, N.Y. Professor of physics and astronomy, and writer. A 1958 magna cum laude graduate of Radcliffe College, Moché received her M.A. and Ph.D. degrees from Columbia University. In 1961 she began her career as a research assistant at that same university's Radiation Laboratory. Through the years, she has taught at various institutions such as the Fashion Institute of Technology and both the Bronx and Queensborough Community Colleges of the City University of New York. During the 1970s she was the recipient of two separate grants from the National Science Foundation. Moché is the author of nine juvenile books that expose children to various facets of astronomy and space exploration. These include: *What's Up There? Questions and Answers about Stars and Space* (Scholastic Book Services, 1975), *Search for Life Beyond Earth* (F. Watts, 1978), *The Star Wars Question and Answer Book about Space* (F. Watts, 1979), and *Astronomy Today* (Random House, 1982). She has also written two books for adults, *Life in Space* (Ridge Press, 1979) and *Astronomy* (2nd edition, Wiley, 1981). A contributor of articles to professional journals, Moché has served as a contributing editor of *Science World,* a member of the editorial board of *Physics Teacher,* and a member of the review board of the *American Journal of Physics. Residence:* Mamaroneck, N.Y.

FOR MORE INFORMATION SEE: Contemporary Authors, Volumes 89-92, Gale, 1980.

MOST, Bernard   1937-

BRIEF ENTRY: Born September 2, 1937, in New York. Advertising executive, and author and illustrator of children's books. Most graduated with honors from Pratt Institute in 1959, and that same year began working for the advertising agency McCann-Erickson, Inc. He later became associate creative director for another agency and since 1978 has been senior vice-president and creative director at MCA Advertising, Inc. Among Most's books for children are two featuring "Anthony," a boy who enjoys finding words within words. In *There's an Ant in Anthony* (Morrow, 1980), he discovers the word in his own name and then looks for it elsewhere. *School Library Journal* found the work a "clever word concept book" and noted its "amusing action-filled line drawings...." In *There's an Ape behind the Drape* (Morrow, 1981), Anthony chases an ape from behind his living room drapes all the way to Mexico and

back. Most emphasizes the word "ape" in fiery red within various words throughout the text. *Publishers Weekly* described the book as "zippy fun" and commented that "the author-illustrator's sure hand and wit have created impressive ... drawings...."

Also by Most is the picture book *My Very Own Octopus* (Harcourt, 1980) in which a young boy imagines what it would be like to have an octopus for a pet. *Publishers Weekly* observed, "Most's blithe, telling and sprightly illustrations convince the reader that his little hero's daydream should come true." The author's other books for young readers are: *If the Dinosaurs Came Back* (1978) and *Whatever Happened to the Dinosaurs?* (1984), both published by Harcourt; as well as *Turn Over* and *Boo!* (both Prentice-Hall, 1980). *Home:* 3 Ridgecrest E., Scarsdale, N.Y. 10583.

FOR MORE INFORMATION SEE: Contemporary Authors, Volume 104, Gale, 1982.

DHAN GOPAL MUKERJI

MUKERJI, Dhan Gopal   1890-1936

PERSONAL: Born July 6, 1890, near Calcutta, India; came to the United States, 1910; died by his own hand, July 14, 1936, in New York, N.Y.; son of Kissori and Bhuban (Goswami) Mukerji; married Ethel Ray Dugan (a teacher), 1918; children: Dhan Gopal II. *Education:* Attended University of Calcutta, 1908, Tokyo University, 1909, and University of California, Berkeley, 1910-13; Stanford University, Ph.B., 1914. *Politics:* Indian Independence Movement. *Religion:* Vendanta.

CAREER: Author and lecturer. *Member:* American Oriental Society. *Awards, honors: Gay Neck: The Story of a Pigeon,* 1927, and *Ghond, the Hunter,* 1928, were both selected as one of the American Institute of Graphic Arts fifty books of the year; Newbery Medal, 1928, for *Gay Neck: The Story of a Pigeon.*

WRITINGS—All fiction for children; all published by Dutton: *Kari, the Elephant* (illustrated by J. E. Allen), 1922, reprinted, 1967; *Jungle Beasts and Men* (illustrated by J. E. Allen), 1923; *Hari, the Jungle Lad* (illustrated by Morgan Stinemetz), 1924, reprinted, 1956; *Gay Neck: The Story of a Pigeon* (illustrated by Boris Artzybasheff), 1927, reprinted, 1968; *Ghond, the*

Hunter (illustrated by B. Artzybasheff), 1928, reprinted, 1962; *The Chief of the Herd* (illustrated by Mahlon Blaine), 1929; *Hindu Fables: For Little Children* (illustrated by Kurt Wiese), 1929; *Rama, the Hero of India: Valmiki's "Ramayana" Done into a Short English Version* (illustrated by Edgar Parin d'Aulaire), 1930; *Bunny, Hound and Clown* (illustrated by K. Wiese), 1931; *The Master Monkey* (illustrated by Florence Weber), 1932; *Fierce-Face: The Story of a Tiger* (illustrated by Dorothy P. Lathrop), 1936.

Adults; all nonfiction, except as noted; all published by Dutton, except as noted: *Rajani: Songs of the Night* (poetry), Paul Elder, 1916; *Sandhya: Songs of Twilight* (poetry), Paul Elder, 1917; *Caste and Outcast* (autobiography), 1923; *My Brother's Face,* 1924; *The Face of Silence,* 1926, reprinted, Servire (Los Angeles), 1973; *The Secret Listeners of the East,* 1926; *A Son of Mother India Answers,* 1928; (translator) *Devotional Passages from the Hindu Bible,* 1929; *Visit India with Me,* 1929; *Disillusioned India,* 1930; (editor and translator) *The Song of God: Translation of the Bhagavadgita,* 1931; *Daily Meditation; or, The Practice of Repose,* 1933; *The Path of Prayer,* 1934; (translator) Nicol Macnicol, editor, *Hindu Scriptures: Hymns from the Rigveda, Five Upanishads, the Bhagavadgita,* 1938; (contributor) *What Is Civilization?,* introduction by Hendrik

"What was my amazement to see a room full of grey dwarf-like figures." ■ (From *Hari, the Jungle Lad* by Dhan Gopal Mukerji. Illustrated by Morgan Stinemetz.)

Van Loon, Books for Libraries, 1968.

Plays: (Adapter and translator) Girish C. Ghose, *Chintamini: A Symbolic Drama*, R. G. Badger, 1914; *Layla-Manju*, Paul Elder, 1916; ''The Judgment of Indra,'' published in *Drama*, edited by A. D. Dickinson, Doubleday, 1922.

ADAPTATIONS—Filmstrips: ''Gay Neck: The Story of a Pigeon'' (with teacher's notes), Miller-Brody, 1973.

SIDELIGHTS: **July 6, 1890.** Born near Calcutta, India. In a small village near the edge of the Indian jungle, Mukerji lived with his grandfather, father, mother, and seven older brothers and sisters. They were Brahmins, the priest caste of India, who had charge of the temple. As a small boy, therefore, Mukerji learned to perform Indian rituals. ''I am a Hindu of Brahmin parentage, and I was born and brought up in a small village near Calcutta. Though the early part of my life was much like that of other children of my caste, I find that in attempting to describe it to English readers, I am at once in a dilemma. The narrative, slight as it is, seems to require continual interruption in order to explain the real meaning of the simple incidents of my childhood and youth—simple, that is, in the Hindu's experience. . . .

''As I look into the past and try to recover my earliest impression, I remember that the most vivid experience of my childhood was the terrific power of faces. From the day consciousness dawned upon me, I saw faces, faces everywhere, and I always noticed the eyes. It was as if the whole Hindu race lived in its eyes. As I grew up, wherever I went on all my pilgrimages and travels, I continued to feel the wonder of faces, the face of nature, the faces of animals, the faces of people. There was a vast procession of ideals and desires moving before me as I watched these faces and behind each I caught the gleam of a thought and began to form an idea of the person himself.

''The jungle is the next thing that I remember. Our house was situated at the edge of the forest not far from the town. In the evenings, after the lights were out we used to sit by the open window looking towards the forest. I remember one evening especially; though I must have been a very little child at the time. I was gazing into the darkness outside when I saw something that appeared to me like a huge jeweled hand. This hand, with rings gleaming on all its fingers, was slowly coming toward me out of the jungle. The movement of the hand in the darkness was intense and terrifying. I cried with fright, and my mother, putting her arms about me, said: 'Fear not, little son. Those are only the eyes of the foxes and jackals and hundreds of other small jungle dwellers coming and going about their business.' I was overawed by the fierce power of life, and I watched in silence the tremendous black masses of dark trees with the emptiness gleaming all around them, and the innumerable fire-flies flitting about. . . .

''. . . As we were Brahmins, we had charge of the village temple which had been in the family for generations. I was the youngest, and of an enquiring turn of mind, I imagine, for my

A challenge to men by the gods of Swarga whose chief was Indra. ■ (From *Ghond, the Hunter* by Dhan Gopal Mukerji. Illustrated by Boris Artzybasheff.)

grandfather used to say I asked more questions than any other child he had ever known. Perhaps that is why I observed and remember many things that to the average Hindu child might be so usual in daily life as to be unconsidered and forgotten.

"I remember every hour of our ritual, and there is a ritual for every hour of the day in India; the ritual peculiar to Brahmin households like ours, and the ritual of the peasant and the workman. The members of my family, the townspeople, the laborers in the field, the many beggars—each followed an intricate and age-old pattern of life, from sudden sunrise, through fervid noon, to the heavy fall of the night and silence. . . .

"In our household, my mother was the first one to rise in the mornings. She got up about five and would always sit and meditate for half an hour so as not to disturb the morning silence. In India a woman is a goddess and must be ready at all times to be worshipped. When we children were up, we would go to her and bow before her and remove the dust from her feet. Every morning I would salute my mother and my father. . . .

"My mother was a very simple woman. She did not know how to read and write. This will seem strange to western readers, but it is in accordance with the traditional education of a lady in India, and my mother being of the old school, considered that anyone who could count beyond a hundred was too forward to be a lady. . . .

"My mother was a busy woman, for in India it is the mother who takes entire charge of the children and their education until they are ten or twelve years old. There were eight of us, and a large household to run, and my mother never spent less than three hours a day in prayer and meditation. Yet her life and personality were so quiet, her duties were conducted so softly and with so much gentleness, that as I look back it seems to me as though it must have been tranquillity and not energy that was the motive power in our home. My mother could cook and did so, for cooking is a sacramental act and is part of the day's religious ritual. At midday she would meditate and no one was allowed to disturb her, but in the afternoon she would recite to us from memory parts of the epics, the old religious tales of India. She had been taught by her mother, and her mother by *her* mother, and so on back for generations. We would listen for about half an hour at a time and then repeat what we had heard. Sometimes she would have two of us chant the lines, sometimes one at a time.

"I gradually absorbed their inner meaning, and when I grew older, the memory of my mother's face as she recited, and the intent yet remote expression of her dark eyes seemed to impress upon me the sense of their spiritual import. We have few books in India, so each mother has to pass on the legends by word of mouth to her child, and he memorizes them, usually before fourteen years of age. By that time he has a thoroughly trained memory and this is the chief part of his early education." [Dhan Gopal Mukerji, *Caste and Outcast*, Dutton, 1923.[1]]

1900. "When I was about ten years old, my father sent me to a Scotch Presbyterian school. . . . When my training was over, I brought a picture of Christ to my mother while she was meditating and asked: 'Why do you meditate in the presence of a false God? This is the real God I have found.'

"She said, 'I have heard of Him from others. He has no quarrel with my God. He is one of my Gods. He is another name.'

"We pushed the image of Vishnu to one side, put the picture of Christ in the sacred niche in the wall and burned incense

Monkey mothers gave birth to sons so luminous that they shamed the sun. ■ (From *The Master Monkey* by Dhan Gopal Mukerji. Illustrated by Florence Weber.)

and meditated before Him. My mother said, 'He who brings about a quarrel between God and God is a more dangerous sinner than he who causes war between man and man. God is one. We have given Him many names. Why should we quarrel about names?'

"An ordinary Indian boy, who was not born like myself into the priest caste, would have gone to an Indian or an English government school. There are certain schools where he could learn to read and write, but not many. There are old Indian schools where he would have studied the Scriptures. I attended school about ten years altogether, as I remember, but in order to be a good Brahmin your studies never stop. You learn even from the Christian saints.'"[1]

1904. Initiated into the priesthood. Before assuming his duties in the village temple, Mukerji made a two-year pilgrimage through India, begging from town to town. "The time came when I was to become a priest. I was asked whether I wanted to be one. At the age of thirteen or fourteen to be a man and bless others is rather an alluring idea, so of course I said yes; I consented at once.

"On the day of my initiation my mother took me to the river bank. We went out to where the dead were being cremated. The lights of the fires seemed to bite the shoulders of the Ganges. I said, 'I don't like it.'

"'But remember there is no death!' she answered. 'We throw off the body as man throws off worn-out garments for new ones. So does the soul rise out of the worn-out body.'

"I asked her, 'Why do you tell me this?'

"She replied, 'How could I have given you life, if I could not explain death?'

"After I had bathed in the Ganges, we went home together, and I went in to my initiation.

"They took me out, shaved my head, gave me an ochre-colored cloth to put on. I came in again. My mother was gone. Only the priests and my father were standing there. . . .

"I took my vow. Then he [the high priest] said the last thing, 'Your parents are dead. Your relatives are dead. You are dead. Only one thing remains—and that is your vagrancy for eternity. Go forth!'

"So it was over. I had renounced the world and entered upon my two-year period of beggary. You cannot be a priest if you do not know how people live, and the best way to find out about people is to beg from them. So there is a law of the priesthood that before officiating in the temple, you must go begging from door to door. But at fourteen, to be turned loose in the world—even after forswearing it, makes one feel rather forlorn. I did not know where to go. So with the child's instinct still strong within me, I went back to my mother's house, knowing that here I would not be refused, and said, 'Give alms to the beggar!' My mother came out with a bowl in her hands and said, "My lord, here is your rice.' She bowed her face to the ground. Before that, every morning, we used to take the dust from her feet; this was the first time she had tried to take the dust from mine.

"I went to the river's edge, made a fire with some charcoal and a few sticks and boiled the rice. I was about to eat it when a beggar came along and said, 'Brother, I have nothing to eat.' At fourteen there is a limit to unselfishness, yet I had to give him the rice and sit there and wait until he was satisfied before I could have any of it myself. I decided that it took even more than the tremendous words of the ceremonial through which I had just passed to enable one to abandon earthly considerations. Then I went to the river bank and wandered through the town and again sat by the river thinking.

"I had some sort of plan for my wanderings, and as I wanted to see Benares and the hills, I joined two or three other young priests who were going in that direction. We traveled by train to Benares. It is older than any other Indian living city today, at least six hundred years older then Rome, and it has no history. When I reached Benares, I realised that the very heart of India was there; I found stone upon stone telling of the ages that had gone before, but leaving the events unrecorded; I found the ruins of a Hindu temple many layers down, and on this a Mohammedan mosque and above this a Buddhist temple.''[1]

When his pilgrimage was completed, Mukerji assumed his priestly duties. "The priest begins the day by opening the temple. He blows the conch, opens the doors, and people come and sit in silence for a few minutes. (Religion in India, as in every other country, is kept up by women, and all the women of the community come in the early morning and sit still in the temple. The priest has to sit still with them to set the example of quiet, and that is hard work!)

"At seven o'clock the children bring flowers with which he decorates the temple, then he goes downstairs and into the kitchen, where there are many servants waiting. After consulting a clerk he gives them the orders for the day: 'I think we may expect fifty poor people by noon, so prepare dinner for fifty.' There is an income for this charity, as all temples are endowed, and the clerk keeps the account if the temple is a large one, otherwise the priest does. The temple remains open all the time and the people come and go and the children play on the stairs.

"Every temple is a theatre, as it used to be in Europe in the middle ages. The priest must give thirteen plays in twelve months. He has to select strolling players as they happen to pass through the town for these performances, which are more or less derived from the epics. The plays are free to all and sometimes two thousand people will come to see them. The temple pays the players, for a special fund from the endowment is set aside for that purpose. When a play is over, the priest says, 'O assembled people, do not talk: go home and meditate and make it part of yourselves!'

"The priest has to do all this; but it is merely routine work. Although he seems to be occupied with holy things, in reality he has no time for God. His duty is that malicious thing, doing good, which is enough to dry up anybody. Very few priests recognize that God has a sense of humor; that is why most of them continue to be priests. Half of them never do anything but sit down to this routine: they are spiritual vultures. But now and then one of them, when he is about forty, renounces the world and goes away from it all.

"When I came back from my pilgrimage I went into the temple, as I have said, and did this routine work. I used to marry young people, take care of the sick and read the epics. Besides performing all these duties, while I was running the temple, I went to the Christian school, and studied the New Testament carefully. It was hardly a year before I gave up being a priest, because I realized that I was not in my right place.

"This may seem very strange to a Westerner after all I had experienced, but to a Hindu it was not strange. A Brahmin boy often fulfills the duties of a priest for a time, but if he finds it is not his vocation he is expected to resign and to seek the Lord in other ways. We think the end is holiness, not a profession. I was very young—hardly sixteen—and I was impelled by an urge which I did not myself fully understand at the time. All I knew was, that after seeing the vast spaces of India, I could not stick to my school, nor could I see myself continuing to sit in a temple giving blessings to people who could do without them.

"Before leaving home again, however, I determined to go on studying for a time and to see what knowledge would do for me. But I only confused myself. I could not find contentment and I soon made up my mind that books were not worth while, and, restless and dissatisfied, I threw them aside and determined to see life from a totally different angle. With the longing for the hills, of which I have spoken, strong within me, I cast about for some occupation that would take me back to them and I hit upon shawl trading. This had the added advantage of the appeal, or the excuse, of usefulness to my family, who made no objection to my going. Fortunately for me, Indian life gives ample opportunity to an unquiet spirit, and, as I have said, there is nothing in our thought or our tradition to bind a restless young man in search of truth to one place or occupation. The significance of the vows I had taken was spiritual and the profession of the priesthood incidental. . . .''[1]

1908. Entered the University of Calcutta, but remained for only

The more they fought, the more fire fell from their beaks. ■ (From *Gay-Neck: The Story of a Pigeon* by Dhan Gopal Mukerji. Illustrated by Boris Artzybasheff.)

a year. "... I was hard at my studies in the University of Calcutta and struggling against the boredom with which my teacher inspired me. Study could not help me, my soul still hungered for space, for some unattainable good that remained unrealized except as a continual goad to my eager, unsatisfied spirit."[1]

Left the university the following year and went to Japan to study engineering. "... When I was offered a chance to go to Japan to study industrial machinery in order to learn Western scientific methods of production, I did not hesitate. We were given a traveling scholarship. My mother bade me go and said, characteristically, 'Go, my son, and study the inner experience of time and make it your own...'

"I was soon to find that my mother had as usual struck to the heart of the matter, and how hard it was to reconcile an alien evolution with the oriental's innate conception of the meaning of time. The West believes in time, in the time process, and consequently, in cause and effect, then in results, then in good and evil. But the East begins by denying the fundamental reality of time, which necessarily changes for us the relative importance of all that results from time. This is the essential difference between the East and the West."[1]

1910. At the age of twenty, emigrated to the United States, which became his adopted country. "Finally I set forth again

to meet this most tremendous change of all, having broken the ties of my country, my past and my caste. For alien though I found Japan to be, it was still an oriental country, but now I was to reach a place where I could keep none of my traditions. Some of this I understood, but I had no conception of the changes that were to come.

"The first American I met on landing was a man very quaintly dressed (later on I learned he was wearing 'overalls'), who had been sent to me to take care of my trunk. I gave him my trunk, which he threw from the deck of the ship down to the wharf— a matter of some eight or ten feet. Not knowing enough colloquial English, I quoted to him the magnificent lines of Milton: 'Him the Almighty Power hurled headlong flaming from the ethereal sky.' The expressman looked at me very quizzically and exclaimed: 'Cut it out! You're too fresh!' This was my initiation into America."[1]

Spent his last dollar toward an entrance fee at the University of California. "... I could not go on exchanging Indian art for American food and so I sought out a Hindu student, who told me to go and get a job. Apparently he had lived in America a very long time. I asked him what kind of a job. He said, 'Dishwashing, taking care of the house—anything. Go and ring the bell of every house until you find a job.' So I went on ringing door bell after door bell. From each opening door came a 'No thank you,' in tones running the whole scale from the

(From the animated filmstrip "Gay-Neck: The Story of a Pigeon," based on the book by Dhan Gopal Mukerji. Produced by Miller-Brody Productions, 1973.)

snarl of a tiger to the smile of a lady.

"But at last I reached a house where they asked, 'What can you do?'

"'Anything,' I said—'washing dishes, taking care of the house.'

"'Can you begin tomorrow?' the lady asked me.

"I replied that I could, but I must first find lodging for the night. 'May I come to you?' I politely inquired.

"In a very businesslike way she replied, 'All right. Your room will be ready in the back yard.'

"However, this employment did not last long. By noon time a huge pile of dishes had accumulated in the kitchen to be washed and my employer said to me during lunch, 'Perhaps you want to wait until your lunch is over before washing the dishes.' I hastily assented and began eating lunch. After lunch

I piled up more dishes in the sink, put on my coat, and went out for a walk in the beautiful sunshine. When I returned from my walk, my employer sternly demanded, 'Why aren't the dishes done?'

"'I said, 'How do you wash them?'

"'Don't you know?' she asked in astonishment.

"I said, 'No.'

"'But,' she said, 'you took the job on the understanding that you would wash dishes.'

"'I will wash dishes if you will show me how,' I replied.

"Then in great dudgeon she said, 'Will you please look for another place tomorrow?'

"'What place?' I replied.

''She answered, 'I mean you are fired.'

''I asked again, 'What is ''fired.''' And I was told, 'In good English, you are discharged!' 'But,' she added with a smile, 'you can stay here tonight.'

''And so I sat in the kitchen chair and watched her wash the dishes. I watched her very carefully to see what steps led up to the washing and wiping of dishes, deciding to make use of my lesson in my next place.

''I was so chagrined at having lost my place that I made up my mind not to accept the invitation to spend another night in the house of my defeat but to set out without more delay in search of another job. So the same ringing of bells and the same snarls and barks from different doors began again for me.''[1]

During his college years, Mukerji managed to support himself with odd jobs other than washing dishes, such as working in fields and even carrying a soapbox for a group of anarchists.

1914. Received a Ph.B. in metaphysics from Leland Stanford University. ''. . . I got my degree, gave a course of lectures on comparative literature in a college and later began to make lecture tours which brought me into contact with many other kinds of Americans.

''I found the United States divided into four psychological groups; the East, the Middle West; the South; and the Pacific Coast. The first section, the East, is in direct touch with Europe and is more like Europe than it is like the rest of America. The second has very little contact with any great external influence. So its culture is more provincial and more indigenous. The South is exremely difficult to make clear. It might seem open to the influence of the Africans, yet that is not the case. It has no great indigenous element. It is full of the eighteenth century European conservatism. But if the climate can be trusted, the Southern men and women will build a tropical culture—sinister and beautiful.

''As regards the Pacific Coast, it cannot resist the culture of Asia, as the East cannot be impervious to Europe. Oriental decorations along with Oriental aloofness are becoming discernible elements. In the homes of the Pacific Coast I have found that the people are aloof. They build a Chinese wall of pride around themselves. On the Pacific Coast one also finds something Spanish, not altogether European, but rather Africo-Saracenic in character.

''Suppose that the forces of race and culture that I have mentioned go on permeating the whole continent. Then will it be too much to say that in five hundred years America will have a culture unique, magnificent and overpowering? America's tradition is her future. A Hindu, who bears the weight of forty centuries of tradition, is drawn by no country as by America. Europe cannot attract a Hindu. It is not old enough to be benign, nor young enough to be blessed. There is nothing outside of Greece that goes to the heart of a Hindu. There is nothing in Europe that matches the sky hunger of the Himalayas and the fierce fatality of life in the jungles. India has space so acrid with loneliness that the greater part of Europe, even Russia, is sweet by comparison, yet Europe is not sweet enough. So a Hindu, who wants to find a complete antithesis to his race and culture, had better avoid Europe and come straight to America.''[1]

1918. Married Ethel Ray Dugan. The couple had one son, Dhan Gopal II.

1923. Published first book, *Kari the Elephant*. The jungle life that Mukerji knew as a child in India became the basis for most of his books.

1928. Awarded the Newbery Medal for *Gay Neck: The Story of a Pigeon*. About the book, Mukerji remarked: ''Most of it is a record of my experience with about forty pigeons and their leader. Alas, as I went on writing the book I had to go beyond my experiences, and had to draw upon those of the trainers of army pigeons. Anyway, the message implicit in the book is that man and the winged animals are brothers. [Dhan Mukerji, ''Fruits from the Living Tree,'' *Newbery Medal Books: 1922-1955,* edited by Bertha Mahony Miller and Elinor Whitney Field, Horn Book, 1955.[2]]

Although *Gay Neck* was awarded the Newbery Medal for ''distinguished contribution to children's literature,'' Mukerji considered his book *Ghond the Hunter* his most valuable contribution to that genre. ''I have sought to render the inmost things of Hindu life into English. It has been the ambition of my life to put into the hands of American boys and girls about sixteen years old a document that will portray the living soul of a Hindu boy. I hope boys and girls between sixteen and eighteen can be persuaded to read *Ghond the Hunter*.''[2]

Among his numerous books, *Hindu Fables* was Mukerji's favorite book. ''The book I love most, and have dedicated to my mother, is *Hindu Fables,* more than one of which I heard from her own lips. Because it is the simplest of my works I dedicated it to her memory.

''I am using the word 'memory' as a matter of form; for to my own conviction her death could not have and has not interrupted her existence.

Dhan Gopal Mukerji in 1936.

"The little *Hindu Fables* I told in English to my mother's grandson who was born in America. My boy heard them again and again until he was seven. By that time they had become clear enough to deserve being set down in writing.

"This transcribing Hindu cradle-tales from Indian folk-speech into modern English is an arduous task, if not an insoluble problem. First of all, today there is hardly any current folk-speech in the English language outside of slang. In the time of Queen Elizabeth, the folk-language of Britain must have been wonderful. India, who still lingers in the Seventeenth Century, has a marvellous common-speech. If in manufacture the English-speaking world has moved on from the hand-loom to industrialism, in the matter of storytelling it has passed from folk-lore to slang and realistic fiction.

"On the contrary, in Hindusthan we are still trying to preserve the spinning wheel, and folk-utterance. Now, as a translator of my people's matchless speech I had a hard time discovering in the English of our Twentieth Century folk an idiom picturesque and direct enough to convey the very simple art of the Orient. Slang is too direct. The so-called picturesque English prevalent in the Senate and the Congress is too involved. At last, worried almost to despair, I tried to invent an arrangement of words that would translate at least a bulk of the grace and directness of my native tongue. My solution of this problem has been the chief preoccupation of all my works.

"There was another thing that I had in mind, too: namely, to convey the wisdom of life that Indians are taught by parents through folk-tales. You will notice in my *Fables* two kinds of morals stressed. The first is a useful everyday business moral, and the second is the transcendental morality through which men find God. The former stresses the science of surviving in our struggle against the unfair bully and the brute. The latter insists that after we have overcome a conscienceless adversary we must eliminate all materialism from our lives and make an effort to find God.

"What has been made explicit in the *Fables* remains implicit in all the other books. In every one of my books hides a lesson."[2]

". . . It is my constant wish that the boys and girls of America should benefit from the ancient lores of India. . . . I hold that until a nation appreciates the common culture of another nation it will not be able to understand the value of international peace. We need peace between nations, because peace alone can augment the forces of true culture. If we know early in life how good our neighbor's culture can be, we shall think twice before we decide to destroy it by warfare. Of the many agencies working for international amity, appreciation of the cultures of other races is a very potent one. And this appreciation should be made into an art and a habit of the young of every land."[1]

July 14, 1936. Hanged himself in his New York City apartment after a six-month nervous breakdown. "My religion teaches and guarantees that birth and death are garments put on by the soul. The soul never dies."[2]

FOR MORE INFORMATION SEE: Dhan Gopal Mukerji, *Caste and Outcast* (autobiography), Dutton, 1923; Stanley J. Kunitz and Howard Haycraft, editors, *The Junior Book of Authors,* H. W. Wilson, 1934; Bertha Mahony Miller and Elinor Whitney Field, editors, *Newbery Medal Books: 1922-1955,* Horn Book, 1955; D. L. Kirkpatrick, editor, *Twentieth-Century Children's Writers,* St. Martin's, 1978. Obituaries: *New York Times,* July 15, 1936; *Publishers Weekly,* July 25, 1936; *Wilson Library Bulletin,* September, 1936.

NAKATANI, Chiyoko   1930-

BRIEF ENTRY: Born January 16, 1930, in Tokyo, Japan. Nakatani received her B.A. from Tokyo National University of Fine Arts in 1952. An internationally known author and illustrator of books for children, she was described by *Publishers Weekly* as an artist "noted for her delicate but far from fragile touch." Nakatani has written and illustrated over a dozen picture books, many of which have been translated from Japanese into English. In a review of *Fumio and the Dolphins* (World Publishing, 1970), *Horn Book* observed: "Her evocative paintings . . . have a strong atmosphere, luminous in color and lively in every scene of action." The same magazine praised her illustrations in *My Teddy Bear* (Crowell, 1976), finding them "imbued with guileless warmth, simplicity, and love. . . ." Nakatani's other translated works include: *The Day Chiro Was Lost* (World Publishing, 1969), *The Zoo in My Garden* (Crowell, 1973), *My Animal Friends* (Bodley Head, 1979), and *Feeding Babies* (Bodley Head, 1981). She has also provided illustrations for more than twenty books written by others, like *The Lion and the Bird's Nest* by Eriko Kishida, *The Animals' Lullaby* by Trude Alberti, and *The Little Old Lady in the Strawberry Patch* by Mutsuko Watari.

FOR MORE INFORMATION SEE: Illustrators of Children's Books: 1967-1976, Horn Book, 1978; *Contemporary Authors,* Volumes 77-80, Gale, 1979; *International Authors and Writers Who's Who,* 9th edition, International Biographical Centre, 1982.

NEWSOM, Carol   1948-

PERSONAL: Born August 15, 1948, in Fort Worth, Tex.; daughter of Elvin (an engineer) and Beth (Bicknell) Bobo;

CAROL NEWSOM

married Tom Newsom (an illustrator), April 4, 1969; children: Andy, Philip. *Education:* Art Center College of Design, Los Angeles, Calif., B.F.A., 1972. *Religion:* Church of Christ. *Home and office:* 7713 Red Rock Cir., Larkspur, Colo. 80118. *Agent:* Dily S. Evans, 40 Park Ave., New York, N.Y. 10016.

CAREER: Free-lance illustrator, 1972—.

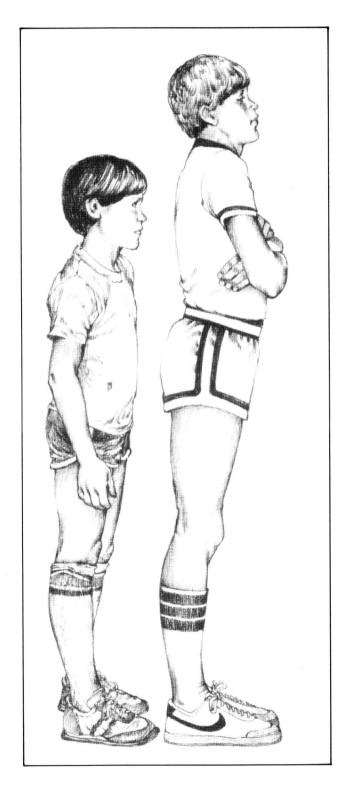

Tryouts were awful. ▪ (From *When the Boys Ran the House* by Joan Carris. Illustrated by Carol Newsom.)

ILLUSTRATOR: Joan Carris, *When the Boys Ran the House,* Lippincott, 1982; Edward Lear, *An Edward Lear Alphabet,* Lothrop, 1983; Stephen Roos, *The Terrible Truth: Secrets of a Sixth Grader,* Delacorte, 1983; Carol Farley, *The Mystery of the Fiery Message,* Avon, 1983; S. Roos, *My Horrible Secret,* Delacorte, 1983; Eve Bunting, *Karen Kepplewhite Is the World's Best Kisser,* Clarion, 1983; Marcia Leonard, *Little Owl Leaves the Nest,* Bantam, 1984; J. Carris, *Pets, Vets, and Marty Howard,* Harper, 1984; Barbara Douglass, *The Great Town and Country Bicycle Balloon Chase,* Lothrop, 1984; S. Roos, *My Secret Admirer,* Delacorte, 1984. Also illustrator of a nursery rhyme book for Avon Products.

WORK IN PROGRESS: Illustrations for: *Owl in the Garden* and *Mother Goose Cats* for Lothrop; *Me, My Goat, and My Sister's Wedding* for Clarion; *Why Me* for Little, Brown; *Little Monkey Sleeps Over* for Bantam; *My War with Mrs. Galloway* for Viking.

SIDELIGHTS: "I'm an illustrator because I love to paint and draw. Since I would rather paint and draw than anything else, it's natural that I wanted to make my living at it. My favorite mediums are watercolor and designer's colors."

OGILVIE, Elisabeth May   1917-

PERSONAL: Born May 20, 1917, in Boston, Mass.; daughter of Frank Everett (in insurance) and Maude (a teacher; maiden name, Coates) Ogilvie. *Education:* Attended public schools in Massachusetts. *Politics:* Republican. *Religion:* Baptist. *Home address:* Gay's Island, Pleasant Point, Me. 04563. *Agent:* A. Watkins, Inc., 77 Park Ave., New York, N.Y. 10016.

CAREER: Writer. *Member:* Authors Guild, Mystery Writers of America, Foster Parents' Plan, Nature Conservancy. *Awards, honors:* New England Press Association fiction award, 1945, for *Storm Tide;* North-East Woman's Press Association Award for fiction, 1946, for *Storm Tide.*

WRITINGS—All published by McGraw, except as noted: *High Tide at Noon,* Crowell, 1944, reprinted, Avon, 1975; *Storm Tide,* Crowell, 1945, reprinted, Avon, 1975; *The Ebbing Tide,* Crowell, 1947, reprinted, Avon, 1976; *Honeymoon* (based on story by Vicki Baum), Bartholomew House, 1947; *Rowan Head,* Whittlesey House, 1949; *My World Is an Island* (personal account; illustrated by Paul Galdone), Whittlesey House, 1950; *The Dawning of the Day,* 1954; *Whistle for a Wind: Maine, 1820* (illustrated by Charles H. Geer), Scribner, 1954; *Blueberry Summer* (juvenile; illustrated by Algot Stenbery; Junior Literary Guild selection), Whittlesey House, 1956; *No Evil Angel,* 1956; *The Fabulous Year* (juvenile), Whittlesey House, 1958; *How Wide the Heart* (juvenile), Whittlesey House, 1959, published as *A Steady Kind of Love,* Scholastic Book Services, 1979; *The Witch Door,* 1959.

The Young Islanders (juvenile; illustrated by Robert Henneberger), Whittlesey House, 1960; *Becky's Island,* Whittlesey House, 1961; *Call Home the Heart,* 1962; *Turn Around Twice,* Whittlesey House, 1962; *The Ceiling of Amber* (juvenile), 1964, published as *Until the End of Summer,* Scholastic Book Services, 1981; *There May Be Heaven,* 1964; *Masquerade at Sea House,* 1965; *The Seasons Hereafter,* 1966; *The Pigeon Pair* (juvenile), 1967; *Waters on a Starry Night,* 1968; *Bellwood,* 1969; *Come Aboard and Bring Your Dory* (juvenile), 1969;

ELISABETH MAY OGILVIE

The Face of Innocence, 1970; *A Theme for Reason,* 1970; *Weep and Know Why,* 1972; *Strawberries in the Sea,* 1973; *Image of a Lover,* 1974; *Where the Lost Aprils Are,* 1975; *The Dreaming Swimmer,* 1976; *An Answer in the Tide,* 1978; *A Dancer in Yellow,* 1979; *The Devil in Tartan,* 1980; *Beautiful Girl,* Scholastic Book Services, 1980; *The Silent Ones,* 1981; *Too Young to Know,* Scholastic Book Services, 1982; *A Forgotton Girl,* Scholastic Book Services, 1982; *The Road to Nowhere,* 1983; *Jennie about to Be,* 1984; *My Summer Love,* Scholastic Book Services, 1985.

Contributor of short stories to magazines, including *Woman's Day.*

WORK IN PROGRESS: A sequel to *Jennie about to Be;* book about Bennetts's Island.

SIDELIGHTS: ''I began writing when I was quite small, because I enjoyed making up stories as much as reading them. One of my best memories concerns the second grade, when the teacher used to pass out pictures cut from magazines for us to write stories about.

''I made up stories to put myself to sleep, and to help me through long boring tasks, and during my walks to and from school. I used to describe what I was doing and seeing as if I were talking about somebody else. 'Elisabeth was walking along Safford Street on one beautiful spring day when she happened to see. . . .' Well, it could be anything that occurred to my imagination, and I'd take off from there.

''But the decision to become a writer for a living didn't come until I was fifteen and saw my work in print in the school

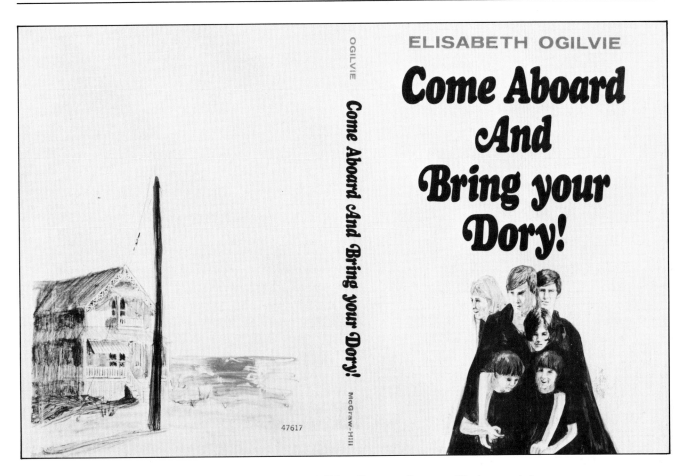

The dusk was coming in like the tide and filling Cameron Cove . . . . The house windows were yellow rectangles against the velvet shadow of the woods. ■ (Jacket illustration by Rob Howard from *Come Aboard and Bring Your Dory!* by Elisabeth Ogilvie.)

magazine. By then I was writing long and complicated stories for my own pleasure. Another student who was a gifted artist used to illustrate them. I had favorite writers whom I imitated, and they were always on the adult side of the public library. This earnest imitation was the best training I could have possibly had, because I tried so hard.

"I couldn't go to college but I had an excellent foundation in English and in writing through the English department of my high school. It was tough, it was demanding, and everyone, no matter what course, was expected to do a good deal of writing—no mercy was shown for poor spelling and punctuation. A university extension course, eight weeks long, started me thinking professionally and commercially. My first professional sale was a short story sold when I was nineteen.

"My first book, *High Tide at Noon* began a saga of some lobstermen's families on an island twenty-five miles off the Maine coast, an island which my family knew very well. I have continued to write books about these people, and they are in some of my juvenile novels as well. I wrote my first young adult novel at the request of a publisher, and it was *Whistle for a Wind,* a historical novel with a Maine background. In fact I used as a hero, a boy who would become the ancestor of my Bennetts of Bennetts's Island.

"Since then I've written quite a few books for younger readers and I've enjoyed this, and the letters I get from the readers a great deal. Lately I have been writing for Scholastic, as well as turning out my adult books, many of which are favorites of teenagers who have gone beyond the juvenile classification."

FOR MORE INFORMATION SEE: Book Week, April 9, 1944; *Weekly Book Review,* April 16, 1944; *New York Times,* April 16, 1944; *Wilson Library Bulletin,* September, 1951; Harry R. Warfel, *American Novelists of Today,* American Book, 1951; Stanley J. Kunitz, *Twentieth-Century Authors,* first supplement, H. W. Wilson, 1955; *Christian Science Monitor,* May 10, 1956; *New York Times Book Review,* Part 2, May 7, 1967; Martha E. Ward and Dorothy A. Marquardt, *Authors of Books for Young People,* Scarecrow Press, 1967.

ORCZY, Emmuska, Baroness   1865-1947

PERSONAL: Surname pronounced "*Or*-see." Full given name cited as Emma Magdalena Rosalia Maria Josefa Barbara; born September 23, 1865, in Tarna-Örs, Hungary; died November 12, 1947, in London, England; daughter of Baron Felix (a composer and conductor) and Countess Emma (Wass) Orczy; married John Montagu Barstow (an artist), 1894; children: John Montagu Orczy. *Education:* Attended West London School of Art and Heatherley School of Art. *Religion:* Church of England. *Residence:* Monte Carlo, France.

BARONESS EMMUSKA ORCZY

CAREER: Author, illustrator, translator, and editor. Best known for her novel *The Scarlet Pimpernel,* 1905, she was also the author of numerous romantic novels and short stories. *Exhibitions:* Her paintings appeared at the Royal Academy, London, England. *Wartime service:* Relief work in Monte Carlo, World War II.

WRITINGS—Of interest to young people: (Translator and editor) *The Enchanted Cat,* Dean & Son, 1895; (translator and editor) *Fairyland's Beauty: Two Fairy Tales,* Dean & Son, 1895; (translator and editor), *Uletka and the White Lizard,* Dean & Son, 1895; (translator and editor with husband, Montagu Barstow) *Old Hungarian Folk Tales,* Wolf, 1895; (adapter with Barstow) *Old Hungarian Fairy Tales* (self-illustrated with Barstow), Dean & Son, 1895, reprinted, Dover, 1969; *The Scarlet Pimpernel,* Putnam, 1905, 62nd edition, Hodder & Stoughton, 1935, reissued, G. K. Hall, 1980 [other editions include those illustrated by Leo Bates, Brockhampton Press, 1951; Richard Kennedy, Brockhampton Press, 1961; and John Falter, Macmillan, 1964]; *Beau Brocade: A Romance* (illustrated by Clarence F. Underwood), Lippincott, 1907, reprinted, Lightyear Press, 1981.

Novels; all published by George H. Doran, except as indicated: *The Emperor's Candlesticks: A Romance,* Pearson, 1899, C. H. Doscher, 1908, reissued, Lightyear Press, 1976 [another edition illustrated by H. M. Brock, Greening (London), 1909]; *By the Gods Beloved,* Greening, 1905, published as *The Beloved of the Gods: A Romance,* Knickerbocker Press (New York), 1905, and *The Gates of Kamt,* Dodd, 1907, reprinted,

White Lion Publishers, 1977; *A Son of the People: A Romance of the Hungarian Plains,* Putnam, 1906; *I Will Repay: A Romance,* Lippincott, 1906, abridged edition, edited by L.R.H. Chapman and L. Robinson, University of London Press, 1938 [another edition illustrated by Bates, Brockhampton Press, 1950]; *In Mary's Reign,* Cupples & Leon, 1907; *The Tangled Skein,* Greening, 1907; *The Elusive Pimpernel,* Dodd, 1908, reissued, Lightyear Press, 1976; *The Nest of the Sparrowhawk: A Romance of the XVIIth Century,* F. A. Stokes, 1909.

Petticoat Rule, 1910 (published in England as *Petticoat Government,* Hutchinson, 1910); *The Heart of a Woman,* 1911 (published in England as *A True Woman,* Hutchinson, 1911); *Meadowsweet,* 1912; *Fire in Stubble,* Methuen, 1912; *The Noble Rogue: A Cavalier's Romance,* 1912; *Eldorado: An Adventure of the Scarlet Pimpernel,* 1913, abridged edition, Knight Books (Leicester, England), 1971, reprinted, Lightyear Press, 1980; *The Laughing Cavalier,* 1914, reissued, Lightyear Press, 1976; *Unto Caesar,* 1914; *The Bronze Eagle: A Story of the Hundred Days* (originally published in serial form under title "Waterloo"), 1915; *A Bride of the Plains,* 1915; *Leatherface: A Tale of Old Flanders,* 1916, reprinted, Darby, 1982; *Lord Tony's Wife: An Adventure of the Scarlet Pimpernel,* 1917; *A Sheaf of Bluebells,* 1917; *Silver-Leg,* 1918; *Flower o' the Lily: A Romance of Old Cambray,* Hodder & Stoughton, 1918, George H. Doran, 1919; *The League of the Scarlet Pimpernel,* 1919, abridged edition, Cassell, 1968, reprinted, Buccaneer, 1981; *His Majesty's Well-Beloved: An Episode in the Life of Mr. Thomas Betterton As Told by His Friend John Honeywood,* 1919.

The First Sir Percy: An Adventure of the Laughing Cavalier, Hodder & Stoughton, 1920, George H. Doran, 1921; *The Triumph of the Scarlet Pimpernel,* 1922, new edition, Knight Books, 1968, reprinted, Buccaneer, 1983; *Nicolette: A Tale of Old Provence,* 1922; *The Honourable Jim,* 1924; *Pimpernel and Rosemary,* Cassell, 1924, George H. Doran, 1925, reprinted, Buccaneer, 1983; *The Celestial City,* 1926; *Sir Percy Hits Back: An Adventure of the Scarlet Pimpernel,* 1927; *Blue Eyes and Grey,* Hodder & Stoughton, 1928, Doubleday, Doran, 1929; *Marivosa,* Cassell, 1930, Doubleday, Doran, 1931; *The Scarlet Pimpernel* (contains *The Scarlet Pimpernel, I Will Repay, Eldorado,* and *Sir Percy Hits Back*), Hodder & Stoughton, 1930; *A Child of the Revolution,* Doubleday, Doran, 1932; *A Joyous Adventure,* Doubleday, Doran, 1932; *The Way of the Scarlet Pimpernel,* Hodder & Stoughton, 1933, Putnam, 1934, reprinted, Buccaneer, 1983; *A Spy of Napoleon,* Putnam, 1934; *The Uncrowned King: A True Romance of the '60's Now First Put on Record,* Putnam, 1935; *Sir Percy Leads the Band,* Hodder & Stoughton, 1936; *The Divine Folly,* Hodder & Stoughton, 1937; *No Greater Love,* Hodder & Stoughton, 1938; *The Gallant Pimpernel* (contains *Lord Tony's Wife, The Way of the Scarlet Pimpernel, Sir Percy Leads the Band,* and *The Triumph of the Scarlet Pimpernel*), Hodder & Stoughton, 1939; *Mam'selle Guillotine: An Adventure of the Scarlet Pimpernel,* Hodder & Stoughton, 1940; *Pride of Race,* Hodder & Stoughton, 1942; *Will-o'-the Wisp,* Hutchinson, 1947.

Short stories: *The Case of Miss Elliot* (reprinted from *Royal Magazine,* 1901-04), T. Fisher Unwin, 1905, reprinted, Remploy, 1978; *The Old Man in the Corner* (illustrated by H. M. Brock; contains "The Fenchurch Street Mystery," "The Mysterious Death on the Underground Railway," "The Mysterious Death in Percy Street," "The Dublin Mystery," "The Glasgow Mystery," "The Liverpool Mystery," "The Case of Miss Elliot," "The Lisson Grove Mystery," "The Tragedy in Dartmoor Terrace," "The Tremarn Case," "The Murder of Miss Pebmarsh," and "The Affair at the Novelty Theatre"; reprinted from *Royal Magazine,* 1901-05), Greening, 1909, pub-

(From the television movie "The Scarlet Pimpernel," starring Anthony Andrews and Jane Seymour. Based on the novels by Baroness Orczy. First broadcast on CBS-TV, November 9, 1982.)

lished as *The Man in the Corner,* Dodd, 1909, reprinted, Light-year Press, 1980; *Lady Molly of Scotland Yard,* Cassell, 1910, reprinted, International Polygonics, 1981; *The Traitor,* Paget Literary Agency, 1912; *Two Good Patriots,* Paget Literary Agency, 1912; *The Old Scarecrow,* Paget Literary Agency, 1916.

The Man in Grey: Being Episodes of the Chouan Conspiracies in Normandy during the First Empire (contains ''Proem,'' ''Silver-Leg,'' ''The Spaniard,'' ''The Mystery of Marie Vaillant,'' ''The Emeralds of Mademoiselle Philippa,'' ''The Bourbon Prince,'' ''The Mystery of a Woman's Heart,'' ''The League of Knaves,'' ''The Arrow Poison,'' and ''The Last Adventure''), George H. Doran, 1918, reissued, Lythway Press, 1975; (reteller) *Castles in the Air: Being the Adventures of M. Hector Ratichon,* Cassell, 1921, George H. Doran, 1922, reissued, Lythway Press, 1974; *The Old Man in the Corner Unravels the Mystery of the Khaki Tunic,* George H. Doran, 1923; *The Old Man in the Corner Unravels the Mystery of the Russian Prince, and of Dog's Tooth Cliff,* George H. Doran, 1924; *The Old Man in the Corner Unravels the Mystery of the Pearl Necklace and the Tragedy in Bishop's Road,* George H. Doran, 1924; *The Old Man in the Corner Unravels the Mystery of Brudenell Court and the Tytherton Case,* George H. Doran, 1924.

The Old Man in the Corner Unravels the Mystery of the White Carnation and the Montmartre Hat, George H. Doran, 1925; *The Old Man in the Corner Unravels the Mystery of the Fulton Gardens Mystery, and the Moorland Tragedy,* George H. Doran, 1925; *A Question of Temptation,* George H. Doran, 1925; *The Miser of Maida Vale,* George H. Doran, 1925; *Unravelled Knots* (contains ''The Mystery of the Khaki Tunic,'' ''The Mystery of the Ingres Masterpiece,'' ''The Mystery of the Pearl Necklace,'' ''The Mystery of the Russian Prince,'' ''The Mysterious Tragedy in Bishop's Road,'' ''The Mystery of the Dog's Tooth Cliff,'' ''The Tytherton Case,'' ''The Mystery of Brudenell Court,'' ''The Mystery of the White Carnation,'' ''The Mystery of the Montmartre Hat,'' ''The Miser of Maida Vale,'' ''The Fulton Gardens Mystery,'' and ''A Moorland Mystery''), Hutchinson, 1925, George H. Doran, 1926; (compiler and editor) *Skin o' My Tooth: His Memoirs, by His Confidential Clerk,* Doubleday, Doran, 1928; *Adventures of the Scarlet Pimpernel,* Doubleday, Doran, 1929, reprinted, Buccaneer, 1983; *In the Rue Monge,* Doubleday, Doran, 1931.

Plays: (With M. Barstow) ''The Scarlet Pimpernel,'' first produced in Nottingham, England, 1903, produced on West End at New Theatre, January 5, 1905; (with Barstow) ''The Sin of William Jackson,'' first produced on West End at Lyric Theatre, 1906; (with Barstow) ''Beau Brocade'' (dramatization of the novel of the same title), produced in Eastbourne, England, in Sussex, and on West End at Wyndham's Theatre, 1908; ''The Duke's Wager,'' first produced in Manchester, England, 1911; ''The Legion of Honour'' (dramatization of the novel *A Sheaf of Bluebells*), first produced in Bradford, England, 1918; ''Leatherface'' (dramatization of the novel of the same title), produced in Portsmouth, England, and London, 1922.

Other: (Author of introduction) Charles Dickens, *Little Dorrit,* Waverly Book, 1913; *Les Beaux et les dandys des grande siecles en Angleterre* (conference), Societe de Conferences (Monaco), 1924; *The Scarlet Pimpernel Looks at the World* (essays), John Heritage, 1933; (author of foreword) John Blakeney (pseudonym of John Montagu Orczy), *A Gay Adventurer: Being the Biography of Sir Percy Blakeney, Bart., Known As the ''Scarlet Pimpernel,''* John Long, 1935; *The Turbulent Duchess (H.R.H. Madame la Duchesse de Berri),* Hodder & Stoughton, 1935; Putnam, 1936; *Links in the Chain*

''Where are you for, lady?'' he said. The lady did not move, and the guard stepped into the carriage, thinking that perhaps the lady was asleep . . . . ■ (From *The Man in the Corner* by Baroness Emmuska Orczy. Illustrated by H. M. Brock.)

of Life (autobiography), Hutchinson, 1947.

ADAPTATIONS—Movies: ''The Scarlet Pimpernel,'' starring Dustin Farnum and Winifred Kingston, Fox Film, 1917, London Film Productions, starring Leslie Howard, Merle Oberon, and Raymond Massey, 1935, reissued, 1966, as ''The Elusive Pimpernel,'' starring David Niven and Cyril Cusack, 1950, as ''The Fighting Pimpernel,'' 1954; ''I Will Repay,'' starring Corinne Griffith, Vitagraph, 1918, starring Henry Kolker and Flora Le Breton, 1923; ''Swords and the Woman,'' R-C Pictures, 1924; ''Two Lovers,'' adaptation of *Leatherface,* starring Vilma Banky, Nigel De Brulier, Paul Lukas, and Ronald Colman, Samuel Goldwyn, 1928; ''Triumph of the Scarlet Pimpernel,'' starring Juliette Compton, Margaret Hume, and Harold Huth, British Dominions, 1928; ''The Scarlet Daredevil,'' adaptation of *The Triumph of the Scarlet Pimpernel,* World Wide Pictures, 1929; ''The Celestial City,'' starring Norah Baring and Malvina Longfellow, British Industrial Films, 1929; ''The Emperor's Candlesticks,'' starring William Powell and Luise Rainer, Metro-Goldwyn-Mayer, 1937; ''The Return of the Scarlet Pimpernel,'' adaptation of *The Scarlet Pimper-*

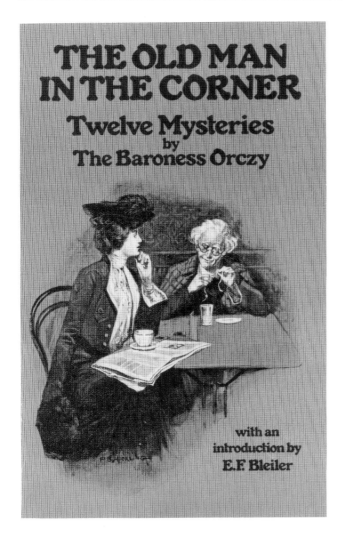

(Jacket illustration by P. B. Hickling from *The Old Man in the Corner* by Baroness Orczy.)

nel, starring Barry K. Barnes, Sophie Stewart, and James Mason, London Film Productions, 1938; "Pimpernel Smith" or "Mister V," adaptation of *The Scarlet Pimpernel*, starring Leslie Howard and Francis Sullivan, Leslie Howard/Anglo-American, 1941.

Radio and television: "The Scarlet Pimpernel" (radio series), starring Marius Goring, Towers of London Syndicate, 1952, NBC-Radio, 1952; "The Scarlet Pimpernel" (television series), starring M. Goring, syndicated, beginning 1954; "The Scarlet Pimpernel" (television program), adapted by George Baxt, aired October 28 and October 29, 1960; "The Scarlet Pimpernel" (television movie), starring Anthony Andrews and Jane Seymour, first broadcast on CBS-TV, November 9, 1982.

SIDELIGHTS: **September 23, 1865.** Born of Hungarian parents in Tarna-Örs, Hungary. "My father and mother lived in Tarna-Örs then, a large agricultural property on the River Tarna—owned and farmed by my grandfather as it had been by many generations before him. . . .

"The house was of the type so often found on the *puszta* (the plains of Hungary) two stories above the ground, rambling, square and huge, with four facades at right angles to one another. The main block contained the reception rooms and the

apartments of the numerous family, together with numberless corridors, halls, and staircases; another had thirty-six guest rooms, and a loggia where one sat on hot summer afternoons looking out over the garden and the park, and beyond these to the village with its little mediaeval church and tower; another consisted of the riding school, gymnasium and swimming bath, whilst kitchens, offices and servants' quarters completed the square. The whole structure was as commodious and as ugly as you like.

"In the centre of the square there was a garden planted with standard rose trees and clipped acacias, in the middle of which a fat stone Cupid spouted water out of its pursed mouth. I remember that Cupid so well, he and a life-sized stone image of Attila, King of the Huns (why Attila I have often wondered since) standing defiant and warlike in a niche on the main staircase, are the two items of ornamentation that have dwelt persistently in my memory." [Baroness Emmuska Orczy, *Links in the Chain of Life,* Hutchinson, 1947.[1]]

1870s. Because of financial unrest in Hungary, Orczy's parents moved the family to Brussels. Her father, having relinquished his land holdings, turned to music. In Budapest, and then in Brussels, he directed the opera. "We were always in town: Budapest first, then Brussels, then Paris for a little while, and finally London. . . . It was in Weimar that the first seeds were sown of my father's friendship with Franz Liszt, then at the apogee of his glorious career, a friendship which endured throughout the life of the great master and influenced not only my father's destiny but strangely enough mine also. It was he who induced my father to accept the position of *Intendant* (Supreme Administrator) of the National Theatres in Budapest—a Court appointment which as so often happens in cases of this sort (and I venture to say in most countries where special appointments are dependent on Court or Government patronage) had hitherto been assigned to gentlemen highly distinguished no doubt in their military or administrative careers, but who knew about as much of music as 'the cock that crows in the morn' or of dramatic art as 'the maiden all forlorn.'

"After Budapest—and always with a view to our future—my parents took us to Brussels where we commenced our education in the convent school of The Visitation. We were only a very little while in Brussels. My beloved sister died there at the age of twelve. My father idolized her and her death did, in a way, break his heart. . . . I was just old enough, too, to realize my own loss to the full. Though I was younger by two years than she was, we had always loved each other devotedly.

"The one year of schooling that we did together in Brussels was made happy for me by the fact that the kind nuns allowed us to be always together both for work and play. My school reports in those days always spoke of me as being *trop dominante avec ses compagnes.* I suppose I was of a domineering disposition. I always wanted to be, and in my own opinion always was, right in any dispute or argument that occurred amongst us schoolgirls. . . .

". . . Indeed, sorrow had become the portion of both my parents at this time. My mother lost both her father and her mother and also a sister of whom she was very fond, and I imagine that both she and my father felt that this overwhelming atmosphere of sorrow was none too healthy for a growing girl as I then was. They were obliged to go to Hungary on business of succession and so forth, and an aunt who had a daughter of her own about my age and who was very fond of me undertook to look after me while my parents were away. She was an aunt *à la mode de Bretagne*— not really an aunt, but distantly related in the way that in Hungary all families are in some way or other linked together.

"Anyway, I fully reciprocated her affection for me. She took me along with her daughter to Paris to give us the educational polish which I daresay was necessary, because the dear little nuns of the Visitation in Brussels were more noted for their piety than for their erudition. Our minds were principally fed on ecclesiastical history, not imparted to us out of printed books but out of copy-books, manuscripts in fact which were copied and re-copied by all of us pupils by way of recreation every Saturday afternoon. We were also grounded in the history of France out of books entirely devoted to the glory of that Catholic country.

"At the Convent School in Paris our studies were certainly on a higher plane than in Brussels, but not much. We learned our *Histoire de l'Eglise* and our *Histoire de France* out of printed books.... Here, too, we had the usual lessons in geography and arithmetic and to these kind nuns am I also indebted for their teaching of *style épistolaire*, the writing of letters to imaginary correspondents, but now these letters were no longer very simple, they were by way of being adapted to our developing intelligence."[1]

1880. "I was ... just on fifteen when my parents took the great and, for me, most momentous steps on which, unknown then by me, the whole course of my life depended: the decision

In the meanwhile Lady Patience, with Betty by her side, had been walking towards the forge.... ■ (From *Beau Brocade* by Baroness Orczy. Illustrated by Clarence F. Underwood.)

to settle down in London for a time. As a matter of fact I am rather vague as to why, or exactly when, they made that decision. The intervening years of my girlhood were, as far as I was concerned, uneventful, and there were no indications whatever in my mind during that time of any tendency towards imaginative or in fact any special kind of talent. Nor do I remember much of the journey to England, except that my first experience of a sea-voyage was a very unpleasant one.

"Of course the first thing to do when one arrives in a foreign country is to learn its language. Both my parents spoke English after a fashion, enough at any rate to make themselves understood by shop people or servants. But I knew not a word. After consultation with the Austro-Hungarian Consul in London—who was an old friend—it was decided that I should first be sent to a small day school where I could pick up the first rudiments of the language....

"'She shall have music wherever she goes,' says the old rhyme. This I certainly did have, which makes me look upon the first years we spent in England as my 'musical life.' Not that I was what is commonly called musical (the French have a better word, *musicienne*). I was not *musicienne*, though very fond of music as most people are—whether intelligent or uneducated—but I had no aptitude for it—to my real sorrow, for my want of musical enthusiasm grieved my father I know. But I could not help it. Enthusiasm comes naturally and from within, it cannot be commanded; and though it was real joy to sit in the twilight and listen to my dear father playing Schumann (his favourite composer) or Liszt, I must confess that concerts rather bored me—classical concerts especially.

"My father tried very hard to develop what little talent I had, and to train my voice, but I had no talent (so-called) and a very poor ear for singing or the violin—which really is rather queer because I have always been an exceptionally good linguist, and before I reached my teens could already jabber in three languages without the slightest trace of a foreign accent—and this proves that the ear may be one of the factors, but not the only one, of linguistic ability."[1]

Attended West London School of Art and then Heatherley School of Art. "... I certainly began my short artistic career at the West London but never distinguished myself sufficiently to obtain admission to other more important schools.

"But there was always 'Heatherley's.' Heatherley's in Newman Street where so many fine, if perhaps not great, English artists served their apprenticeship. Heatherley's demanded no special qualifications for joining the life class, *i.e.* working from the living model. One paid one's two guineas a month and was at liberty to work either from the nude or the costume model every day from 9 a.m. till dusk, with an interval for luncheon. All this I learned from fellow-students at the West London, and it all sounded very attractive. It suggested freedom for the exercise of one's special talents (if one had any) and I was bound to admit that the tuition which I was receiving at the time was on the dull and uninspired side, for it only meant drawing from plaster casts in charcoal or in chalk, and I hated drawing. I wanted to paint. I wanted to run before I had learned to walk. I wanted to go to Heatherley's and paint pictures. I saw pictures floating like visions before my mind, pictures that I was going to paint and that would be epoch-making when they were hung on the walls of the Royal Academy, and this I should never attain by making representations of plaster casts in charcoal and in chalk.

"Happily I encountered no opposition from my parents when I broached the question of Heatherley's by way of a change.

(From the stage production of "The Scarlet Pimpernel," written by Baroness Orczy and Montagu Barstow. It opened at the New Theatre in London, January 5, 1905, and subsequently transferred to the Knickerbocker Theatre in New York.)

I imagine that the poor darlings looked upon me now as an emancipated product of English education and felt that 'in for a penny, in for a pound' of this emancipation was the best course to pursue in the interests of peace in the home. And I was allowed to go to Heatherley's. . . .

"'Old Heatherley,' as he was familiarly called, went round the studios once in the mornings and once in the afternoons. He would make sarcastic remarks or criticize the work if it was worthy of criticism, and left one entirely to one's own devices. The rest of the day he spent upstairs in his private apartments playing the flute, practising scales and exercises on that delectable instrument. He was a funny old boy, in appearance like *Faust* in the first act; he wore a long sort of velvet garment, down to his heels, very much the worse for wear and shuffled about in faded red leather slippers. His face was really very noble both in features and in expression, with light blue eyes and a transparent pale skin. His hair was snow-white and scanty, and he wore a straggly kind of beard.

". . . Though I loved the life in the studio and worked regularly and enthusiastically it soon began to dawn upon me that I had not the real *feu sacré* which would one day carry me to the pinnacle of fame.

"The atmosphere of the studio was more congenial to my temperament than the concert halls and the fashionable opera. The students were for the most part simple girls and boys, most of them from the City of London or St. Paul's school; some were possessed of ambition as I was, others just content to look upon the craft of the brush as a likely means of earning a livelihood. As a matter of fact not one of these aspirants to fame or fortune who passed in and out of 'Heatherley's' during the three or four years I worked there, achieved greatness. I certainly did not. We all made pictures; oh yes! pictures which we would hopefully send in to the Royal Academy every year, looking forward to seeing them hung and possibly sold to an art patron, and more often than not had them returned 'unhung for want of space' the little bit of sugar to disguise the bitterness of the pill. As a matter of fact pictures of mine were accepted and hung in the Royal Academy three successive years. . . .

"Let me confess at once that though my incursions into an artistic career are not worth recording and my attempts at pictorial art were anything but glorious there is a thing for which I shall always be profoundly grateful, and that is that my artistic training enabled me to see *pictorially* what later on I attempted to describe with my pen. . . ."[1]

1894. Married fellow art student John Montagu Barstow. ". . . It was in the studio at 'Heatherley's' that I met the man who from that day became and remained all the world to me. The subject is secret and sacred to me so I will not speak of it except to say this, that the whole of my life, every step in my career has been bound up with what Swinburne glorifies in such exquisite words: *Love that keeps all the choir of lives in chime....* My marriage was for close on half a century one of perfect happiness and understanding, of perfect friendship and communion of thought. The great link in my chain of life which brought me everything that makes life worth living.

"My dear father was dead, my mother who was in delicate health and who had never really cared for England—not as my father and I did—had gone back to Hungary as soon as she saw me happily and contentedly married. Travelling across the continent of Europe was no longer the slow and complicated affair of one's young days and one could get over from London to Budapest in less than thirty-six hours without stepping out of one's comfortable *lit-salon*.

"However we were not thinking of *lits-salon* and of Hungary just then. We were going to settle down to work and to work very hard.

(From the cartoon satire "The Scarlet Pumpernickle" by Chuck Jones, a parody of the original by Baroness Orczy.)

"... Those early days of our married life were indeed jolly and happy and, above all, care-free. We had plenty of work to occupy us and plenty of ways to amuse ourselves. Our boy was born the last year of the century.

"We were both of us great readers and it was interesting—yes! and stimulating—to witness the gradual infiltration of American light literature into the hitherto rather close borough of English fiction.

"Many of us had always loved our Bret Harte. I was a passionate worshipper at his shrine. I still feel, even to this day, that no other author with the exception of Dickens has ever come near him either in pathos or in humor, and I loved his own devotion to Dickens."[1]

1895. Translated and edited several fairy tales, which were published in five seperate books.

1899. First novel, *The Emperor's Candlesticks: A Romance,* was published. "Its appearance coincided with Kruger's ultimatum to Great Britain, immediately followed by the outbreak of the Boer War. My first effort, like many first efforts during that eventful year, fell quite flat. I believe that only ninety copies were sold. Somehow I did not break my heart over that initial failure. I was interested in my stories of detection and crime and in my funny old man with his piece of string, and ready to give my whole mind to the proposed series."[1]

1905. Her most famous book, *The Scarlet Pimpernel,* was published. "Strangely enough that personality of the Scarlet Pimpernel came to me in a very curious way. I first saw him standing before me ... on the platform of an underground station, The Temple. I had been to see someone on the *Daily Express, à propos* of some minor work, and was waiting for my Inner Circle train for Kensington. Now, of all the dull, prosy places in the world, can you beat an Underground Railway Station? It was foggy too, and smelly and cold. . . .

Caricature of Julia Neilson dated 1905, the same year she played Lady Blakeney in the London stage production of "The Scarlet Pimpernel."

When Chauvelin reached the supper room it was quite deserted. ■ (From *The Scarlet Pimpernel* by Baroness Orczy. Illustrated by John Falter.)

. . . **The old hag whipped up her lean nag and drove her cart out of the gate.** ■ (From *The Scarlet Pimpernel* by Baroness Orczy. Illustrated by John Falter.)

"I saw him in his exquisite clothes, his slender hands holding up his spy-glass: I heard his lazy drawling speech, his quaint laugh. I can't tell you in detail everything I saw and heard—it was a mental vision, of course, and lasted but a few seconds—but it was the whole life-story of the Scarlet Pimpernel that was there and then revealed to me. The rest of the day has remained a blur in my mind, but my thoughts were clear enough for me to tell my beloved husband about the wonder that had occurred; the birth of the Scarlet Pimpernel.

"Everything else was easy. I set to work the very next day and wrote *The Scarlet Pimpernel,* as it now stands, in five weeks. I wrote it as a book; I thought of it as a possible play. Scenes, pictures, love-scenes, adventures both comic and tragic, thrilling moments, dramatic scenes, and above all character—always character—after running riot in my brain all settled themselves down into a simple and complete whole.

"I think I may look on those five weeks as some of the happiest in my life. To feel my creation become more and more real, to feel it growing into something that would live, into something vivid that would not fail to stir the imagination of all those who, on reading about that imaginary personage, would in their turn feel that he was absolutely real, that he had indeed lived and laughed and loved, that was my happiness and my joy. And I know that Sir Percy Blakeney has become such a real living personality to so many millions of readers that books of biography and history have been consulted by the studios to discover his prototype somehow, somewhere; that for over forty years now I have been bombarded with letters from all over the world demanding a pronouncement from me, 'Who was the original of your Scarlet Pimpernel?'

"Well, anyway, there he was, quite ready now at last to make his bow before the reading public. His triumphs of course came a bit later, for let me tell you at once that things did not go quite so easily for me as I had so confidently anticipated. The book was ready for publication: the most important thing now was to find a publisher. My husband and I had put the play together in collaboration, and it was ready for production. The thing was to find a theatrical manager who would produce it. But the book first. In my ignorance I thought that the choice of a publisher for my book rested with me. And so it started on its weary way. Yes! weary way indeed, for my beloved book on which I had built such hopes was refused by a round dozen of publishers in London. Starting at the top of the publishing world, I sent it to Macmillan and to Heinemann, to Murray, and so on, and always with monotonous recurrence came that fatal rejection slip. However, I was not discouraged. I thought and thought. I tried this, that, and the other. Personal introduction, personal interviews.

"In the offices of the powers that be people were always very kind and sympathetic. I spoke about having dramatized the book and this aroused a glimmer of interest, for I remember Mr. Heinemann, to whom I had a personal introduction, saying to me: 'Well! if your play is produced and is successful, you bring me back your book, and I'll see what I can do.'

"The reader at Cassell's liked it too and recommended it for publication. It was kept three weeks in the office pending final decision. And 'final decision' was again the rejection slip. One firm offered me publication and a certain amount of publicity if I paid all expenses connected with the printing and general advertising of the book. That I never would agree to; and never throughout my whole life did I ever spend one penny for the pushing of any of my works. . . .

"Anyway, no one wanted to publish *The Scarlet Pimpernel* until—almost in desperation—I bethought myself of a small firm who brought out a weekly publication, *The Play Pictorial.* I argued to myself that the powers that be in that particular firm were especially interested in theatrical matters. I obtained a personal interview and offered my book, explaining about the play and its future production. Mr. Greening was very kind, though a little doubtful, as all of them were. I left the book with him and when I saw him he was good enough to say that personally he liked the book but was not inclined to back his opinion; 'but,' he added, 'I'll tell you what I can do. When I am doubtful about a book I submit it to my dear old mother, who lives down in Cornwall. She is quite unsophisticated but knows what she likes. If she likes the book I publish it, because I take her to be a criterion of the taste of the great reading public for whom I wish to cater.' That was in substance what he said and what he did. Evidently the unsophisticated old lady from Cornwall liked the *Scarlet Pimpernel,* for the firm of Greening & Co. accepted the book for publication (publication to be co-incident with the production of the play) and gave me quite a good contract for it, considering that I was then an unknown writer.

"Since the days of *The Scarlet Pimpernel* I have written a number of historical romances. History always fascinated me, and as I never really cared for social life I didn't find that modern thought and modern views of life attracted me sufficiently to place my romantic stories in the setting of to-day. I don't mean to suggest by that that there is no romance in the life of to-day. There is plenty and to spare, more perhaps than there was in the olden days. All I mean is, that somehow I am not in tune with it. Never, even in my young days, was I fond of social life. I am something of a hermit and the company of my husband and a few intimate friends was all I ever craved for in the way of society. I always found going to parties a terrible waste of time. . . .''[1]

1908. "It was about this time that we finally decided to settle down in the country. We were both of us country lovers at heart . . . and we had had enough and to spare of town life, its bustle and its noise. What we wanted was peace and quietude. What we hoped for was the opportunity of buying some small property not too far from town but with a nice garden where we could indulge our passionate love of flowers and trees and birds and the broad expanse of heaven above us. But of course that was not an undertaking that could be gone into in a hurry, and in the meanwhile we rented a nice old dower house near Minster, in Thanet. Thanet is not a beautiful part of England. It is flat; there are no hills, few trees, only big fields and wide spaces with the tang and smell of the sea all around. We spent three very happy years there.

"My reputation was now on a solid foundation. I could write just whatever I wanted to. I could let my imagination and my love of romance have free play. Whatever I wrote was eagerly sought for publication and welcomed by an ever widening circle of readers. Bless 'em for their goodness and loyalty to me. It was in Thanet that I wrote *The Nest of the Sparrowhawk,* the scene of which was laid in our neighbouring village of Acol. That book is one of the few romances of mine with an English background. I have often been asked why that was so. English history is every bit as colourful, and picturesque, and as romantic as that of any other country, and I loved it and studied it with all the ardour which my love for my spiritual home had engendered in my heart. So I was always a little bit at a loss how to reply to that question.

"The real reason was the difficulty of dealing with names of places and persons. I have never disguised these in my ro-

(From the movie "The Elusive Pimpernel," starring David Niven. Released by British Lion Films, 1950.)

mances, as fiction-writers almost invariably do. In writing of Paris or Boulogne, of Clichy or Anjou they were always Paris or Boulogne, and so on in my books. The streets of Paris and Nantes bear the same names to-day as they do in *Eldorado* or in *Lord Tony's Wife*. I have old maps of all the towns which, to my ears, still echo the footsteps of the Scarlet Pimpernel and his devoted followers. There is not a country lane the configuration of which I have in any way distorted. To me, had I changed the names or the positions of any actual place I would, I feel sure, have lost something of their reality and had been unable to infuse that reality into my narrative."[1]

1912. "... I wrote two romances ... *Fire in Stubble* and *Meadowsweet* and started (at I am happy to say, public request) yet another adventure of my always popular Scarlet Pimpernel, namedly, *Eldorado*, which was completed and finished the following year. It has always seemed to me strange how universally popular that hero of mine had become. In fact his popularity had grown and spread with the years.

"As in all my books the dominant idea for me was always character rather than story. I have always begun my books with the conception of a character and then built my romance around that. *Unto Caesar* gave me immense pleasure to write: that book and *By the Gods Beloved* have always remained my favourite works—leaving *The Scarlet Pimpernel* as one apart from anything else I have ever done. In those books I could

allow my imagination and my love for the picturesque to run absolutely riot. I am happy to say that both have been among the most popular, the most widely read, and the most frequently translated into European languages."[1]

1915. "It was during our short stay in Monte Carlo ... that I first conceived the romance which I think was, next to the Scarlet Pimpernel books, my most popular one. Already in *The Laughing Cavalier* I had indulged in glimpses of the Low Countries and of their heroic fight for independence against the political and religious tyranny of Spain. I had for some time before this been absorbed in that romantic period of history. Monttram's *Rise of the Dutch Republic* and his *John of Barneveld* had thrilled me and sown in my mind the seeds of those imaginings which were now about to bear fruit. It was while sitting on the terrace of the little villa during those months of February and March of that year—months so full of sorrow and anxiety for us and for all those we cared for—that I mapped out the romance of *Leatherface*."[1]

1918. Bought a villa in Monte Carlo.

1920-1940. "... Through all these days of gaieties and of varied experiences of life and character I carried on assiduously with my work. Between the years 1920—after we were finally and comfortably settled in Villa Bijou—and 1940 I brought out some of my most successful books: *The Uncrowned King*,

(From the movie "The Scarlet Pimpernel," starring Leslie Howard and Merle Oberon. Copyright by London Films Productions, Ltd., 1935.)

A Spy of Napoleon (a story of the Second Empire), *The Hon'ble Jim.''* [1]

During World War II Orczy and her husband were forced to stay at their villa in Monte Carlo, and were unable to return to England. ''We were not molested in any way, but we were unofficially advised not to speak English in the streets, and not to meet in restaurants more than four of us at one table. We were also advised not to cross the frontier into France. But there was no definite order about this and many went over day after day to some favourite restaurant in Beausoleile where meals were decidedly cheaper than in Monte Carlo.

''The question of money began to loom unpleasantly ahead by now for some of us, I am afraid. I am speaking of 1941. Our money at home had been blocked for close on two years and many were driven to selling little bits of jewellery to meet necessary expenses. But I want to put it on record that the Monégasque Government was most kind and considerate to us Britishers and repeatedly assured us that we were under its protection and could count on its help in case of distress.

''I think we all of us felt that this sensation of being 'cut off' from everything at home was more cruel to bear than anything else. English and American papers were no longer allowed to come through the post, and very soon even Swiss ones failed us. . . . And all we had by way of news (*sic*) in German controlled papers, was a welter of ridiculous lies and garbled versions of what was going on in Egypt and in Greece. And thus we were kept in complete ignorance of what the French—*i.e.* the Laval-Pétain clique were up to, and what they meant to do. Would they end by turning definitely against us and signing a treaty of alliance with Germany and Italy and declaring war against England or what? Impossible to know. One thing was certain, the *collaborationistes* were getting more and more numerous, and hatred of the British was fanned to devouring flames by the local papers, dirty rags all under German control. . . .'' [1]

1943. Husband died. ''Then came the end of everything that for close on half a century had meant the very breath of life to me, and all I felt that I could do was to trail my spirit along like a bit of drift-wood tossed about by the torrent of existing circumstances.

''The war went on. Men, women, even children suffered as much as I did. I know that . . . and I was sorry—oh! ever so sorry for them . . . for nothing, not even sorrow seemed real to me during those weeks, those months, those years that I supposed went on as before . . . for time does not stand still.

(From the movie "The Emperor's Candlesticks," starring William Powell. Copyright by Metro-Goldwyn-Mayer Corp., 1937.)

(From the movie "Two Lovers," based on the novel *Leatherface* by Baroness Orczy. Starring Ronald Colman and Vilma Banky. Copyright by Samuel Goldwyn, 1928.)

"Only two events during the next two years reached my consciousness. I mean that I knew that they happened. One was the arrest of my devoted English maid, Julia Purkis, my constant companion who knew and who understood everything. In spite of the many mealy-mouthed assurances that I had received from the Italian Commando then in occupation, she was sent to Barcelonette in the Basses Alpes, a twenty-four hours' journey from Monte Carlo. And then began my weekly pilgrimage up to Castelleretto, the G.H.Q. of the Italian Army of Occupation on the heights above Monte Carlo, in order to beg almost on my knees for the release of the one companion in my loneliness. Let me admit at once that the Colonel Commanding and all his officers were always full of kindness and consideration for me. They knew me well by reputation, knew and loved my books, would feel happy they said, if I presented each of them with an autographed copy of *La Primula Rossa*. They assured me that they were doing their utmost to obtain the release of Miss Julia Purkis, for Captain Matteotti had himself journeyed expressly to Rome for this purpose, for permission had to come from Rome, and so on. So kind, so friendly always, and already then so entirely pro-British.

"Of Mussolini and the Fascist party, never a word, and already one felt that Italy was learning her lesson, and was ready to make amends for her adherence to the Axis Party, the enemies of civilization and of liberty.

"The second event which reached my consciousness—it could not very well fail to do so—was the bombardment of Monte Carlo. The bubble of the status of Monaco as a neutral state had soon burst as soap bubbles are apt to do and the Germans occupied the little Principality, turning every available locality into armament works or ammunition dumps and forcing the population to work for them both with their hands and with their brains in the way of propaganda for a friendly *entente* with the army of occupation."[1]

November 12, 1947. Died in London, England. ". . . It is experience—of this I am absolutely certain—which is the only word to real and *lasting* success. Experience of life, of humanity, of its virtues and its failings. Mine has been a long life, and I have seen much and studied a great deal, and in my old age now I am more convinced than I ever was that youth is far too readily inclined to give out to the world all that it has learned and absorbed in the very few years of development out of childhood. In the essence of things that 'all' can only be very little."[1]

FOR MORE INFORMATION SEE: Patrick Braybrooke, "Baroness Orczy," in his *Some Goddesses of the Pen,* Daniel, 1928;

Baroness Orczy, *The Scarlet Pimpernel Looks at the World* (essays), John Heritage, 1933; Howard Haycraft, *Murder for Pleasure: The Life and Times of the Detective Story,* D. Appleton-Century, 1941; *Twentieth Century Authors: A Biographical Dictionary of Modern Literature,* H. W. Wilson, 1942; Orczy, *Links in the Chain of Life* (autobiography), Hutchinson, 1947; *Who Was Who in Literature, 1906-1934,* Omnigraphics, 1979.

Obituaries: *Times* (London), November 13, 1947; *New York Times,* November 13, 1947; *Newsweek,* November 24, 1947; *Time,* November 24, 1947; *Publishers Weekly,* November 29, 1947; *Wilson Library Bulletin,* January, 1948.

PALLADINI, David (Mario) 1946-

PERSONAL: Born April 1, 1946, in Roteglia, Italy; son of Aldo (a landscaper) and Ada Palladini. *Education:* Attended Pratt Institute, 1964-68. *Home:* Sagaponack, N.Y.

CAREER: Free-lance illustrator. Photographer, Olympic Games, Mexico City, 1968; illustrator, Push Pin Studios, New York, N.Y. *Exhibitions:* American Institute of Graphic Arts, 1969-80; Society of Illustrators, 1969-83; Saks Fifth Avenue Gallery, 1974. Palladini's works are in the collection of the Metropolitan Museum of Art, New York, N.Y. and the Museum of Warsaw, Poland. *Awards, honors: The Girl Who Cried Flowers and Other Tales* was selected for the American Institute of Graphic Arts Children's Books Show, 1973-74, was named one of the best illustrated children's books of the year, 1974, by the *New York Times,* won a Golden Kite Award, 1974, and was a National Book Award nomination, children's book category, 1975; *The Moon Ribbon and Other Tales* was named a Golden Kite honor book, 1976.

ILLUSTRATOR—All for young people: Constance B. Hieatt, *The Sword and the Grail,* Crowell, 1972; Ruth Goode, *People of the Ice Age,* Crowell, 1973; Franklyn M. Branley, *The End*

She takes comfort in infamous dreams. ■ (From *Twenty-Six Starlings Will Fly through Your Mind* by Barbara Wersba. Illustrated by David Palladini.)

of the World, Crowell, 1974; Jane H. Yolen, *The Girl Who Cried Flowers and Other Tales* (ALA Notable Book) Crowell, 1974; J. H. Yolen, *The Moon Ribbon and Other Tales,* Crowell, 1976; J. H. Yolen, *The Hundredth Dove and Other Tales,* Crowell, 1977; Barbara Wersba, *Twenty-Six Starlings Will Fly through Your Mind,* Harper, 1980; Crescent Dragonwagon, *If You Call My Name,* Harper, 1981. Has also done numerous book jackets including Jane Yolen's *Cards of Grief,* Ace, 1984.

WORK IN PROGRESS: Another book.

SIDELIGHTS: **April 1, 1946.** Born in Roteglia, Italy, Palladini came to the United States with his parents in 1948. "We lived in Illinois, outside of Chicago in Highland Park. The Midwest

(From *If You Call My Name* by Crescent Dragonwagon. Illustrated by David Palladini.)

(From "Sans Soleil," in *The Moon Ribbon and Other Tales* by Jane Yolen. Illustrated by David Palladini.)

is not a very exciting place.

"Although I drew as a kid, I never really thought about be-

coming an artist. An immigrant family, we had never been exposed to art and didn't really know what it was. Drawing was for me, as it was for many artists I've met since, an escape.

. . .She floated like a swan and the river bore her on, on past houses and hills, past high places and low. And strange to say, she was not well at all.

■ (From *The Moon Ribbon and Other Tales* by Jane Yolen. Illustrated by David Palladini.)

I was always drawing or reading and was well known in Highland Park as the kid who had read all the books in the children's library by the time he was twelve. After that, I moved to the adult library.

"The books that first interested me were, of course, those with illustrations and drawings. Howard Pyle became one of my favorite artists because he did many romantic, inspiring Arthurian legends with paintings of men in armor. The first drawings that I did as an illustrator were all based on that era, and I still work with the medieval period. I believe in reincarnation and that I was in fact from medieval times which is why I seem to understand that period so well without ever having researched it. The images flow very naturally.

"I didn't have any thought of becoming an artist until high school when during my junior year I decided to take an art course. I had exhausted every elective course available and art was, in fact, the only course remaining. The second class day the teacher was so excited and impressed with my work that she brought another art teacher in to see my drawings. The same year a representative from Pratt Institute offered me a four-year scholarship to the art school. I accepted.

"Most of the teachers at Pratt were uninspiring except Herbert Beerman, who would, for instance, repeat the same words for half an hour. At first I didn't know what to make of all this until I began to realize that he was trying to teach us the inherent freedom in art. Beerman inspired me by showing me that 'anything goes,' and that creativity has to do with breaking boundaries and *not* with being like 'normal people.' Art really comes from other places, which has nothing to do with politics or economics, but rather, has to do with being a creative soul. I still remember working harder for Beerman than anyone else. There is something about the way he taught that I've tried to emulate in my own teaching and it works.

"I didn't study illustration at Pratt; nor did I study art, although I had painting and drawing classes. I studied film and photography. I left school in 1968, the middle of my senior year, to work as a photographer for the Olympics in Mexico City. I was a good photographer and when I returned to New York, I had every intention of setting up a studio and becoming a professional. I soon discovered the reality of that world: you need a lot of money to set up and equip a studio. I couldn't afford it so I went to Push Pin Studios, 'the place' for commercial artists in New York. After I showed them my portfolio of drawings from art school they hired me on the spot. I began to work on full blown professional projects and I've been doing it ever since."

1972. Illustrated his first children's book, *The Sword and the Grail* by Constance B. Hieatt. "As I became known in New York I was approached by publishers. When a publisher handed me a manuscript he gave me the freedom to conceive an entire body of work based on my imagination. I found that children's books—although they make no money and take a great deal of time—were the most satisfying projects of all because I got a finished product which looks exactly the way I wanted it to look."

Palladini has illustrated three books by author Jane Yolen. "I was given the manuscript, *The Girl Who Cried Flowers,* by the publisher, then Jane and I formed an author/illustrator relationship. I did the jacket for her new novel, *Cards of Grief.* I have never actually worked with her on the writing of a story, but our ideas are sympathetic. We have a similar view of the medieval, romantic ideas and so our work has been a nice creative blend.

"Several years ago I had a show of my children's books at the Metropolitan Museum of Art. Jane came and told stories to the children and I talked to them about making drawings for books. Watching her tell her stories was a marvelous experience. She uses facial expressions and voice changes for the different characters much like a storyteller of ancient times.

"Kids are much smarter than adults. They see more clearly, they know when a lie is a lie, and they know what fantasy is. Interestingly, a few years ago, the *New York Times* put out a 'Best Illustrated' list judged by two juries: an adult jury made up of art directors and artists, and a children's jury. Contrary to all our expectations the children's jury chose books with mostly black and white drawings which were not heavily illustrated. Their imaginations are apparently so active that they often prefer to invent their own private pictures for the stories they read. Creating illustrations which are both convincing and fascinating to children is a challenge to me, and that's what I like about it.

"I enjoy working in both black and white and full-color illustrations. The problem with children's books these days is that they have become very expensive to produce. If, for instance, *The Girl Who Cried Flowers,* was published now, the illustrations would be black and white with perhaps one or two in color. As an artist you have to be able to do both and make them convincing. For my black and white drawings, I use very dark pencils. This has the effect of charcoal. I've worked on almost every kind of surface, although my favorite surface is velour paper, which has a velvet surface and gives a very soft, beautiful finish to the drawing.

"The amount of research I do for illustrations depends on the subject matter. For the medieval period, as I've mentioned, I have ready information in my head which is fairly accurate. But many projects involve research. I once illustrated a scientific book which dealt with ions and nuclei, which required research. *People of the Ice Age* was also heavily researched.

"Artists don't make much money. When I lived in New York and couldn't afford an apartment, I found an inexpensive alternate lifestyle by living on a boat at the end of West 79th Street. The boat basin was a fabulous place, wonderful in the sense that it provided freedom—I could pick up the anchor and go anywhere I wanted! It made working a little rough until I became used to the constant motion of the boat. As a matter of fact, I became so used to it that when on land I would become landsick. I would go to art director's offices, sit in the chair, and sway back and forth."

The image of hands recurs frequently in Palladini's illustrations. "Hands are very expressive. Musician's hands in particular are quite expressive, as are the hands of sculptors. You can tell everything about a person by studying his hands. Art teachers were always telling me that I couldn't draw hands, so I spent a number of years concentrating on hands, trying to prove them wrong. Many of my artistic developments have come about as a reaction to criticism. I'm a particularly sensitive person, and when my feelings are hurt I immediately attempt to overcome so as never to hear the criticism again.

"I've been teaching at the School of Visual Arts for nine years. I've also lectured at Philadelphia Museum School and Pratt Institute. The first exercise I do in my classes every year is to send students home to create a 'masterpiece.' They all look at me with bewilderment. The following week, hoping that they've struggled all week with the assignment, I go down the rows and tear up their masterpieces. The students go crazy, not believing what I'm doing. Many of them arrive at art school

Olivia looked at him, blossoms streaming from her eyes. ■ (From *The Girl Who Cried Flowers and Other Tales* by Jane Yolen. Illustrated by David Palladini.)

with the notion that they're good artists. Maybe they worked on the yearbook or did posters for the prom, as I did. That, however, has nothing to do with art. Art has to do with thinking, and has to do with trying to fit yourself into the world. So I start my students off by shocking them; by shaking them up a bit.

"I try to be very sensitive about giving criticism. I had an art teacher who told me that I couldn't paint and consequently for twelve years I didn't actually paint. Most of the books I've illustrated, even the color work, have been done in pencil. It took me a long time to overcome the pain of that comment and actually get the courage to paint again. I think most people who try to become creative writers or actors or artists do so by overcoming the discouraging remarks of other people—all the 'shouldn'ts' and the 'can'ts.' It is characteristic of all the artists I know to continue to create despite the pain.

"Teaching affords contact with other creative people and that contact is one of the things I like best. It is a process of constant reaffirmation of new ideas. Sometimes when I teach I realize that 'My God, I'm not doing these things myself,' and run home and try to do just that.

"I don't like most contemporary illustration because much of it is devoid of aesthetics and ability. Many illustrators, it seems to me, can't draw. My favorite illustrators are Howard Pyle and N. C. Wyeth. The contemporary illustration I respect most is Japanese illustration, which I believe is the best art in the world. Kinuko Craft's work is full of imagination and detail.

"It's extremely important for artists to have contact with other artists. Unfortunately, illustrating becomes a very monastic existence—you sit in your room alone and draw. When I've

met other illustrators at such organizations as the Society of Illustrators all they talk about is business, which is the last thing I want to talk about when I'm doing something social. The contact I've had with other artists has been professional and I haven't had much of that. Now that I'm painting and drawing landscapes outdoors, I have even less contact with other artists than I used to.

"I am presently living with an artist, and find that it keeps me on my toes, and makes me more creative. It challenges me when she does a drawing that's better than mine. The same is true for her. It forces us to grow.

"I've become less involved with illustration during the last two years because the illustration field has become extremely frustrating for me. Being told what to do after fifteen years finally got to me as did the long hours between six a.m. until dark, usually skipping meals, 365 days a year. It was bad for my brain and my life; my friends disappeared because I never spoke to them. If there is one lesson to be learned from the experience of being an illustrator, it is that everyone may take advantage of you. Artists are so naive. We believe that everyone is honorable and appreciative of art when in fact money is their priority."

Palladini's illustrations have won many awards. "I don't put much stock in awards. I've been in judging situations and find that the judges become a committee, which means compromise and therefore the unusual works are never chosen. Whenever I've been given awards, it's always for the worst thing I've done. The work that was entered into the Society of Illustrators shows was consistently the worst piece of work I'd done all year. The show at the Met in 1977, however, was the nicest thing that's ever happened to me. Leonardo DaVinci and I shared a show at the Met. The entire day I walked around the museum smiling.

"When I first became an illustrator, I did many movie and theater posters. I did a series of posters for Lincoln Center and the Vivian Beaumont Theater, which went on a traveling exhibition throughout Europe and ended up at the Warsaw Museum, where they are now. I am very proud, but there again, the work I considered my best was not chosen for the exhibition.

"One of the problems in the field of illustration is that it is really difficult to earn a living, especially since the fees haven't changed in thirty years. The only way to protect yourself would be to form a union, as writers and photographers have, although artists shy away from organizations.

"I find an attitude in many artists, and in my students as well, that if you are paid for your work, it's not art. I point out that the Sistine chapel was a book illustration of the Bible and was paid for. In fact, the Pope, was always yelling at Michelangelo, 'When is it going to be finished?'

"Art collectors are finally beginning to appreciate that illustration is a modern form of art and should be collected and respected as much as any other art form. It has taken many years for illustration to make the breakthrough. It is one of the most powerful art forms around. It makes a statement about our culture. And in a commercial culture, which we are, commercial art makes sense."

Palladini's interests in the arts are diversified. "I participate in and am influenced by other art forms as well. I play keyboards and guitar, and I used to sing. I had a band for awhile. Didn't everyone? If I could have been anything other than an artist I would have loved to have been a musician. Sculpture interests me very much, as does photography. I would love to make a serious film someday, but that is a major financial undertaking. I've tried writing and have submitted several manuscripts without success. I am afraid to push it because I don't like rejections. But lately, I've been reconsidering.

"I don't read fiction any more because there is not enough time. I'd rather get information than read fiction. I'm in the process of reading the 1911 *Encyclopedia Brittanica* which contains a lot of information that encyclopedias nowadays exclude. For relaxation I play music for hours. Happiness comes from being outdoors painting, the best experience in my life. Watching the clouds move and the shadows change has taught me more about life than I ever knew before. I don't have hobbies; everything I do is related to staying alive and trying to become a better artist.

"When I don't have inspiration it has to be sought out by looking through the work of other artists, a Michelangelo at the Uffizi Gallery in Florence, Italy. One of the things I like about art is that you can sit in a corner with a paper, a pencil and nothing else and create a new reality. For most other creative people, that's not possible. The photographer, for instance, needs a subject. Writers, however, are like artists—with words they construct new realities."

Palladini's advice to young people who are hoping to become artists is to "color outside the lines. The best advice is that you have to believe way beyond believing. You have to believe beyond what your parents try to discourage you from, beyond the fear that everybody's going to laugh. If you believe in your work, you will survive all the obstacles."

PARENTEAU, Shirley (Laurolyn) 1935-

BRIEF ENTRY: Born January 22, 1935, in Garibaldi, Ore. Parenteau's writing career began as a result of her love for the outdoors. She and her family have camped across the United States and cruised waters in British Columbia, the Canadian Gulf Islands, and elsewhere. Aside from contributing articles to magazines like *Boating* and *Field and Stream*, she began writing the column "Outdoor Wife" for a local newspaper in 1972. Several years later, she became interested in writing for children and has since concentrated her efforts in that area. Parenteau's books cover a variety of subjects for ages ranging from kindergarten to young adult. For primary-grade readers, she has written two fictional works that explore the history of natural color from plants and insects. Although they differ immensely in locale, both books effectively describe the techniques of their particular topics. *Blue Hands, Blue Cloth* (Childrens Press, 1978), relates the story of a young West African girl who eagerly begins to learn the craft of indigo dyeing as practiced by the women of her tribe. In *Secrets of Scarlet* (Childrens Press, 1979), the setting is eighteenth-century Southern France where villagers earn their living by picking scarlet bugs for dyemakers. Also for primary-grade readers are *Crunch It, Munch It, and Other Ways to Eat Vegetables* (Coward, 1978), and *A Space Age Cookbook for Kids* (Prentice-Hall, 1979), both of which contain nutritional information in anecdotes and easy recipes.

For a younger age group, *I'll Bet You Thought I Was Lost* (Lothrop, 1981) is a picture book that deals with an easily identifiable situation—getting lost in the supermarket. As a small boy anxiously searches for his father down crowded aisles, items on the shelves become menacing objects. *School Library Journal* commended the use of "realistic suspense . . . built on an ordinary situation, and described in the images that inhabit kids' minds." In yet another genre, Parenteau exhibits a long-time love for science fiction with *Jelly and the Spaceboat* (Coward, 1981), aimed at middle-school readers, and *The Talking Coffins of Cryo-City* (Elsevier/Nelson, 1979), for young adults. "In writing books for children," she relates, "I hope to share with readers my own love for books and adventure, and to keep them turning pages by offering humor and suspense." She is also the author of two romance novels published by Ballantine: *Hot Springs* (1983) and *Vulnerable* (1984). *Home:* 9815 Emerald Park Dr., Elk Grove, Calif. 95624.

FOR MORE INFORMATION SEE: Contemporary Authors, Volumes 85-88, Gale, 1980.

PARK, Barbara 1947-

PERSONAL: Born April 21, 1947, in Mt. Holly, N.J.; daughter of Brooke (a merchant) and Doris (a secretary; maiden name, Mickle) Tidswell; married Richard A. Park (in real estate), June 28, 1969; children: Steven Allen, David Matthew. *Education:* Attended Rider College, 1965-67; University of Alabama, B.S., 1969. *Residence:* Phoenix, Ariz.

CAREER: Author of books for young people.

WRITINGS—All juvenile: *Don't Make Me Smile,* Knopf, 1981; *Operation: Dump the Chump* (illustrated by Rob Sauber), Knopf, 1982; *Skinnybones,* Knopf, 1982; *Beanpole,* Knopf, 1983.

WORK IN PROGRESS: Juvenile fiction, for junior high grade

levels, that ''deals with the age-old struggle to become popular and the tremendous pressure put on kids to associate with the 'right' people, which often necessitates cruelly 'dumping' the undesirables.''

SIDELIGHTS: ''The nicest thing about writing humor for children is that they are such an appreciative audience. You don't have to be droll or dry or sardonic. Kids are eager to laugh and, I think, they enjoy laughing at themselves the most.

''I have fun with my books by writing about characters who are 'uncool' and never quite in control. It's not nearly as fun or funny to write about the school's star athlete as it is to focus on the bumbling, skinny kid in charge of the athletic equipment. And since it's the bumble in all of us that brings out life's funniest moments, my readers can empathize and chuckle at the same time. Maybe if kids could grow up laughing at their own 'uncoolness,' then as adults we could put the 'stuffed shirt' on the shelf.

''Certainly, my writing is influenced by my two sons, Steven and David, though not in obvious ways. While I sometimes use things that actually happen to them in my books, most of their help is just keeping me in touch with the kinds of things that make kids laugh. Underwear, spitballs, and adults (of course!) are good examples. Having boys has made me feel comfortable writing about them, but I've found that girls can be just as much fun.

I've never really liked my brother. Never. And it's silly to pretend I do. ▪ (Jacket illustration by Rob Sauber from *Operation: Dump the Chump* by Barbara Park.)

''The parents in my books also get caught acting 'uncool' and in moments of awkwardness. In *Don't Make Me Smile,* Charlie's parents are in the process of splitting up, and they really don't understand it anymore than he does—sometimes even less! Kids don't believe we adults know it all, so why should we pretend that we do?

''For all their faults, the families in my books have a lot of fun as they muddle through life. Though I'm not big on fairy tales, I do like to think that I leave my readers with a sense that the moments of laughter and joy in life more than make up for the sadness.''

BARBARA PARK

PETROVICH, Michael B(oro) 1922-

PERSONAL: Born October 18, 1922, in Cleveland, Ohio; children: two. *Education:* Western Reserve University (now Case Western Reserve University), B.A., 1943; Columbia University, M.A., 1947, Russian Institute Certificate, 1948, Ph.D., 1955. *Office:* 199 Bascom Hall, University of Wisconsin—Madison, Madison, Wis. 53706.

CAREER: University of Wisconsin (now University of Wisconsin—Madison), Madison, began as instructor, 1950, became professor of modern European history, 1957—. Visiting associate professor, University of California, Berkeley, 1956, Harvard University, 1957. *Wartime service:* Office of Strategic Services, 1943-46, Balkan desk analyst. *Member:* American Historical Association, American Association for the Advancement of Slavic Studies. *Awards, honors:* Recipient of fellowships from Rockefeller Foundation, 1946, Social Science Research Council, 1948-49, 1959-60, Ford Foundation, 1953-54, and Harvard University Russian Research Center, 1957.

WRITINGS: The Emergence of Russian Panslavism, 1856-1870, Columbia University Press, 1956; (contributor) *The Social Studies and the Social Sciences,* Harcourt, 1962; (contributor) *Essays in Russian and Social History in Honor of Geroid Tanquary Robinson,* Columbia University Press, 1963; (with Philip D. Curtin) *The Human Achievement* (juvenile), Silver Burdett, 1967; (with P. D. Curtin) *India and Southeast Asia* (juvenile), Silver Burdett, 1970; *The Soviet Union,* Ginn, 1970; *Yugoslavia: A Bibliographic Guide,* Library of Congress, 1974; *A History of Modern Serbia, 1804-1918,* two volumes, Harcourt, 1976.

Translator; all published by Harcourt: Milovan Djilas, *Conversations with Stalin,* 1962; Ivan Kusan, *The Mystery of Green Hill* (juvenile; illustrated by Kermit Adler), 1962; M. Djilas, *Njegos: Poet, Prince, Bishop,* 1966; M. Djilas, *Wartime,* 1977.

Little Cat said, "Service station man, do you know where my mother is?" ■ (From *Where Did My Mother Go?* by Edna Mitchell Preston. Illustrated by Chris Conover.)

PRESTON, Edna Mitchell

CAREER: Teacher, editor, and author of books for young people. *Awards, honors: Pop Corn and Ma Goodness* was chosen as a Caldecott Honor Book by the American Library Association, and was a finalist, National Book Award, Children's Book Category, both 1970; *Where Did My Mother Go?* chosen for the American Institute of Graphic Arts Book Show, 1979.

WRITINGS—All for children: (Editor) *Arrow Book of Spooky Stories,* Scholastic Book Services, 1962; *Air* (illustrated by Joseph Rogers), Follett, 1965; *Marco Polo: A Story of the Middle Ages* (illustrated by Edward Leight), Crowell, 1968; *Monkey in the Jungle* (illustrated by Clement Hurd), Viking, 1968; *One Dark Night* (illustrated by Kurt Werth; Junior Literary Guild selection), Viking, 1969; *Pop Corn and Ma Goodness* (illustrated by Robert Andrew Parker), Viking, 1969; *The Temper Tantrum Book* (illustrated by Rainey Bennett), Viking, 1969; *Toolittle* (illustrated by Joe Servello; Junior Literary Guild selection), Viking, 1969; *The Boy Who Could Make Things* (illustrated by Leonard Kessler), Viking, 1970; *Horrible Hepzibah* (illustrated by Ray Cruz), Viking, 1971; *Ickle Bickle Robin* (illustrated by Joan Sandin), F. Watts, 1973; *Squawk to the Moon, Little Goose* (illustrated by Barbara Cooney; ALA Notable Book), Viking, 1974; *The Sad Story of the Little Bluebird and the Hungry Cat* (illustrated by B. Cooney), Four Winds Press, 1975; *Where Did My Mother Go?* (illustrated by Chris Conover), Four Winds Press, 1978. Also editor of *Barrel of Chuckles* and *Barrel of Fun,* both published by Scholastic Book Services.

SIDELIGHTS: Two of Preston's books for children, *One Dark Night* and *Squawk to the Moon, Little Goose,* have been adapted into filmstrips by Miller-Brody.

REINIGER, Lotte   1899-1981

PERSONAL: Born June 2, 1899, in Berlin, Germany; died June 19, 1981, in Dettenhausen, West Germany; married Carl Koch (an art historian and film producer), in 1921 (died, 1963). *Education:* Attended Max Reinhardt Theater School, Berlin, about 1916-17; Berlin Institut für Kulturforschung, 1918-19.

LOTTE REINIGER

CAREER: Filmmaker, creator of animated silhouette films, author, and illustrator. Began career cutting title vignettes for Paul Wegener's film ''The Pied Piper of Hamelin,'' 1918; silhouette filmmaker, Berlin, Germany, beginning 1919; producer with husband Carl Koch of ''The Adventures of Prince Achmed,'' first full-length feature film, 1923-26; General Post Office Film Unit (later Crown Film Unit), London, England, filmmaker, beginning 1933 (some sources cite 1936-39); John Art Centre, New Barnet, England, filmmaker, beginning about 1939, and 1949-80; producer of children's television programs, beginning 1951; commissioned by National Film Board of Canada to produce film, ''Aucassin and Nicolette,'' 1974. Lecturer in shadow animation, United States, Europe, Turkey, and Canada, 1974-80; founder, Fantasia Productions, Ltd. (film-production group). *Exhibitions:* Victoria and Albert Museum, London, about 1935.

AWARDS, HONORS: First prize in the television category, Venice Film Festival, 1955, for ''The Gallant Little Tailor''; Deutsche Film Prize, Berlin Film Festival, 1972; Jury Prize, International Animated Film Festival, Ottawa, 1976, for the animated film ''Aucassin and Nicolette''; subject of special program and symposium, American Film Festival, 1980; Cross of the Order of the Federal Republic of Germany.

WRITINGS: Lotte Reiniger Story-Plays, Hutchinson, 1957; *Shadow Theatres and Shadow Films* (young adult), Batsford, 1970, published as *Shadow Puppets, Shadow Theatres, and Shadow Films,* Plays, 1975. Also co-author with husband, Carl Koch, of film script ''Una Signora dell'Ovest,'' [Italy], 194(?).

Illustrator: *Die Abenteuer des Prinzen Achmed* (title means ''The Adventures of Prince Achmed''), Wasmuth (Tuebingen, West Germany), 1972; Roger L. Green, *King Arthur and His Knights of the Round Table,* Penguin, 1980.

FILMS—All animated short subjects, except as indicated: ''The Ornament of the Loving Heart,'' Berlin Institut für Kulturforschung, 1919; ''Cupid and the Constant Lovers,'' Berlin Institut für Kulturforschung, 1920; ''The Flying Coffer,'' Berlin Institut für Kulturforschung, 1921; ''The Star of Bethlehem,'' Berlin Institut für Kulturforschung, 1921; ''Cinderella,'' Berlin

Photograph from the television film ''Cinderella,'' Primrose Productions. ■ (From *Shadow Puppets, Shadow Theatres and Shadow Films* by Lotte Reiniger. Illustrated by the author.)

Institut für Kulturforschung, 1922; ''Sleeping Beauty,'' 1922; (contributor of animated sequence) ''Die Niebelungen,'' [Berlin], 1923; (with C. Koch, Walter Ruttman, and Berthold Bastosch) ''The Adventures of Prince Achmed'' (feature-length film), Berlin Comenius Film, 1926; ''The Shamming Chinese,'' Berlin Comenius Film, 1927; ''The Chinese Nightingale,'' 1927; ''Dr. Doolittle and His Animals,'' [Berlin], 1927; ''The Adventures of Dr. Doolittle'' (contains ''The Journey to Africa,'' ''The Monkey Business,'' and ''The Monkey's Illness''), Berlin Comenius Film, 1928; ''Cinderella,'' 1929.

''Running after Luck'' (live-action, feature-length film), Berlin Comenius Film, 1930; (contributor of animated sequence) ''Ten Minutes with Mozart,'' [Berlin], 1930; ''Harlequin,'' Berlin Town Film, 1931; ''Sissi,'' 1932; ''Carmen,'' Lotte Reiniger Films (Berlin), 1933; (contributor of animated sequence), ''Don Quichote,'' [Paris], 1933; ''The Rolling Wheel,'' Lotte Reiniger Films, 1934; ''The Count of Carabas (Puss in Boots),'' Lotte Reiniger Films, 1934; ''The Stolen Heart,'' Lotte Reiniger Films, 1934; ''The Little Chimney Sweep,'' Lotte Reiniger Films, 1935; ''Caliph Stork,'' 1935; ''Galathea,'' Lotte Reiniger Films, 1935; ''Papageno,'' Lotte Reiniger Films, 1935; ''Mary's Birthday,'' [England], circa 1936; ''The King's Breakfast,'' Facts and Fantasies (London), 1936; ''Silhouetten,'' 1936; ''Puss in Boots,'' 1936.

(Contributor with C. Koch of animated sequence) ''La Marseillaise,'' 1937; ''Tochter,'' London General Post Office, 1937; ''Dream Circus,'' (unfinished work), Scalera Film (Rome), 1939; ''The Golden Goose'' (unfinished work), [Berlin], 1944; ''The Daughter,'' [London], 1949; ''The Frog Prince,'' 1950; ''Mary's Birthday,'' Crown Film Unit (London), 1951; ''The Seraglio,'' 1958; ''Aucassin and Nicolette,'' National Film Board of Canada, 1976; ''Walter Ruttman Seeks His Liberation,'' 1977; ''The Rose and the Ring,'' 1979.

Television films: ''Puss in Boots,'' 1953; ''Snow White and Rose Red,'' Primrose Productions (London), 1953; ''The Magic Horse,'' Primrose Productions, 1953; ''You've Asked for It,'' 1953; ''Aladdin,'' Primrose Productions, 1953; ''Sleeping Beauty,'' Primrose Productions, 1954; ''The Frog Prince,'' Primrose Productions, 1954; ''The Gallant Little Tailor,'' Primrose Productions, 1954; ''The Three Wishes,'' Primrose Productions, 1954; ''Caliph Stork,'' Primrose Productions, 1954; ''Cinderella,'' Primrose Productions, 1954; ''Grasshopper and the Ant,'' Primrose Productions, 1954; ''Thumbelina,'' Primrose Productions, 1955; ''Hansel and Gretel,'' Primrose Productions, 1955; ''Jack and the Beanstalk,'' Primrose Productions, 1955, also released as ''Jack and the Giant Killer,'' 1955.

''The Star of Bethlehem,'' Primrose Productions, 1956; ''Helen la Belle'' (some sources cite ''La Belle Helene''), Fantasia Productions (London), 1957; ''A Night in the Harem,'' Fantasia Productions, 1958; ''The Pied Piper of Hamelin,'' circa 1960; ''The Frog Prince,'' circa 1961; ''Wee Sandy,'' circa 1962; ''Cinderella,'' 1963.

SIDELIGHTS: **June 2, 1899.** Born in Berlin, Germany. ''I could cut silhouettes almost as soon as I could manage to hold a pair of scissors. I could paint, too, and read, and recite; but these things did not surprise anyone very much. But everybody was astonished about the scissor cuts, which seemed a more unusual accomplishment. The silhouettes were very much praised, and I cut out silhouettes for all the birthdays in the family. Did anyone warn me as to where this path would lead? Not in the least; I was encouraged to continue.

''Now I was very fond of the theater and acting. But performing plays in a small flat made rather a confusion, so it was a great

Lotte Reiniger at the animation table with her husband, Carl Koch.

relief to all when I began to use my silhouettes for my play-acting, constructing a little shadow theater in which to stage Shakespeare.'' [Robert Russett and Cecile Starr, *Experimental Animation: An Illustrated Anthology,* Van Nostrand Reinhold, 1976.[1]]

1916. While studying art in Berlin with Max Rheinhart, met the German filmmaker Paul Wegener. ''. . . He produced a number of beautiful and unusual films, and his ambition was to utilise [sic] to the full the possibilities of the camera for the development of the film. . . . Wegener saw me cutting silhouettes behind the stage in Reinhardt's theater, and he became interested. He liked my silhouettes; he thought they showed a rare sense of movement. He therefore introduced me to a group of young artists who had started a new trick [animation] film studio. Here I first began to photograph my silhouette figures, just as drawings are photographed for the cartoon film, and I was successful in making a film with my shadow figures.

''The technique of this type of film is very simple. As with cartoon drawings, the silhouette films are photographed movement by movement. But instead of using drawings, silhouette marionettes are used. These marionettes are cut out of black cardboard and thin lead, every limb being cut separately and joined with wire hinges. A study of natural movement is very important, so that the little figures appear to move just as men and women and animals do. But this is not a technical problem. The backgrounds for the characters are cut out with scissors as well, and designed to give a unified style to the whole

(From the feature-length silhouette film "The Adventures of Prince Achmed." Produced by Berlin Comenius Films, 1926.)

picture. They are cut from layers of transparent paper.

"When the story is ready, the music chosen, and the sound track recorded, then the work for the picture itself begins. Figures and backgrounds are laid out on a glass table. A strong light from underneath makes the wire hinges, etc., disappear and throws up the black figures in relief, while the background appears as a more or less fantastic landscape in keeping with the story. The camera hangs above this table, looking down at the picture arranged below. By means of a wire contrivance the film in the camera can be moved one frame at a time. After the first photograph, the figures are moved into their next position, and the whole photographed again. And so on. . . . The important thing at this stage is to know how much to move the figures so that a lifelike effect may be obtained when the film is run through.

"The synchronization between sight and sound is secured by carefully measuring the sound track, and preparing a very exactly worked out scenario, in which the number of shots are calculated according to the musical value. These calculations are the basis for the picture which is then painstakingly photographed.''[1]

1923. Began work on "The Adventures of Prince Achmed," a 65-minute silhouette film based on tales from the Arabian

Nights. "At that time animation was in its infancy, there was just Felix the Cat, Fleischer's cartoons and so forth; Mickey Mouse was far away in the future. For the filmmakers of this period, those were the days: with each film we could make new discoveries, find new problems, new possibilities, technical and artistic, we were most eager to execute. The whole field was virgin soil and we had all the joys of explorers in an unknown country. It was wonderful.

"Yet, when . . . a Berlin banker, Louis Hagen, visited the Institute and saw us at work, and asked us whether we could consider making a full-length picture in silhouettes, we had to think twice. This was a never heard of thing. Animated films were supposed to make people roar with laughter, and nobody had dared to entertain an audience with them for more than ten minutes. Everybody to whom we talked in the industry about that proposition was horrified.

"But we did not belong to the industry. We always had been outsiders and we always had done what we wanted to do. Our friends were artists of the same calibre who approached films in their own ways, such as Ruttmann, Bartosch, Richter and Eggeling and others. So we were not afraid of the challenge.

"As the making of those silhouette films did not require very expensive equipment nor a great personnel, and money in this

(From the silhouette film "The Adventures of Prince Achmed." Produced by Berlin Comenius Films, 1926.)

time of inflation became less valuable from day to day, our conscience was not overburdened in that direction. So we decided to accept that most tempting proposal.

"The banker did not want this film to be made in the framework of the Institute and offered to install a studio for us above his garages in the vegetable gardens of his house in Potsdam. So we went there. We being me and my husband Carl Koch, who had married me meantime, and later on Berthold Bartosch, who had also worked with us in the Institute.

"So we started in 1923 and finished in 1926. Starting with black-and-white only and gradually developing more scenery as movable backgrounds, using soap and sand and paint on different layers, sometimes two negatives, each done on different animation benches and composed by the different artists entirely after their own conception. The anxiety of this process was sometimes almost unbearable. Whilst working you only see your figures on your composition in one position. What will it look like when it moves, or what the two compositions, which might look all right in themselves, will look like when they are printed together, were riddles whose solution could only be awaited with hope. Many of the things we did are

nowadays a household word, but we really did them for the first time. Often we had to experiment for weeks until we got them ready for shooting.

"Although this was the time of the silent film, we were anxious to provide our picture with every support to ensure its coming over well to its audience. So we had the musician Wolfgang Zeller collaborating with us throughout this time, composing the score. When for instance a procession was wanted he composed a march; we measured with stop watches and tried to move the figures according to its beat. Or a Glockenspiel was executed to measure. In this period the better theaters employed an orchestra and for the more ambitious films special music was composed. In our own score, for this purpose, small pictures of the film were cut out and pasted in, so that the conductor knew where he had to place his intended effects. . . .'"[1]

1926. "When the film was finished, we did not find any theater which wished to play it. So we arranged on our own a first performance at the Volksbuehne, a theater in the North of Berlin, where Wolfgang Zeller was in charge of the orchestra. His musicians had consented to play for us on a Sunday morning for his sake. We invited the press and all the people we could think of on postcards. As we had led a very remote life during the production, we had not had much contact with the press; our friend Bert Brecht helped us a great deal to invite the right people. It had to be on a Sunday morning, and as it was Spring and good weather had broken out, we did not think that many people would sacrifice a beautiful morning to see a mysterious, never-heard-of silhouette film in an out-of-the-way theater. But they all came and the theater was over-crowded. . . .''[1]

The film was a resounding success, and was followed by an-imated adaptations of *Doctor Doolittle* by Hugh Lofting in 1928 and cartoon shorts.

1930s. Moved to England with her husband. The two artists worked together on a variety of projects, utilizing both sil-houette and colored flat-figure techniques. Their projects in-cluded films for the General Post Office Film Unit in Britain and the John Art Centre in New Barnett, England. About the technical production of their collaborated films, Reiniger ex-plained: ''The kind of life we are trying to achieve through these figures is, of course, an artificial one of its own; we are creating a special sort of world of character and setting and action. Our figures move within their own simplified limits, freed from the restrictions of actuality. They are the timeless creatures of fantasy with their own laws of movement and action—their own style or stylization, in fact.

''Paralled with this work of designing and cutting out the fig-ures comes the design of the sets. Like the performing figures these, too, are cut-outs. We use no painted backgrounds on sheets of paper as in normal animation. The sets are cut out in sections, and the figures can move in and out of these sections with the controlled timing necessary for the action. Some of our settings are made of translucent materials (in particular, coloured gelatines) which lie on top of each other and give various coloured densities of light.

''The lighting of silhouette films comes exclusively from be-neath the table on which the sets or figures are manipulated beneath the camera; the silhouette film registers its pictures in terms of various shades black to white.

''The shooting stage is first reached when all the preparations are complete for photographing whatever sequence in the film we happen to have chosen with which to initiate ourselves into the subject. We like to ease our way into a film in this manner, chosing the particular sequence which we think will act as the best guide to our work on the rest of the film. It becomes a kind of test sequence.

''We complete our shooting frame by frame, recording each exposure in a shooting book. The action is controlled by means of the original music chart, which acts as a guide to each frame-by-frame phase of the movements. We are thinking in terms of so many frames to each beat of music, and we adjust the limbs and the expressions of our characters in such a way that they respond to the music as subtly as we can make them.

''This for us is the crucial part of the work in our medium, at once the root and the climax of its artistry. It is so because we have to be able to sense intuitively how we may create a living action in terms of our particular characters in the time dictated to us by the needs of the music. We rehearse the movements in sketch form as well as by manipulating the figures them-selves. But the final result depends on our intuitive understand-ing of what our flat, jointed cut-out characters can perform most expressively. That for us is our art.'' [John Halas and

(Filmstrip from the silhouette film "Papageno." Pro-duced by Lotte Reiniger Films, 1935.)

Roger Manvell, *The Technique of Film Animation*, Hastings House, 1971.²]

At the start of World War II, Reiniger and her husband moved to Italy, where they continued to make silhouette films until they returned to Berlin in 1944.

1949. Returned to England. Began making films for English and American television.

1963. After the death of her husband, Carl Koch, Reiniger retired from making silhouette films for eleven years.

1974. Commissioned to make a new film, "Aucassin and Ni-colette," by the National Film Board of Canada. The film won a special prize at the 1976 Ottawa International Animated Film Festival. From 1974 until 1980, Reiniger lectured in the United States, Canada, Europe, and Turkey on shadow animation. "There remains a good deal to say about the artistic problems of this type of film, about its future, and about its value. But I am content to leave these matters to those people whose profession it is to bother about such problems. I feel that I do better to concentrate on making the films—and on making as many as my good luck allows. Each new film raises new problems and questions, and I can only hope to live long enough to do justice to them all."¹

1980. In failing health, Reiniger moved to Dettenhausen, West Germany.

June 19, 1981. Died in Dettenhausen at the age of eighty-two.

FOR MORE INFORMATION SEE: Illustrators of Children's Books: 1946-1956, Horn Book, 1958; John Halas and Roger Manvell, *The Technique of Film Animation*, 3rd edition, Focal Press, 1971; Robert Russett and Cecile Starr, *Experimental Animation: An Illustrated Anthology*, Van Nostrand, 1976; *Film Library Quarterly*, Volume 10, number 1-2, 1977; "The Art of Lotte Reiniger" (motion picture). Obituaries: *Annual Obituary 1981*, St. Martin's, 1982; *Contemporary Authors*, Volume 108, Gale, 1983.

They stayed on the so-called big country road for about three miles. After the woods came meadows, fences, and then more stretches of woods. ■ (From *Doctor's Boy* by Karin Anckarsvärd. Illustrated by Fermin Rocker.)

ROCKER, Fermin   1907-

PERSONAL: Born December 22, 1907, in London, England; came to United States; married Ruth (a free-lance copy editor); children: one son. *Education:* Attended Municipal School of Arts and Crafts, Berlin, Germany.

CAREER: Illustrator. Has worked as a commercial lithographer, animated cartoonist, and commercial artist. Work has been exhibited at various museums, including Library of Congress, Metropolitan Museum of Art, and Brooklyn Museum.

ILLUSTRATOR—All for young people: Natalie Carlson, *A Pet for the Orphelines*, Harper, 1962; N. Carlson, *Carnival in Paris*, Harper, 1962; Virginia Sorensen, *Lotte's Locket* (*Horn Book* honor list), Harcourt, 1964; Eden V. Stevens, *The Piper*, Atheneum, 1964; Wilhelmina Harper, editor, *Merry Christmas to You: Stories for Christmas*, revised edition (Rocker was not associated with earlier edition), Dutton, 1965; Ruth M. Arthur, *My Daughter, Nicola*, Atheneum, 1965; Karin Anckarsvärd, *Doctor's Boy* (*Horn Book* honor list), translated from the Swedish by Annabelle MacMillan, Harcourt, 1965; Vera Henry, *Ong, the Wild Gander*, Lippincott, 1966; Nellie Burchardt,

Project Cat, F. Watts, 1966; Betty F. Horvath, *Hooray for Jasper*, F. Watts, 1966; B. F. Horvath, *Jasper Makes Music*, F. Watts, 1967; O. Henry, *Gift of the Magi, and Five Other Stories*, F. Watts, 1967; James J. Poling, *The Man Who Saved Robinson Crusoe*, Norton, 1967; Elizabeth Foster and Slim Williams, *The Friend of the Singing One*, Atheneum, 1967; K. Anckarsvärd, *Struggle at Soltuna*, translated from the Swedish by A. MacMillan, Harcourt, 1968; Carol R. Brink, *Two Are Better than One*, Macmillan, 1968; C. R. Brink, *Winter Cottage*, Macmillan, 1968; Henry James, *The Jolly Corner* [*and*] *The Real Thing*, F. Watts, 1968; Thomas Fall (pseudonym of Donald Clifford Snow), *Goat Boy of Brooklyn*, Dial, 1968.

Hila Colman, *Andy's Landmark House*, Parents Magazine Press, 1969; Elizabeth Coatsworth, *Indian Mound Farm*, Macmillan, 1969; Bertha Stemm Norton and Andre Norton, *Bertie and May*, World Publishing, 1969; Stanley Steiner, *George Washington: The Indian Influence* (biography), Putnam, 1970; Jean Bothwell, *The Mystery Candlestick*, Dial, 1970; Robert Burch,

(From *Lotte's Locket* by Virginia Sorensen. Illustrated by Fermin Rocker.)

Simon and the Game of Chance, Viking, 1970; Lorraine Henriod, *Marie Curie* (biography), Putnam, 1970; Patricia Miles Martin, *Thomas Alva Edison* (biography), Putnam, 1971; Charles P. Graves, *Mark Twain* (biography), Putnam, 1972; C. P. Graves, *The Wright Brothers* (biography), Putnam, 1973; James M. Marks, *Jason,* Oxford University Press (London), 1973; Peter Carter, *Gates of Paradise* (biography), Oxford University Press (London), 1974, Oxford University Press, 1979; Winifred Cawley, *Gran at Coalgate,* Oxford University Press (London), 1974, Holt, 1975; Bernard Ashley, *The Trouble with Donovan Croft,* Oxford University Press (London), 1974; Johanna Reiss, *The Journey Back,* Oxford University Press (London), 1977; J. M. Marks, *Hijacked!,* Penguin (London), 1977.

SIDELIGHTS: "I have come to most things rather late in life and book illustration is one of them. The first book I illustrated, *A Pet for the Orphelines,* was published by Harper in 1962. I actually manifested an early interest in drawing and painting but it was not until I reached my thirties that I devoted all my time to those pursuits. After finishing school in Germany I worked for five years as a commercial lithographer, serving a full apprenticeship in that trade. Later when I came to the United States, I drifted into the animated cartoon field. From about 1938 on I devoted all my time to painting, etching, and lithography. I tried my hand—not too successfully—at commercial work. I finally discovered that of all the commercial applications of art, book illustration, while not the most remunerative, was the most satisfying one. An added factor may have been my inability to come to terms with art and music that need to be 'explained' before they can be enjoyed. Children, before they received their cultural brainwashing at least, seem to share my sentiments in this regard. I have not found working with a simple, uncompromising ink line too easy, yet with the exception of *The Piper,* which used wash drawings, this is the technique I have used in almost all my books. On most of my jackets the key drawing was done in ink and the added colors with pencil or crayon on acetate or dinobase." [Lee Kingman and others, compilers, *Illustrators of Children's Books: 1957-1966,* Horn Book, 1968.]

Rocker's works are included in the Kerlan Collection at the University of Minnesota.

Eat no green apples or you'll droop,
Be careful not to get the croup,
Avoid the chicken-pox and such,
And don't fall out of windows much.

—Edward Anthony

ROSEN, Michael (Wayne) 1946-

BRIEF ENTRY: Born May 9, 1946, in Harrow, Middlesex, England. British poet, playwright, free-lance writer, and broadcaster. Rosen has gained the reputation of being an innovative poet of children's verse who employs nonsensical humor in dialogue form. Dealing with subjects easily identifiable and appealing to young readers, he has the ability to pinpoint the child's view of everyday situations—tying your shoes, having your hair cut, sharing a bedroom. The result is an amusing look at childhood's many idiosyncrasies. *School Library Journal* described his first book of poems, *Mind Your Own Business* (Phillips, 1974), as "lighthearted earthy and unintrospective," appropriately accompanied by Quentin Blake's cartoon-like "slapdash drawings." This book was followed by seven others, including two additional ones illustrated by Blake: *Wouldn't You Like to Know* (Deutsch, 1977) and *You Can't Catch Me!* (Deutsch, 1981). Rosen's latest book of verse is *Bloody L.I.A.R.S.*, which he published himself in 1984.

In 1982 Rosen was the recipient of the Signal Poetry Award for *You Can't Catch Me!*. That same year marked the beginning of "Everybody Here," a children's series on poetry he created for Thames Television in London. In 1983 he received the Other Award for a miscellany of material taken from the show and published under the same title. In addition to poetry, Rosen is the author of several juvenile stories such as *Once There Was a King Who Promised He Would Never Chop Anyone's Head Off* (Deutsch, 1976), *The Bakerloo Flea* (Longman, 1979), and *Nasty!* (Longman, 1982). He has also written three plays for adults: "Backbone" and "Stewed Figs," both for stage, and "Regis Debray," for radio. *Home:* 11 Meeson St., London E5 0EA, England.

FOR MORE INFORMATION SEE: Contemporary Authors, Volumes 25-28, revised, Gale, 1977; *Twentieth-Century Children's Writers,* 2nd edition, St. Martin's, 1983.

ROSENBERG, Dorothy 1906-
(Dorothy Young Croman)

PERSONAL: Born December 25, 1906, in Waverly, Wash.; daughter of Edward Henry (a chemist) and Blanche (Bennett) Young; married Harrison Croman, August 1, 1943 (divorced, 1952); married George Rosenberg, August 21, 1970 (died, 1970); children: (first marriage) Garry Croman, Sherrill (Mrs. Orville Taylor), Maureen (Mrs. Paul Travis). *Education:* Attended Reed College, 1937-39, and University of Washington, Seattle, 1956, 1957, and 1962. *Religion:* Protestant. *Home:* 3505 Northeast 95th St., Apt. 306, Seattle, Wash. 98115.

CAREER: Seattle (Wash.) public schools, secretary and writer, 1954-64; University of Washington, Seattle, night supervisor of two dormitories, 1965-69. Volunteer worker at Orthopedic Hospital, Seattle. *Member:* Smithsonian Associates, American Association of Retired Persons, Orthopedic Hospital (Seattle), National League of American Pen Women (secretary of Seattle branch, 1968-70; president of Seattle branch, 1984-86), Pioneer Association of State of Washington, Seattle Historical Society, Seattle Art Museum, Seattle Urban League, Reed College Alumni Association, Hamilton House Senior Citizens.

WRITINGS—All under name Dorothy Young Croman: *Mystery of Steamboat Rock,* Putnam, 1956; *Danger in Sagebrush Coun-*

try, Tyndale, 1984; *Trouble on the Blue Fox Islands,* Tyndale, 1985; *Poison Ring Mystery,* Tyndale, 1985.

Readers for slow learners; all published by Stanwix: *Something to Do,* two books, 1962, 1966; *World of Wonder,* 1965; *Gather Around,* two books, 1966, 1971. Also author of *Bright Courage.* Contributor to adult publications and children's magazines. Editor, *Whistling Swan* (newsletter of Seattle branch of National League of American Pen Women), 1976-80.

WORK IN PROGRESS: Oil Spurts for Sandy, a children's novel with an Alaskan setting.

SIDELIGHTS: "I've often wondered what my life would have been had my mother not died when I was nine years old. I have heard wonderful things about her, her good character, her musical ability, her kindness. I learned to play the piano but not as well as she, I'm sure. I also loved to play the pump organ at my grandparent's home.

"I needed my mother most in high school. I was a sensitive, withdrawn young girl and the beloved grandparents with whom my two younger brothers, Bennett and Edward, and I grew up in central Oregon gave us good care, but there was not the emotional support a young girl needs from a mother. My father, a kindly and good man, was a chemist for the Utah-Idaho Sugar Company and was away most of the time.

DOROTHY ROSENBERG

"I loved the animals around the farm, the new-born calves and kittens, the baby chicks, a lamb now and then, and of course my own riding pony. I spent hours catching little wild bunnies to tame. For two summers I even had two wild magpies which became tame enough to eat from my hands. The first summer I kept them caged but the second summer they returned on their own. My brothers shot gophers to help feed them. I tried to teach the lovely black and white, long-tailed birds to talk but they never did. I couldn't stand the thought of slitting their tongues which I was told had to be done if they were to speak. I couldn't bear to hurt anything.

"My first short story was written when I was in my teens. Later, the first story sold was a short story about a kitten for a little religious Sunday School paper, *Dew Drops*. I walked on air for days after that. From time to time I'd sell children's stories to juvenile magazines.

"After I was married, my father came to live with us and he told many stories of his childhood. In 1883 his family arrived by mule-drawn covered wagons from Iowa to eastern Washington near the present site of the Grand Coulee Dam. The party included the parents, paternal grandparents and four uncles. Dad told his childhood activities so often that I finally wrote my first juvenile novel, *Mystery of Steamboat Rock,* using him as the main character.

"While working for the Seattle Public Schools I became interested in racial matters. During the 1950s I discovered that pioneering included blacks as well as many other ethnic groups. *Danger in Sagebrush Country* is about two early pioneer families, one white (my own family) and one black (friendly neighbors) and how they adjusted to each other and conditions through their children during those pioneer days.

"Also while working for the Seattle Public Schools for the ten years of my life, I wrote five readers for slow learning children. These books were made up of forty short stories each and covered many subjects."

HOBBIES AND OTHER INTERESTS: Dancing and swimming (particularly as a volunteer worker, teaching senior citizens creative writing, pattern dance and swimming).

ROY, Ron(ald) 1940-

PERSONAL: Born April 29, 1940, in Hartford, Conn.; son of Leo Joseph and Marie (Ouellette) Roy. *Education:* University of Connecticut, B.A., 1965; University of Hartford, M.Ed., 1974. *Residence:* New York, N.Y. *Agent:* Carol Mann Literary Agency, 174 Pacific St., Brooklyn, N.Y. 11201.

CAREER: Author of children's books, 1978—. West Hill School, Rocky Hill, Conn., teacher, 1975-79. Instructor, Institute of Children's Literature, 1982-84. *Military service:* U.S. Navy, 1958-60, hospital corpsman. *Member:* Society of Children's Book Writers, Authors Guild. *Awards, honors: Nightmare Island* and *Frankie Is Staying Back* were chosen as "Children's Choices," 1982, by the International Reading Association.

*WRITINGS—*All for children: *Old Tiger, New Tiger* (illustrated by Patricia M. Bargielski), Abingdon, 1978; *A Thousand Pails of Water* (illustrated by Vo-Dinh Mai), Knopf, 1978; *Awful Thursday* (illustrated by Lillian Hoban), Pantheon, 1979; *Three Ducks Went Wandering* (illustrated by Paul Galdone; Junior

RON ROY

Literary Guild selection), Clarion Books, 1979; *The Shadow in the Pond* (paperback; cover illustration by Gil Cohen), Scholastic Book Services, 1979; *Breakfast with My Father* (illustrated by Troy Howell), Clarion Books, 1980; *Nightmare Island* (illustrated by Robert MacLean), Dutton, 1981; *Frankie Is Staying Back* (illustrated by Walter Kessell), Clarion Books, 1981; *The Great Frog Swap* (illustrated by Victoria Chess), Pantheon, 1981; *Avalanche!* (illustrated by R. MacLean), Dutton, 1981; *What Has Ten Legs and Eats Corn Flakes?: A Pet Book* (illustrated by Lynne Cherry), Clarion Books, 1982; *I Am a Thief* (illustrated by Mel Williges), Dutton, 1982; *Where's Buddy?* (illustrated by T. Howell), Clarion Books, 1982; *Million Dollar Jeans* (illustrated by Joyce A. dos Santos), Dutton, 1983; *Move Over, Wheelchairs Coming Through!*, Clarion Books, 1985; *The Chimp Kid,* Clarion Books, 1985.

SIDELIGHTS: "When I was ten my family moved to a quiet street in East Hartford, Connecticut. I knew no one in the neighborhood. There was a library on the corner, and one day I wandered in. I never really wandered out again.

"I found myself spending several hours a week in the library hunting for things to read. It was not unusual to see me on a summer day surrounded by a stack of books. We were too poor to vacation, but vicariously, I was vacationing all over the world.

"As a kid I spent a lot of time caring for baby animals which I would scoop up whenever I happened to come across one that seemed to need my ministration. My mother seemed to understand my need for their company and allowed small creatures to invade her home regularly. Squirrels, snakes, owls,

"Hi, Harriet," said Wally. "What a cute little tiny frog." ■ (From *The Great Frog Swap* by Ron Roy. Illustrated by Victoria Chess.)

fish, turtles, it didn't matter. Most of my stories have animals lurking somewhere in the text.

"Since that summer in 1950 I have been a reader. Reading is perhaps the biggest influence in my writing of children's books. It is also my chief hobby.

"I started writing in 1974 and have not stopped since. After I received my first rejection letter in the mail, I was hooked. The fact that I knew nothing about preparing manuscripts and approaching editors was all beside the point. I wanted to write so I wrote. I bought a copy of Jane Yolen's book *Writing Books for Children* and the writing world suddenly began to make sense. *Three Ducks Went Wandering* had its beginnings while I was driving my father home from visiting his ninety-seven-year-old mother in Boston. We were together in the car for two hours, and I asked him to help me put together an idea

I'd had about three baby ducks who wander off. At the end of the trip the story was complete.

"I like kids a lot. I write for them, to them, about them. I remember how important books were to me when I was young. One of the reasons I write is to try to bring to kids some of the joy I derive from books.

"I try to fill my life with the things and people I like. My current family consists of a black cat named Updike and my friends.

"When I'm not working, I like to cook. I'm a vegetarian and between paragraphs I make soup, bread, yogurt, and just mess around in the kitchen. When I'm not reading or cooking I run, visit schools, travel, play with my friends.

"But there aren't any dinosaurs," Marty said. "They all died." ■ (From *Awful Thursday* by Ron Roy. Illustrated by Lillian Hoban.)

"My dream is to have a farm and lots of pets. I really love ducks, so I think one day I'd like to raise them.

"My favorite things are kids, animals, sunshine, laughter, peace, good books and music.

"My favorite writers are John Updike, E. B. White, and Anne Tyler."

Roy's works are included in the deGrummond Collection at the University of Southern Mississippi.

RUCK-PAUQUÈT, Gina   1931-

PERSONAL: Born October 17, 1931, in Cologne, West Germany; daughter of Wilhelm (a dentist) and Walburga (Odendah) Pauquèt; married Robert Ruck (a writer). *Education:* Kaiserin Augusta Lyzeum, 1941-45. *Home:* Buchberg, D-8170 Bad Tölz, West Germany.

CAREER: Has worked as a dental hygienist, a model, an advertising assistant, contract agent, court reporter and photojournalist. Author of books for children and young adults, 1958—. Works as a therapist in Munich, 1980—. *Awards, honors:* Oesterreichischer Staatspreis für Kinder- und Jugen-

dliteratur in the youth book category, 1967, for *Joschko;* "Golden Pocketbook" from O. Maier Publisher for the sale of over one million paperbacks out of the Ravensburg publishing house, 1977.

WRITINGS—In English translation; all juvenile fiction: *Der kleine Igel,* Verlag Herder, 1959, translation published as *Little Hedgehog* (illustrated by Marianne Richter), Hastings House, 1959; *Gespenster essen kein Sauerkraut,* Lentz Verlag, 1959, translation by Marion Koenig published as *Ghosts Don't Eat Sausages* (illustrated by Lilo Fromm), Albert Whitman, 1964; *Zweiundzwanzig kleine Katzen,* Verlag Herder, 1961, translation published as *Twenty-Two Little Cats* (illustrated by Eva Hohrath), McGraw, 1962; *Vierzehn hoellenschwarze Kisten,* Lentz Verlag, 1962, translation by Edite Kroll published as *Fourteen Cases of Dynamite* (illustrated by Fromm), Seymour Lawrence, 1968; *Joschko,* Cecilie Dressler Verlag, 1963, translation by Edelgard von Heydekampf Bruehl published as *The Most Beautiful Place* (illustrated by Sigrid Heuck), Dutton, 1965.

Die Tante und der Seehund (illustrated by Herbert Lentz), Annette Betz Verlag, 1965, translation by Anthony Graham published as *Aunt Matilda and the Sea-Lion* (illustrated by Lentz), World's Work, 1967, another translation published as *Aunt Matilda and the Baby Seal* (illustrated by Lentz), Hart Publishing, 1968; *Waehrend du schlaefst* (illustrated by Gisela Degler-Rummel), Bertelsmann Jugendbuchverlag, 1969, translation published as *Red Peppers for a Donkey* (illustrated by Degler-Rummel), Blackie & Son, 1970, adaptation by Euan Cooper-Willis published as *Helen's Dream* (illustrated by De-

GINA RUCK-PAUQUÈT

gler-Rummel), Blackie & Son, 1970; *Der Koala-Baer,* [West Germany], 1976, translation published as *Oh, That Koala!* (illustrated by Anna Mossakowska), McGraw, 1979.

Honey Bear (illustrated by Erika Dietzsch-Capelle), Kestrel Books, 1979; *Murmelbaer,* Annette Betz Verlag, 1979, translation by Anthea Bell published as *Mumble Bear* (illustrated by Dietzsch-Capelle), Putnam, 1980; *Kai-to, der Elefant, der sang,* Annette Betz Verlag, 1981, translation by Bell published as *The Singing Elephant* (illustrated by Monika Laimgruber), Hodder & Stoughton, 1983.

Also author of numerous additional books in German.

WORK IN PROGRESS: "In contrast to earlier days when I committed to work with deadlines two years in advance, I am no longer willing to plan my future to such an extent. So there are at this point no other projects pending. But it is certain that I will continue to write for children, that I will tell them stories that are exciting or funny, realistic or fanciful."

SIDELIGHTS: Since 1958 Ruck-Pauquèt has had more than eighty books published and translated into fifteen languages. She has contributed to children's theaters, children's radio, television, magazines, textbooks and anthologies. "[This is what] I am—a woman who has written books, many poems, lyrics for songs, stories, radio plays and musicals, a woman who enjoys success.

"I am also—a woman who has learned to live for the moment, at the place between past and future, on a mountain surrounded by people and cats.

"I started writing as a child. I wrote down what I found to be pleasing, funny, bad or sad, everything that affected me. I believe the real reason for my writing is that I would like to hold on to life. My life has always been rather unsettled, chaotic, fast-moving. I have tried my hand at many professions and have had relationships with many different kinds of people. Much was constantly happening in my life. I would gladly have been able to control time in order to stop it or at least to slow it down, to keep things from being over so soon.

"Time, however, cannot be controlled. Therefore, I wrote everything down. I produced my first children's book when I was twenty-five and have stayed with it since.

"People often ask which books influenced me in my childhood. In those days I did actually read a lot. But I found life around me to be bolder, more beautiful, more awful, more fascinating, simply more powerful than books.

"That still remains to be the case today. My friends include people from all social strata. I think adulthood is wonderful, for I consider childhood to be a difficult time. As a child one is judged to be extrinsic, incapable of living one's own life. One is inexperienced, inept at articulating and bodily weak. Often a child represents to his guardians something like a hopeful continuation of their own not optimally developed personality.

"Adulthood is not paradise. But at least it allows for a certain measure of freedom of movement, of independence, which makes it possible to decide when to go to bed and whether or not to eat spinach. Yet by the time a person is old enough to jump into a puddle without the objection [encountered during childhood], he is unfortunately most often so inhibited, he no longer enjoys it. For me the joy in doing such wonderful things

has remained intact. All that I do, I do seriously, and yet with a measure of playfulness.

"I detested schools. Even today it makes my skin crawl when I enter a school. In school, besides vocabulary, I learned historic dates, mathematical skills and similar things, most significantly an achievement mentality, extreme conformity and resulting insincerity. I learned nothing about people, nothing about affection; nothing about all that for which we have such pressing need.

"I do not actually work at my writing. I am not diligent, I have never been. I draw from intuition. What entices me to write is the creative process, the creation, the development, the eruptive process of being swept along as in a crashing torrent.

"I put all the text which I have written aside for a few days, then read it again, but seldom change anything. That does not mean that I perceive any of my stories to be perfect. The dream of the 'absolute' is fortunately never fulfilled. Therefore, interest is maintained and with it the incentive to try again.

"Every character I write about is also a piece of me, a small part of myself. We can only draw out feelings from inside ourselves. I take reality and filter it through my own personality. The stories do not come from reality. The age group for which I write is determined by the subject matter.

"Now and again someone asks if I fear the day I run out of material. I do not fear that. Even if I become very old, will my time be sufficient to write down everything I consider to be worthwhile. If, in spite of that fact, I write less in the future, it will be to spend more time in direct contact with people.

"During the last years I have in my young adult books written authentic stories, stories about people I know. At the moment I'm working on 'Menschen-Portraits' (working title). In it I describe people who come to visit me in my home—the old neighbor woman, the farmer, the rebellious youth, the advice-seeker, the mentally-ill, the alternative life-style seeker, the mild revolutionary and the dreamer.

"I have always dealt with the subject of being different, which is the theme of man's uniqueness. If I have one concern, it is promoting tolerance in the right of the individual to seek a suitable life-style even if that life style belongs to someone on the fringes of society.

"I don't put much store in raising children. The word for me personifies the image of pulling at someone until he fits the desired mold. Care is better, regard for the life of the other, the rendering of opportunity.

"'You certainly must like children very much,' I am often asked. Were I to answer this question affirmatively, I would be limiting myself unnecessarily. I like children, hobos, musicians, the girls in the communes, cats, trees, and old men who sit on park benches.

"I keep myself as far removed as possible from literary circles. Too many intellectuals. Too much talk. I feel easily imprisoned in small rooms. I suffered from that in school already.

They turned up the strangest things—a bicycle without wheels, two cow bells, an ear trumpet, a church tower weather vane, a broken drum, a bath tub, a trolley brake, 300 rusty razor blades....

■ (From *Fourteen Cases of Dynamite* by Gina Ruck-Pauquèt. Illustrated by Lilo Fromm.)

"I am not an intellectual. I write down thoughts as they come to me. I describe slips of paper and cigarette boxes.

"It is very time-consuming to answer mail from my readers. I receive letters from children, parents, from the elderly, from people who are pursuing writing, from autograph collectors, letters from both home and abroad. A little boy once asked me for support, because his cat was to be put to sleep. Another time a desperate woman and her five children wanted to move in with me. I receive love letters and mail from young people who seek guidance.

"My relationship with my publishers is good. Over the years I have been able to prevail with friendly persistence, so that the conditions under which our collaboration exists, is now acceptable to both."

HOBBIES AND OTHER INTERESTS: Music, painting, the countryside, and "the stories of unspoiled people."

FOR MORE INFORMATION SEE: Cricket, February, 1975.

SALVADORI, Mario (George) 1907-

PERSONAL: Born March 19, 1907, in Rome, Italy; came to United States, 1939; naturalized U.S. citizen, 1944; son of Riccardo (an engineer) and Ermelinda (Alatri) Salvadori; married first wife, Giuseppina Tagliacozzo, June 30, 1935 (divorced, 1975); married Carol Bookman (a market researcher), May 5, 1975; children: (first marriage) Vieri R.; (second marriage) a stepson, Michael Kazin. *Education:* University of Rome, doctor of civil engineering, 1930, doctor of pure mathematics (cum laude), 1933, Libero Docente in theory of structures, 1936; additional study at University College, London, England, 1933-34. *Home:* 2 Beekman Place, New York, N.Y. 10022. *Office:* Weidlinger Associates, 333 Seventh Ave., New York, N.Y. 10001.

CAREER: University of Rome, Rome, Italy, instructor, 1933-37, assistant professor of theory of structures, 1937-38; Columbia University, New York City, lecturer, 1940-41, instructor, 1941-46, professor of civil engineering, 1946-75, professor of architecture, 1959-75, chairman of Architectural Technology Division, 1965-73, professor emeritus of architecture and James Renwick Professor Emeritus of Civil Engineering, 1975—. Consulting engineer, Istituto Nazionale di Calcolo, Rome, 1932-38; time and motion engineer, The Lionel Corp., Irvington, N.J., 1939; vice-president of Industrial Products Trading Corp., New York City, 1939-42; consultant to Manhattan Project, 1942-44; consulting engineer to Paul Weidlinger, New York City, 1954-63, partner, Weidlinger Associates, 1963-83; principal, 1983—; vice-president of Advanced Computer Techniques Corp., New York City, 1962-65. Consultant to government agencies and industries. Lecturer, with the rank of professor of architecture, Princeton University, 1954-60. Teacher in grade and junior high schools in Harlem, North Bronx, and South Bronx, N.Y., 1975—. *Military service:* Italian Army, 1931-32; became second lieutenant.

MEMBER: International Association for Shell Structures, International Association for Bridge and Structural Engineering, International Union of Theoretical and Applied Mechanics (member of assembly), American Society of Mechanical Engineers (fellow), American Society of Civil Engineers (fellow; member of committee on applied mechanics, 1944-50; member of committee on thin shells, structural division, 1949-52; chairman of committee on mathematical methods in engineering, mechanics division, 1952-54; honorary member, 1982), American Concrete Institute (fellow), New York Academy of Sciences (fellow), American Institute of Architects (honorary member, 1980—), National Academy of Engineering (member, 1983), Tau Beta Pi, Sigma Xi, Academic Alpine Club of Italy.

AWARDS, HONORS: Honorary professor of University of Minas Gerais, Brazil, 1954; Engineer of the Year, 1977, from Drexel University; D.Sc. from Columbia University, 1978; award for children's nonfiction from New York Academy of Sciences, and *Boston Globe-Horn Book* Award, both 1980, both for *Building: The Fight against Gravity.*

WRITINGS: Differential Equations in Engineering Problems, Columbia University Press, 1947, revised edition (with Ralph J. Schwarz), Prentice-Hall, 1954; *The Mathematical Solution of Engineering Problems,* problems by Kenneth S. Miller, McGraw-Hill, 1948, revised edition, Columbia University Press, 1957; (with Melvin L. Baron) *Numerical Methods in Engineering,* Prentice-Hall, 1952, 2nd edition, 1961; (translator with Giuseppina T. Salvadori) Pier Luigi Nervi, *Structures,* F. W. Dodge Corp. (New York), 1956.

(Translator with G. T. Salvadori) Giovanni Ponti, *In Praise of Architecture,* F. W. Dodge Corp., 1960; (with Robert Heller) *Structure in Architecture,* Prentice-Hall, 1963, second edition, 1975; (with John Michael McCormick) *Numerical Methods in FORTRAN,* Prentice-Hall, 1964; (with Matthys Levy) *Structural Design in Architecture,* problem solutions by John J. Farrell, Prentice-Hall, 1967, second edition, problem solutions by Howard H. M. Hwang, 1981; *Mathematics in Architecture,* Prentice-Hall, 1968; (with Jeremiah Eck and Giuseppe de Campoli) *Statics and Strength of Structures,* Prentice-Hall, 1971; *Building: The Fight against Gravity* (juvenile; drawings by Saralinda Hooker and Christopher Ragus; *Horn Book* honor list), Atheneum, 1979; *Why Buildings Stand Up: The Strength of Architecture* (drawings by S. Hooker and C. Ragus), Norton, 1980; *Architecture and Engineering* (teacher's manual), New York Academy of Sciences, 1982.

Translator into Italian of short poems of Emily Dickinson. Contributor to professional journals in many countries, including the United States, England, Italy, France, and Romania.

MARIO SALVADORI

WORK IN PROGRESS: An autobiography.

SIDELIGHTS: "I began writing books to satisfy the requests of my students for textbooks. I thus learned that there is no better way of understanding a subject than to write about it. My children's book first confronted me with the problems of the writer. My book for the layman showed me how difficult and fascinating it is to learn the writer's trade. Now my autobiography gives me the agony and the joy of dealing with words."

A university-level teacher at Columbia University for more than four decades, Salvadori introduced himself to a new teaching arena in 1975. Under the sponsorship of the New York Academy of Sciences, Salvadori began teaching a fourteen-week course in basic principles of architectural structures to junior-high students in New York's South Bronx and Harlem. Salvadori related in the *New York Times* some of the personal delights of teaching this course. "To my surprise, the children seem to absorb the ideas better and quicker than do my university students. Their enthusiasm is unbounded and their questions come like bullets from a machine gun. . . . I had asked some teachers to attend the classes, and even during our first meeting I got as many questions from them as from the children. The next time they came with twice as many students. . . . When one of my Columbia students graduates with honors, I am happy. But when the first graduate of my [junior high school] course, who six years ago was twelve, entered the school of architecture at Pratt Institute . . . , I was really proud.''

Part of the popularity that Salvadori had with his young students grew out of the respect that he showed for them. ''. . . Children should be treated as honest, bright, enthusiastic adults. They are ready for such treatment from their early years and, certainly, from the moment they enter school. Nothing is so damaging to children as condescension—either by considering them inferior in sensitivity or intelligence or, more subtly and more dangerously, by simplifying things for them. Children are so psychologically alert that tricks and games do not fool them. It is essential that in education, as in any other human activity, a spade be called a spade. Of course, I do not mean that one should brutally compel children to acquire knowledge and accept ideas against their will. Education is by its own nature a voluntary phenomenon, and no amount of force, authority, or violence will ever succeed in imparting it. Hence, motivation is the key word in the educational process, in which success is measured by the knowledge and the ideas the child gladly makes his or her own.

''In my opinion, authoritarian education is a contradiction in terms and leads to unavoidable failure. Unfortunately, the kind of education I am most familiar with—science education—often has an authoritarian bent. When confronted with the statement that a negative number multiplied by another negative number gives a positive result, the child asks, 'Why?' Most of the time the unsatisfactory answer is 'This is a rule.' It is so much simpler to explain—by using the analogy of numbers and distances along an axis—that *minus* means change direction and that if one is moving to the right, which is the plus direction, and is asked to change direction twice, one ends up by still moving to the right, that is, with a plus. Thus, once the 'rule' is visualized, it becomes clear and easily accepted.

''The second principle I suggest is that the child be allowed to follow freely his or her imagination, even if it leads to unexpected results. As a corollary to this suggestion, I also believe that the child should be allowed to reach an answer by the path he or she spontaneously chooses and that the path in the book should not necessarily be considered best for all. Demonstrating the principles of structures to a kindergarten class, I once asked a boy of five, who had told me he knew all about gravity, 'Although the earth is pulling on you, why are you not falling to the next floor below?' His answer was a real eye-opener to me. 'That's because of the floor. You see, if there were no gravity, we would all fall *upwards*.' I must confess that I had never thought about the absence of gravity in this manner, but the boy, in a sense, was right.

''The third principle I am proposing is really an axiom of life. One can teach only those one loves. You have all seen a loving teacher make more difference than a well-furnished classroom, a well-stacked library, or an efficient principal. You have all heard of the teacher who had charisma and gets more out of the children than a better-trained and more knowledgeable one. The trouble with this axiom is that love cannot be taught—either we have it in us, or we don't. We cannot force ourselves to love if we don't feel like loving. But those blessed individuals who are born loving and have chosen to become educators instinctively know a number of additional truths: that we should never underestimate a child, that we should always expect the best from a child, that we should bring the child up to our own level rather than descend to his or her supposedly lower level. Such attitudes not only do not diminish the authority of the teacher, but they actually enhance it, making the teacher spontaneously acceptable. A particularly important aspect of this

approach is a candid confession of our ignorance and our mistakes. The greatest compliment I ever received from a student came from a twelve-year-old girl at the end of the course. She was asked suggestions on how to improve the course, for something she would like to change in the teacher's approach. The girl wrote, 'The only thing wrong with Mario is that there is nothing wrong with Mario. He is the first teacher I ever had who did not get mad when we caught him wrong.'

''Our good luck has entrusted to us those young human beings on whom the future of the world rests. It is fortunate that although other sources of energy on our planet may be exhaustible, human energy is not. But its inexhaustibility does not make it less precious or delicate. If 'Handle with Care' is written on all essential components of a nuclear reactor, this same motto should appear on the door of each classroom in the world and should be permanently imprinted on the brains of all of us who write for children. Ours is an awesome and exhilarating task. May we be inspired, loving, and dedicated enough to live up to our responsibility. A lesser life is not worth living.'' [Mario Salvadori, ''Children: The Inexhaustible Source of Human Energy,'' *Horn Book,* December, 1983.]

HOBBIES AND OTHER INTERESTS: Music, collecting art, engineering large sculptures, mountain climbing (retired), graphology, and the scientific investigation of thought transmission.

FOR MORE INFORMATION SEE: Civil Engineering, June, 1974; *Long Island Press,* February 1, 1977; *New York Times,* February 21, 1977, May 5, 1981, November 15, 1981; *American Society of Civil Engineers (ASCE) News,* March, 1978; *New York Daily News,* May 13, 1979; *Columbia,* winter, 1979; *Scientific American,* December, 1980, April, 1981; *Horn Book,* April, 1981, December, 1983; *Times Literary Supplement,* July 10, 1981.

SAMPSON, Fay (Elizabeth)   1935-

BRIEF ENTRY: Born June 10, 1935, in Plymouth, England. A graduate of the University College of the Southwest, Sampson received a certificate in education from the University of Exeter. She has worked as an assistant mathematics teacher, and as an evening class lecturer in writing since 1979. As an author of ten juvenile books, including novels for young adults, Sampson commented: ''. . . For me the essential motivation in writing is curiosity. 'What would it be like if . . .?' 'What if they *had* . . .?' Or just 'Why?' My books are an exploration of these questions. . . .'' Among her young adult novels are *The Watch on Patterick Fell* (Dobson, 1978, Greenwillow, 1980) and its sequel *Landfall on Innis Michael* (Dobson, 1980). Both books look at the subject of nuclear technology through the differing perspectives of the main characters, teenagers Roger and Elspeth Lowman. *Junior Bookshelf* described the novels as ''a grim peep into what could happen in the future . . . ,'' filled ''with pace and purpose . . . [and] serious overtones of the effect of nuclear energy on ordinary people, young and old.''

In contrast to the futuristic environment of these two novels, Sampson chose turn-of-the-century England as her setting for *The Hungry Snow* (Dobson, 1980). *Junior Bookshelf* again commented on this story of a fourteen-year-old Dartmoor girl growing up amidst the harsh realities of famine, describing it as a ''frighteningly real'' tale in which ''the narrative is gripping . . . and the characterisation . . . vividly created.'' In another young adult book, *Sus* (Dobson, 1982), Sampson deals with the present times as she delves into the problem of law and order vs. young people, a confrontation that ends in major riot. Her other writings are: *F.67* (Hamish Hamilton, 1975), *Half a Welcome* (Dobson, 1977), *The Empty House* (Dobson, 1979), *The Chains of Sleep* (Dobson, 1981), *Pangur Ban: The White Cat* (Lion, 1983), and *Jenny and the Wreckers* (Hamilton, 1984). *Home:* Christie Cottage, Tedburn St. Mary, Exeter, Devonshire EX6 6AZ, England.

FOR MORE INFORMATION SEE: Contemporary Authors, Volume 101, Gale, 1981.

SAN SOUCI, Robert D.   1946-

PERSONAL: Surname is pronounced ''San *Sue*-see''; born October 10, 1946, in San Francisco, Calif.; son of Robert Abraham (a business consultant) and Mary Ellen (Kelleher) San Souci. *Education:* St. Mary's College, Moraga, Calif., B.A.,

1968; graduate study, California State University, Hayward, 1968-70. *Address:* 2000 Center St., Box 1113, Berkeley, Calif. 94704. *Agent:* Barbara S. Kouts, Philip G. Spitzer Literary Agency, 1465 Third Ave., New York, N.Y. 10028. *Office:* Harper & Row Publishers, Inc., 1700 Montgomery St., Suite 250, San Francisco, Calif. 94111.

CAREER: Books Inc., Walnut Creek, Calif., book buyer, 1966-72; California State University, Hayward, Hayward, Calif., lecturer in English, 1969-70; Campus Textbook Exchange, Berkeley, Calif., assistant store manager and book department manager, 1972-73; Graduate Theological Union Bookstore, Berkeley, Calif., general manager, 1973-79; free-lance writer, editor, and consultant, 1974—; Harper & Row Publishers, Inc., San Francisco, Calif., promotion coordinator, copywriter, and editorial coordinator, 1979—; Downey Place Publishing House, Inc., El Cerrito, Calif., consulting editor, 1984—. *Awards, honors: The Legend of Scarface: A Blackfeet Indian Tale* was selected as one of the ten best illustrated children's books of 1978 by the *New York Times,* and as an honor list book of 1979 by *Horn Book; The Song of Sedna, Sea-Goddess of the North* was named one of the notable children's trade books in social studies, 1981, by the National Council for

Mattak grew huge wings and soared into the sky. ■ (From *Song of Sedna: Sea-Goddess of the North,* adapted by Robert D. San Souci. Illustrated by Daniel San Souci.)

ROBERT D. SAN SOUCI

Social Studies and the Children's Book Council, and was selected one of International Reading Association's "Children's Choices," 1982.

WRITINGS—Adapter; all for children: *The Legend of Scarface: A Blackfeet Indian Tale* (illustrated by brother, Daniel San Souci; *Horn Book* honor list), Doubleday, 1978; *Song of Sedna: Sea-Goddess of the North* (illustrated by D. San Souci), Doubleday, 1981; Jacob Grimm and Wilhelm Grimm, *The Brave Little Tailor* (illustrated by D. San Souci), Doubleday, 1982.

Adult: *Emergence* (novel), Avon, 1981; *Blood Offerings* (novel), Dorchester Press, 1985. Also contributor of short stories, book reviews, articles, and theater criticism to various journals, newspapers, and magazines.

WORK IN PROGRESS: Daddy's Boy, a novel for adults; several juvenile, young adult, and adult works of fiction.

SIDELIGHTS: "I plan to continue writing for both children and adults, as long as I have stories to tell—and an audience that is willing to listen. My usual procedure is to work on projects for both levels simultaneously; something about the back-and-forth keeps everything a little fresher and more energized. In a way there's really a lot more similarities than might be at first evident. Retelling a Grimm Brothers' fairytale or building an adult novel based on Pueblo Indian myths allows me scope to tell a story that has a solid structure derived from the inner truths that are the kernels of all legends, myths, and fairytales.

"In all my writing I'm first of all concerned with the story;

but (and I see this more and more as I write) I'm also using the narrative to explore ideas and suggest answers to questions about why and how the world works. I hope my books are entertaining, and I also get a pleasure from thinking they may be sharing a little more substance with readers.

"Right now I've got several novels in various states of completeness and have several proposals for children's books out. On some I will plan to work with my brother, Daniel; on two, I hope to work with a friend who is a designer with a very different visual approach to the material. But Dan and I are a solid team. While we will develop projects independent of each other, we have every confidence that we've just begun to produce what we hope will be a long line of shared works. After all, we share the same birthday, October 10 (although there is two years' difference in our ages), so, I guess you might say that 'it was in the stars that we were going to be collaborators.' Anyhow, it makes for a nice myth, so I'm happy to subscribe to it."

FOR MORE INFORMATION SEE: Chico Enterprise-Record, March 15, 1982; *Contemporary Authors,* Volume 108, Gale, 1983.

SCHEIER, Michael   1943-

PERSONAL: Born May 1, 1943, in New York, N.Y.; married Julie Frankel (an author and illustrator), 1977. *Education:* New York University, B.S. (honors), 1966; graduate study at Columbia University Teachers' College. *Address:* P.O. Box 694, Putnam Valley, N.Y. 10579.

CAREER: Teacher and author of children's books. *Member:* Authors' Guild, Society of Children's Book Writers. *Awards, honors:* Readers Choice Award, for *Ridiculous World Records,* and for *Digging for My Roots;* Children's Choice Award, International Reading Association, 1979, for *The Whole Mirth Catalog: A Super Complete Collection of Things.*

WRITINGS—All with wife, Julie Frankel; all juvenile: *Ridiculous World Records,* Scholastic Book Services, 1976; *Digging for My Roots,* Scholastic Book Services, 1977; *The Whole Mirth Catalog: A Super Complete Collection of Things* (illustrated by J. Frankel), F. Watts, 1978; *What to Do with the Rocks in Your Head: Things to Make and Do Alone, with Friends, with Family, Inside, and Outside,* F. Watts, 1980; *Me by Me,* Scholastic Book Services, 1982; *More Ridiculous World Records,* Scholastic Book Services, 1983; *The Wildlife Romance Fill-In-Book,* Scholastic Book Services, 1984. Also contributor of cartoons to *Animals, Animals, Animals* (cartoon collection), edited by George Booth and others, Harper, 1979, and to the periodicals *Cosmopolitan, Audubon Magazine,* and *The Runner Magazine.*

WORK IN PROGRESS: "Books relating to puns, imaginative activities, fill-in formats, adoption, and humor relating to birds, plants, and wildlife, all with elaborate illustrations."

SIDELIGHTS: "I was raised in Westchester and moved to New York City to attend New York University.

"I met Julie in 1968 and we started our working relationship as teacher-teacher trainee, sharing a third grade classroom on the lower east side of New York City. For a time we lived in

(From *The Whole Mirth Catalog: A Super Complete Collection of Things* by Michael Scheier and Julie Frankel. Illustrated by Julie Frankel.)

Michael Scheier with wife, Julie Frankel.

Berkeley, California, where we made and sold finely crafted imaginative jig-saw puzzles.

"Upon returning east, I began teaching again, and in 1976 Julie and I embarked on collaborative efforts in publishing.

"I have lived in many neighborhoods in New York, but find real fulfillment in our Putnam Valley home nestled in over ten acres of woods with a small stream, a cat, and a working vegetable garden, still an easy drive to the city.

"I am currently enrolled at Columbia University Teachers' College in a master's degree program in computers."

SIMON, Solomon   1895-1970

PERSONAL: Born July 4, 1895, in Kolinkovich, Russia (now U.S.S.R.); came to the United States in 1913; died November 8, 1970, in Miami, Fla.; son of Eurichim and Mere (Lifschitz) Simon; married Lena Fischer, March 27, 1920; children: David, Judith Simon Bloch, Miriam Simon Forman. *Education:* New York University, D.D.S., 1924. *Religion:* Jewish. *Residence:* Brooklyn, N.Y.

CAREER: Dentist, beginning in 1924. Staff member, *Di Presse of Argentina*, beginning 1949, and *New York Morning Journal*, beginning 1951; associate professor of Bible literature, Jewish Teachers Seminary, beginning 1964. *Military service:* U.S. Army, 1918. *Member:* Kings County Dental Society (past chairman of membership committee), Allied Dentist Council (past executive member), Yiddish Scientific Institute, Poets, Playwrights, Editors, Essayists, and Novelists Club, Jewish Ethical Culture Society (past vice-president), Society of Bible Literature. *Awards, honors:* Mordecai Stolier Literature Award, 1956; Kessel Library Award, Mexico.

WRITINGS: H. Leiviks Golem, [New York], 1927; *Shmerl nar* (juvenile), Farlag Matones (New York), 1931, translation from the Yiddish by the author and his son, David Simon, published as *The Wandering Beggar; or, The Adventures of Simple Shmerl* (illustrated by Lillian Fischel), Behrman's Jewish Book House, 1942; *Dos Kluge schneiderl*, Farlag Matones, 1933; (coauthor) *Maises Fun Agadata*, 1936; *Kinder yorn fun idishe schreiber*, Farlag Matones, Volume I, 1936, Volume II, 1945; *Roberts wentures*, [New York], 1938; *H. Leiviks kinderyorn* (juvenile biography), 1938; (coauthor) *Chumesh far Kinder*, 1940; *Di heldn fun Chelm* (juvenile folklore), Posy-Shoulson Press (New York), 1942, translation by Ben Bengal and D. Simon published as *The Wise Men of Helm and Their Merry Tales* (illustrated by Fischel), Behrman, 1945, reprinted, 1965; *In di teg fun di nevi'im* (title means "In the Days of the Prophets"), [New York], 1947; *Yidn tsvishn felker* (history; title means "Israel among Nations"), [New York], 1949; *Medinas Yisrael un Erets Yisrael* (travel), [Buenos Aires], 1950; *Amolike Yidn*, [Buenos Aires], 1952; (editor and translator) *Yehoshua un Shoftim* (title means "Joshua and Judges"), [New York], 1952.

Tokh-Yidishkayt (essays), [Buenos Aires], 1954; *Vortslen* (autobiography), Yidbukh (Buenos Aires), 1956, translation by Shlomo Katz published as *My Jewish Roots*, Jewish Publication Society, 1956; *Hakhomim, 'akshonim un naronim* (title means "Wisemen, Dullards, and Donkeys"), [Buenos Aires], 1959; *In di teg fun di ershte neviim*, [Buenos Aires], 1959; *Tsvaygn* (title means "Branches"), 1960; *Oyf eygene drokhim* (title means "On Own Ways"), [Buenos Aires], 1962; *Chachomim*

un Akshonim, 1963; *Emuneh fun a dor* (essays), 1970; *Kuge hent*, 1973.

Other works translated into English: *In the Thicket* (autobiographical novel), translation by Moshe Spiegel, Jewish Publication Society, 1963; *More Wise Men of Helm and Their Merry Tales* (juvenile; illustrated by Stephen Kraft), edited by Hannah Goodman, Behrman, 1965, reprinted, 1979; (with Morrison D. Bial) *The Rabbis' Bible*, editorial assistance by Goodman, Behrman, 1966; (coauthor) *The Rabbis' and Bible Teachers' Resource Book on the Pentateuch*, 1966; (coauthor) *The Early Prophets*, 1969.

Also associate editor, *Kinder Journal*, 1940-47, editor, 1947-50; editor, *Schulblatt*, 1940; and contributor to *Jewish Day-Journal*, beginning 1951.

SIDELIGHTS: **July 4, 1895.** Born into a poor Russian family, whose members for generations had been simple artisans. In his autobiography, *My Jewish Roots*, Simon recalled his earliest years, referring to himself in the third person as "Shimon." "All the children except Shimon were healthy and sound in mind and in body. Only he was not up to par. He suffered from rickets—'the English disease,' as they called it—and his legs would not hold him up. He was a *sidun*—a sitter. No doctor was consulted. Why bother? The child would outgrow his ailment, the family said.

"The first thing that Shimon remembers is terror. Because he always sat on the floor and could not even crawl on all fours, he was afraid. He reasoned that the table, the chairs, the kitchen bench could all walk, because they stood upright. But he could

(From *Shmerl nar* by Solomon Simon. Illustrated by Aaron Goodelman.)

. . . They stumbled upon Yossel standing among the little boys, holding a lighted candle in his hand and gazing expectantly at the bride along with all the other Helmites. ■ (From *The Wise Men of Helm and Their Merry Tales* by Solomon Simon. Illustrated by Lillian Fischel.)

not walk, so he had to beware of them. Should they take it into their heads to start walking, it would be necessary to make way for them, to move aside; but he could not run away from them; his situation was desperate.

"At dusk all the objects in the house loomed bigger, thick with shadows. The boy looked up to the red table and saw it flex its thick legs. It would start walking any minute.

"The dawns terrified Shimon even more. His Father, Ben-Zion the shoemaker, was a poor provider, and Mother had to operate a bakery to supplement his earnings. She would rise before dawn and start a fire in the oven; then she would knead the dough for the bread, rolls and beigel. When the fire in the oven was in full blast, she would rouse the older children, Gitte, Simcha and Rochel-Leah. But Shimon would awaken as soon as Mother left her bed. He slept on the long couch, with his head near the door to the kitchen, and watched her every move." [Solomon Simon, *My Jewish Roots*, Jewish Publication Society, 1956.[1]]

The town where Simon spent his childhood was a small Russian village. "Kalinkovich was a minute island of Jewish life in the midst of an ocean of Gentiles; a few steps the other side of 'The Sand,' the new suburb, there began an alien world.

"The town was surrounded by scores of peasant villages. Every day scores of peasants came to Kalinkovich to stock up on necessities. On Sundays, holidays or Fair days, hundreds of peasants would come to town. The Jews depended on the peasants for their livelihood. The peasants depended on the Jews to supply them with their household needs and their few luxuries—boots, head gear, beads, combs, nails, needles, sickles, kerchiefs, clothes and all the other necessities of civilized existence.

"But though a social island, Kalinkovich was not nearly as isolated as other towns like it. . . . Kalinkovich had both a church and a sizable railroad station. Three trains stopped daily at Kalinkovich and about the station was gathered a compact community of skilled Gentile workers whom the Jews supplied with all their needs, excepting only pork. One third the Jewish population of the town derived its livelihood from the station; and these Jews could also speak Russian fluently.

"But despite these contacts, Jews and Gentiles remained two distinct and separate entities, living according to different concepts. They were two worlds, culturally as far apart as if they had been separated by oceans." [Solomon Simon, *In the Thicket*, Jewish Publication Society, 1963.[2]]

1901. In his autobiography, Simon vividly remembered when he began to walk. "A few days before Shevuous, Shimon, who was then almost six years old, stood on his feet for the first time, and within a matter of weeks he shot up in height. His protruding belly flattened out; his back straightened and became broader. His complexion, which had been a sickly gray, changed to a healthy tan, and a flush of health now played on his cheeks. His hair became denser and its former dullness gave way to a healthy sheen. Only his eyes did not change and remained as before, wide open and bright blue, and they examined with much wonder and curiosity everything they beheld.

"At this stage Shimon became very active and childishly mercurial. He could not stay put for a moment. Speech and laughter constantly tumbled from his mouth, and his hands were ever busy.

"'He is trying to catch up on lost time,' Mother said. 'For almost six years he couldn't even crawl, so now he is in a hurry to make up for it.'

"At this time Shimon no longer cried, and lost all his fears. Now Mother complained that he had lost all sense of fear."[1]

1908. Early on the family discovered, much to their amazement, that Simon was endowed with a gifted intelligence. "Shimon had sensed even when he was still very young that he differed from other boys and was a Chosen One. That feeling probably stemmed from the fact that his family held him in high esteem, regarding him as its prodigy and taking pride in him as the only scholar in a tribe of common craftsmen.

"Inscribed indelibly on his mind is a remark his mother made at that time. The two had been sitting on the steps of the porch, discussing his coming departure for the yeshiva. She said: 'My son, I want you to bear one thing in mind. When you become a rabbi, or a doctor, or an author—and some such thing will surely come to pass, for like all Jewish mothers, I used to sing to you as a child 'You will study the Torah, you will write books'—remember that there are many cobblers in this world, and they deserve some consideration.'

"Whereupon her son had protested: 'You've already ordained me, and also made a doctor and an author of me. But I am

(From *Robert Ventures* by Solomon Simon. Illustrated by Nata Kazalovski.)

only thirteen, and I'm going to a yeshiva [a school for Talmudic studies] where I will have to depend on "eating days."'

"'A mother's heart knows whereof she speaks,' she had answered confidently: 'My heart told me, even when you were still a *siddun* (a 'sitter') unable to walk because of rickets, that you would be a scholar. I know that you will be a distinguished Jew among Jews. Some day, you will recall what I have just told you.'

"Remembering this required no undue effort. Shimon had faith in her words, words that would come true only four years after their utterance."[2]

1912-1913. Of his adolescent years and emigration to America, Simon recalled in his book, *In the Thicket:* "... Shimon was barely seventeen when he published a rhymed epigram in the journal *Ha-Hayyim v'Hatevah*. He felt then that he would become a man of letters, and he began to jot things down in a diary which he kept throughout his life with only occasional lapses. He also preserved all his correspondence, short stories, poems, and essays. In general, he liked to maintain a balanced view of things.

"His parents preserved his letters from the yeshiva, just as he,

in turn, kept the letters which his own son sent to him from various universities. Parents, especially from the poorer class, naturally take pride in their gifted children. When Shimon left for the United States at the age of eighteen, he took the letters he had sent to his parents from the yeshiva. He also took everything he had ever written. After a decade in America, when he had graduated from college and opened an office, he examined all his youthful writings, and winnowed the chaff from the wheat. At that time he was contributing stories and essays to various publications, and considered himself a man of letters. He discarded most of this 'heritage' that lacked literary value, retaining only about a hundred pages, all in Hebrew."[2]

After emigrating to the United States, Simon became a dentist. He married Lena Fischer in 1920, and had three children.

Besides his dental practice, Simon was an author of numerous articles and books, which were written in Yiddish. From 1940 to 1947 he was associate editor of *Kinder Journal*, becoming editor until 1950. For children, he wrote *The Wandering Beggar; or, The Adventures of Simple Shmerl, The Wise Men of Helm, More Wise Men of Helm and Their Merry Tales,* and other Jewish tales. He died at his winter home in Miami on November 8, 1970.

FOR MORE INFORMATION SEE: New York Times, February 24, 1946. Obituaries: *New York Times,* November 10, 1970; *AB Bookman's Weekly,* January 4, 1971.

SMITH, E(dric) Brooks   1917-

PERSONAL: Born April 23, 1917, in Brooklyn, N.Y.; son of Edric B. (a businessman) and Laura (Seaver) Smith; married Elizabeth Williamson, June 29, 1946; children: Jonathan, *Education:* Harvard University, A.B. (cum laude), 1939, M.A., 1950; Columbia University, Ed.D., 1955. *Home:* R.F.D. Greengate, Marlboro, N.H. 03455.

CAREER: Teacher at North Shore Country Day School, Winnetka, Ill., 1946-49, and in Scarsdale (N.Y.) public schools, 1949-55; Columbia University, New York, N.Y., instructor, 1952-55; Wheelock College, Boston, Mass., coordinator of teacher education, 1955-62; Wayne State University, Detroit, Mich., professor of education and chairman of elementary education department, since 1962. *Military service:* U.S. Army Air Forces, 1941-45; became captain. *Member:* Association for Student Teaching (executive committee), Northeastern Association for Student Teaching (past president), American Association of Colleges for Teacher Education (chairman, subcommittee on school-college relationships), National Education Association.

WRITINGS—All with Robert Meredith, except as noted; all published by Little, Brown, except as noted: *Pilgrim Courage* (*Horn Book* honor list; illustrated by Leonard Everett Fisher), 1962; *The Coming of the Pilgrims* (illustrated by L. E. Fisher), 1964; (with P. Johnson) *Report of Cooperation Ventures in Teacher Education,* Colleges for Teacher Education, 1964; *Riding with Coronado,* 1965; (editor) *The Quest of Columbus* (illustrated by L. E. Fisher), 1966; *Pere Marquette,* 1967; (with others) *Partnership in Teacher Education,* American Association of Colleges for Teacher Education, 1968; *Exploring the Great River* (illustrated by L. E. Fisher), 1969. Contributor to yearbooks and to professional journals.

(From *The Quest of Columbus,* edited and adapted by Robert Meredith and E. Brooks Smith. Illustrated by Leonard Everett Fisher.)

SNELL, Nigel (Edward Creagh) 1936-

BRIEF ENTRY: Born November 9, 1936, in London, England. British author and illustrator of books for children. Snell studied art at the Central School of Art and Design and, since 1966, has been employed by an advertising company located in London. He is the author of a series of sixteen books designed to aid young children in coping with everyday situations that they may find stressful, such as getting new glasses, undergoing a tonsillectomy, moving to a new house, and so on. All published by Hamish Hamilton, these six-inch square "mini-books" are self-illustrated and fulfill Snell's desire "to bring some humor into situations that frighten children." The titles include: *Johnny Gets Some Glasses* (1978), *Jane Has Asthma* (1981), *Danny Is Afraid of the Dark* (1982), *Sam's New Dad* (1983), and *Jenny Learns to Swim* (1983). Snell has also written and illustrated four books that introduce young readers to the mechanisms of the five senses—*Tasting and Smelling, Hearing, Touching,* and *Seeing* (all Hamish Hamilton, 1983). An active participant in many kinds of sports and outdoor activities, Snell also takes a great interest in animal environments. He is currently working on additional children's books that center around wildlife preservation and conservation. *Home:* Hambleden near Henley-on-Thames, Oxfordshire, England.

FOR MORE INFORMATION SEE: Contemporary Authors, Volume 111, Gale, 1984.

SOLOMON, Joan 1930(?)-

BRIEF ENTRY: Born November 26, 1930 (another source cites 1932), in Johannesburg, South Africa. A graduate of both the University of Witwatersrand and the University of Cape Town, Solomon has been employed as a lecturer in English at London's Open University since 1981. Her career has included positions as English teacher and social worker in Johannesburg and Cape Town, as well as manager of her own advertising art studio in Upington, South Africa. Solomon has written nearly a dozen books aimed at preschool and early primary-grade readers in which she strives to emphasize the importance of racial harmony among children of Asian, black, and white ethnic backgrounds. All published by Hamish Hamilton, these books combine simple stories with color photographs (many of them taken by Solomon and her son, Ryan) of actual children in realistic situations, such as amidst balloons and birthday candles in *Kate's Party* (1978), at school in *Berron's Tooth* (1978), on a seaside outing in *A Day by the Sea* (1978), and playing "pretend" in *Wedding Day* (1981).

For an older reading audience, Solomon is the author of eight textbooks published in 1983 by the Association for Science Education. Part of the "Science in a Social Context (SIS-CON)" series, the books are intended to supply middle-school students with a higher awareness of scientific and technological developments through a multimedia format. The topics covered include *Ways of Living, Evolution and the Human Population, Space, Cosmology and Fiction, The Atomic Bomb,* and *Energy.* Solomon has also written *Teaching Children in the Laboratory* (Croom Helm, 1980), a science curriculum guide for educators. In addition to other work, she is currently researching the existence of racism, sexism, and classicism in children's literature. *Residence:* London, England.

FOR MORE INFORMATION SEE: Contemporary Authors, Volume 109, Gale, 1983.

SPRINGSTUBB, Tricia 1950-

BRIEF ENTRY: Born September 15, 1950, in New York, N.Y. Author of fiction for children and young adults. A 1972 graduate of State University of New York at Albany, Springstubb did not begin writing professionally until she was twenty-six years old. Up until that time, she had planned a career as a social worker. She now has six books to her credit, alternating between picture books for early primary-grade readers and novels for young adults. Her first picture book, *My Minnie Is a Jewel* (Carolrhoda, 1980), relates the story of an old woodcutter and his absent-minded wife who find the best riches of life in each other. *Booklist* described it as a ". . . romantic little fable . . . [with] neatness and character . . . [that] have real appeal." In her next book, Springstubb turned her attention toward an older reading audience. *Give and Take* (Little, Brown, 1981) explores the friendship between two high school girls as they encounter their first real relationships with boys. *Voice of Youth Advocates* called it "a spring-green, refreshingly clean adult/

young adult novel,'' filled with ''honesty, sense of balance, and perspective.''

Springstubb's picture books *The Blueberry Troll* (Carolrhoda, 1981) and *The Magic Guinea Pig* (Morrow, 1982) tell the stories of a greedy, lazy troll with a passion for blueberries and a small boy who, with the help of a bungling witch, wishes for a puppy and ends up with a guinea pig. In *Moon on a String* (Little, Brown, 1982), seventeen-year-old Deirdre escapes from a boring small town for life in the big city and eventually gains valuable insight into herself and those around her. *School Library Journal* labeled this young adult novel ''a perceptive, muted study of a particular rite of passage.'' Likewise, in *Which Way to the Nearest Wilderness?* (Little, Brown, 1984), eleven-year-old Eunice seeks refuge from a home that has become the battleground for a strife-torn marriage. *Bulletin of the Center for Children's Books* observed: ''In a very funny novel, alive with . . . wit and snappy dialogue . . . , Springstubb poignantly depicts the groping, complicated quality of relationships.'' Throughout her works, Springstubb adheres to ''. . . the necessity of extending ourselves.'' She adds, ''Taking risks, letting life suprise you: these seem to me key ingredients of happiness. . . .'' *Home:* 2399 Woodmere Dr., Cleveland Heights, Ohio 44106.

FOR MORE INFORMATION SEE: Contemporary Authors, Volume 105, Gale, 1982.

TABACK, Simms 1932-

PERSONAL: Born February 13, 1932, in New York, N.Y.; son of Leon (a housepainter and contractor) and Thelma (a seamstress) Taback; married Gail Baugher Kuenstler (a writer), March 1, 1980; children: Lisa, Jason, Emily. *Education:* Cooper Union, B.F.A., 1953. *Home:* 532 West 111th St., New York,

SIMMS TABACK

(From *Fishy Riddles* by Katy Hall and Lisa Eisenberg. Illustrated by Simms Taback.)

N.Y. 10025. *Agent:* Milton Newborn, 135 East 54th St., New York, N.Y. 10022. *Studio:* 38 East 21st St., New York, N.Y. 10010.

CAREER: CBS Records, New York, N.Y., graphic designer, 1956-57; *New York Times,* New York, N.Y., designer, 1957-58; William Douglas McAdams, New York, N.Y., art director, 1958-60; free-lance illustrator, 1960-63, 1970—; Ruffins/Taback Design Studio, New York, N.Y., partner, 1963-70. *Exhibitions:* Society of Illustrators, New York, N.Y., 1961-82. *Military service:* U.S. Army, private first class, 1953-55. *Member:* Illustrators Guild (president, 1976-78), New York Graphics Artists Guild (president, 1978-83), Society of Illustrators, Art Directors Club. *Awards, honors: Please Share That Peanut!: A Preposterous Pageant in Fourteen Acts* was named one of *New York Times* Best Illustrated Books, 1965; *There's Motion Everywhere, Joseph Had a Little Overcoat,* and *Laughing Together* were named one of American Institute of Graphic Arts Children's Books, 1970, 1979, and 1980, respectively; over fifty Certificates of Merit, Society of Illustrators, 1961-83.

WRITINGS: Joseph Had a Little Overcoat (self-illustrated), Random House, 1978.

Illustrator: Sesyle Joslin, *Please Share That Peanut!: A Preposterous Pageant in Fourteen Acts,* Harcourt, 1965; Lewis Carroll, *Jabberwocky and Other Favorites,* Harlan Quist, 1966; Ann McGovern, *Too Much Noise,* Houghton, 1967; John Travers Moore, *There's Motion Everywhere,* Houghton, 1970; (with Reynold Ruffins) Harry Hartwick, *The Amazing Maze,* Dutton, 1970; Mary Calhoun, *Euphonia and the Flood,* Parents Magazine Press, 1976; Barbara K. Walker, compiler, *Laughing Together: Giggles and Grins from Around the World,* Four Winds Press, 1977; Katy Hall, *Fishy Riddles,* Dial, 1983; Harriet Ziefert, *Where Is My House?,* Grosset, 1984; H. Ziefert, *Where Is My Dinner?,* Grosset, 1984; H. Ziefert, *Where Is My Family?,* Grosset, 1984; H. Ziefert, *Where Is My Friend?,* Grosset, 1984; H. Ziefert, *On Our Way* (series of four books), Harper, 1985; K. Hall, *Buggy Riddles,* Dial, 1985.

SIDELIGHTS: "Though I was interested in art since a small child, the study of art was my second choice. I originally wanted to be a painter. I work in all media, but mostly pen and ink and watercolor.

"Milton Glaser, Seymour Chwast, Reynold Ruffins, Saul Steinberg are strong influences. I was a student of Ray Baxter Dowden and Sid Delevanty."

Taback's works are included in the Kerlan Collection at the University of Minnesota.

FOR MORE INFORMATION SEE: New York Herald Tribune Book Review, October 17, 1965.

THOMAS, Joyce Carol 1938-

PERSONAL: Born May 25, 1938, in Ponca City, Okla.; daughter of Floyd Dave (a bricklayer) and Leona (a homemaker; maiden name, Thompson) Haynes; married Gettis L. Withers (a chemist), May 31, 1959 (divorced, 1968); married Roy T. Thomas, Jr. (a professor), September 7, 1968 (divorced, 1979); children: Monica Pecot, Gregory Withers, Michael Withers, Roy T. Thomas, III. *Education:* College of San Mateo, A.A., 1964; San Jose State University, B.A., 1966; Stanford University, M.A., 1967. *Residence:* Berkeley, Calif. *Agent:* Mitch Douglas, International Creative Management, 40 West 57th St., New York, N.Y. 10019.

CAREER: Author and educator. Ravenwood School District, East Palo Alto, Calif., teacher of French and Spanish, 1968-70; San Jose State University, San Jose, Calif., assistant professor of Black studies, 1969-72, reading program director, 1979-82, professor of English, 1982-83; Contra Costa College, San Pablo, Calif., teacher of drama and English, 1973-75; St. Mary's College, Moraga, Calif., professor of English, 1975-77; Purdue University, associate professor of English, spring, 1984; full-time writer, 1982—. Commissioner, Berkeley Civic Arts; visiting scholar at Center for Research on Women, Stanford University, 1980-81. *Member:* International Reading Association, Author's Guild, Western Reading Association, Sigma Delta Pi, Spanish Honors Society. *Awards, honors:* Djerassi visiting artist in fiction, 1982, 1983; Before Columbus Foundation Award, 1982, and American Book Award for children's fiction in paperback, 1983, both for *Marked by Fire,* also named outstanding book of the year, 1982, by *New York Times* and best book of the year by American Library Association, 1982; Coretta Scott King Citation from the American Library Association for *Bright Shadow,* 1984.

WRITINGS: Bittersweet (poetry), Firesign, 1973; *Crystal Breezes* (poetry), Firesign, 1974; *Blessing* (poetry), Jocato, 1975; *Inside the Rainbow* (poetry), Zikawuna, 1981; *Black Child* (poetry), Zamani, 1981; *Marked by Fire* (young adult novel), Avon, 1982; *Bright Shadow* (young adult novel; sequel to *Marked by Fire),* Avon, 1983; *An Act of God,* Scholastic, 1985.

Plays: "A Song in the Sky," first produced in San Francisco at Montgomery Theatre, 1976; "Look! What a Wonder," first produced in Berkeley at Berkeley Community Theatre, 1976; "Magnolia," first produced in San Francisco at Old San Francisco Opera House, 1977; "Ambrosia," first produced in San Francisco at Little Fox Theatre, 1978; "Gospel Roots," first produced in Carson, Calif. at California State University, 1981.

WORK IN PROGRESS: Four more novels about Abyssinia Jackson and her people: *Water Girl, Amber, House of Light,* and *Green Pastures.*

SIDELIGHTS: "I have always been a writer, although I never thought of myself as being that in a formal sense until 1973 when I published my first book of poetry. I say always, because my earliest memories are of making up songs under the porch and of composing poems for fun. In retrospect the incident that I think marked me as a budding writer stands out in sharp relief in my mind. It is about what happened to my father's hat.

"When I was a child, I was forever running into difficulty with my musing. I loved to read and create stories and poems. This enchantment with the written word was sometimes so engrossing that I paid scant attention to some of my household duties.

JOYCE CAROL THOMAS

"On the occasion of the hat story, my chore was to clean the kitchen, clear the breakfast table, wash the dishes, wipe off the stove and refrigerator, and sweep and mop the floor.

"I hurried through these tasks for I was intent upon completing a poem I'd started before breakfast.

"Just about the time I'd finished the kitchen and plopped down comfortably on the couch with pad and pencil, my father came in to announce he could not find his hat. He thought he'd left it on top of the refrigerator, but it was nowhere to be found.

"My mother looked and I looked, but we could not find the hat. Under the table, no hat. Behind the refrigerator, no hat. In the living room, no hat. In the closet, no hat. Finally, my father gave up. Realizing he would be late for work, he decided to brew a nerve-settling pot of coffee. He poured himself a cup and opened the refrigerator to get the cream. Then I heard him yell to my mother, 'Come here, Leona, and see what this gal done done!'

"Of course, I swiftly followed my mother into the kitchen to see what the matter was. My father was standing glaring into the refrigerator. There, as neatly placed as you please, next to the cream, the butter, the eggs, and the orange juice, sat my father's hat.

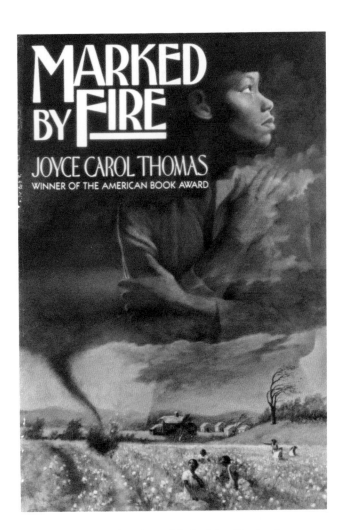

(Cover illustration from *Marked by Fire* by Joyce Carol Thomas.)

"I think I've always been an optimist. I even used to think it was fun playing catch up in school. Nearly always, I missed the first month of the school year because I was in the fields picking cotton with my eight brothers and sister. I've often welcomed challenge in my life and looked upon it as a bright opportunity. Finding time to be alone was another challenge. I was part of a big family where sometimes the only place to be by myself was under the house. I think my ability to concentrate on writing may be part of the legacy of surviving amidst the chaos of a big family. In my work, concentration is paramount, since I write about five drafts for each of the completed novels.

"I grew up in a rural setting and in my writing of books for young people, I steep my words in the peculiar idiom and rural image of Abyssinia Jackson, the Oklahoma character in my series of books. In these books of Abyssinia, *Marked by Fire* and *Bright Shadow*, I work for authenticity of voice, fidelity to detail, and naturalness of development representative of the baffling multiverse of the country heroine functioning in a country environment. In my treatment of Abyssinia Jackson I try to capture language (its rhythm and pace) in movement and in thought pattern. For example, before I wrote Abyssinia's snake story in *Marked by Fire,* I had to recall the voices of the porch sitters as they told the stories I heard as a child sitting on my own rough and splintered porch on a dark Oklahoma night.

"In telling Abyssinia's story I must recall conflict, for without conflict and courage this cannot be her story. She is born with courage—with both vision and the will to live bravely and heroically.

"As a writer I work to create books filled with conflict. Indeed, that is my principal quest. I address this quest in part by matching the pitiful absurdities and heady contradictions of life itself, in part by leading the heroine to twin fountains of magic and the macabre, and evoking the holy and the horrible in the same breath. Nor is it ever enough to match these. Through the character of Abyssinia, I strive for what is beyond these, seeking, as do many writers, to find newer worlds.

"My travels as an author, lecturer and educator include journeys throughout North America, to Latin America, Africa, the Carribean, the Far East and Europe. I love to travel; I enjoy speaking foreign languages and prefer to communicate in the tongue of the people whose countries I visit. I fell in love with Latin in high school and later chose to major in Spanish and French at the universities of San Jose State and Stanford. I read Latin fluently and am fluent as a reader and speaker in English, Spanish and French.

"I feel at home in the world and on my national and international visits aim to scatter Abyssinia's story everywhere I stop."

FOR MORE INFORMATION SEE: Who's Who Among Black Americans, Who's Who Among Black Americans, Inc., 2nd edition, 1977; Patricia Holt, ''A Stunning New Talent Emerges,'' *San Francisco Chronicle,* April 12, 1982; *New York Times Book Review,* December 5, 1982; *Women Writers of the West,* edited by Marilyn Yalom, Capra Press, 1982; Camille Gavin, ''Optimism Abounds . . . ,'' *The Bakersfield Californian,* February 9, 1983; Frances Starn, ''First Novel Award-Winner for Thomas,'' *Berkeley Gazette,* July 21, 1983; Susan C. Griffith, ''Alternative to Shallow Romances,'' *New Directions,* January/February, 1984.

THOMPSON, Julian F(rancis) 1927-

BRIEF ENTRY: Born November 16, 1927, in New York, N.Y. Author of novels for young adults. A graduate of Princeton University, Thompson received his M.A. from Columbia University in 1955. From 1949 to 1961 he was employed as teacher, coach, and director at a private school in Lawrenceville, N.J. In 1971 he and a group of students founded Changes, Inc., an alternative high school where he spent seven years as director/ teacher. It was the experience he gained through conducting writing workshops at Changes that led Thompson to become a writer himself. With the publication of his first novel, *The Grounding of Group Six* (Avon, 1983), he was hailed by *Publishers Weekly* as "an author with a remarkable literary style and frightening inventiveness. . . ."

The novel relates the story of five sixteen-year olds who are shipped off to an alternative boarding school located in the isolated hills of Vermont. Labeled "problem children" by their rich parents, they have actually been sent to the school for a permanent "grounding," namely, extermination. The headmaster is well paid for this annual event in which six groups of youths are sent into the woods for a weekend forage—but only five return. Noting that Thompson writes "fluently about adolescents in one key (romantic realism) and about adults in another (surrealistic black comedy)," *Horn Book* called *The Grounding of Group Six* "humorously antiestablishment and slick . . . pure, page-turning entertainment." *Booklist* agreed, observing that "an intriguingly scary premise, well-differentiated characters, and some romantic . . . entanglements . . . make this an unusually satisfying adventure. . . ."

Thompson realizes that some readers might "take what I write completely literally. That would be a bad mistake; by and large, my novels have (as, thank heaven, reviewers have noticed) a certain amount of surrealistic (and even black) humor in them. I'm pretty sure most kids . . . understand and relax with what I'm up to, sometimes even before they learn what it's called." Thompson's other novels are *Facing It* (Avon, 1983), *A Question of Survival* (Avon, 1984), and *Discontinued*, in press. He is currently working on his fifth young adult novel, *A Band of Angels. Address:* P.O. Box 138, West Rupert, Vt. 05776.

FOR MORE INFORMATION SEE: Contemporary Authors, Volume 111, Gale, 1984.

THOMSON, David (Robert Alexander) 1914-

PERSONAL: Born February 17, 1914, in Quetta, India; son of Alexander G. (an army officer) and Annie W. (a nurse; maiden name, Finlay) Thomson; married Martina Mayne (an art therapist); children: three sons. *Education:* Lincoln College, Oxford, B.A., 1936. *Home:* 22 Regent's Park Ter., London N.W.1, England.

CAREER: Private tutor of history and English in County Roscommon, Ireland, 1932-43; British Broadcasting Corp., London, England, writer and producer in features department, 1943-69; writer, 1969—. *Member:* Association of Broadcasting Staff, Society of Authors, Zoological Society (London, associate), United Arts Club (Dublin).

WRITINGS—Children's books: *Danny Fox,* Penguin, 1966; *Danny Fox Meets a Stranger,* Penguin, 1968; *Danny Fox at the Palace,* Puffin Books, 1976; *Ronan and Other Stories,* Macmillan, 1984.

Other: *The People of the Sea: A Journey in Search of the Seal Legend,* Turnstile Press, 1954, John Day, 1955, 3rd edition, Granada, 1980; *Daniel* (novel), Barrie & Rockliff, 1962; *Break in the Sun* (novel), Barrie & Rockliff, 1965; (with George Ewart Evans) *The Leaping Hare,* Faber, 1972; *Woodbrook,* Barrie & Jenkins, 1974, Universe Books, 1976; (editor with Moyra McGusty) *The Irish Journals of Elizabeth Smith, 1840-1850: A Selection,* Oxford University Press, 1980; *In Camden Town* (nonfiction), Hutchinson, 1983; *Dandiprat's Days* (novel), Dent, 1983.

SIDELIGHTS: "The first pets I remember were a fox-terrier puppy—white with light brown patches—and a crow—an ordinary rook with shiny black feathers and a harsh cawing voice. The puppy and the crow each had a terrible adventure which frightened me and thrilled me. This was when I was seven and living with my three sisters and our parents in Derbyshire, in the village of Burbage about two miles from Buxton, where I went every day by bus to school.

"My mother used to fetch me from school every afternoon. One day she brought my sister Joan with her and the little dog which we called Kuti, and left us together in the park while she went to do some shopping.

"That park and my school are the only places I remember in Buxton and I'm sure I wouldn't have remembered the park if Kuti hadn't fallen into the river that ran through it. There had been heavy rain the night before and the river was all muddy with thick red mud that the rushing water had dislodged from its banks. The river banks were steep and the water swift and deep—bright sun, speckled shadows from the leafy trees, green grass thick and lush and the muddy red stream.

"I don't know how Kuti fell in. Perhaps she thought the mud was thick enough to walk on. But there was a splash and suddenly I saw her in the water and the next second she was swept away by the current downstream far from us. Joan ran and I ran after her. Joan was quicker and reached a bend in the river where Kuti had managed to swim to the edge—she was scrabbling with her paws at the bank but it was too high for her and the earth fell away as she clawed it and she went under. By lying face down on the grass, Joan reached down to the water and managed to grab Kuti and pull her out. Joan was nine, two years older than me.

"Joan seemed even more heroic to me a few weeks after that on the day when she rescued Jim Crow. On her way home from school she saw a crowd of boys throwing stones at something—she heard a bird squawk, and when she came nearer she saw that the 'something' was a young crow. It was hopping along as fast as it could and flapping its wings, but it could not fly. The boys were stoning it. Joan pushed her way through them and caught the crow and brought it home. The boys were laughing at her, jeering at her, threatening her, but they dared not touch her.

"The crow had one broken wing. My mother made a splint for it; and after a few weeks of hopping round our house and garden, he was able to fly. And as soon as he could fly he began to steal. He loved anything made of bright metal. It was because of this that we named him Jim Crow—after the Jackdaw of Rheims who stole the Archbishop's ring.

"We only lived in that Derbyshire house for about a year, but that year, 1921, when I had my seventh birthday is easy for me to remember, too, because it was then that I started writing. I wrote stories and one of them even won a prize in a children's magazine competition for the best short story written by a child under ten.

"As I grew older, my favourite subject at school was natural history, and I learned a good deal about how animals live from farmers, woodsmen and fishermen, as well. But at the same time I heard animal legends and fairy stories. There is a connection between natural history and legends. Foxes, for instance, really are clever, cunning and full of tricks and in real life they play some of the tricks that Danny Fox plays in my books.

"Something went wrong with my eyes when I was eleven—I wasn't allowed to read or write—so I was taken away from school and sent to Nairn in the North of Scotland to live with my grandmother and have lessons all by myself. My teachers were a parson and a retired schoolmaster. The parson was very pale and mournful and the schoolmaster was usually happy— he had cheeks like apples reddened by the sun—but when he was reading aloud to me and came to a sad bit he would burst into tears. I liked him very much. Not being able to read to myself made me very good at listening.

"Nairn was a small town by the sea—very cold and dark in winter when the sun didn't rise till about ten in the morning and darkness fell about three in the afternoon. But in the summer the days were long and bright. The town was divided rather unnaturally into two parts—the Upper Town with its High Street and little shops and big stone houses with two storeys, where people like my grandmother lived—and the fishertown, where nearly all the houses had thatched roofs and only one floor—the ground floor. All the families in the fishertown made their living from the sea.

"Almost everything in Nairn had something to do with the sea. A great number of the people were fishermen. Many of the farms outside the town had fields stretching down to the beach and the farmers had their own boats and spent part of their time sea-fishing. I made friends with a farming family called MacDonald. Their farm was two miles from the town and I used to bicycle out there every day. When I was twelve I was given the milk cart to drive. Some of the fisher people would come out to the street with their jugs, when they heard the milk cart jangling, and after a while I made friends among them, and sometimes when the milk round was finished I'd be asked in for tea.

"In this way I came to know a lot of old people—farmers and fishermen and their wives. Some were good storytellers, and some would tell me about their own parents or grandparents— musicians and story-tellers—who couldn't read or write but went to each other's houses to play or sing or listen to music and to tell and listen to stories. Most of their stories were connected with the sea, and the ones that intrigued me most were about that mysterious animal the seal. The old people believed that every animal on the land had its counterpart in the sea and it is almost true if you go by names—sea lion, sea horse, sea cow and so on. There's a sea mouse and even a sea louse. Well, the seals were supposed to be the *people* of the sea. They were supposed to be able to turn into people and back again into seals.

"Well, I have told you some of the things I have written about. I believe I can only write well when I put something of my own into the subject I am dealing with. It must come from the

DAVID THOMSON

heart. And it isn't easy. In fact it's very hard work. But in the end you enjoy it.

"Even if you are given a subject that seems dull—and you have to do it for a magazine editor, or at school for a teacher— use your imagination and always say what you really mean— not what you think other people expect you to say. It's you that matters and even the most unlikely things—buttons or bootlaces—become exciting if you think about them for long enough.

"If anybody wants to be a writer and asks my advice I'd say write about yourself to start with, about animals or people you know, about what you have seen with your own eyes and heard with your own ears and about what you think of it all. That doesn't mean describing exactly what really happened. You allow your imagination to add to it as you go along. It's rather like a dream where real people appear but your imagination makes them do extraordinary things.

"My other bit of advice is to keep a diary. I kept a really dull and stupid one when I was a boy. For instance: 'Saturday. Had lunch. Went for a walk—had tea' without even saying what we ate or where we walked. I wrote that kind of thing because I had a diary printed with dates. I thought I should write something down every day. It is far better to have an ordinary notebook and only write in it when there is something you really want to put down. That's what I do nowadays. I carry it about with me."

A house full of books, and a garden of flowers.
—Andrew Lang

TRESILIAN, (Cecil) Stuart 1891-19(?)

PERSONAL: Born July 12, 1891, in Bristol, England; deceased; married an artist, 1919; children: one son, one daughter. *Education:* Attended Regent Street Polytechnic School and the Royal College of Art. *Residence:* Winslow, near Bletchley Bucks, England.

CAREER: Artist and illustrator; taught art for many years at Regent Street Polytechnic School, London, England. Several of his paintings, made as a prisoner-of-war during World War I, hang in the War Museum, London. *Military service:* Served with 12th London Territorial Regiment ("The Rangers"), during World War I. *Member:* Art Workers' Guild (master, 1960), Society of Graphic Artists (president, 1962-65), Savage Club (London).

ILLUSTRATOR—All for young readers, except as noted: Rudyard Kipling, *Animal Stories from Rudyard Kipling,* Macmillan (London), 1932, Doubleday, Doran, 1938; R. Kipling, *All the Mowgli Stories,* Macmillan (London), 1933; Mary Treadgold, *We Couldn't Leave Dinah,* J. Cape, 1941, Merrimack Book Service, 1980 (Tresilian was not associated with original edi-

(Jacket illustration by Stuart Tresilian from *Puck of Pooks Hill* by Rudyard Kipling.)

She forgot she felt sick and skipped so nimbly over the little running rivulets left by the storm that Mick had to break into a stiff trot to keep up. ■ (From *We Couldn't Leave Dinah* by Mary Treadgold. Illustrated by Stuart Tresilian.)

tion published as *Left Till Called For*); Enid Blyton, *The Island of Adventure,* Macmillan (London), 1944, published as *Mystery Island,* Macmillan (New York), 1945; E. Blyton, *The Castle of Adventure,* Macmillan, 1946; E. Blyton, *The Valley of Adventure,* Macmillan, 1947; E. Blyton, *The Sea of Adventure,* Macmillan, 1948; E. Blyton, *The Mountain of Adventure,* Macmillan, 1949; Ellis Dillon, *Midsummer Magic,* Macmillan (London), 1950; E. Blyton, *The Ship of Adventure,* Macmillan, 1950; E. Blyton, *The Circus of Adventure,* Macmillan (London), 1952, St. Martin's, 1953.

R. Kipling, *The Jungle Books,* Reprint Society, 1955; E. Blyton, *The River of Adventure,* St. Martin's, 1955; Sir Vivian Fuchs, *Antarctic Adventure: The Commonwealth Trans-Antarctic Expedition, 1955-58,* British Book Service, 1959; Joseph E. Chipperfield, *Petrus, Dog of the Hill Country,* Heinemann, 1960; Mary E. Patchett, *The Quest of Ati Manu,* Lutterworth, 1960; M. E. Patchett, *Come Home, Brumby,* Lutterworth, 1961; J. E. Chipperfield, *The Grey Dog from Galtymore,* Heinemann, 1961; (and author of accompanying text, with Herbert J. Williams) *Human Anatomy for Art Students,* Chapman & Hall, 1961; M. E. Patchett, *Circus Brumby,* Lutterworth, 1962; Michael Gaunt, *Brim's Boat,* J. Cape, 1964, Coward, 1966; M. E. Patchett, *Stranger in the Herd: A Brumby Book,* Lutterworth, 1964, Duell, Sloan & Pearce, 1966; Michael J. Barrett, *Antarctic Secret,* Dent, 1965; M. Gaunt, *Brim Sails Out,* J.

Cape, 1966.

SIDELIGHTS: Tresilian spent his childhood in London and in Liverpool, England, where he used to draw pictures of the ships and shipping industry in Liverpool. His interest in art led him to study at the Polytechnic School. After completing his art studies there, he taught art at the school until gaining a Royal Exhibition Scholarship to the Royal College of Art. ''After studying at the Polytechnic for a few years, I taught as a pupil-teacher, then gained a Royal Exhibition Scholarship to the Royal College of Art. I had an enjoyable time until war broke out in 1914. Serving with the 12th London Territorial Regiment ('The Rangers'), I was wounded three times, the last time being taken prisoner. I did some drawing and painting and started a class among my fellow prisoners. When I returned to London, I resumed my work as an illustrator, as well as that of a teacher at the Polytechnic. . . .'' [Bertha E. Mahony and others, compilers, *Illustrators of Children's Books: 1744-1945*, Horn Book, 1947.[1]]

The drawings that he made while a prisoner in World War I are now housed in the War Museum in London.

Besides teaching art for many years at the Polytechnic School, Tresilian illustrated numerous children's books, including storis by Rudyard Kipling, Enid Blyton, and Mary Patchett. ''I work very much on my own as I live in an old thatched house in Winslow near Bletchley Bucks (England) dated about 1560, renovated, of course, but delightful to live in. I was Master of the Art Workers' Guild for the year 1960 and was President of the Society of Graphic Artists from 1962 to 1965.'' [Lee Kingman and others, compilers, *Illustrators of Children's Books: 1957-1966*, Horn Book, 1968.[2]]

TRIMBY, Elisa   1948-

BRIEF ENTRY: Born June 30, 1948, in Reigate, Surrey, England. British author and illustrator of books for children. After leaving the Brighton College of Art in 1971, Trimby moved to London where she worked as a free-lance illustrator of everything from books to wine labels. She has also been employed as a teacher of life drawing at Thames Polytechnic and as a geriatric art therapist. As an author, Trimby keeps her texts simple yet direct. She has written and illustrated three picture books published in the United States by Lothrop: *Mr. Plum's Paradise* (1977), its sequel, *Mr. Plum's Oasis* (1981), and *The Christmas Story* (1984). *Booklist* described her water-colored pen-and-ink drawings as ''intricate, precise . . . , sparkling with clear, vibrant colors,'' while *School Library Journal* noted that they ''are alive with detail and display some unusual perspectives that will intrigue and absorb young children.'' In addition to her own writings, Trimby has supplied the illustrations for Ruth Morris's *The Cornerstone* (Heinemann, 1976), Ann Lawrence's *Mr. Robertson's Hundred Pounds* (Kestrel Books, 1976), an edition of Clement C. Moore's *The Night Before Christmas* (Doubleday, 1977), and Ruth Craft's *The King's Collection* (Doubleday, 1978).

FOR MORE INFORMATION SEE: Illustrators of Children's Books: 1967-1976, Horn Book, 1978.

Books and friends should be few and good.
—Proverb

TROYER, Johannes   1902-1969

BRIEF ENTRY: Born in 1902, in South Tirol, Austria (now Italy); died July 13, 1969, in Innsbruck, Austria. An internationally known illustrator, designer, and calligrapher, Troyer studied art in Austria and Germany. He was a long-time resident of Vienna and Innsbruck where he worked as an illustrator and calligrapher for German, Swiss, and American publishers. Also a designer of posters, he received numerous awards in competitions on both the national and international levels. With the onset of World War II, Troyer fled Austria and the invading Nazi troops for the small principality of Liechtenstein where he designed a number of postage stamps for the government. In 1949 he emigrated to the United States, remaining until the death of his wife in 1962. During that time he executed work for various publishers and was involved in the creation of typographic ornaments and new designs for type faces. Troyer's illustrated books for children include Augusta Baker's *Talking Tree* and *The Golden Lynx and Other Tales*, and Michel-Aime Baudouy's *Bruno, King of the Mountain*. Currently in print are Baudouy's *Old One-Toe*, and Thomas B. Leekley's *King Herla's Quest and Other Medieval Stories from Walter Map*.

FOR MORE INFORMATION SEE: Illustrators of Children's Books: 1957-1966, Horn Book, 1968. *Obituaries: Publishers Weekly*, September 1, 1969.

VINCENT, Eric Douglas   1953-

PERSONAL: Born June 4, 1953, in Gainesville, Fla.; son of Walter Ernest (a professor) and Theodora Ann (a teacher; maiden name Johnson) Vincent; married Elisabeth Ann Porter (a registered nurse), December 3, 1978. *Education:* University of Southwestern Louisiana, B.A. (magna cum laude), 1978. *Politics:* Democrat. *Home:* Houston, Tex.

ERIC DOUGLAS VINCENT

CAREER: Author and illustrator. Lafayette Natural History Museum and Planetarium, Lafayette, La., curatorial and lab assistant, 1970; *Acadiana Journal*, Lafayette, La., managing editor, 1974; *Media Associates*, Lafayette, La., art director, 1976-78; free-lance author and illustrator, 1978—. Prepared portable display "The Kingdom of Kush—Africa's Oldest and Greatest Inland Empire," Lafayette Natural History Museum, 1974. *Exhibitions:* The Original Art Exhibit, New York, N.Y., 1982; 24th Society of Illustrators Show, New York, N.Y., 1983. *Awards, honors: Clovis Crawfish and the Singing Cigales* was awarded a rating of "excellent" by Southern Books Competition, 1981.

ILLUSTRATOR: Mary Alice Fontenot, *Clovis Crawfish and Etienne Escargot*, Acadiana Press, 1979, Pelican, 1982; M. A. Fontenot, *Clovis Crawfish and the Singing Cigales*, Pelican, 1981; Marilyn Redmond, *Henry Hamilton, Graduate Ghost*, Pelican, 1982; M. A. Fontenot, *Clovis Crawfish and the Orphan Zo-Zo*, Pelican, 1983. Contributor to *Westtimes, Houston Post, Houston Chronicle, Imp Magazine.*

WORK IN PROGRESS: Roottangle; Puss in Boots; Edward; Cajun nursery rhymes for adults.

SIDELIGHTS: "Animal fantasy gives a child a first sense of separate worlds, places independent of man. A child's sense of self is enriched by animal tales because they can change an egocentric world-view to one of respect and thoughtful stewardship. The bonus is the lasting impression moral lessons can make when acted out by animals; tales entertain while illustrating difficult points.

"Best of all, a sense of wonder can be cultivated. Good fantasy gives health; it nurtures and reconciles the broken parts of our lives. Dealing with life takes a variety of skills, and a powerful imagination gives reach and resilience to the mind. What a painful emptiness those without fantasy must have, those with no secret garden."

WABER, Bernard   1924-

BRIEF ENTRY: Born September 27, 1924, in Philadelphia, Pa. Graphic designer, and author and illustrator of children's books. Waber attended the University of Pennsylvania, Museum School of Fine Art in Philadelphia, and Pennsylvania Academy of Fine Arts before becoming a commercial artist for Conde Nast Publications and *Seventeen* magazine. He has also been a graphic designer for *Life* magazine and, since 1974, for *People*. His interest in picture books evolved as he began reading them aloud to his children. Realizing his enjoyment of the books, he became increasingly absorbed in them; in 1961 he entered the picture book field with a self-illustrated story, *Lorenzo*. He has since written and illustrated over twenty additional books, all published by Houghton. Waber is probably best known for his books featuring "Lyle the Crocodile." Lyle first appeared in *The House on East 88th Street* (1962), and later in the books *Lyle, Lyle, Crocodile* (1965), *Lyle and the Birthday Party* (1966), *Lovable Lyle* (1969), and *Lyle Finds His Mother* (1974). "Lyle," a play based loosely on Waber's books, was produced off-Broadway at the McAlpin Rooftop Theatre in 1970.

Humor plays a major role in much of Waber's work. In a review of *You're a Little Kid with a Big Heart* (1980), *Publishers Weekly* took note of Waber's "rare ability to balance nonsense and pathos. . . ." Similarly, *Booklist* observed that *Ira Sleeps Over* (1972) "depicts common childhood qualms with empathy and humor. . . ." *Horn Book* also applauded Waber's "brilliant nonsense" that was "cleverly shown" in *A Firefly Named Torchy*. His other books include *An Anteater Named Arthur* (1967), *But Names Will Never Hurt Me* (1976), *The Snake: A Very Long Story* (1978), and *Bernard* (1982). Waber has received several awards for his books, among them a Lewis Carroll Shelf Award for *Lyle, Lyle, Crocodile* in 1979. *Office: People* Magazine, Time, Inc., Time & Life Bldg., Rockefeller Center, New York, N.Y. 10020.

FOR MORE INFORMATION SEE: Illustrators of Children's Books: 1957-1966, Horn Book, 1968; *Third Book of Junior Authors*, H. W. Wilson, 1972; *Elementary English*, September, 1974; *Contemporary Authors, New Revision Series*, Volume 2, Gale, 1981; *Twentieth-Century Children's Writers*, 2nd edition, St. Martin's, 1983.

WALCK, Henry Z(eigler)   1908-1984

OBITUARY NOTICE: Born March 30, 1908, in Greencastle, Pa.; died December 24, 1984, in Plandome, N.Y. Publisher. A well-known publisher of children's books, Walck began his career as an accountant with the publishing firms of G. P. Putnam's Sons and Prentice-Hall in the early 1930s. In 1936 he joined the staff of Oxford University Press, advancing to the position of president by 1948. Ten years later, he bought the children's book division of Oxford University Press and formed his own publishing company—Henry Z. Walck, Inc. Walck retired during the mid-1970s when his company was sold to David McKay.

FOR MORE INFORMATION SEE—Obituaries: *Publishers Weekly*, January 18, 1985.

WALTNER, Elma   1912-

PERSONAL: Born November 30, 1912, in Yankton, S.D.; daughter of Emil J. (a teacher and farmer) and Mary (Goering) Waltner. *Education:* Freeman Junior College, Freeman, S.D., student, 1930-32; Yankton College, A.B. (cum laude), 1935; additional study at Bethel College, 1938. *Religion:* General Conference Mennonite Church. *Address:* Box 190, Freeman, S.D. 57029.

CAREER: Free-lance nonfiction writer teaming with brother, Willard Waltner, a photographer, early 1940s-1961; writer, 1961—; dairy farmer.

WRITINGS—All with brother, Willard Waltner; all illustrated with photos by W. Waltner; all published by Lantern, except where indicated: *Carving Animal Caricatures*, McKnight & McKnight, 1951; *Wonders of Hobbycraft*, 1962; *The New Hobbycraft Book*, 1963; *Holiday Hobbycraft*, 1964; *Hobbycraft Toys and Games*, 1965; *Hobbycraft around the World*, 1966; *Hobbycraft for Juniors*, 1967; *Year Round Hobbycraft*, 1968; *A New Look at Old Crafts*, 1971; *Heritage Hobbycraft*, 1977. Contributor of adult and juvenile articles to magazines and trade journals.

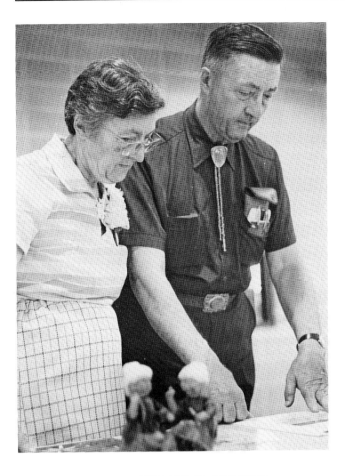

ELMA and WILLARD H. WALTNER

WORK IN PROGRESS: Nonfiction feature writing.

SIDELIGHTS: "My brother Willard and I grew up as South Dakota 'farm kids.' Since he was older by three years he often took the lead in our various games and pastimes so I was a hopeless tomboy. We spent endless hours in the creek that circles the farmstead, sailing homemade boats, building dams and pools to hold the shiny minnows we scooped up by hand or with a gunny sack seine. Many summer afternoons were spent with our willow or cane poles wandering the creek from fishing hole to fishing hole. We usually returned with half a pailful. The understanding was that we had to clean them and mom would fry them. Nothing ever tasted as good as those sardine-sized fish fried crisp and brown so we could eat them, crunchy bones and all.

"Many of our toys were 'homemade' and both of us grew up with the 'making things' fever. Our parents always encouraged us in this.

"We never outgrew the pleasure of creating 'originals' in numerous craft areas and eventually reached the point where we wanted to share our designs and the 'how to' of making them with others. The very first article sold was of a set of little peanut animal party favors. We needed photographs to illustrate the articles and the first ones were taken with dad's folding Kodak, with the objects set out on the porch while we waited for the sun to come out from the clouds to make the proper exposure. By the early 40s we were regularly selling nonfiction features, many of them craft pieces, to various magazines. Under the dual by-line of 'Willard and Elma Waltner,' we continued to expand our output in both volume and subject matter, selling to various juvenile and adult publications. We continued as a part-time photojournalism duo until 1961, sandwiching in as many articles as possible between farming and dairying. That fall we dispersed the herd and went into full-time photojournalism. The 'Hobbycraft' series, published by Lantern Press, are a set of books in which previously published craft articles are compiled.

"Though now semi-retired, we continue to produce and illustrate nonfiction features. In theory, Willard is the photographer and I am the writer. In practice, we work together so closely that the end result is truly a piece originated and prepared by Willard and Elma Waltner."

WALTNER, Willard H.   1909-

PERSONAL: Born September 10, 1909, in Freeman, S.D.; son of Emil J. (a teacher and farmer) and Mary (Goering) Waltner; married Florence Leigh, August 8, 1981; children: Winona (Mrs. Leslie Senner), Dianne (Mrs. Anthony Epp). *Education:* Yankton College, B.A., 1930. *Religion:* General Conference Mennonite Church.

CAREER: Dairy operator; photographer. Free-lance nonfiction writer with sister, Elma Waltner, early 1940s-1961; writer, 1961—.

WRITINGS—All with sister, Elma Waltner; all self-illustrated with photographs; all published by Lantern, except where indicated: *Carving Animal Caricatures,* Mcknight & Mcknight, 1951; *Wonders of Hobbycraft,* 1962; *The New Hobbycraft Book,* 1963; *Holiday Hobbycraft,* 1964; *Hobbycraft Toys and Games,* 1965; *Hobbycraft around the World,* 1966; *Hobbycraft for Juniors,* 1967; *Year Round Hobbycraft,* 1968; *A New Look at Old Crafts,* 1971; *Heritage Hobbycraft,* 1977. Contributor of adult and juvenile articles to magazines and trade journals.

WORK IN PROGRESS: Nonfiction feature writing.

WEST, Anna   1938-

PERSONAL: Born April 5, 1938, in Crete, Ill.; daughter of A. E. (in sales) and Helen (Janota) Wood; married Paul West (a broadcaster and craftsman), November 28, 1969. *Education:* University of Michigan, B.A., 1959; San Francisco State University, M.A., 1971. *Residence:* Palermo, Calif.

CAREER: Writer. *Awards, honors:* Avery Hopwood Award from University of Michigan, 1955, for a story, "The Revivalists."

WRITINGS: Revenge at the Spy-Catchers' Picnic (juvenile; Volume I of "The Messina Trilogy"), Addison-Wesley, 1981. Work represented in anthologies, including *Coast to Coast,* Angus & Robertson, 1968.

WORK IN PROGRESS: A novel for adults.

SIDELIGHTS: "When I was a child I lived here and there,

If there were enough kids in the hills to have a school, you can be sure that we had enough for a summer gang. ■ (Jacket illustration by Susan Paradis from *Revenge at the Spy-Catcher's Picnic* by Anna West.)

ANNA WEST

with mother, with an aunt, and with grandmother. If I wandered in childhood, I continued to do so when I grew up. That peripateticism took me to Alaska, Hawaii, Mexico, England, Morocco, Spain, Greece, and Australia. Now it has brought me to northern California, where my husband is building a home among oak, manzanita, and digger-pine, on a hill that is thistle-dry in summer and mushroom-moist in winter. I love the opposites of this land.

"In order to help us stay here, I took work as a substitute elementary school teacher. As I worked with the children and observed their intrigues, I remembered the games *we* used to play! Those memories compelled me to write a spy novel for children."

FOR MORE INFORMATION SEE: Oroville Mercury Register, December 14, 1981.

WHEELER, Cindy 1955-

BRIEF ENTRY: Born May 17, 1955, in Montgomery, Ala. A graduate of Auburn University, Wheeler began her career as a free-lance illustrator and author of books for children in 1980. Prior to that time, she worked as a children's book buyer and sales clerk in Nashville, Tenn., and as an editorial secretary for the New York publishing firm of Alfred A. Knopf. Her self-illustrated picture book, *A Good Day, a Good Night* (Lippincott, 1980), is the first in a series featuring the antics of a mischievous cat named Marmalade. These stories are designed for young children who are just starting to grasp the basic concepts of shapes and colors. *School Library Journal* observed: "Wheeler has done beginning readers a great service in creating a fun character, placing him in humorous situations, and presenting it all in simple language." *Booklist* took special note of her illustrative technique in which "objects of importance on each page are featured in warm tones, while black lines sketch out background details against plenty of white space. . . ." All published by Knopf, the titles are: *Marmalade's Snowy Day* (1982), *Marmalade's Yellow Leaf* (1982), *Marmalade's Nap* (1983), *Marmalade's Picnic* (1983), and *Marmalade's Christmas Present* (1984).

In addition to the "Marmalade" series, Wheeler has illustrated several books written by others, among them Charlotte Zolotow's *One Step, Two* (Lothrop, 1981), Susan Talanda's *Dad Told Me Not To* and Carol A. Marron's *Someone Just Like Me* (both Carnival Press, 1983). As an author and illustrator, Wheeler strives to inject into her books those feelings she best remembers as a child, namely, "uncomplicated, unsuspicious, happiness in its purest and most all-encompassing form." *Home and office:* Box 157, Glynwood Farm, Cold Spring, N.Y. 10516.

FOR MORE INFORMATION SEE: Contemporary Authors, Volume 110, Gale, 1984.

WIBERG, Harald (Albin) 1908-

BRIEF ENTRY: Born March 1, 1908, in Ankarsrum, Sweden. Swedish artist, illustrator, and writer. Wiberg's affinity for drawing was developed as a child when he began sketching the animals around his home, notably, the pigs and hens that were customarily kept by families of that time. In his early twenties, he traveled to Stockholm where he studied art at Konstfack and Edvin Ollers Malarskola. Eventually, he became established as a writer and painter of outdoor life. In 1961 Wiberg illustrated Astrid Lindgren's adaptation *The Tomten.* Reprinted in 1979, reviews of the illustrations remained favorable. *New York Times Book Review* cited their "luminous beauty" while *Publishers Weekly* called them "lovely, full-color paintings [that] convey the hushed atmosphere of night in the Swedish countryside. . . ."

Wiberg has since illustrated numerous picture books that have been translated from their original Swedish into English. These include Lindgren's *Christmas in the Stable* and *The Tomten and the Fox,* Edor Burman's *Three Wolverines of Rushing Valley* and *Bears of Big Stream Valley,* Hans Petersen's *When Peter Was Lost in the Forest* and *The Big Snowstorm,* and Viktor Rydberg's *The Christmas Tomten.* In 1976 Wiberg was the recipient of the Elsa Beskow Award, given to the illustrator of the best Swedish picture book, for *The Big Snowstorm.* Three years later he received the Osterreichischer Staatspreis fur Kinder- und Jugendliteratur for the same book. He has written and illustrated one of his own picture books, translated as *Christmas at the Tomten's Farm.*

FOR MORE INFORMATION SEE: Illustrators of Children's Books: 1957-1966, Horn Book, 1968.

WISEMAN, David 1916-

BRIEF ENTRY: Born January 13, 1916, in Manchester England. British author of novels for children and adults. Wiseman became a full-time writer in 1978, following a twenty-five year career as teacher, principal, and advisor at high schools in Yorkshire and Cornwall. Prior to teaching, he spent several years as editor of the *Journal of Adult Education* in London. To date, he has written four novels for young readers which reflect his interest in fantasy and historical events. In his first two novels, *Jeremy Visick* (Houghton, 1981) and *Thimbles* (Houghton, 1982), the modern-day main characters are transported back in time for encounters with personages of another era. In *Jeremy Visick,* it is young Matthew Clemens who experiences the horrors of mining in nineteenth-century Cornwall as he attempts to bring to rest the ghost of a boy who died in the mines. "This story," observed *School Library Journal,* "blends the mystery and awe of the supernatural with the real terror and peril of descending the shaft of an 1850 Cornish copper mine." *Horn Book* praised Wiseman's "seamless fusion of illusion and reality. . . ." in which "the historical material [is] rich and dramatic, and the fantasy . . . entirely convincing."

In *Thimbles,* Wiseman's focus is on the struggle for universal suffrage in early nineteenth-century Britain as young Cathy Aitken's very being becomes immeshed in the bodies of two girls during the Peterloo Massacre of 1819. According to *Booklist,* "civil-rights concerns, parental relationships, and interest in family historical ties provide a solid frame through which the story gleams with intensity and drama." Wiseman keeps the setting contemporary in *Blodwen and the Guardians* (Houghton, 1983) as ten-year-old Blodwen meets the invisible, imp-like protectors of a nearby tomb. *Booklist* took note of "a remarkable range of characters [that] emerges as Wiseman individualizes both his human and fantasy characters with vivid detail." His latest novel, *Adam's Common* (Houghton, 1984), again transports the reader back in time as a fourteen-year-old American girl and a nineteenth-century British boy struggle to preserve a special piece of land. Currently, Wiseman's projects include a trilogy of adult novels that deal with the political adversities of women at various points in history. *Home:* 25 Ellers Lane, Auckley, Doncaster, Yorkshire, England.

FOR MORE INFORMATION SEE: Contemporary Authors, Volume 109, Gale, 1983; *Fifth Book of Junior Authors and Illustrators,* H. W. Wilson, 1983.

YOLEN, Jane H. 1939-

PERSONAL: Born February 11, 1939, in New York, N.Y.; daughter of Will Hyatt (author, public relations man) and Isabelle (Berlin) Yolen; married David W. Stemple (a professor of computer science), September 2, 1962; children: Heidi Elisabet, Adam Douglas, Jason Frederic. *Education:* Smith College, B.A., 1960; University of Massachusetts, M.Ed., 1976. *Politics:* Liberal Democrat. *Religion:* Quaker. *Mailing address:* Phoenix Farm, Box 27, 31 School St., Hatfield, Mass. 01038. *Agent:* Marilyn Marlow, Curtis Brown Ltd., 575 Madison Ave., New York, N.Y. 10022.

CAREER: Saturday Review, New York, N.Y., production assistant, 1960-61; Gold Medal Books (publishers), New York, N.Y., assistant editor, 1961-62; Rutledge Books (publishers),

Jane Yolen in Hatfield, Massachusetts, 1981.

New York, N.Y., associate editor, 1962-63; Alfred A. Knopf, Inc. (publishers), New York, N.Y., assistant juvenile editor, 1963-65; full-time professional writer, 1965—; teacher of writing and lecturer, 1966—. Chairman of board of library trustees, Hatfield, Mass., 1976-83; member of arts council, Hatfield, Mass. *Member:* Society of Children's Book Writers, Society of Friends, International Kitefliers Association, Smith College Alumnae Association, Science Fiction Writers of America, Bay State Writers Guild, Children's Literature Association, Science Fiction Poetry Association, National Association for the Preservation and Perpetuation of Storytelling. *Awards, honors:* Boys' Club of America Junior Book Award, 1968, for *The Minstrel and the Mountain; The Emperor and the Kite* received the Lewis Carroll Shelf Award, and was a Caldecott honor book, both 1968; Lewis Carroll Shelf Award, 1973, for *The Girl Who Loved the Wind; The Girl Who Loved the Wind,* 1973, and *The Little Spotted Fish,* 1976, were both selected for the Children's Book Showcase; Society of Children's Book Writers Golden Kite Award, 1974, and National Book Award nomination, 1975, both for *The Girl Who Cried Flowers and Other Tales; The Transfigured Hart,* 1975, and *The Moon Ribbon and Other Tales,* 1976, were both named Golden Kite honor books; Christopher Medal, 1978, for *The Seeing Stick;* honorary L.L.D. from College of Our Lady of the Elm, 1981; *The Gift of Sarah Barker* was selected one of *School Library Journal's* "Best Books for Young Adults", 1982; Garden State Children's Book Award, 1983, for *Commander Toad in Space.*

WRITINGS—All juvenile, except as noted; fiction: *See This Little Line?* (illustrated by Kathleen Elgin), McKay, 1963; *The Witch Who Wasn't* (illustrated by Arnold Roth), Macmillan, 1964; *Gwinellen, the Princess Who Could Not Sleep,* Macmillan, 1965; (with Anne Houston) *Trust a City Kid,* Lothrop, 1966; *The Emperor and the Kite* (illustrated by Ed Young), World Publishing, 1967; *The Minstrel and the Mountain* (illustrated by Anne Rockwell), World Publishing, 1967; "Robin Hood" (musical play), first produced in Boston, Mass., 1967; *The Longest Name on the Block* (illustrated by P. Madden), Funk, 1967; *Isabel's Noel* (illustrated by A. Roth), Funk, 1967; *Greyling: A Picture Story from the Islands of Shetland* (illustrated by William Stobbs; *Horn Book* honor list), World Publishing, 1968; *The Wizard of Washington Square* (illustrated by Ray Cruz), World Publishing, 1969.

Hobo Toad and the Motorcycle Gang (illustrated by Emily McCully), World Publishing, 1970; *It All Depends* (illustrated by D. Bolognese), Funk, 1970; *The Inway Investigators; or, the Mystery at Maccracken's Place* (illustrated by Allan Eitzen), Seabury, 1970; *The Seventh Mandarin* (illustrated by E. Young; Junior Literary Guild selection), Seabury, 1971; *The Bird of Time* (illustrated by Mercer Mayer), Crowell, 1971; *The Girl Who Loved the Wind* (illustrated by E. Young), Crowell, 1972; (editor) *Zoo 2000: Twelve Stories of Science Fiction and Fantasy Beasts,* Seabury, 1973; *The Girl Who Cried Flowers and Other Tales* (illustrated by David Palladini; ALA Notable Book), Crowell, 1974; *The Boy Who Had Wings* (illustrated by Helga Aichenger), Crowell, 1974; *The Adventures of Eeka Mouse* (illustrated by Myra McGee), Xerox Education Publications, 1974; *The Magic Three of Solatia* (illustrated by Julia Noonan), Crowell, 1974; *The Rainbow Rider* (illustrated by Michael Foreman), Crowell, 1974; *The Little Spotted Fish* (illustrated by Friso Henstra; Junior Literary Guild selection), Seabury, 1974.

The Transfigured Hart (illustrated by Donna Diamond), Crowell, 1975; *An Invitation to the Butterfly Ball: A Counting Rhyme* (illustrated by Jane B. Zalben), Parents Magazine Press, 1976; *Milkweed Days* (photographs by Gabriel A. Cooney), Crowell, 1976; *The Moon Ribbon and Other Tales* (illustrated by D. Palladini), Crowell, 1976; *The Seeing Stick* (illustrated by Remy Charlip and Demetra Marsalis), Crowell, 1977; *The Sultan's Perfect Tree* (illustrated by Barbara Garrison), Parents Magazine Press, 1977; *The Giants' Farm* (illustrated by Tomie de Paola; *Weekly Reader* Book Club selection), Seabury, 1977; *The Hundredth Dove and Other Tales* (illustrated by D. Palladini), Crowell, 1977; *The Lady and the Merman* (adult; illustrated by Barry Moser), Pennyroyal, 1977; *Hannah Dreaming* (photographs by Alan R. Epstein), Museum of Fine Art (Springfield, Mass.), 1977; *Spider Jane* (illustrated by Stefan Bernath), Coward, 1978; *The Simple Prince* (illustrated by Jack Kent), Parents Magazine Press, 1978; *No Bath Tonight* (illustrated by Nancy W. Parker; Junior Literary Guild selection), Crowell, 1978; *The Mermaid's Three Wisdoms* (illustrated by Laura Rader), Collins & World, 1978; (editor) *Shape Shifters: Fantasy and Science Fiction Tales about Humans Who Can Change Their Shapes,* Seabury, 1978; *Dream Weaver* (illustrated by Michael Hague), Collins, 1979; *The Giants Go Camping* (illustrated by T. de Paola; Junior Literary Guild selection), Seabury, 1979; *All in the Woodland Early: An ABC Book* (illustrated by J. B. Zalben; Junior Literary Guild selection), Collins, 1979.

Commander Toad in Space (illustrated by B. Degen; Junior Literary Guild selection), Coward, 1980; *Spider Jane on the Move* (illustrated by S. Bernath), Coward, 1980; *Mice on Ice* (illustrated by Lawrence Di Fiori), Dutton, 1980; *The Robot and Rebecca: The Mystery of the Code-Carrying Kids* (illustrated by Jurg Obrist), Knopf, 1980; *Shirlick Holmes and the Case of the Wandering Wardrobe* (illustrated by Anthony Rao), Coward, 1981; *The Robot and Rebecca and the Missing Owser* (illustrated by Lady McCrady), Knopf, 1981; *The Acorn Quest* (illustrated by Susanna Natti), Harper, 1981; *Brothers of the Wind* (illustrated by Barbara Berger), Philomel, 1981; *Sleeping Ugly* (illustrated by Diane Stanley; Junior Literary Guild selection), Coward, 1981; *The Boy Who Spoke Chimp* (illustrated by David Wiesner), Knopf, 1981; *Uncle Lemon's Spring* (illustrated by Glen Rounds), Unicorn/Dutton, 1981; *The Gift of Sarah Barker,* Viking, 1981; *Dragon's Blood,* Delacorte, 1982; *Neptune Rising: Songs and Tales of the Undersea Folk* (story

collection; young adult; illustrated by D. Wiesner), Philomel, 1982; *Commander Toad and the Planet of the Grapes* (illustrated by B. Degen; Junior Literary Guild selection), Coward, 1982; *Tales of Wonder* (adult collection of thirty stories), Schocken, 1983; *Commander Toad and the Big Black Hole* (illustrated by B. Degen), Coward, 1983; *Heart's Blood,* Delacorte, 1984; *Cards of Grief* (adult science fiction novel), Ace, 1984; *The Stone Silenus,* Philomel, 1984; *Children of the Wolf* (historical novel), Viking, 1984; *Commander Toad and the Dis-Asteroid* (illustrated by B. Degen; Junior Literary Guild selection), Coward, 1985; *Dragonfield and Other Stories* (adult collection), Ace, 1985.

Miss Rosa smiled. Her skates touched the ice. The band began to play. From the sides of the tent skated nineteen other mice. The Mice Capades had begun. ■ (From *Mice on Ice* by Jane Yolen. Illustrated by Lawrence DiFiori.)

Nonfiction: *Pirates in Petticoats* (illustrated by Leonard Vosburgh), McKay, 1963; *World on a String: The Story of Kites,* World Publishing, 1968; *Friend: The Story of George Fox and the Quakers,* Seabury, 1972; (editor with Barbara Green) *The Fireside Song Book of Birds and Beasts* (illustrated by Peter Parnall), Simon & Schuster, 1972; *The Wizard Islands* (illustrated by Robert Quackenbush), Crowell, 1973; *Writing Books for Children* (adult), Writer, Inc., 1973, revised, 1983; *Ring Out!: A Book of Bells* (illustrated by R. Cuffari; Junior Literary Guild selection), Seabury, 1974; *Simple Gifts: The Story of the Shakers* (illustrated by Betty Fraser), Viking, 1976; (compiler) *Rounds about Rounds* (illustrated by Gail Gibbons), F. Watts, 1977; *Touch Magic: Fantasy, Faerie and Folklore in the Literature of Childhood* (adult), Philomel, 1981; *The Lullaby Book* (illustrated by Charles Mikolaycak), Harcourt, 1985.

Poetry: *How Beastly! A Menagerie of Nonsense Poems* (illustrated by James Marshall), Philomel, 1980; *Dragon Night and Other Lullabies* (illustrated by Demi), Methuen, 1980.

Contributor: Orson Scott Card, editor, *Dragons of Light,* Ace Books, 1981; Terri Windling and Mark Alan Arnold, editors, *Elsewhere: Volume I,* Ace Books, 1981; T. Windling and M. A. Arnold, editors, *Elsewhere: Volume II,* Ace Books, 1982; Susan Schwartz, editor, *Hecate's Cauldron,* Daw Books, 1982; Jessica Amanda Salmonson, editor, *Heroic Visions,* Ace Books, 1983; T. Windling, editor, *Faery!,* Ace Books, 1985; Will Shetterly and Emma Bull, editors, *Liavek,* Ace Books, 1985; S. Schwartz, editor, *Moonsinger's Friends,* Bluejay, 1985; Robin McKinley, editor, *Imaginary Lands,* Greenwillow, 1985.

Yolen at a bridge game, Wesleyan College, 1959.

Author of column "Children's Bookfare," *Daily Hampshire Gazette.* Contributor of articles, reviews, poems, and short stories to *The Writer, Parabola, New York Times, Horn Book, Wilson Library Journal, Magazine of Fantasy and Science Fiction, Isaac Asimov's Science Fiction Magazine, Language Arts,* and other periodicals. Member of editorial board, *Advocate,* and *The National Storytelling Journal.*

ADAPTATIONS: "The Seventh Mandarin" (movie), Xerox Films, 1973; "The Emperor and the Kite" (filmstrip with cassette), Listening Library, 1976; "The Girl Who Cried Flowers and Other Tales" (cassette), Weston Woods, 1983; "Dragon's Blood" (movie), CBS Storybook, 1985.

WORK IN PROGRESS: A Sending of Dragons, the final book in the trilogy which includes *Heart's Blood* and *Dragon's Blood; Ring of Earth,* a picture book; *The Shouting Fey,* an adult novel; *Sister Light, Sister Dark,* an adult novel; a folklore collection for Pantheon; *Chaya,* a time travel novel for young adults; *Mermen: An Unnatural History,* with Shulamith Oppenheim; *Merlin's Booke,* a short story collection; picture books.

SIDELIGHTS: **February 11, 1939.** Born in New York City. "When I was growing up, New York City was a much freer and more carefree place for a nine and ten year-old to roam in. I lived across the street from Central Park where I played alone or with friends. Now, I wouldn't even *walk* across the park alone; it has become very dangerous. The city has changed.

"When I wasn't in school or in ballet class (I studied at Balanchine's school for eight years, until I hit puberty), I played elaborate fantasy games in Central Park, such as Robin Hood and King Arthur, or I spent long hours traveling the subway which stopped right near my house. A nickel could buy hours of riding on the subway with changeovers. We'd all check the gum machines for pennies or dimes."

Museums were familiar playgrounds. "The Museum of Natural History was fifteen blocks from home and the Museum of the City of New York across the park from our house."

Yolen demonstrated an early interest in writing. For her initial endeavor, she wrote both music and script for a first grade play. "All the characters were vegetables. I played the lead and we all ended up in a salad together—that was the grand finale! Music and theater have always interested me. I did do some drawing as well, but haven't any talent for it—it's as if my head and eye were disconnected. I have to make images in words.

"I left New York City at thirteen and did the rest of my growing up in Westport, Connecticut. Though we lived only an hour out of New York, we were focused on Westport which was, and still is, a very culturally exciting community. It was a hotbed of writers and artists, so I just assumed that when you grew up, you became a writer. For me that seemed a logical explanation for all the writers around.

"My mother was a not-very-successful short story writer. What she was successful at was making and creating crossword puzzles and acrostics. She would have graph paper and plot out the words and clues. She used to be able to do the *New York Times* Sunday crossword—in pen—in an hour! She had an incredible vocabulary. It wasn't a speaking vocabulary but, rather, a reading and crossword puzzle vocabulary. She spoke very well but I never heard enormous words in her everyday speech.

**The Pythong ties itself in knots
But has a tiny brain
And so it cannot ever get
Itself untied again . . . .**

■ (From "The Pythong," in _How Beastly! A Menagerie of Nonsense Poems_ by Jane Yolen.
Illustrated by James Marshall.)

For days he used the magic golden net. ■ (From *The Little Spotted Fish* by Jane Yolen. Illustrated by Friso Henstra.)

"I was very involved in high school as captain of the girls' basketball team, staff member of both the newspaper and literary magazine, and member of the Jazz, Spanish, and Latin clubs. We had one of the best choirs in the country, touring and performing.

"I would often write my term papers in verse. I'm more at ease with verse than prose. It's a party trick. I recall how during my senior year in college I wrote the final exam for American Intellectual History in verse. The teacher was so astounded he gave me an 'A+,' even though it was really a 'C' paper in terms of content. He gave me the grade for grace under fire. He didn't know how easily I could write verse."

1956-1960. Attended Smith College. "In college I started publishing in magazines and newspapers. Between junior and senior year, I had my first poem published in a 'real' poetry magazine.

"First I thought I'd be a journalist, but found out that I made up facts. When I had to interview poor people in terrible straits, I'd get so upset I'd start crying. I ended up writing stories off the top of my head, which these days could win you a Pulitzer Prize, but in those days was frowned upon if you wanted to be a journalist. It became clear that I was a fiction writer.

"I wrote a lot of poetry. At that time, I made a distinction between poetry and journalism. I didn't think the two could ever meet. I won all the poetry prizes at Smith as well as the journalism prize. I saw poetry and journalism as two very separate strands of my writing. Although both of them run very strongly within me, the poetry has really won out. When I write fantasy books, I like to think that I see my fantasy world with a journalist's eye, as well as a poet's eye. I know how the imaginary country runs, what the gross national product is, even if I don't write it down. That's where the journalistic eye comes into my writing.

"I'm just starting to write adult books. My first adult fantasy book, *Cards of Grief,* was chosen for the Science Fiction Book Club, so I feel very good about it. It is a combination of science fiction and fantasy and is very poetic. It's about the life of art in a culture on a planet in which grieving is the highest art, and about the religion and the structure around which the entire

society is ordered. Grieving really is an art form; perhaps *Cards of Grief* is my manifesto."

An avid reader, Yolen read "all the Andrew Lang fairy books as a child and any kind of fairy stories I could get my hands on. I vividly remember *Treasure Island* and the Louisa May Alcott books. All of the Alcott books, *Jo's Boys,* and even the Alcott books that nobody else had heard of, became part of my adolescent reading. I read *Wind in the Willows* and the Mowgli stories. We didn't have 'young adult' fiction, so I skipped right into adult books which tended to be very morose Russian novels—my Dostoevsky phase—then I got hooked on Joseph Conrad. Adventure novels or lugubrious emotional books are what I preferred. Then I went back into my fairy tale and fantasy stage: Tolkien and C. S. Lewis, metaphysical and folkloric fantasy.

"Literature should begin in the cradle. If we didn't have literature in childhood, we wouldn't have an adult literature or adult readers. The best readers are those who develop a love of reading early from the strong, beautiful, moving books of childhood.

"The only time I *don't* like to be identified as a 'children's writer' is when people try to put me in a box with, 'Oh, you write kids books . . .' or 'Oh, you write science fiction,' or 'poetry' or 'fantasy.' I'm a storyteller. I tell a story, then someone else decides how it should be packaged—for children or adults. That is a blurry line in many of my works.

"It is very rewarding to read how my stories have affected readers. But I am very embarrassed when it happens in public because it puts emphasis on me, not the story. I'm a conduit for the story, but the reader invests that story with power. The story by itself has only the power that one allows it to have. A little boy once wrote me, 'Your stories will live forever. I hope you live to be 99 or 100, but who cares!' He was right. I think the problem, especially in this country, is that the storyteller, the writer, becomes more important than the writing itself. We have a 'cult' of the writer, just as we do for rock singers. Their followers shout and scream so loudly you can't hear the songs. That's ridiculous. I feel if one is not really listening, one is in a sense, cursing the singer, denying his power.

"One of the problems people have with me is that they can't label me. Librarians sometimes say 'We don't know where to shelve you. . . .' That's not my problem. I just tell stories. I hope my stories amuse and entertain and move people. But in truth, I'm just telling a story and what happens between the story and the listener is between the story and the listener.

"Many of my stories are about a girl trying to please her father. That's me. But my father doesn't know. He has really never read anything that I've written. He was an international kite flying champion who singlehandedly created a renaissance for kites in this country. He's written several books on kites as well as edited many others for the Overseas Press Club, of which he was president for a while. He was a journalist for a number of years and a public relations man. He knows the value of books and reading. He likes to tell people I'm a writer; he likes to see my books on display, but he doesn't read them, because he feels they are not 'real' books because they are kids books. My brother on the other hand is a journalist, an economic and political reporter about South America, and he is considered a 'real' writer by my father."

About her writing technique, Yolen admits: "I have no idea where the first draft which comes pouring off my fingers comes from. I'm often surprised during the first draft, and think, 'Oh! Is *that* how the story ends!' But in revision I know that I have a hand in it. I tidy it up and I look for the right word and I rephrase. I truly enjoy that part. On a book or a story I might do up to twenty revisions—sometimes simply going through and polishing, sometimes tearing apart and putting back together again. I would say that each book I ever worked on has had at least three or four major revisions. I take things out, throw them away and re-shape. That comes from being a poet. I read everything aloud and when you read aloud you hear it again, the way you would a poem. People are amazed that someone as prolific as I am would be able to do that many revisions but when I'm writing I am totally involved. There are times when I don't even hear the phone ring.

"I compose on the typewriter because I visualize better in print, but the revision process is both by hand and typewriter. We have a word processor—my husband is a computer scientist and my children all use it—but one of the things I have to do is run drafts through the typewriter again and again. I am a 'skim reader,' I need to hear it again. Also, I'm faintly annoyed at something called a 'word processor.' It smells of nitrates.

"In the beginning I didn't know much about children's books. I started reading them when I started writing them. I don't think you should ever write something without having some knowledge of the field. It's as if to say 'I don't need to know this stuff, what I write is good enough.' That attitude betrays an absurd lack of self-knowledge.

"I really started to learn more about children's books when people began asking me to give speeches. I wanted to be able to say something fundamental, something about the whole process of writing, but I also wanted to be able to link it to what people throughout the ages had written. I looked through books about children's literature and I discovered I knew very little. Then I started reading the books themselves. As it turned out, I am a good lecturer, so I have become more and more in demand. The more I was in demand the more I had to find out about the various genres that I was writing in. When I began working on my book, [*Writing for Children*], which came out of a number of those lectures, I had to do even more research to find out about those topics which I didn't spend a lot of time writing myself."

Yolen taught Children's Literature at Smith College for six years. "There are different periods in children's literature, different specialties, genres. . . . It's absurd to try and teach children's literature in one semester (as I have to at Smith College). It's like trying to teach World Literature in one semester. I mention a few signpost books, look at some trends and give people ways of evaluating the literature that's there. You can't possibly choose three fantasy books for students to read. I could choose thirty-three more easily than I could choose three."

Yolen feels her most significant contribution to literature for children has been her literary fairy tales. "There was a heyday for literary fairy tales around the time of Laurence Housman and Howard Pyle. Before that, there was Oscar Wilde and the Rossetti crew (who were trying to live like fairy tales as well as create them!), Hans Christian Andersen, and then back further to the French Comtesse d'Aulnoy. But literary fairy tales were not something that had been done much in this century. There have been single picture books, but no romantic fairy tales that grew out of the folk mode, and yet were original stories until *The Girl Who Cried Flowers*.

"*The Girl Who Cried Flowers* continues to be a good seller, and it is the collection I am most known for. I have written others which I feel are better collections, such as *Dream Weaver* and *Neptune Rising*, but they haven't done as well. I think people say, 'I already have one collection, I don't need another,' as if there is a finite number of fairy tales you can have.

"I am an incorrigible punster. I am probably the best punster writing for children today since I make the *worst* puns. Big

Jane Yolen. Photograph courtesy of the *Honolulu Advertiser*.

"He has done it. He has stared the sun down, too." ■ (From "The Lad Who Stared Everyone Down," in *The Girl Who Cried Flowers and Other Tales* by Jane Yolen. Illustrated by David Palladini.)

Long ago there were five giants who lived together on a farm. ■ (From *The Giants Go Camping* by Jane Yolen. Illustrated by Tomie de Paola.)

distinction. I read the last *Commander Toad* book to my two sons. Adam rolled his eyes and said 'Oh, God, I hope nobody knows she's my mother.' Jason put his head down on the table. David, my husband, laughed out loud. When you are over forty-five you can laugh aloud at silly puns. Heidi, my daughter who is eighteen, refused to come in and listen. But the next day I got a note from her that said, 'I read the manuscript last night and I laughed out loud.' That was wonderful.

"I was very close to my mother. I really respected her. She was not a very open, demonstrative woman but when she gave advice, I listened. In fact, she never bothered learning the last names of my boyfriends because the turnover was so fast! It took her a year before she learned my husband's last name. When we got engaged she finally asked. She figured it was serious enough then to listen. On the other hand, I have a

tendency to give unsolicited advice to my children."

1971. A fantasy tale, *The Bird of Time,* dedicated to the memory of her mother, was published. "Ostensibly, the book was started when I misheard the lyrics of a Righteous Brothers song on the car radio. I thought the words were 'time bird,' since the singers mumbled a lot. Before I had quite caught the real lyrics (which had nothing to do with either a bird or time), I found myself consciously thinking about a time bird. I started writing the first paragraph of *Bird of Time* on the day that I was told my mother had incurable cancer. The story, a classic fairy tale, is about a miller's son who finds a bird that can speed up time or slow it down.

"When the book was accepted for publication, I gave the manuscript to my mother. It was the last time I saw her alive.

**But the leader of them all
is COMMANDER TOAD,
brave and bright,
bright and brave.**

■ (From *Commander Toad in Space* by Jane Yolen. Illustrated by Bruce Degen.)

She had come up to visit us. She knew she had cancer but we didn't talk about it because my father didn't want her 'to know.' My mother was a very bright woman with a master's degree in social work. *She knew*. She was respecting his wishes not to talk about it. I, on the other hand, was desperate to talk about it. Heidi was almost four, Adam was two, and I was very pregnant with Jason. Mother sat in a big chair (she was a very tiny woman), finished reading the story, looked up at me and said, 'Intimations of mortality?' I knew she was telling me, 'It's all right. I know I have cancer; I know I don't have long to live.' Then she added, 'You know where the book comes from, don't you? Remember how you loved to read the *Rubaiyat of Omar Khayyam*?' I hadn't thought of that book in years, but then I realized that my favorite quotation from it was 'Lo into the fire of spring, the winter garment of repentance

bring, the Bird of Time has but a little way to flutter, and Lo the Bird is on the Wing.' Which, like my story, evokes a sense of time passing and seems to say, 'Don't worry, there will be a renewal.'

''Jason was born nine days before my mother died. It was about a year later, after the book was published and dedicated to my mother's memory, that I began to understand that it was a book for her, about my desire to stop time. That happens often with my stories. I find out long after that they were about more than the story itself. For example, one morning, eight years after my mother died, I was reading out loud a story in *Dream Weaver* called 'The Boy Who Sang for Death.' There is a line in which the boy says, 'Any gift I have I would give to get my mother back.' I started to sob. I realized that 'The

Yolen talks with students at Jefferson Davis School in Denton, Texas.

Boy who Sang for Death,' written eight years after her death, was a story in which I was still mourning my mother. I hadn't realized it when I wrote it; I only realized it when I spoke it out loud. Stories do give us permission to have feelings; not only do they give permission to the author, but they also give it to the reader. Stories help people, heal people.''

Yolen has kept an idea file for many years. ''My idea file is very big, fat and messy. The minute something becomes more than just an idea, it comes out of the file and is put into its own file folder. I just pop anything in the idea file, and figure out what I can do with it later. I took a photograph of a bear in Central Park with his paws cupped under his chin and its been sitting in the idea file for about nineteen years. I haven't a clue as to what most of the material will be used for. I had a phrase from a Vermont tombstone, 'It is a dreadful thing to love what death can touch,' in the file for eight or ten years, and I finally found a use for it in *Cards of Grief*. It stunned me that it suddenly was there when I needed it. There are frogs in Australia that live in the mud. During a dry spell, they burrow and stay under for a year or two until it starts raining again. Then they resurface. That is the metaphor for my idea file. Sometimes nothing happens for years and suddenly an idea or a note will have meaning. There's no predicting it and no guarantees.''

1972. While working on her biography of George Fox, *Friend: The Story of George Fox and the Quakers,* Yolen was inspired to embrace the Quaker religion. ''My aunt's sister by marriage was very involved with the Quakers and was a seminal influence on me during my teens. When I was sixteen, she gave me a copy of George Fox's journals. Since then, I've been interested in the Quakers. I grew up during the Viet Nam war and pacifism was an alternative.''

1981. *The Gift of Sarah Barker* was published. ''The crafts of the Shakers had also interested me but, I didn't know much about their culture. Though the Shakers did grow out of the Quakers, they have totally different religious beliefs. The Shakers are a millennium religion, and believe that Mother Anne is the female incarnation of Christ. After a visit with the few remaining Shakers, I felt I could go ahead and write the book.

''My only daughter was becoming interested in boys right about the time I was writing the book. I kept wondering how, in a Shaker community, you could keep the boys away from a girl like Heidi or keep Heidi away from the boys. I imagined a Romeo and Juliet story within the Shaker setting.'' Yolen took two to three years to think about the story before coming up with the right theme.

''It later occurred to me that *Dragon's Blood* and *The Gift of Sarah Barker* are in some ways the same book. They are both set in farm communities where men and women are separated with rigidly set roles within the communities. There is even a large central mow in the big Dragon barn which comes right out of a description of the Shaker mow in *The Gift of Sarah Barker*. A boy and a girl fall in love, without really understanding what's happening to them or that they will eventually be thrust out of the community. In some ways the two books lean on each other. I've noticed the same phenomenon with my third 'Dragon' book and my new *Children of the Wolf*—the idea of muteness and language is very important in both. It's interesting to find out about these similarities afterwards, but while I'm right in the middle of writing I don't think about it. Once a class of sixth graders said to me, 'Why do you have so many walls in your stories?' We started exploring the possible meanings together. I said, 'Walls could mean the difference between freedom and imprisonment . . . the difference

**But on a spaceship
all the meals
look the same.**

■ (From *Commander Toad and the Big Black Hole* by Jane Yolen. Illustrated by Bruce Degen.)

I could see into his kitchen and danged if that man wasn't still eatin' and jawin' at the root cellar. ■ (From *Uncle Lemon's Spring* by Jane Yolen. Illustrated by Glen Rounds.)

between cozy and comfortable. Walls could mean being out in the scary but real world.' *The Girl Who Loved the Wind* and *The Seventh Mandarin* are both about what's beyond the wall, as is *The Seeing Stick,* in which a girl goes beyond the walls of the city. I had never thought of walls as a kind of thematic tic, but those kids were right.

"I don't understand how any writer, woman or man, can have the 'significant other' in their life, whether it's a lover or husband or wife, not be supportive. My husband is the most constant, supportive, critical eye I know. He's the only one in the world who's read absolutely everything I've written. He's read even more than my agent who hasn't read the failures. David is the single most important influence in my writing. When the draft is readable (many of my early drafts aren't readable because I've written all over them), he reads it. Sometimes I read things out loud to him, sometimes I just talk to him about a problem I'm having. He's always there.

"I have two pieces of advice for young people interested in writing: read and write. Read and read and read. It's the only way you will discover what great stories have been told, and what stories you want to tell better. Write every day because writing is like a muscle that needs to be flexed. I don't [physically] exercise as much as I should, but I do exercise my writing every day. Faulkner said, 'I only write when I'm inspired. Fortunately, I'm inspired at nine o'clock every morning.' It's true, you can't wait around for inspiration. You just have to get up and go to your desk and write."

Yolen's present goal as a writer is to become "better at telling stories. I do a lot of storytelling and I love it. I am involved in NAPPS, the National Association for the Preservation and Perpetuation of Storytelling. A great deal of storytelling has gone on in this country.

"I can't start my writing day until I get my mail. There are times when I'll work for just one or two hours in a day, but when I was finishing each of the 'Dragon' books, and *Cards of Grief,* I worked for about two weeks for ten solid hours a day. The rest of the time, I was thinking about the book. In fact, I was probably very bad company, not responding to anyone because I was busy thinking and running upstairs to my studio whenever I could.

"I also feel very strongly that nobody gets to be a writer without help. I feel that one of our responsibilities as established writers is to reach out and pass our knowledge, passion, and information on to others. That's why I teach and conduct workshops. You don't become who you are without a helping hand from somewhere, even if it's just from reading other people's work. I run a monthly Society of Children's Books workshop and go to children's literature conferences. I was an editor. I know many people have more talent than I do, but they often don't know how to focus or how to start; they don't know the right questions to ask, so they're afraid to ask questions at all. I feel it's vital for aspiring writers to get the answers early so they won't have to spend years and years making the same mistakes."

Yolen's works are included in the Kerlan Collection at the University of Minnesota.

FOR MORE INFORMATION SEE: Horn Book, August, 1970, October, 1975; *Publishers Weekly,* February 22, 1971, May 7, 1979; *New York Times Book Review,* September 10, 1972, May 5, 1974, September 19, 1976, November 20, 1977, January 1, 1978, February 18, 1979, October 28, 1979, May 23, 1982; *Library Journal,* March 15, 1973; *Wilson Library Bulletin,* October, 1973; Jane H. Yolen, *Writing Books for Children,* Writer, Inc., 1973, revised, 1983; *The Writer,* April, 1975, December, 1978, January, 1981, August, 1983, May, 1984; *Cricket,* September, 1975; Doris de Montreville and Elizabeth D. Crawford, editors, *The Fourth Book of Junior Authors and Illustrators,* H. W. Wilson, 1978; D. L. Kirkpatrick, *Twentieth-Century Children's Writers,* St. Martin's Press, 1978; *Children's Literature in Education,* Volume II, number 3, 1980; J. H. Yolen, *Touch Magic: Fantasy, Faerie and Folklore in the Literature of Childhood,* Philomel, 1981; *Children's Literature Review,* Volume IV, Gale, 1982; *Language Arts,* May, 1982; *Chicago Tribune Book World,* November 7, 1982; *Fantasy Newsletter,* September, 1983.

Children have more need of models than of critics.
—Joseph Joubert

ZARING, Jane (Thomas) 1936-

BRIEF ENTRY: Born December 26, 1936, in Nelson, Wales. Zaring graduated from the University of London in 1959, and later received a Diploma in Education from Cambridge University and her M.A. from Indiana University. A full-time children's writer since 1978, Zaring has also been employed as a geography teacher, a lecturer in education, and an instructor in earth sciences at Iowa State University. She is the author of *The Return of the Dragon* (Houghton, 1981), a fantasy based on elements of Welsh legend and folklore. In this story, an exiled dragon named Caradoc finds he has one year to accomplish twelve good deeds so that he may return to his home in the hills of Caernarfon. *Horn Book* described the tale as "... warm and glowing, full of friendship and good cheer as well as of brisk, exciting action." Zaring also wrote *Sharkes in the North Woods; or, Nish Na Bosh Na Is Nicer Now* (Houghton, 1982), a farce about a no-good family that turns a summer camp into one of hard labor. *School Library Journal* labeled it "ludicrous, lively, deliciously horrifying," while *Booklist* took special note of "the overdrawn characterizations of the horrendous Sharkes, whom readers will love to hate." Zaring intends to write another spoof and anticipates the publication of a book about Latin-speaking snails. "My books try to give pleasure rather than improve," she observes, "probably a result of my happy memories as a child bookworm."

FOR MORE INFORMATION SEE: Columbus Republic, October 12, 1981; *Ames Tribune,* October 31, 1981; *Ninnau,* February 1, 1982; *Contemporary Authors,* Volume 108, Gale, 1983.

ZECK, Gerald Anthony 1939-
(Gerry Zeck; G. Anthony Zupa, a pseudonym)

PERSONAL: Born December 29, 1939, in Minneapolis, Minn.; son of Robert E. (an attorney) and Mary (a homemaker, maiden name, Bachler) Zeck; married Sandra Athelstan, August 13, 1960 (divorced, 1970); married Pamela Tuke (a banker and writer), October 30, 1971; children: Christopher, Cynthia, Adrian. *Education:* University of Minnesota, B.A., 1964; University of California, Los Angeles, M.A., 1967, Ph.D., 1972. *Home and office:* 2506 Randa Blvd., Sarasota, Fla. 33580.

CAREER: San Fernando Valley State College, Northridge, Calif., lecturer, 1968-69; Ohio University, Athens, assistant professor, 1969-71; Syracuse University, Syracuse, N.Y., assistant professor of geography, 1971-73; Zeck & Associates (communications/public relations firm), Minneapolis, Minn., president, photographer, and writer, 1979-83; Gerry Zeck Photography, Sarasota, Fla, owner, 1984—. Textbook consultant to John Wiley & Sons, Inc., 1969-71. *Military service:* U.S. Marine Corps, 1957-59, private first class. *Member:* The Loft: A Place for Literature and the Arts (member of board of directors, 1977-78).

WRITINGS—Under name Gerry Zeck, except as noted: (Under pseudonym G. Anthony Zupa) *The Turning Point* (adult poetry), White Cottage Press, 1974; (with wife, Pam Zeck) *Mississippi Sternwheelers* (juvenile nonfiction; illustrated by George Overlie; photographs by P. and G. Zeck), Carolrhoda, 1982;

Gerry Zeck with son, Adrian, in 1982.

By the time I'm fifteen years old, I'll be in two or three dance classes a day, seven days a week. ■
(From *I Love to Dance* by Gerry Zeck. Photograph by the author.)

I Love to Dance!: A True Story about Tony Jones (juvenile nonfiction; self-illustrated with photographs), Carolrhoda, 1982.

Illustrator: *Forest Resources Atlas*, Ohio University, 1970; Kevin R. Cox, *Man, Location, and Behavior: An Introduction to Human Geography*, Wiley, 1972.

WORK IN PROGRESS: ''Photo essays and photojournalism on my home place, Florida.''

SIDELIGHTS: ''I am the third of seven children. I grew up in the Midwest, attended a seminary in Alabama, and dropped out of public high school in Minnesota. Bored and socially awkward, I joined the Marine Corps at age seventeen.

''My interest in art led to a map-making job in the Corps. After my service I worked my way through college using my mapping skills for various employers.

''I concentrated my graduate studies in applied photography, ethnocinematography, and environmental perception and behavior. My doctoral dissertation in geography, ''Images of American Cities,'' was an inquiry into urban imagery. Most of my academic research centered on perceptual and cognitive maps and how we come to 'know' about places, and how that understanding, in turn, affects our behavior.

''I terminated my academic career in 1973 and closed myself off in a basement office-writing room where, after several months, I came to regard myself as 'Moleman.' Today, I have a drawerful of notes about that character. I also wrote my first, unpublished novel in that basement. It is an adventure story about Harvey Edsel Wumper, a misfortunate hero who falls in love with a red leather boot named Rosey.

''I think graphically. I visualize that which I am attempting to understand. Since 1979 I have been writing and photographing for people in business. I use old skills of draftmanship and photography whilst assembling brochures and annual reports. I test my skills by assigning myself photo-stories when not working for other people. I find something interesting, then I pursue my ignorance with pen and camera.

'''Doing' is the difficult part of my life. Thoughts are cheap. I must constantly push my body to do what my head wants. I write myself encouraging notes and leave them in places I will look. I have evolved a litany of good advice for myself, like, 'work your own garden first.' Although I complain about it a lot, I am really happiest when I am moving.

''When I am moving, I believe I can do just about anything imaginable. And that is what *I Love to Dance* is all about.

''Ten-year-old Tony Jones makes great progress toward his goal of becoming a danseur because he already knows he must dance to be happy. And he has already learned some of the secrets of turning his work into play. I followed Tony from classroom to classroom and from theater stage to backyard theater over six months before I tried to write anything. I made photographs and notes, but in the end the story assembled itself. All I had to do was suffer over the typewriter.

''I am constantly writing. I write to my brothers or my sisters to explain what I see and feel. I write to my young son so he might read my thoughts when he grows enough to care. If I can't tell you why it is important to me and how it bears on my life and your life, then I do other things until the time is right and the Muse begins to stir my soul. I look for relationships that give us an awareness of our common origins and paths through life. I'm very basic, very simple.''

CUMULATIVE INDEX TO ILLUSTRATIONS AND AUTHORS

Illustrations Index

(In the following index, the number of the volume in which an illustrator's work appears is given *before* the colon, and the page on which it appears is given *after* the colon. For example, a drawing by Adams, Adrienne appears in Volume 2 on page 6, another drawing by her appears in Volume 3 on page 80, another drawing in Volume 8 on page 1, and another drawing in Volume 15 on page 107.)

YABC

Index citations including this abbreviation refer to listings appearing in *Yesterday's Authors of Books for Children,* also published by the Gale Research Company, which covers authors who died prior to 1960.

Author Index

The following index gives the number of the volume in which an author's biographical sketch, Brief Entry, or Obituary appears.

This index includes references to all entries in the following series, which are also published by Gale Research Company.

YABC—*Yesterday's Authors of Books for Children: Facts and Pictures about Authors and Illustrators of Books for Young People from Early Times to 1960*, Volumes 1-2

CLR—*Children's Literature Review: Excerpts from Reviews, Criticism, and Commentary on Books for Children*, Volumes 1-8

B

Author Index

Author Index